DATE DUE			
OCT 5 '00			

THE POWER
OF
THEIR GLORY

THE POWER
of
THEIR GLORY

America's Ruling Class:
The Episcopalians

KIT & FREDERICA
KONOLIGE

Wyden Books

Grateful acknowledgment is made to the following for permission to reprint from the sources cited:

Cleveland Amory. From Amory, Cleveland. *The Last Resorts*. New York: Harper and Brothers, 1948. Amory, Cleveland. *The Proper Bostonians*. New York: E. P. Dutton, 1947. Amory, Cleveland, *Who Killed Society?* New York: Harper and Brothers, 1960.

E. Digby Baltzell. From E. Digby Baltzell, *Philadelphia Gentlemen: The Making of a National Upper Class*. Glencoe, Illinois: The Free Press, 1958.

Crown Publishers, Inc. Taken from *Man of the World: My Life on Five Continents* by Cornelius Vanderbilt, Jr. Copyright © 1959 by Cornelius Vanderbilt, Jr. Used by permission of Crown Publishers, Inc.

Doubleday & Company, Inc. Excerpts from *A Casual Past* by Francis Biddle. Copyright © 1961 by Francis Biddle; copyright © 1961 by American Heritage Publishing Co., Inc. Used by permission of Doubleday & Company, Inc.

Henry Lee Higginson, From Perry, Bliss. *Life and Letters of Henry Lee Higginson*. Boston: Atlantic Monthly Press, 1921.

Houghton Mifflin Company. From
    George Wolfskill, *The Revolt of the Conservative*.
    Copyright © 1962 by George Wolfskill
    Reprinted by permission of Houghton Mifflin Company

    Orville H. Bullitt, *For the President*
    Copyright © 1972 by Orville H. Bullitt
    Reprinted by permission of Houghton Mifflin Company

Alfred A. Knopf, Inc. From Day, Clarence. *God and My Father*, from *The Best of Clarence Day*. New York: Alfred A. Knopf, 1948. Copyright © 1948 Clarence Day.

Rt. Rev. Frederic C. Lawrence. From Lawrence, William. *Memories of a Happy Life*. Cambridge, Mass.: Houghton Mifflin Co., 1926.

Henry F. May. From May, Henry F. *Protestant Churches and Industrial America*. New York: Harper and Brothers, 1949.

National Publishing Co. From Ingersoll, R. Sturgis. *Recollections at Eighty*. Philadelphia: National Publishing Co., 1971.

Random House, Inc. From Halberstam, David. *The Best and the Brightest*. New York: Random House, 1969. Copyright © 1969 David Halberstam.

Yale University Press. From Ahlstrom, Sydney. *A Religious History of the American People*. New Haven: Yale University Press, 1972. Copyright © 1972 Yale University Press.

    The author and publisher also gratefully acknowledge the picture research by Research Reports, New York.

Manufactured in the United States of America.

FIRST EDITION

Trade distribution by Simon and Schuster
A Division of Gulf + Western Corporation
New York, New York 10020

Designed by Tere LoPrete

Library of Congress Cataloging in Publication Data

Konolige, Kit.
    The power of their glory.

    Bibliography: p.
    Includes index.
    1. Episcopalians in the United States.   2. United
States—Church history.   3. United States—Social life
and customs.   I. Konolige, Frederica, joint author.
II. Title.
BX5883.K66   283'.73   78–12517
ISBN 0–88326–155–3

To Robert

Contents

viii   *Contents*

THE POWER
OF
THEIR GLORY

C H A P T E R

I

Links

Robert Amory, Jr., has been in his career successively a military
engineer, the second youngest professor ever at Harvard Law
School, deputy director for intelligence (DDI) of the Central
Intelligence Agency, treasurer of the national group that bank-
rolled the construction of America's own version of Westminster
Abbey, the National Cathedral. Now he officiates as the prin-
cipal business administrator of the Mellon-dominated National
Gallery of Art.

Amory looks every inch the successful soldier, thinker, and
man of action. He stands tall above his professional landscape,
his personality carved by a lifetime of remarkable experiences
and associations—a human reflection of the tall, broad-
shouldered trees dominating the sharp hills of Washington's
exclusive Wesley Heights neighborhood that Amory overlooks
when he stands at his living-room window. The man his law
school students called Bullet Bob.

Amory looks so at home in his craggily handsome surroundings because he is, in a sense, part of the landscape. By family
background, he need yield to no oak in deep, firm rooting.
Amory's grandfather on his mother's side was Henry Ives
Cobb, the official government architect who helped convert
Washington from a muddy cow pasture into the neo-imperialist
capital of the fastest-growing society in history. Amory's
mother, Leonore Cobb, used to ford Rock Creek while riding

with "Princess" Alice Roosevelt, daughter of Episcopalian President Roosevelt the First, who married Congressman Nicholas Longworth and still survives as a witty nonagenarian tribute to the glories of America's early aristocracy.

On his father's side, Amory (like Mrs. Longworth, for that matter) was cultivated in the far deeper soil of the ancient aristocracy of Boston. Back there, the roots get so confused through intermarriages of the grand old families—the Coolidges, Lawrences, Peabodys, Lymans, Lodges, Cabots, and Lowells—that it's a wonder the trees managed to grow straight at all. From inside the forest, though, the views are clear.

It is distinctly clear, for example, that Robert Amory's great-grandfather, old Gus Amory, from whom all present-day Amorys descend, was the man responsible for rebuilding Boston's famous old Trinity Church when it burned down and had to be rebuilt. Rebuilt it was, in glorious Gothic in 1877, on Copley Square. Copley Square is named after John Copley, the great portraitist whose name on an ancestor's painting is a sure sign of proper breeding in the descendants of America's old families. John Copley not only painted early Amorys for later Amorys to hang on their walls but was an ancestor of the latter-day Amory himself.

To have one ancestor rebuild Boston's most important church on a square named after another ancestor who painted portraits of still other ancestors—that is the sort of viny grip on the past that has sprouted such a man as Robert Amory. His brother Cleveland Amory has spent the great part of a journalistic career charting the social twists and turns of those familial roots.

But unlike some of his background, the man Amory does not dwell in the past. He is so aggressive and fast a talker, so vivid an anecdotist, so sharp a bargainer, so coldly competent, and so inexhaustibly friendly and entertaining that he glows with a larger-than-life feeling of aristocracy in the flesh, not on canvas.

His house, in the tall, righteous trees of exclusive Wesley Heights, seeps history of a living sort, background of use every day, belief in a religion, Episcopalianism, that hardly bothers to exact ecclesiastical discipline from its followers but implants in them a feeling for nothing less than a culture.

His silver cigarette cases are Amory's most notable manifestation of his life among his people, the Episcocrats—the Episcopalian aristocrats of America. June 17, 1938, says one—his wedding date to the former Mary Armstrong, a young lady of good background like his, a graduate of Rosemary Hall, one of the Connecticut countryside's handsome Episcopalian-oriented boarding schools for women. (Like many other of the exclusive boarding schools, Rosemary Hall has abandoned its single-sex commitment for fiscal reasons. It is now combined into one school with Choate, its male equivalent.)

There are perhaps even more Episcocratic low-key ways than Amory's to decorate a silver cigarette case. Across the Potomac River in McLean, Virginia, another hilly suburb, the son of Amory's first law partner has a cigarette case covered with the engraved signatures of his ushers. Amory's other cigarette case, on the living-room windowsill, is engraved to THE SKIPPER—from his World War II crew. Amory calls himself "an old military engineer," describes landscapes in terms of how easily an army could defend them, and is obviously proud of having risen from private to colonel during the war, of commanding an amphibian engineering battalion in the South Pacific. The man of thought, the man of action. An aristocrat in a tradition going back to medieval knights and beyond.

The Amory house has a very typical appeal to sight and smell and to some sixth, social sense. The colors of rug and wall and even books are muted, as though the great bold outdoors were being confidently invited to creep inside. Edges of the blond-wood, post-Bauhaus furniture are peacefully shredding, trying to revert to roots and twigs. There is a smell of living wood, of mildew before it turns offensive. A disorder that signals minds willing to allow the Greater Laws of nature a little room to move. An amazing ability to persuade bright new book covers, can openers, antiques, and bottles of prepackaged Bloody Mary mix to coexist peacefully.

One does not arrange things too neatly; "pretty" is not something a house should be. Nor should women. Episcocratic houses and women are *handsome*. The house has a life of its own. The Amorys leave it to live frequently by itself, take care of its own problems, while they travel to their Maine cottage for extended working vacations. One treats one's house as one does the children: with respect, some distance, some slack, some confidence in their eventual triumph.

In the Amory dining room glows an enormous picture of the Virgin Mary with the Christ Child, vivid, charged with more color than the rest of the house put together. Even that does not, somehow, look out of place. When Episcopalians suddenly get serious about their religion, as Mary Amory, the painter of the picture, has done, it is considered a somewhat unusual but, if done properly, natural and acceptable thing. "Properly" means you don't sneak off to six-thirty mass before anyone else is awake; you splash your convictions on canvas and hang them in the dining room.

Robert Amory, sixty-three, greets visitors on a warm early-spring Saturday noontime in a plaid shirt that makes him look like a lumberjack and a tweed elbow-patched jacket that makes him look like a professor. He is both. This morning he has been engineering a cradle for his first grandchild, who is still, as Amory puts it in his military parlance, at "D minus ninety days." And a warm welcome to the new Amory.

He comes in and talks fast with visitors—very fast, very fluently, very wittily. It is an unscientific but unquestionable fact that, as a religious grouping, Episcopalians talk faster and with less prompting than anyone else. Also, as a professor at the University of Pennsylvania has shown, they are thinner than any other religious denomination—and that *is* a fact.*

Any reserve Episcocrats might feel to begin with falls victim, early in life, to that upper-class holy water, the cocktail. Amory pours his visitors prelunch Bloody Marys, then settles himself behind a Gibson with ambitions to be straight gin. The talk radiates from him, into the familial web and beyond to the

---

* Dr. Albert J. Stunkard, a psychiatrist at the University of Pennsylvania School of Medicine, whose specialty is obesity, testified about his research before the Senate Subcommitte on Nutrition. Stunkard conducted a study in 1975 from data collected in the Midtown Study, a huge collection of raw information from the early 1960s. He found that Jews are the fattest religious group, followed by Catholics and Protestants. Among Protestants, Lutherans are skinnier than Methodists, and Episcopalians are thinnest of all. Those findings correspond closely to Stunkard's general observation that social class and socioeconomic status are important factors in obesity. Six times as many lower-class people studied were obese as upper-class people, and that was the same ratio between subjects who had been in the country for only one generation compared with those who had been here for four. Only one fourth-generation American in every twenty-five is overweight.

network of connections of school, work, and church. As a group, Episcocrats are influenced by the long-held values of Episcocratic families and institutions.

Amory is not devoutly religious. His involvement with the Washington Cathedral, crowning glory of the power of the semiofficial church of America, has been financial and aesthetic: Amory is enamored of Gothic architecture. "To me, the value of the cathedral is in its ecumenical approach," Amory says. That attitude has not stopped him from contributing $10,000 to build a balustrade with wings of stone in the giant structure on Mount St. Alban, the highest point in Washington, a few miles down the road from Amory's home.

For his fund-raising duties, family was useful, too. He got a contribution from a man who does not even live in the United States—Viscount Amory, Robert Amory's "distant cousin and close friend," who donated the cathedral's limestone porch, named after Winston Churchill. Churchill happens to be the one man besides Viscount Amory who was a commoner when chosen a member of England's ancient and honorable Order of the Garter.

A few years ago Amory had brunch with Joseph Alsop, the rarefied Washington author and once widely feared columnist, who shares with Robert Amory old friendship, a Harvard education, old New England ancestry, current membership in Washington's ne plus ultra Metropolitan Club, and an Episcopal upbringing.

Amory's eldest, also Robert, was getting to the age when young Episcocrats' fancies lightly turn to thoughts of career. In Episcocratic families, this is about twelve. This has traditionally been the age at which young men go off to boarding school. As the two strolled, after brunch, among the tall timber that rolls down from Amory's house into a national forest, young Bob Amory's future came up. The time had come, Alsop suggested, to send him away to one of the great New England prep schools that train the leaders of Wall Street and Washington for the next generation.

Alsop had gone to Groton. His family had gone to Groton since the school began in 1884. It is the strength of family dynasties like the Alsops, with their politicians, businessmen, and columnists, that has made Groton what it is—probably the greatest single school in the country.

At Groton young men get as good an education as is available anywhere; no one questions that. They also get an early introduction to Alsops from Connecticut, Biddles from Philadelphia, Auchinclosses, Harrimans, Whitneys from New York, and the tribe of other young scions who—if six or eight generations of their ancestors are any guide—will someday hold positions of immense power in the United States. Young men—and, recently, young women—also get religion at Groton.

Groton is a school of the Episcopal Church. As expressed at Groton, Episcopalianism is a religion very much part of old families of English descent, part of an expectation of high achievement in the national government, part of comfortable old wealth, part of an ethic of success. Groton has a faculty without peer in terms of its links between the church, the state, and aristocratic American families. Until the summer of 1977 it was headed by the Reverend Malcolm Cox, brother of Archibald Cox, the Harvard law professor and special prosecutor.

Not long ago there would have been little question that Amory would have sent his children to such a school. It was an inevitable reflex for Episcocrats of his rank. He himself had been remanded to Milton Academy, which differs somewhat from Groton and a number of other schools in lacking formal connections with the church and in its long history of coeducation, but operates on essentially Episcopal wavelengths. Amory told Alsop, though, that it was no longer *de rigueur* to send a child to boarding school. Not only not necessary, but "frightfully expensive." Episcocrats become very concerned about money when they don't *have* to spend it.

Amory suggested to Alsop that while Groton was, certainly, a very good school, nobody would get down on him, or on his son in the future, if he did not go to Groton. For one thing, the schools had stopped producing Episcocrats of the old school and started making Episcocrats of the new school, which are very different. In the old days, the boys from Groton and St. Paul's and St. George's and all the New England schools were the richest, handsomest, cleanest, most clothes-conscious, most morally upright young men the country could produce.

Amory recently heard of a friend, he told Alsop, who had visited St. Paul's and found it a "pig pile."

This, if you please, was St. Paul's School in Concord, New Hampshire, where Cornelius Vanderbilt III and John D. Rockefeller, Jr., competed for first place in the class at the end of the nineteenth century, where brokers and statesmen and even some saints, and seemingly half of Yale, had been the chief produce for as long as any Episcocrat could remember. It is the alma mater of former New York City Mayor John V. Lindsay, who referred to it in the campaigns as his "high school," trying to play down his Episcocratic background for his constituents. But Episcocratic needs and wants change with the decades. Amory noted that, in the past, close contact with teachers had produced adulation in the boys—with teachers like John Gilbert Winant, later governor of New Hampshire and ambassador to Britain. Now at St. Paul's the students rarely saw the masters, Amory had heard, except when the masters came charging through the dormitory halls with trained dogs to sniff out marijuana.

Another reason for not going to Groton or St. Paul's was that young Robert Amory was already going to a school that was, for practical purposes, just as good—St. Alban's School, the church-affiliated institution on the grounds of the National Cathedral. Much is unique about St. Alban's. It is probably the only school in the world to get an inquiry from *Time* magazine about the identity of the boy voted "best potential centerfold" in a putative liberated yearbook by the students of the National Cathedral School for Girls, St. Alban's sister institution. The young man in question was Mark Percy, son of the senator from Illinois and brother-in-law of West Virginia governor John D. ("Jay") Rockefeller.

St. Alban's turned *Time* magazine down. It has probably turned down *Time* more than any other institution in the country. No pictures when another student, twelve-year-old Edward Kennedy, Jr., had a leg amputated. No interviews with Billy Mondale, the vice president's son, when he first showed up for classes. Nothing about the Secret Service agents following around the daughter of Vice President Spiro Agnew at the Cathedral School. Nor about Lynda Bird and Luci Baines Johnson before that (though they were hardly in demand, then children of a lowly senator, a dime a dozen at St. Alban's). No special treatment for anybody, in fact. No swelled heads—that is a prime tenet of Episcopal schools. At this level we are all equal.

"We know how to deal with children of so-called prominence," remarks Richard Downes, the school's chaplain, in the breezy, dismissive manner that people of so-called prominence have always loved in the people who work for them.

St. Alban's sprang from the same fertile Episcocratic domination of Washington at the turn of the century that saw the Amory family first establish itself there. It was begun with a bequest from Harriet Lane Johnston, niece of President James Buchanan, in 1909—two years after a gala crowd of 20,000, including J. P. Morgan, heard President Theodore Roosevelt speak at the dedication of the cornerstone of the National Cathedral. The National Cathedral School for Girls was begun in 1900 in a house donated by Mrs. Phoebe Apperson Hearst, wife of silver millionaire California Senator George Hearst, mother of press baron William Randolph Hearst. Since those beginnings, St. Alban's has remained the premier school of the nation's capital and one of the best in the country, training the children of important, frequently famous men to assume their fathers' places in the cosmos.

The official religion of the school, Episcopalianism, serves as a link between the celestial and the secular glory of Washington. As Robert Amory pointed out to Joe Alsop when they strolled after lunch a few years back, it is impossible to imagine a better way for a young man like young Robert to be introduced to Episcocratic Washington than by attending St. Alban's.

"The other day," Amory remarked, "he had a debate with Dean Acheson over foreign policy." The retired secretary of state, like many other prominent men, made it a habit to appear occasionally at the Episcocratic school near his home—Washington.

David Acheson, fifty-seven, son of Dean and grandson of an Episcopal bishop of Connecticut, turns away from the windows of his downtown Washington law office and seats his lanky body on one of the soft modern sofas.

"I thought my sons would get more out of school if they went to the one *they* chose," Acheson explains in his slow, careful accents. "So to give it a semblance of democratic procedure, I showed them Groton, Exeter, and two other topnotch schools. Both picked Exeter. They thought Groton was a little too small."

Exeter and Andover, the two Phillips academies, are the other type of major prep school in the nation. They were founded not as Episcopal Church schools like Groton, St. Paul's Middlesex, Kent, Taft, Brooks, Pomfret, Noble and Greenough, St. George's, and Choate, but much earlier, at the time of the Revolution, as Congregationalist seminaries. Later they became larger and more nonsectarian than the church schools, but have essentially the same function of providing the brightest and wealthiest young men in the country with adequate academic and social preparation for Harvard, Yale, and Princeton. Though the Phillips academies and the great universities were founded long before the church schools, they came to be dominated, in the highest Episcocratic age at the end of the nineteenth century, by the upper-class mores that the church schools created. Traditionally the Phillips academies have been somewhat less "social" and snobbish than the church schools.

The church schools and the Phillips academies are responsible for most of the high concentration of Episcocrats in Washington in high government positions. The schools have long instilled in their students a worldliness available nowhere else, combined with a drive for success in all endeavors, that has traditionally led to the top of Wall Street, the State Department, and the Central Intelligence Agency. Over the years there has been a direct and personal line of church-school-educated Episcocrats passing down the mantle of government, especially in foreign service, from one generation to the next: from Theodore Roosevelt and Elihu Root and John Hay to John W. Davis (presidential candidate and ambassador to England) to Franklin D. Roosevelt (Groton) and Secretaries of State Frank B. Kellogg, Henry L. Stimson, Christian Herter (St. Paul's), Dean Acheson (Groton), and Cyrus Vance (Kent), secretaries of the treasury like C. Douglas Dillon (Groton), secretaries of defense like James Forrestal, Thomas S. Gates, Jr., and Elliot Richardson, and the cream of assistant secretaries of state and deputy directors of the CIA.

Going to the great, self-important prep schools was a guaran-

tee of neither a strong belief in religious Episcopalianism afterward—compulsory daily chapel at Groton left David Acheson
with "enough of a dose of it" to dodge church effectively for
years later—nor an automatic career in government. If nothing
else intervenes, a lucrative Wall Street law or brokerage post
frequently siphons off the most aggressive potential assistant
secretaries. But Groton was no handicap when Dean Acheson
came to Washington for the first time.

President Roosevelt "had left our school ten years before I
got there, but he regarded my having gone there as a recommendation," the future secretary of state noted in his autobiography. Acheson was soon joined by Attorney General
Francis Biddle and Undersecretary of State Sumner Welles as
part of a sort of Groton Mafia with a formidable hold on federal
policy. But this highly personal government that began under
Theodore Roosevelt continued through Cousin Franklin's New
Deal and into the New Frontier days could work against an
aspiring bright young Episcocrat as well, Dean Acheson found.
His great ambition in 1933 was to become solicitor general,
the second highest post in the Justice Department. He had
been law clerk of Felix Frankfurter, and that august jurist, who
had been Roosevelt's first choice for the position, recommended
Acheson. The reaction from Attorney General Homer Cummings "being immediate, violent, and adverse, the proposal was
withdrawn."

Acheson was rather amazed that he had produced such
enmity in a man he really knew nothing of. He learned the
explanation when he visited his dying father. The Episcopalian
Cummings, it appeared, had been married more than once, and
Acheson's father, the bishop of Connecticut—Cummings's home
state—forbade the Episcopal Church under him to allow such
goings-on within its churches. Outraged, Cummings sought
marital blessings outside the church, and when Bishop Acheson's
son was proposed as his second-in-command, he sought revenge
by vetoing young Dean's appointment.

Dean Acheson was not the only Episcocrat who found that
while going to Groton is generally a boost to progress in official
Washington, the church itself can be rather unbending when

it comes to making it easy for people to stay on good terms with it. Jonathan Bingham is the son of Hiram Bingham, a self-made New York millionaire who capped his career by heading to Washington as a senator, much in the tradition of many other rich businessmen at the turn of the century, when the Senate was known, perhaps with even more justice than today, as the "Millionaires' Club."*

Young Jonathan, headed for a future as a New York congressman, went to Groton in the 1930s. His family was Congregationalist, but the young man was so much taken by the overwhelming presence of Endicott Peabody, the headmaster, that he asked to be confirmed into the Episcopal Church. Peabody, who had founded Groton in 1884 and was still its tall, commanding, revered headmaster fifty years later, refused to allow Bingham to join the church officially at that point. "You are taken only by me, not by the church," Peabody warned the youth.

Bingham's subsequent history says much about Episcocrats' arm's-length treatment of their religion while they embrace its peripheral apparatus. He was married in 1939 to the former June Rossbach. She was Jewish, but from an upper-class family. A grandniece of New York's Governor Herbert Lehman, she had attended Rosemary Hall at the same time as Mary Armstrong Amory. The two were and remain close friends, especially after June Bingham was a bridesmaid at the Amorys' nuptials. The wedding was written up as quite the social event by the *New York Times*, joining, as it did, two such distinguished and yet disparate families.

The incongruities were remarkable. After a ceremony in the Episcopal chapel at Rosemary Hall, St. Bede's, the guests repaired to the home of June's uncle, Irving Lehman, the chief justice of the New York Court of Appeals. There the beautiful young couple greeted their guests, the Jewish ones already bedazzled by the culture shock of an Episcopal ceremony, the Episcocrats perhaps puzzled by the appearance of a menorah on the mantelpiece over the couple's head.†

---

* With his work in the foreign service, Jonathan's brother, Hiram, carried on the family's Episcocratic tradition of government service.

† Jonathan Bingham was recently made an honorary member of the local B'nai B'rith, apparently the first non-Jew to be so honored.

Rough Rider Theodore Roosevelt during the Spanish–American War, 1898—an inspiration to a generation of Episcocratic public servants.

"Cousin Franklin" Roosevelt, April 1917, as assistant secretary of the Navy, a post four other Roosevelts held.

Elihu Root, one of TR's Public-minded Patricians (as secretary of war), later secretary of state and senator from New York.

Mr. and Mrs. John W. Davis attend a funeral at upper Fifth Avenue's Church of the Heavenly Rest, 1934. One of the country's first great corporate lawyers and unsuccessful presidential candidate in 1924, he later introduced his cousin Cyrus Vance to law and government.

Secretary of State Dean Acheson and wife, 1950. Acheson was a son of an Episcopal bishop and father of the head of the National Cathedral Association.

C. Douglas Dillon—investment banker, museum chairman, treasury secretary, vintner, hunter, Grotonian, shown here just before leaving for France as ambassador in 1953.

Secretary of State Cyrus W. Vance as U.S. negotiator at the Paris peace talks, 1968. His Kent School crew coach called him "very aggressive, but a perfect sport and gentleman."

One St. Paul's graduate, New York Mayor John V. Lindsay (at right), watching another—Paul Moore, Jr. (extreme left) being installed as Episcopal bishop of New York, September 23, 1972, in the Cathedral of St. John the Divine.

The Bingham children have all been baptized, or, as their great-uncle would have put it in haughty Yiddish, "gedunked," into the Episcopal Church. One of their daughters is married to Father Downes of St. Alban's school, a very religious man.

The sort of family-and-friends link that connects the Binghams to the Amorys and both to St. Alban's School ripples outward in widening circles throughout the Episcocratic community in Washington, for the Episcopal Church is a gregarious one, comfortable with personal relationships. There are, for example, the club links, especially those extending back to Harvard days. Amory was a member of Harvard's Spee Club, one of the modestly housed but subtly powerful groups at the Big Three colleges that choose members each year much on the basis of family reputation, personal charm, and (sometimes) achievement. A few years after Amory was graduated, Spee took John Harper, who recently celebrated his fifteenth anniversary as rector of St. John's Episcopal Church on Washington's Lafayette Square, one of the most historically and socially important congregations in the country.

Besides their joint interest in the health of the organized Episcopal Church in Washington, Harper and Amory share relationships in the old-line Boston church. Harper married the daughter of John Quarles, the longtime financial wizard of the diocese of Massachusetts; later he was an usher at the wedding of Stephen W. Howe, the current chancellor of the diocese. Much of the time of both men was spent administering the donations of the diocese's largest contributor, William Appleton Coolidge, Robert Amory's cousin. They're all related.*

Like virtually everyone else in the capital's Episcocratic com-

---

* It is typical of the Boston Coolidges that they have been far more concerned with true Boston Coolidges—including a famous historian and a famous mathematician at Harvard, as well as a number of diplomats and scores of buinessmen —than with establishing their link to President Calvin Coolidge. Indeed, *that* Coolidge's assumption of the presidency on the death of Warren G. Harding in 1923 touched off a crisis at a Coolidge family dinner. Since everybody was *some* relation, then as now, exactly what relation was this Coolidge from Vermont? Fortunately the Coolidges had available the mental resources of Julian Coolidge, the famous mathematician, who not only was pithy, like all Coolidges, but had an extremely precise mind. He thought for a moment and decided: "Calvin is my seventh cousin once removed." Which turned out to be correct—of course; for in Boston they are always *some* relation.

munity, the two families have also sent children to St. Alban's at the same time.

John F. Kennedy was another member of the Spee Club. Kennedy made a major point of his Catholic religion—or, more likely, suffered to have it made a big point by political enemies —but his educational and social background, personal tastes and styles were primarily shared by Episcocrats and their institutions. He had gone to Choate and so was acquainted with Episcopal services, which are not noticeably different from the Catholic Mass.

John Harper had a tradition to uphold, the one embodied in the nickname for St. John's, the Church of the Presidents. That title conveys the uneasy but distinct yearning of the Episcopal Church to be the instrument through which the American people sing to God as with one voice. De facto, this tradition has become one characteristic of the national upper-class set of mores that applies to high government officials in Washington and to important leaders of business, law, and opinion outside it. And St. John's Church, conveniently across Lafayette Square from the White House and built as all but its private chapel, has continued to display ambitions of its own along those lines.

Harper makes no secret of his desire to continue the tradition of every president since James Monroe attending services there (though Grover Cleveland was the last to become a member). He gave his old friend Jack Kennedy several calls; they were on a first-name basis, had met in 1946 during the president's first campaign for office, and had sealed a sort of Spee Club bond over the Kennedyesque gift of a pair of skis. And Kennedy responded to an old clubmate. When John Harper was installed in March 1963 as the thirteenth rector of the prestigious parish, President Kennedy was there listening to the sermon.

Harper's connections also go back into the educational system that produces Episcocrats. He spent the years between Harvard and seminary teaching at the Taft School, in Watertown, Connecticut, founded in 1890 by Horace Dutton Taft, the president's brother, at the height of the high-Episcocratic era in America. It was not an experience he enjoyed overmuch, but it did not change his opinion that the church boarding schools in New England are "really first-rate schools." He was able,

St. John's Lafayette Square, across from the White House, has been visited by every sitting president since James Madison. All chief executives since Herbert Hoover have signed its prayer book.

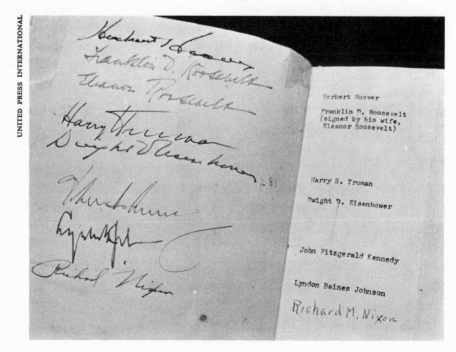

Harper relates in an account of his life as a minister, to get the son of a parishioner a scholarship to another church school in Connecticut—through the offices of a longtime St. John's parishioner who was also a fixture on the school's board of trustees. Once there, unfortunately, the young man demolished this careful plan to inject him into the upper-class educational system by getting caught in chapel with his, and a young lady's, pants down. An illustration, perhaps, of Robert Amory's contention that the prep schools have changed in the past decade or so.

Another of Amory's links to the upper-crust hierarchy of the Episcopal Church is considerably more solid: Paul Moore, Jr., now the bishop of New York. Moore sprang from precisely the same social background as Amory: old family, current wealth, Boston, church schools after a Boston childhood. Moore grew up in the fabulous, Grand Trianon type of mansion of Mrs. Paul Moore, Sr., one of the jewels of Boston's North Shore. Like a number of other Episcocrats before him with a St. Paul's breeding and all the money they need, Moore became a "radical" clergyman (radical, certainly, in contrast with the Louis XIV conservatism of his social milieu). Today he is possibly the leading symbol of the strains in the church between radical and old-line elements, a schism which some predict could ultimately lead to its dissolution; Moore's ordination of a lesbian to the Episcopal priesthood early in 1977 produced probably the biggest outcry from Episcopalians since the American Revolution.

Robert Amory knew Moore well before all that happened. Their lives intersected closely on a number of occasions. For one, "he damned near got my son killed," Amory says jokingly. Robert III went with Moore, then a suffragan (assistant) bishop in Washington, to Mississippi on a civil rights march in 1964, the summer after three young northerners came to their end in an earthen dam in Philadelphia, Mississippi.

Amory's ties to his current job, secretary and chief counsel of the National Gallery of Art, go well beyond showing up at nine and collecting a paycheck. His professional roots there extend back in lengthening tendrils through his previous, part-time position as treasurer of the National Cathedral Association. One of the most important clerical families of the Episcopal Church, members of which he dealt with constantly at the National Cathedral—the Kinsolvings of Baltimore—also provided the current wife of J. Carter Brown, the director of the National Gallery. Both institutions, moreover, to a great extent owe their existence to the Mellon family of Pittsburgh.

This is one of the major old-line examples of cross-pollination among government, business, the arts, and Episcopal institutions. The National Cathedral contains a Mellon Bay honoring the family's contribution to its progress—though reportedly with an amount of square footage dismissed by the family as too little for a monument to the richest family in America. One of the Mellon Bay's pillars is carved with the facade of the National Gallery, which Andrew Mellon, the secretary of the treasury, money machine, and philanthropist, created single-handedly in 1937 and which his son, Paul, has continued to endow and strongly to influence.

The Mellons and J. Carter Brown maintain their own tight web that encourages close communication and cooperation. One step was very direct: Brown married Constance Mellon, Paul Mellon's second cousin. The marriage did not last, but it brought the two men into close contact, and the commonality of background helped them overcome reservations they may have had about each other's value. They shared the experience of family members becoming high officials in the federal government (Brown's father was assistant secretary of the navy under Truman, a post that is catnip to Episcocrats, including FDR), families that endowed educational institutions—Brown is Brown, Carnegie-Mellon is Mellon—and many friends, interests (including art, of course), and styles of living.

Although he lists himself as a Presbyterian, Mellon illustrates how the mores of the Episcocrats permeate upper-class America. A graduate of Episcopal-oriented Choate, once a banker, now a horse farmer in Virginia's hunt country, Mellon is one of the great living examples of an Anglophiliac country gentleman. Despite his formal religious affiliation, Mellon is one of the few Americans who have given a church building to the Episcopal church—a faithful reproduction of a Norman-style church that he donated in 1960 to the parish of Upperville,

Virginia, the town near his Oak Spring estate. The English-
country-gentleman image is further enhanced by Mellon's pas-
sionate devotion to fox hunting. Mellon's feeling for his steeds
was so great that his first wife, Mary Conover Mellon, felt
obliged to ignore an asthmatic condition aggravated by the
animals. She rode with her husband. In October 1946, she died
of a heart attack only a few hours after a ride with the Piedmont
Hunt Club. Mellon built the Upperville church as a memorial
to her.

Particularly Episcocratic is the link between Paul Mellon and
Carter Brown extending back another generation. Ailsa Mellon,
Paul's sister, married David K. E. Bruce, a future diplomat of
high rank and cousin of Brown's mother, among other links to
the Episcocratic gentry of Maryland and Virginia. Their 1926
wedding has been one of the Washington Cathedral's grandest
gifts to the Mellons, and vice versa. David Bruce's links to the
National Gallery through his family connections with Brown
and Mellon were formalized in 1939, when Bruce took over
the presidency of the young institution upon Paul Mellon's
resigning to attend to business and travel in Europe. Bruce's
multiple interests in the men and the business of the National
Gallery proved classically useful in 1975, when, as director of
the U.S. Liaison Office in Peking, Bruce captured a fabulous
exhibit of Chinese architectural finds for the National Gallery
over the protestations of New York's Metropolitan Museum.
It was a great coup.

The world of law is one of the great subnetworks through
which Episcocrats have consistently extended their influence,
contacts, and opportunities. Law is a catalyst of professions,
turning one rapidly into another, sometimes flowing through
every conceivable activity of powerful men. Episcocrats are
among the chief navigators manipulating the flow. A law degree
not only helps them advance in whatever direction they happen
to be advancing but is of immense value in confirming and
expanding their importance to other people who might deal
with them.

Amory was something of a token Episcopalian in the law firm
of Corcoran, Foley, Youngman & Rowe, primarily an outlet

for the debatable talents of Tommy ("The Cork") Corcoran, one of FDR's closest advisers and still an insider's insider in Washington. An even more impressive figure of the continuing presence of old Episcopalian stock in the Washington law firms, which in turn feed the governmental structure, is David Acheson. Acheson's figure looks a great deal like that of his father, the secretary of state—tall, spare, self-possessed, fastidious. David Acheson is a partner in the Washington firm of Jones, Day, Reavis & Pogue. But his heritage is more august. For he started his law career at Covington & Burling. And before him, Dean Acheson, the bishop's son who became secretary of state, was one of the first and towering partners in Covington & Burling, the first and towering of Washington's law firms, the combine that made the mold for dealing in a sophisticated, insider's, Episcocrat's manner with presidents and bureaucrats.

The growth of Covington & Burling, a product of the high-Episcocratic age, too, was a very personal matter: Judge J. Harry Covington's connections with the Du Pont family, which consisted of knowing just about every one of them personally. Through Du Pont, in those days, General Motors became a valued client.

Dean Acheson's contribution, as he moved in and out of the firm from the early New Deal days until he died in 1971, was to solidify the close personal advice and effort which the firm could offer to potential foreign clients, who now began to flock to it. It was only coincidence, the firm says officially now, that two of its major foreign clients, Iran and Greece, came into the C&B fold during the immediate postwar period, when Acheson, former name partner, was toiling to defeat the Communist menace there as undersecretary of state. Coincidence, perhaps. It is the sort of coincidence generated by close personal contact between government official and powerful law firm.

Covington & Burling was responsible for the furtherance— actually the creation—of another important Episcocratic institution: the direct pipeline between prep school and major law firm that would come to dominate American law, business, and government in the rest of the century. The man responsible was George Rublee, who was no less than the first young man ever graduated from Groton. Appropriately, Rublee single-handedly created the firm itself.

CHAPTER
2

The Power of Their Glory

Episcocratic society is not only a fine linkage of the best names and families in the United States; it is also the most important single religious denomination in the country—the richest and most generally prominent of any American sect. While the organized church has undergone earthquake upon typhoon, the people who identify themselves as Episcopalians continue to prosper and enjoy the use of their power. The religion as such appears to play no substantial part in their success, but it has contributed to the establishment of institutions like church schools that are a distinct element of the group's hold on American power. In a subtler way, the Englishness, formality, grace, intellectuality, rationality, and fundamental conservatism of the Episcopal religion have nurtured and accompanied the development of a distinctly upper-class way of life and system of values that have dominated American business, law, and politics for 100 years.

As a cultural phenomenon, much more than a religious organization, Episcopalianism remains a dominant force of upper-middle-class life in America. Though formal membership has declined from a peak of 3,647,000 baptized members in 1966 to fewer than 3 million, with no end to the slide in sight, the number of Americans over eighteen who identify themselves as Episcopalians to pollsters for George Gallup's religion surveys has remained constant at 4.5 million for ten years. That represents about 3 percent of the population.

Strength is not necessarily in numbers. As a group, Episcopalians are by far the wealthiest, most eastern, best educated, and most highly placed professionally of any Christian denomination in the United States. In 1976, according to Gallup's studies, nearly half of all Episcopalians, 48 percent, had incomes over $20,000, compared with 21 percent of the overall American population. Of those polled, 43 percent said their occupation was professional and business, and 45 percent had gone to college; the corresponding national figures are much lower—25 and 29 percent respectively.

Episcopalians were heavily concentrated in the eastern part of the country—45 percent of them lived there, compared with only about 25 percent of other Christian denominations. (The Midwest was the Episcopalians' least favorite region; only 11 percent lived there, as opposed to 27 percent of the American population.) Except for Jews, Episcopalians are the most urban denomination, with one-third living in cities of more than 1 million people and nearly half in urban centers over 500,000. The eastern, big-city concentration is an indication of the Episcopalians' identification with the first American settlers, with the original growth of industrial development, with the current corporate elite, and with a preference for family expansion rather than missionary activity as a means of growing as a religion.

The fierce opposition on the part of many Episcopalians to the ordination of women is ironic, as Gallup pointed out to the church's 1976 general convention, because the Episcopal Church is more predominantly female than any other religious group in the country. Fully 58 percent of its members are women—a radical change from 1966, when the church membership was split almost equally between men and women.

The church is heavily white, as might be expected—94 percent to be exact. However, its attraction to upwardly mobile professionals and men of public affairs appears to cut across color lines. The only black U.S. senator, Edward Brooke of Massachusetts, is an Episcopalian; so is Andrew Brimmer, the first black head of the Federal Reserve Board. John Walker, the newly installed black bishop of Washington and dean of the cathedral, not only was the first black master at St. Paul's School and the first black admitted to Washington's exclusive Metropolitan Club, but is also married to the first black member of D.C.'s Junior League. For blacks as well as whites, Episcopalianism and other status symbols—especially upward mobility—frequently go hand in hand.

The statistics also confirm the impression that Episcopalians, while belonging to a socially liberal church, are socially conservative. They are easily the most heavily Republican denomination in the country, with 38 percent favoring the GOP and only 27 percent the Democrats. (Presbyterians are the only other religious denomination in the country that is also predominantly Republican, by a margin of 39 to 32 percent.) Gallup found that before the 1976 election Episcopalians were the only religious group that favored President Gerald Ford, a coreligionist, over Jimmy Carter—and they favored him by a whopping 2 to 1 margin.

Episcopalianism is the oldest religion in America in average age of members; only one in five Episcopalians is under thirty years old, Gallup says, and the paucity of young people seems to be permanent, with obvious implications for the church's future strength. Among Jews and Catholics, young people make up a share half again as great.

As befits a church that belongs to the worldwide Anglican Communion, Episcopalianism has the United Kingdom to thank for the ancestors of fully 49 percent of its members. Germany and Austria, with 15 percent, and Scandinavia, with 8, are the only other areas that contributed significantly to the church's current membership, leaving it the most ethnically homogeneous Christian denomination in America. The stereotype of the White Anglo-Saxon Protestant (WASP) finds its fullest expression in the Episcopal Church.

Jews challenge Episcopalians as leaders in almost every statistical category measured by Gallup. Episcopalians have a noticeable edge in the income race—48 percent make over $20,000, compared with 43 percent of Jews. But more Jews go to college. They show a higher concentration in business and the professions and live even more exclusively in the big cities of the East.

The differences between the two groups are not very large in any category. Jews and Episcopalians are much more like one another, demographically speaking, than either is like any other religious denomination. They even have almost exactly the same number of members as measured by Gallup. The composite pictures of Jews and Episcopalians are so strikingly similar that it suggests there may well be similarities in cultural emphases, family structure, ethnic cohesiveness, self-assurance or other sociological factors. A sense of the demographic challenge from Jews may also be a contributing factor in the persistent, though diminishing, anti-Semitism among upper-class Episcopalians.

Even these characteristics—noticeably higher income, education, and status levels than those of most or all other denominations—do not make Episcopalians the uniquely influential group they have been in America. Episcopalians are outstandingly powerful because they have bred a small, supersuccessful, and superwealthy elite that has become, historically and today, America's aristocracy. These are the people we have called Episcocrats. What has made them so important to the country is that their set of attitudes and mores, fertilized by a distinctly Anglophiliac and Episcopal atmosphere of feeling, has been adopted by non-Episcopalians as the standard for upper-class conduct. The influence of the distinctly Episcopalian institutions—the prep schools, the men's colleges, and the metropolitan clubs—can hardly be overstated.

As we shall see in more detail later, the major professional paths of modern corporate America—law, business, politics, even the arts—were cast in an unmistakably Episcocratic mold as they developed in the four decades around 1900, the age of the inseparable and triumphant rise of American industrial might and, not coincidentally, of Episcopalians' influence and panache.

Any number of unarguable statistical indicators gauge the Episcocrats' grip on the uppermost ranks of the American corporate state. Of the 500 largest business concerns in the United States, fully 20 percent are run by an Episcopalian chief executive officer, *Fortune* magazine reported in 1976. The concentration is even more striking in the traditional Episcocratic stronghold of Wall Street banking. Of the banking companies in the *Fortune* 500, no fewer than one-third are headed by Episcopalian CEOs. Episcocrats, then, not only are generously represented in the highest salaried positions—chairmanships and presidencies paying $200,000 and up as a matter of course—but are the largest religious denomination that decides the direction of the trillion-dollar American economy.

Perhaps even more decisive than the Episcocrats' high salaries and their exercise of corporate muscle is the enormous wealth they have managed to accumulate and ice away because they were, in Dean Acheson's phrase, "present at the creation," participating from the ground floor upward in the growth of the country's business might. Despite the waning of the staggering turn-of-the-century fortunes built by such clans as the Vanderbilts, Morgans, Whitneys, Astors, Stillmans, and Hearsts—Episcocrats all—Episcopalians still control an estimated one-third of all the mass of corporate wealth in the country.

Economic domination and the system of elite church-affiliated prep schools—which leads to positions of first rank in the important eastern colleges—have in turn given Episcopalians national political power far out of proportion to their numbers. Eighteen of the men made U.S. senators by the 1976 elections were Episcopalians—again, by far the largest single denomination in that "Millionaires' Club." David Acheson says it is "probably true" that more cabinet officials have been Episcopalian than any other religion in the twentieth century. If one examines such favorite Episcocratic government posts as secretary of state, secretary of the navy, ambassador to England, and deputy director of the CIA, these have probably been occupied more by Episcopalians than *all* other denominations combined.

The deeply rooted network that selects and appoints government officers at the highest level ensures that Episcopalians will continue to be widely represented. The system has not changed substantially from the days before the First World War, when Frank Knox, later to be secretary of the navy, arrived in the office of Henry L. Stimson, later to be the great secretary of war and of state, bearing a note from Stimson's fellow Episcocrat Teddy Roosevelt with the career-making words "He is just our type!"

McGeorge Bundy, the son of one of Henry Stimson's assistant

secretaries of war, knows that the deep-rooted network still grows giant Episcocrats. Bundy's career got its start when, as a bright young man fresh from Groton and Yale, he was tapped as a right-hand man by Alan Kirk, a society vice admiral who happened to be an old friend of the Bundy family. After participating in the planning for D-Day, Mac Bundy was handed another major, career-making assignment: He coauthored the memoirs of Henry L. Stimson. Those two steps on the Episcocratic ladder not only established Bundy's reputation and helped him become dean of Harvard at the age of thirty-four but gave him his first knowledge of the people he would have first to impress, then to dominate, as President Kennedy's national security adviser.

Once he took that post in 1961, Bundy started doing his part to perpetuate the network into the next generation. He first got his old friend Admiral Kirk a job in government. A good one: ambassador to Taiwan. Next Bundy took care of Peter Solbert, who had been at Groton with Bundy and then married Admiral Kirk's daughter Deborah. Solbert, a lawyer for the prestigious, socially correct Wall Street law firm of Davis, Polk & Wardwell, was referred by Mac Bundy to William P. Bundy, who was not only Mac's older brother but also Dean Acheson's son-in-law and so had become, to no one's surprise, assistant secretary of defense. Solbert became, in 1963, William Bundy's aide at Defense.

Having helped the son-in-law of Admiral Kirk, the Bundys could hardly ignore the son of Admiral Kirk. Roger Kirk, it happened, had already landed a State Department job; however, when William Bundy moved over to become an assistant secretary of state soon afterward, he could and did give young Kirk a handsome raise and a handsome new title.

Mac Bundy now rules the Ford Foundation as president, distributing its many millions. Bill Bundy is editor of *Foreign Affairs*, the enormously influential magazine of the Council on Foreign Relations. Solbert is back in New York as a partner in Davis, Polk and a resident of swank Sutton Place. All are in their places in the great Episcocratic forest, ready to help along the young sprouts who have branched off from them or their peers.

As David Acheson, William Bundy's brother-in-law, puts it: "Episcopalians in the federal government have been synonymous with what is loosely called the Eastern Establishment. They are somehow bunched in national office."

Somehow.

We will not dwell much on the religion that Episcopalians believe in, partly because this church, like many others, now tends to downplay the beliefs that distinguish it from other churches. "Episcopal," from the Greek for "bishop," refers to the hierarchical structure of the church, as opposed to "Congregational" and other sects, which emphasize decentralized organizations and the value of individual beliefs. Theologically, the Protestant Episcopal Church, as it is officially called, is the United States branch of the worldwide Anglican Communion. That means the body of doctrine is nearly identical with that of Roman Catholicism: Episcopal services are called masses; their clergymen and clergywomen are called priests; the doctrine holds that bread and wine are changed into Christ's body and blood and that the Catholic "sacraments"—baptism, confirmation, matrimony, and penance—have real, not symbolic, power to bestow divine grace.

But Anglicanism also means that the church, unlike Roman Catholicism, has received a heavy dose of influences from English character and history—a sense of moderation and rationality, suspicion of fanatics, love of literate sermons, a suspicion of absolute power in the hands of the bishops. Present-day Episcopalians have gone far beyond their initial disagreement with Rome merely over the pope's final authority; they have become much more liberal than Catholics, more relaxed even than most other Protestant sects on such social doctrines as divorce, women priests, birth control, and the independence of the local parish.

Episcopalianism is a faith for rational people. If that is a contradiction, it is both evident and troublesome to Episcopalians and accepted with benign insouciance. The Episcopal Church has made history of surviving doctrinal troubles that threatened to split it; as many current observers point out, a church that could get through the Civil War intact—the only major denomination to do so—can also survive a few harsh words over women priests and prayer books.

Episcopalians take a very English, stiff-upper-lip attitude toward their church; it is the sort of thing one should accept or reject personally, internally, without unduly annoying other people with theological disputations, even in church. Episcopal clerics almost universally deny having ever received a direct divine order to the ministry, a "calling," in the sense most other ministers speak of, and the laity is even less concerned with public acknowledgment of God or His people on earth.

George Gallup found (and he didn't like it) that Episcopalians attend church less frequently than any other Christian group; have had far fewer "born again" experiences per capita; "bear witness" (tell someone about the religion) far less frequently; tend strongly to deny that the Bible is literal truth; and in general place less importance on their religious lives than any other Americans who identify themselves with a religion.

At St. Alban's School, to use one example of the prevailing temper, "Jesus freaks" are actively discouraged by the school's religious authorities; one priest there talks disdainfully about their propensity to "go off to Presbyterian camps or something in the summer." Hence the seeming paradox: a very formal, elaborate, orthodox religion with an extremely worldly, wealthy, and rationalistic congregation. It is a religion for sophisticates—for people who can "believe" a religious philosophy of life without letting it interfere in their workaday world.

Not that there is a lack of substance to the doctrinal controversies that have been the main claim to fame of modern Episcopalianism. These disputes are expressions of the ongoing, fundamental split between the well-educated, socially progressive segment of the church that includes many clergymen and some of the more important urban, eastern congregations, and the more conservative, archly Republican, "social" parts of the laity. The split rumbled during the 1960s, when clerics like Bishop Moore charged to the front of the civil rights struggles and Dean Francis B. Sayre, Jr., denounced Goldwater *and* Johnson in a famous "plague on both your houses" sermon from the National Cathedral's pulpit during the 1964 presidential campaign.

Although there has been no actively racist backlash in the

Episcopal Church, many communicants did not hide their feeling that their priests were going too far in the late 1960s, when people like the Reverend David Gracie in Philadelphia were leading the drive to collect "reparations" for slavery and oppression on behalf of black militants. Quietly many parishes cut back or eliminated their contributions to the diocesan headquarters, which were usually more likely to support priests of Gracie's political and social convictions. Then, in 1974, the more conservative elements in the church managed to elect one of their own, Bishop John Allin, the bishop of Mississippi, presiding bishop of the national church. Allin turned the organized church's emphasis from the sixties radicals' agenda for social change to more "churchy," less controversial and ambitious attempts to alleviate shortages of food and housing. Theologically, Allin was looked on as a savior by the small but growing charismatic movement—a sign of evangelism and "religiosity" that much annoys the rationalistic, sociologically minded majority.

Allin and Bishop Moore quickly became opponents, if not enemies. Allin was given to understand that he was hardly welcome to cross the border into the diocese of Washington, even though the National Cathedral is his official seat. Ironically, though the liberals dislike him, Allin has also presided over the first overt symptoms of conservative unrest in the church—the gathering of 1700 dissidents in a St. Louis convention in September 1977, the formation of a rival "Episcopal" diocese, and the consecration in Denver of schismatic bishops.

At the heart of this controversy was the decision by the church's 1976 general convention in Minneapolis to allow women to become priests.* (General conventions meet once every three years to set overall policy in the church.) Theological conservatives and "orthodox" churchmen, Episcopalian priests have been an all-male brotherhood for 400 years, conforming

* The 1976 general convention caused a brouhaha over a number of other issues, perhaps less sensationalized than the ordination of women. The Book of Common Prayer—familiar, comfortable, "elegant," and unchanged since the early twentieth century—underwent revisions that raised some eyebrows, although a comparison of the new text with the old does not show glaring changes. Some Episcopalians are afraid of losing their Elizabethan English in modern America, but it does not seem they have very much to fear. Another cause of concern to some more conservative priests was changes in the liturgy. These changes essentially allow individual priests more flexibility in their services.

to the indubitable ban on female importance handed down from the Bible through the earlier Catholic Church. What do you call a priest who has been "Father" for centuries?

Traditional values run deep in Episcopalians, and the habits of ages are deeply ingrained in most of them. Even for many of the female majority, the issue of women priests was more one of theological purity than of "fairness" or "liberation" in a modern sense. Episcopalian women as well as men have always conformed strongly to the upper-class notion that the proper roles of the sexes mean that essential control—in religion as well as business—rests in the hands of men, with women alleviating the harsher conditions the men create. Yet the social and political liberals who have dominated the organized Episcopal Church over the past decade could hardly fail to support the ideal of sexual egalitarianism among the church's leaders. The conflicting pulls of long-standing religious belief and modern notions of a free society provoked deep conflicts in the church—and in many individual Episcopalians.

The dispute sometimes degenerated into outright name-calling and personal vindictiveness. Antiordinationists remarked on how "all kinds of homely women" were sneaking into the priesthood, sometimes within the hearing of the allegedly homely women. Supporters of women priests responded by suggesting that the opposition was acting more out of sexual-psychological cramps than theological motives. Robert Terwilliger, the suffragan bishop of Dallas and a staunch opponent of female clerics, had a difficult marriage that surely must have influenced his views on whether women could handle sacramental power, they said.

Bishop Moore's decision to ordain the lesbian Ellen Barrett appalled and infuriated conservatives—it condoned "sin," they asserted—and it added to suspicions that Moore was a moral poseur interested more in stirring things up on earth than helping people to heaven. But when cries of outrage arose at Ms. Barrett's homosexuality, liberal churchmen like the outspoken Reverend William Wendt of Washington estimated confidently that fully one-third of the 7500 or so male priests were homosexuals. Only they were quiet about it. Should hypocrisy be rewarded with ordination, Wendt asked, while Ms. Barrett's honesty kept her out?

Even in the worst days of the controversy, the indefatigable good nature of Episcopalians prevailed. It continued to be a mellow, polite church; except for a few bishops, nobody seemed much concerned by the threat of secession by a socially conservative splinter group. The dispassionate attitude among the majority of Episcopalians, including the regular churchgoers, is that if the secessionists want to get apocalyptic about every issue that comes down the pike, then the church of sophisticated, affable people is probably better off without them. Episcopalians do not get excited. They've never had to. Things have always managed to work out by themselves as long as Episcopalians continued to set a straight, smooth course through American life, powered by divine right.

CHAPTER
3

A Church of Contradictions

On Sunday, September 29, 1907, one of the greatest crowds ever seen in Washington until that time, some 20,000 people, went up to Mount St. Alban for the ceremonial laying of the cornerstone for the National Cathedral, the "great church for national purposes in the capital city" that had been envisioned by George Washington and dozens of Episcocrats after him. The participants at the outdoor ceremonies that dedicated the foundation stone of the great church represented the full glory of American political, economic, and social might, gathered to erect a cathedral that would symbolize their taste and ambition. President Theodore Roosevelt, the shrewd, tough-living descendant of a long line of distinguished New York Episcocrats, leading a government of aristocrats and eventually to inspire another under his cousin Franklin, gave the main address. The Marine Band lent muscular support to a massed choir that sang the cathedral's praises.

The American ecclesiastic establishment naturally attended in force—men like Bishop William Lawrence of Massachusetts, friend of the rich, famous, and Harvard; and Washington's Bishop Henry Y. Satterlee, who just the year before had celebrated the most famous and lavish White House wedding of all, the one which turned Alice Roosevelt into Mrs. Longworth. The bishop of London was there, too, suggesting not only the

Anglican ties of the religion but also the close political and social relationship that created an international Victorian elite under the aegis of the Anglican Church.

The most powerful and striking figure at the dedication had no official position at all. J. Pierpont Morgan, in his full, portly glory, the most dominant banker who ever lived, the most aggressive and important art collector, sailor, "gentleman," and censor of his time or probably any other, was also the supremely commanding lay figure in the Episcopal Church.

Morgan had not, it was true, been involved in the real beginning of the cathedral, which occurred on December 8, 1891, at the home of Charles Carroll Glover. From the beginning, it was the work of a small, powerful group of leaders. Glover used to discuss the project with his friends at the Metropolitan Club over lunch and dinner; they continually joked that the Mount St. Alban site he had chosen was so far out of the city that it might as well have been in Frederick, Maryland (about sixty miles away).

In 1893, the cathedral obtained a charter from Congress. That did not mean public funds, since the United States is officially nonsectarian. The funds came from the quasi-public men who ruled the nation's miraculously fecund economy— men like Morgan. Only the onset of construction was affirmed by Teddy Roosevelt and the Marine Band. No question, though: Like the Episcopal Church itself, the National Cathedral had become a semiofficial repository of national pride, national hope, and national unity.

J. P. Morgan had the same sort of religious accompaniment the next day, when no fewer than three Episcopal bishops went with him on a pilgrimage to George Washington's seat at Mount Vernon, where, in an act of homage from one national leader to another, the banker planted a mulberry tree on the lawn.

Both occasions were stops along the road to Morgan's ultimate destination—the general convention held by the Episcopal Church every three years to determine matters of national policy. Morgan had long been its leading layman. "No matter how weighty his cares were in New York, he left his business for the Church's Council, was punctual and faithful at the sessions, sitting patiently through dull debates," his good friend Bishop Lawrence noted.

Morgan's visits became combinations of pilgrimages and

Bishop Henry Codman Potter of New York, "pastor of the rich," about 1908.

William A. Lawrence, bishop of Massachusetts, fund raiser for the church and for Harvard, in 1898.

Bishop William E. Doane of Albany helped turn Mt. Desert Island into a resort with proper tone.

grand tours of his country. Gathering into his two private railroad cars all he would need on the way—bishops, excellent
food and wine, and a certain Mrs. Markoe from Philadelphia,
whose presence was widely noted and speculated upon (but
naturally not discussed with the reasonably discreet and un-
reasonably powerful Morgan)—in 1901 he spanned all of a
continent to attend the convention in San Francisco, where he
and his entourage were entertained by William H. Crocker,
head of the bank that was something of a western counterpart
of Morgan's Wall Street empire.

In 1907, Morgan's presence at the convention was an even
more inescapable reminder of the closeness of the religious and
financial power of the booming country. The Panic of 1907 was
astir. Morgan's associates back in New York could ill afford to
allow him to concentrate on nonfinancial affairs. He received
telegrams during dinner, meditated on them for a few moments,
then rejoined the discussion. Once a member of the party decided to draw the great financier out a bit, remarking puckishly,
"Mr. Morgan, you seem to have some bad news." At that point,
Bishop Lawrence remarks, Morgan "shot his eyes across the
table at the speaker and said nothing. No question of that sort
was asked again."

Caught in the business of the convention, most churchmen
did not pay much attention to the trouble on Wall Street—
though a number, like Lawrence, had substantial inherited
wealth invested there. Morgan, staunch churchman though he
was, kept his ear to the ground and watched for the interests
of them all. His easygoing megalomania in dealing with the
crisis and his matter-of-fact discussion of it with his Episcopalian comrades are striking testaments to a centralization of
American power in a particular ethnic and religious elite.

The story is from Bishop Lawrence's diary:

As I was going out of the door to the House of Bishops on
Saturday morning, Mr. Morgan called me into his room
and said, "Bishop, I am going back to New York on the
noon train." I said, "Why do that?" He answered, "They
are in trouble in New York; they do not know what to do,
and I don't know what to do, but I am going back." I replied, "Why do you go back at noon? You will arrive in

New York in the middle of the night. Why not get Mr. Sherry to have your two cars hitched onto the early evening train tonight: we will all pack up and go with you." He said, "I had not thought of that: I do not believe it can be done, but I will try." It was done, and off we went by the evening train. Still, there was no suggestion of care or anxiety on his part, indeed rather the contrary: he was in the best of spirits. Held at Washington for an hour at midnight, he sat on the rear platform smoking until the train should start.

Sunday morning, as we ran into Jersey, we went into Mr. Morgan's car for some bread and coffee before arrival, and found him sitting at the table with a tumbler turned upside down in each hand, singing lustily some tune which no one could recognize.

It is a precious picture: Pierpont Morgan charging into New York, drunk and confident, to save the country. With perhaps understandable exaggeration (especially given what he knew about Morgan's state of mind), Lawrence exulted in his autobiography: "The masterful way in which during that week he called upon the leaders in finance, the banks, and the life insurance companies, to pledge enormous sums to check the panic and his success in so doing are unique in financial history."

Morgan even managed to persuade the Roman Catholic archbishop of New York, John M. Farley, to state in St. Patrick's Cathedral, "I have confidence in the banks," and other religious leaders followed suit. The Rockefellers, those Baptists, could not repeat the trick the next time the abyss yawned, in 1929. Morgan did not succeed through any particular divine favoritism to Episcopalians, of course, but it is perhaps significant that the tight-knit business aristocracy of the turn of the century, pulled together by its common Anglican ancestry and religion, was the last that could preserve its own capitalistic system without government intervention. Episcopalianism was a large part of the bond that pulled together the great capitalists of the age—the Morgans, Harrimans, Whitneys, Astors, Vanderbilts, Stillmans, Fricks, and thousands of lesser lights—into a social, political, and business aristocracy that ran America in, and like, their private clubs.

Today Episcopalianism is a church of contradictions. It practices an elaborate, Catholic ritual and full-blown cosmology, yet is the most worldly of churches. It preaches a gospel of poverty to the richest denomination in America. It is an English church for English people, created through a revolution against English rule. There are hardly any Episcopal priests left who will say it is better to be Episcopalian than not, yet the church exercises an uncanny pull on its birthright members when it comes time to get married. It is a church of American industry whose clergy was the single-handed creator of church support for the rights of labor. Its leaders were banning books in Boston while their coreligionists were scandalizing America with the sexual openness of "café society." And yet no group has ever dominated American society more than 3 million Episcopalians. Where these select 3 million came from—and how they managed to latch onto their property, power, and prestige—is a fascinating quilt of ancestry, snobbishness, money, intelligence, schooling, and common sense.

Anglican means English. The Anglican Church is the Church of England—the established church of the country, supported by grants from the kings since England went Christian in A.D. 597, the church whose bishops are members of the House of Lords. Though such a formal alliance was not possible after the American Revolution, leaders of the Episcopal Church—the Anglican Church in America—have historically perceived their organization as the expression of all that is good and great in the national character. Because people of English descent have dominated the United States since its founding, their national church has always had a quasi-official tone. Because its adherents became so rich—and also because the rich became its adherents—the Episcopal Church has acquired through private donations the land for churches and schools that have given it a solid approximation of the self-generating character of the Church of England. Nor has its numerical inferiority hurt the Episcopal Church; as in England, the upper classes have become largely Episcopalian, while the masses seek churches that are livelier and friendlier.

In short, the Episcopal Church has achieved through evolution what the Anglican Church received as a royal gift: the

dominant religious expression of the nation's culture and the
most influential creator of the nation's mores. As in England,
America's upper class has not been unanimously Episcopalian,
but it has always laid down the moral and social rules even for
aristocrats who were not Episcopalian.

The Anglican Church in America has not been exclusively
upper-class. After all, England used to export its criminals and
misfits to the colonial shores. There also remains a leavening
force of Episcopalians throughout middle-class America. The
chief product of this Anglican yeast is an admiration for things
and styles English. Even more than the other American denominations of English and Scottish descent, the Methodists
and Presbyterians, the Episcopalians have been responsible
for the consistently English molding of American society.
Through formative institutions like the prep schools and men's
clubs, both copied from England, the Episcopalians created an
international aristocracy.

In the beginning, the Anglican Church in America was a
rather sorry creature. It barely existed in the nascent English
colonies except in the royal areas of Maryland, Virginia, and
the Carolinas. There developments foreshadowed the future
breakdown of American religion along class lines. Virginia
was the dominant colony—the Old Dominion—and the established church was correspondingly important there. Its hold
was strengthened by the colony's geography, which favored the
development of vast riverfront plantations and a self-sufficient
economy founded on slaves. That economy left nearly feudal
power in the aristocratic hands of the great landowners, Anglican nearly to the man and consequently inclined to impose the
religion in their fiefdoms. In the class strife that developed in
Virginia, the backwoods farmers began to adopt a dissenting
religious position as a reflection of their economic and political
disaffection.

Maryland was an even more significant precursor of religious
trends in the future nation. The Calvert family started the
colony in 1632, but they were dispossessed by land-hungry
settlers who used the Calverts' Catholicism as a political wedge
against them. The colony was rapidly Anglicized.*

---

* The English Reformation was barely 100 years old when Maryland was being
settled, and continuing European wars with religious overtones, like the contemporaneous Thirty Years' War in Germany, made good Englishmen violently

Seeing the handwriting on the wall, Benedict Leonard Calvert, descendant of the colony's founder, became a member of the Church of England in 1713—the first recorded example of social conversion in America. When he died two years later, his son and heir, Charles, the fourth Lord Baltimore, was given back the charter that his family had used to found the colony. That religious signal was enough for the few landowners who had doggedly held to their Catholicism through the years of the Calverts' exile. So Maryland began the tradition of social conversion that is carried on today by young assistant vice-presidents in blue-chip corporations.

The eventual stronghold of the Episcopal Church, the North Atlantic seaboard, had a particularly unpromising introduction to the established church. The Puritans and Pilgrims of Massachusetts and the other New England colonies had fled England precisely to rid themselves of oppressive church taxes and distasteful "Babylonian" ceremonial. They had no intention of letting Anglicans live among them, much less practice or proselytize. Instead, they established the great American tradition that the first settlers are free to impose their own form of bigotry.

In the seventeenth century, it was only royal power that created any Anglican presence in the colonies north of Maryland.

As America grew richer and more cosmopolitan in the eighteenth century, conversion to Anglicanism became pleasant and useful for many of the upwardly mobile. In the sloppy but yearning society of young America, Anglicanism was like a fashionable, charming boarding-school girl returning to outshine the rather common lasses around her. It was more refined, more intellectual, more dignified than the puritanism and revivalism that most Americans preferred. Then, as now, men

---

anti-"papist" as a matter of nationalism. That prejudice was nurtured by the isolation of American life.

The hatred was reinforced by the arrival in the late 1840s of the hungry Irish refugees of the potato famine, the most despised immigrant group in America until Jews began arriving in numbers later in the century. Anti-Catholicism in social matters has been combined by the Episcopalian with a pro-Catholic stand on liturgical matters—that is, a rejection of the austerity of low-church (and low-class) Protestants. Anti-Catholicism was an even more visceral force among the lowest of low Protestants, the Southern Baptists.

William White, first presiding bishop of the Episcopal Church after its break from England.

Phillips Brooks, the Church's greatest preacher of the nineteenth-century days of glory.

The church of refinement: Trinity Church New York, 1737, stands in sedate contrast to a religious revival in Kentucky, 1800 (below).

Queen Elizabeth and Prince Philip visit their American ecclesiastical cousins at Old North Church, Boston, 1976.

Francis B. Sayre, Jr., retired dean of the National Cathedral in Washington, welcomes Senator Stuart Symington and Representative James W. Symington, both of Missouri, to memorial service for Evelyn Wadsworth Symington, wife and mother respectively, 1972.

Pollster George Gallup, Jr., a leading Episcopal layman, keeps track of his church's statistics.

Tiffany head Walter Hoving, an "ex-Episcopagan," found the Church too tame and was reborn. His son Thomas, former director of the Metropolitan Museum, returned to the fold.

Bishop John M. Allin (above), here being installed as presiding bishop in 1974, is leading a centrist backlash against radical trends, exemplified by New York Bishop Paul Moore, Jr. (below left), seated near his predecessor, Horace W. B. Donegan, 1970. Moore stoked the Church's biggest modern fire storm by ordaining avowed lesbian Ellen Marie Barrett (below) to the priesthood in 1977.

with the time and money for refinement looked down on vulgar excess, while those with nothing else to do crammed inexpensive and concentrated religious revivalism into the few free hours.

The church became the religion for people who had other things to do with their time than be formally religious—the new-wealthy landowners and merchants. Their religion became an integral part of their society, not a mystical force to assure them of a better life than this one. This life was very pleasant, and Anglicanism was a pleasant religion. The joke now told about Episcopalians applied then as well. A newcomer to heaven asks St. Peter why the first few rooms are so raucous— reeking of alcohol, sounding like laughing and dancing.

"Why, those are the Methodists, Baptists, and Presbyterians," explains St. Peter.

"But why is it so quiet in the last room?" asks the man.

"Oh. Those are the Episcopalians. They drank, laughed, and danced on earth. They don't need to do it here."

Philadelphians provided the clearest example in the American colonies of an entire ruling class turning abruptly from the dissenting principles of its founders to the theologically less exclusive ritual of Anglicanism, which its Quaker fathers had hated. Quakerism was a difficult burden for the powerful and newly wealthy gentlemen of Philadelphia, the biggest city in the colonies. The Friends not only frowned on such practices as drinking, gambling, and marrying out of meeting but rejected members for engaging in them. Anglicanism happily embraced new spouses if they were *socially* acceptable, and the traditional tolerance of drinking and other "vices" in the church goes back well before the Revolution.

The great apostasy from Quaker ideals was symbolized and led by the heirs of William Penn, who inherited the colony when he died in 1718. Of his three sons, Richard joined the Church of England outright in young adulthood; Thomas did not hesitate to chafe publicly under Friendly restraints and eventually joined the church, too, in later life; John, the only one who remained Quaker, did not bother to attend meeting frequently. John Penn, William's grandson, was a pewholder first at Christ Church and then at St. Peter's during the Revolutionary era. Those were the two most fashionable churches in the country at the time, the preferred houses of worship when the Continental Congress and Constitutional Convention gathered in Philadelphia. After all, two-thirds of the signers of the Declaration of Independence were Anglicans.

St. Peter's Church was the first Episcopal church to become a center of fashion and power. The church historian noted that its opening in 1761 was attended by "fine gentlemen and beautiful belles, in damasks and brocades, velvet breeches and silk stockings, powdered hair and periwigs."

They heard a sermon from Provost William Smith of the newly founded College of Pennsylvania (now the University of Pennsylvania), an important center of the increasing strength and intellectual aggressiveness of converts to Anglicanism. Aside from William and Mary in Virginia, the most prominent colonial colleges—Harvard, Yale, and Princeton—were founded by dissenters who came to America to escape Anglicans.

The College of Pennsylvania was created in 1740 specifically to enhance the rising social, intellectual, and professional position of the Anglicans. Fourteen years later the same impulses gave birth to the little charity school that would become Columbia College. That school, originally King's College, had a board of trustees drawn heavily from New York's famous Trinity Church, and its charter provided that its president must "forever and for the time being" belong to the Anglican Church. Though that proviso was deleted from the college's charter in 1810, it remained in the grant deed through which Trinity provided the land for Columbia. In 1950 the Columbia board had to obtain a formal waiver of the rule from the Trinity vestry to allow it to elect the first non-Episcopalian president—Dwight David Eisenhower.

What finally broke the power of the Quakers in Philadelphia was the Revolutionary War, which efficiently eliminated from proper society all those, like religious Friends who would not fight. "Fighting Quakers" such as Owen and Clement Biddle and "Christian Sam" Morris took up the sword and the Book of Common Prayer at the same time, establishing families that would continue an Episcocratic tradition for two centuries. And when the smoke of the bitter War of Independence cleared, it became obvious that in fact, if not in law, the United States would be ruled politically, as well as financially and socially, by Episcopalians.

CHAPTER

4

The Church of the Presidents

When George Washington was inaugurated in New York City, then the capital of the country, in 1789, the oath of office was administered by Robert R. Livingston, chancellor of New York State and a former warden of Trinity Church, then, as now, the richest parish in the country. After the ceremony at Federal Hall, momentarily marred by the absence of a Bible, the assembled crowd marched up Broadway to St. Paul's Chapel, on Division Street (now Fulton), the oldest building standing on Manhattan Island today, a part of Trinity Parish. Washington filed into the special pew prepared for him (a rebuilt pew is still set apart as Washington's Pew) and heard appropriate prayers for his success from the mouth of the Episcopal bishop of New York (and former rector of Trinity), Samuel Prevoost, recently appointed chaplain of the country's Senate. And later in the same year the Episcopalians' general convention, meeting in Philadelphia, adopted a resolution praising Washington as one "who has happily united a tender regard for other Churches with an inviolable attachment to his own."

The theocratic nature of the first inauguration was emphasized by the members of the vestry of the same Trinity Parish, many of whom attended. Besides Chancellor Livingston, they included James Duane, mayor of New York; Francis Lewis and Lewis Morris, signers of the Declaration of Independence; Wil-

liam Bedloe, first postmaster general of the United States; Isaac
Sears, former leader of the Sons of Liberty; Richard Morris,
chief justice of New York State; and Marinus Willett, a general
in the Continental Army. Other areas of the country, such as the
English strongholds of Philadelphia and Virginia, contributed
to the new republic's service an equally impressive number of
communicants of what had just become the Protestant Episcopal Church in America. Four of the first five presidents (the
exception was John Adams) came from Virginia—the Old
Dominion, and the seat of the highest Church of England
sentiment.

But the layer of nominally Anglican leaders of the new
country disguised a gutted church. The church's connection to
the British establishment had all but demolished it when the
colonies fought that very establishment.

The clergymen and active laymen of the great Anglican
churches of Boston, New York, and New Haven were among
the most despised traitors to the American cause. As a group,
Anglicans were by far the least patriotic segment of the colonial
population. In Boston the priest and many of the lay leaders of
the Old Stone Church—King's Chapel—either left or were
deported during the Revolution. The church itself turned Unitarian and remained that way for the next century as a major
symbol of the religious preference of Massachusetts's elite. The
Old Stone Church remains the oldest Unitarian congregation
in America.

In New York, Trinity Parish was torn apart by partisan passions; its rector, Charles Inglis, fled the city to join the lines of
the British as they approached, taking with him information
about American troop placements and the irredeemable hatred
of the patriots. Shortly after the city was occupied by the
British, old Trinity Church burned to the ground amid accusa-
tions by both sides that it had been torched. After the war the
struggle for control of what even then was a rich parish bitterly, if briefly, pitted Whig Anglicans against Tory Anglicans.

Philadelphia, though its rebellion was led by Anglicans, saw
the disturbing cultural and historical tug of Anglicanism make
Tories out of would-be patriots. John Penn, grandson of William, was only the most famous of the royalist Anglicans
arrested by the patriots. Perhaps the most shocking reversion
to England was that of Jacob Duché, who before the war was

rector of the fashionable parish containing St. Peter's and Christ Church. Duché was such a patriot—and it was so unusual for an Anglican divine to oppose the king—that John Adams selected him as chaplain of the First Continental Congress, where Duché gave a moving invocation. Duché lost his patriotism once hostilities started and was removed from the parish and the city.

At the end of a hard struggle on the wrong side of the war, the Anglicans' fragments were left scattered from Portsmouth to Savannah. The church was torn apart. By the time peace was declared, only five priests were left in all of New Jersey, four in Massachusetts, one in New Hampshire, and none at all in Rhode Island or Maine. Even in heavily Anglican Pennsylvania during the war, William White, the first Episcopal presiding bishop, was for a time the only remaining Anglican clergyman. Two-thirds of the clergymen in Virginia left their parishes. Even worse, perhaps, was the situation among the laity. An incredible total of 70,000 Anglicans fled the colonies during the war or immediately after. The more prominent a citizen—merchant, landowner, or royal official—the more likely he was to leave the uncertain new nation, and since those classes had been substantially Anglican, many of the country's most prominent parishes were grievously wounded.

It was also during the Revolution that King's (Columbia) College and the future University of Pennsylvania were forcefully torn from their connection with the official Anglican Church. It was to be many years before there would again be a significant presence of Anglicans among the students of the nation's universities—although the administrations at Penn and Columbia continued to be informally associated with the Episcopal Church. When the students did become Episcopalian again, it happened mainly at newly fashionable Harvard and Yale, leaving Penn and Columbia as collegiate backwaters in social prestige.

Naturally, the church was severely hurt by its disestablishment—that is, by the forced loss of financial and political support from the government. The newly independent Americans made it a cornerstone of their Constitution that no church would possess political power, collect taxes, or force people to attend services.

Cut off by the outside world, the Anglicans were now also

stabbed in the back by their former brethren, the neo-dissent-
ing movement known as Methodism. When John Wesley
founded the sect, he intended it to remain inside the national
church; but its direction was against the formality and hierarchical structure of the Anglican service, and Methodists viewed
their wealthy and refined religious neighbors with suspicion
and distaste. In 1784 the American Methodists officially walked
out. That desertion strongly hinted that the Anglican Church
in the new country would attract mainly people of refinement
and wealth.

It either had to emphasize those traits or disappear altogether,
for the Anglican Church, facing suspicion all around it, could
muster little religious vitality to respond. The eighteenth-
century deist movement had infected the entire church, making those who still belonged to it wonder just what they were
supposed to be doing in church at all. Deism said that God had
set the world in motion, as though He were winding a clock,
and then left it to run by the laws of reason. The logical religious response would be not to sit in an Anglican service, but
to run through an orchard or look through a telescope. John
Adams, Thomas Jefferson, and even Ethan Allen, among the
Revolution's heroes, considered Christianity in general nothing
more than a pale foreshadowing of the true "religion of nature"
that every man could think of for himself.

Right after the Revolution, then, Anglicanism all but disappeared as a major religion, though it still held the allegiance
of a small minority—the oldest, proudest, and richest families
in the country.

From the beginning of the country, Episcocrats were identified
more strongly than any other groups with politics of an elitist,
Tory tendency. They tended to develop such leaders as Nicholas
Biddle, the self-consciously aristocratic Philadelphian who
sneered at democracy as "a mere rabble" led by "demagogues"
and by "political gamblers and gambling politicians." Biddle
rose through a tight, family-oriented circle that, even at the
beginning of the nineteenth century, showed its stubborn control over national policy without the need for popular election.

When Biddle was graduated from Princeton at the age of

eighteen, his father, Charles, asked General John Armstrong, a former U.S. senator just departing as minister to France in 1804, if he would take along young Nicholas as his private secretary. Armstrong agreed. The career was off and running. Upon his return from Paris, Biddle practiced law in Philadelphia and had an easy time, in those days of property qualifications for voting, winning a seat in the state legislature. In short order, Biddle was appointed a director of the fledgling Bank of the United States. Four years later he was elected its president and quickly turned to enhancing its power to control the currency and the economy in the manner of such great national institutions as the Bank of England.

Andrew Jackson was Biddle's great opponent. Lines were already being drawn between Episcocrat and democrat: Jackson was elected through sheer personal popularity and flooded the government with his political followers through the spoils system, a concept always alien to the Episcocratic establishment of foreign-policy and economics "experts," who try to survive political changes. Jackson's ascendancy was also a sign that political power was shifting to the West. Since, as the saying went, Episcopalians didn't go west until they invented the Pullman car, that meant the voting power of the Episcocrats would inevitably continue to shrink. Jackson correctly perceived that Episcocrats like Biddle made excellent political cannon fodder. Biddle, like future Episcocrats, responded with economic power. His giant bank had made a series of strategic loans to congressmen and newspapers. By calling in such IOUs, Biddle managed to get Congress to renew his charter. Jackson, however, simply vetoed the act—and the bank's victory. Its expiration signaled the eclipse of the old-line Episcocrats in the middle of the nineteenth century.

What with the Irish immigration of the 1840s, the continuing expansion of the western frontier, the rough-and-tumble beginnings of industrialism, and internal strife culminating in the Civil War, squabbling young America was far too rugged a battleground for the proper old families. With some exceptions—especially in the well-ordered South—they took their money and religion, sanctified by age, and began a long tradition of Episcocratic withdrawal from local political and societal affairs. In most American cities, especially after the Civil War, political

machines of immigrants and newly rich low Protestants seized
all the political and much of the economic power.

On a national level, public standards were, if anything, worse.
Variously dubbed "The Gilded Age" and "The Age of Boodle,"
the half century after the Civi War turned into one long period
of political corruption and the mightiest industrial expansion the
world has ever seen. Railroad barons like E. H. Harriman,
James J. Hill, and Commodore Vanderbilt, the Rockefellers and
assorted partners in oil, steel kings like Henry Clay Frick and
Andrew Carnegie, sugar lord Henry O. Havemeyer, pork baron
Norman Armour, the McCormicks of reapers, the Hearsts of
mining first and newspapers next—as these men consolidated
their economic power and grew bolder about exercising their
influence, the federal government became no more than a playground for them or their creatures.

Constitutionally the U.S. Senate was designed as the American upper house of Parliament, a body of steady aristocratic
men to check the passions of the mob that directly elected the
House of Representatives. But toward the end of the nineteenth
century the Senate had been invaded by the most bizarre, uncouth collection of millionaires a rugged country could produce.
While in the East the state legislatures, which elected senators
then, had traditionally been controlled by the state's old-rich,
and more refined citizens, the new-hatched western states had
governments that were little more than retail office-buying
shops—and they got the senators they deserved.

The famous Comstock silver mines in Nevada produced for
that unfortunate state two of the least qualified national legislators ever to stalk the halls of Congress. Senator James G. Fair's
reputation may be deduced from his nickname—Slippery Jim
—while his fellow senator from Nevada, William Sharon, was a
ferretlike fellow notorious even in those days for attending Senate sessions as infrequently as he did the opera.

George Hearst was no prize gentleman either; he had made
his fortune at the Comstock Lode, too, and begun his family's
investment in San Francisco newspapers and society. He
smoked, drank, swore, ran around openly with unseemly women, and in general was a crusty enough old miner to cause an
acquaintance to write: "Hearst was bitten on the privates by a
scorpion; the latter fell dead."

Hearst's good friend in the California delegation to the Senate was Leland Stanford—£eland $tanford, as Ambrose Bierce loved to write his name—who had built the Southern Pacific Railroad, together with Collis P. Huntington, largely by borrowing government money and refusing to pay it back. He spent the profits on a $100,000 necklace for his wife, racehorses, paintings, and a $30-million university. Stanford's most notable action in the Senate was throwing $20 gold pieces to newsboys to watch them scramble. The most straightforward of all the purchasers of Senate seats was Ohio's Henry B. Payne, a sanctimonious functionary of John D. Rockefeller; Payne's son Oliver, treasurer of the Standard Oil Company, distributed $100,000 around the Ohio legislature for that specific purpose.

Proper Episcocrats everywhere were revolted by people like these. Socially they were cut dead. While they seemed, for a time in the 1880s, to own the country outright, there was a developing countercurrent of Episcocratic righteousness that would soon turn mining fortunes and spittoon use into social gaffes of the same magnitude—a tide of proper opinion that would sweep all before it. And the sons and grandsons of the uncouth millionaires would be swept along, too.

CHAPTER
5

Cultivating "Episcopal Emotions"

In 1861, while the Civil War was bringing not only bloodshed but the onset of economic expansion that would usher in the Gilded Age, a young man who, several decades later, would come to dominate that expansion was undergoing another experience that would have a profound effect on American social history. He was converting.

Young J. P., the Episcopal Church's most dominating lay figure during its golden age, was far from the rough-edged robber barons whose financial activities he abetted so well later in the century. Unlike Rockefeller, Morgan had no fundamentalist belief that God was making his money for him; it was clear enough, in his case, that the money came from his father, Junius, who had founded a thriving international banking house with the father of Endicott Peabody, another signal Episcopal figure, as a partner. With that background, young Morgan naturally grew up the polar opposite of uncouth parvenus like Commodore Vanderbilt or Henry Clay Frick; instead of rising, like them, from poverty and fundamentalist Protestantism to wealth and social ambition, Morgan received the best education England and world travel could offer. Morgan did not grow up

Episcopalian. His decision to convert, just at the start of his business career, not only was an ultimately influential choice in making Episcopalianism *the* American aristocrat's religion but also reflects the sociophilosophical winds blowing across the landscape of an industrializing American society.

Morgan's grandparents on both the Pierpont and Morgan sides had been staunch Congregationalists in Connecticut. Joseph Morgan was a flinty type common to New England, reading his Bible incessantly on Sunday and his account books incessantly the rest of the week. Grandfather Morgan began as a hotelkeeper in Hartford and ended with profitable investments in the new Aetna Insurance Company. The father of J. P.'s mother was a Congregationalist minister, notable more for his religious fervor and his combative—even romantic—mien than for his business acumen. The crossing of the Midas-touch moneymaker and a man with a certain overall dream—plus a faith God would help him achieve it—is evident in the colossal figure of the mature J. P. Morgan.

The conversion of the young Morgan showed a telling mixture of motive, too—partly the lush romanticism of the high-church sensibility of the late Victorian age, partly marital ambition, partly social rectitude. Though his fiduciary propensities resulted in a stockbrokerage partnership before he was twenty-five, Morgan grew up a sickly, well-traveled, and rather dreamy young man. His unusual and suggestive hobby as a youth was collecting autographs of Episcopal bishops.

Morgan's first romantic attachment also indicated a personality reflective of the ritualistic, stylized sensitivity of Victorian times—a sensibility that would eventually dominate feeling in the high-Episcopal era of Morgan's maturity. Following his heart, Morgan became involved with a family named Sturges, particularly with their daughter Mimi. The family represented a refinement that attracted wealthy young men reared on harsher precepts and religions. Also of New England ancestry, they ran a cultured salon and filled it with music.

Two major events occurred in Morgan's life in 1861, almost certainly out of the same romantic impulse. He became engaged to Mimi despite her rapidly progressing tuberculosis (or perhaps because of it—it was the age's most fashionable disease), and he was confirmed into the Episcopal Church by the Rever-

end Stephen H. Tyng of St. George's Church, soon to become
New York's most fashionable. Later that year, in a lachrymose
Episcopal ceremony, Morgan carried the rapidly failing Mimi
downstairs in his arms to be married by Dr. Tyng. She died
soon afterward, freeing the financier from the burden of his
imagination and releasing him to marry the decorous, sturdy
Fannie Tracy, with whom he had four children.

The growing Episcopal Church after 1860 rapidly exchanged
its original high-church ceremony and beliefs for a comfortable and stately ritual that eventually shut down the religious
vigor it had shown for a brief period. That, no doubt, was what
most of the newly respectable Episcopalians wanted.

A big man who did things in a big way, Morgan became the
country's leading Episcopal layman as swiftly and inevitably
as he became its leading banker and leading art collector. To
Morgan's mind the Episcopal Church was another agency for the
improvement of America and the American aristocracy. His
devotion was very public and very widespread. Morgan was a
critical factor, socially and financially, in the resounding success
of the new Groton School, which standardized elegant and influential Episcocratic mores for an entire class. He was a senior
warden for much of his life at St. George's, frequently inviting
the entire vestry over to his massive Greek-temple house on
Madison Avenue for a meeting, but he also managed to attend
newer and more elegant St. Thomas's Fifth Avenue with some
frequency. Two of his closest friends and advisers were bishops
—William Lawrence and Henry Codman Potter, "pastor to the
rich"—and his interest in turn gave their opinions significant
social influence in the country.

Morgan was the key supporter of the triennial church conventions for decades. He was instrumental in founding the New
York Society for the Suppression of Vice, which burned,
banned, and badgered publications that did not meet its straitlaced standard, giving the country the term *Comstockery* (after
founder Anthony Comstock) along the way. (In Boston, Episcopal leaders like Endicott Peabody were the drive behind the
Watch and Ward Society, whose activities made *banned in
Boston* a household phrase.)

Morgan was such a caricature of the upright, uptight, socially
religious man that some of the more cynical members of the

Episcopal clergy took to calling him Pierpontifex Morgan. And St. Thomas's Church, built on Fifth Avenue at Fifty-third Street at the height of the high-Victorian Gothic revival—and still one of the nation's most fashionable churches—contains two tongue-in-stone architectural details that suggest even some Episcopalians were bemused by their church's wealth. One is a dollar sign worked into the tracery over the Bride's Door; the other is three moneybags carved above the choir stalls, initialed J., P., and M.

Practical jokes aside, Morgan's twin roles as moneybags and vestryman became the type and, for many a roughhewn new millionaire, the ideal of the Episcocratic gentleman.

One of the major reasons Episcopalianism succeeded in becoming the upper-class religion par excellence was that its clergy trod lightly, not to say hypocritically, around the social mores of its adherents. Morgan, the bankroller of Comstockery, was again the *locus classicus* of the church's double standard between rich and poor. It was an open secret for much of Morgan's life that he entertained ladies of questionable moral, if impeccable social, credentials. The joke was that the portly financier had three female members of a distinguished Philadelphia family to participte (one each) in the three leisure-time activities he found most important: his Church, his Art, and his Bed; they were dubbed his Church Markoe, his Art Markoe, and his Bed Markoe. One of them, identified only as Mrs. John Markoe, certainly accompanied him on a number of journeys for which it would have been pleasant to have female company—the 1907 church convention and an arduous journey up the Nile to collect things Egyptian in 1912.

When Morgan sailed his *Corsair* to Bar Harbor during his restless wanderings—one wonders how he ever got any business done—his interest was clearly more in ladies than in people like Harvard's President Charles W. Eliot who came out in an official delegation to offer him the resort's welcome. So apparent were his attentions to two ladies who lived in High Street that the street was renamed Rotten Row.

Morgan's dual interest in ladies and art was duly noted. "Morgan not only collected Old Masters, he also collected Old

Mistresses," said the painter A. E. Gallatin, referring to the solid blue-chip quality the banker preferred even in his women. Morgan's attitude toward extramarital maneuvers was indicated when a young man in his office became involved in a well-publicized scandal and was promptly dismissed.

"But all I did was what you've been doing behind closed doors for years," the unfortunate blade pleaded.

"That, sir," Morgan responded emphatically, "is what doors are for."

Despite his discreet philandering, Morgan never had trouble darkening the door of a church. Whenever he was about to depart Bar Harbor after one of his whirlwind visits, he invariably drove to Northeast Harbor on the other side of Maine's Mount Desert Island to deliver a new $100 bill to Bishop William Doane as a donation to his St. Mary's Church. Doane, the Episcopal bishop of Albany and a strong influence on the social customs of the resort in its turn-of-the-century days, would proudly announce the donation at the eleven o'clock service the next Sunday.

Morgan's sublime belief in the church as a concrete building block of a Business-Aristocratic society was not necessarily shared by every newly minted Episcopalian. Conformity was the prime motive for conversion.

Henry Clay Frick, the Coke King who got his start as a Morgan protégé, began his life in the bosom of the Lutheran Church. In the rolling hills of Pennsylvania Dutch country where young Frick sprouted, the embellishments of the Episcopal service were frowned upon, if not ignored as altogether too alien. The Lutheran faith had been good enough for the four generations of Fricks who had remained in Pennsylvania. But Henry Clay Frick, his biographer records, later in life "attended the Protestant Episcopal Church whose form of service appealed strongly to his sense of dignity, harmony and beauty."

One may assume that, while the Episcopal Church certainly possessed those qualities, Frick was not especially aware of them, any more than he apparently could appreciate the Renaissance thrones that he used to perch on casually while perusing the newspaper in his glorious and tasteful mansion on Fifth

Avenue. Though both the art world and the Episcopal Church benefited from Frick's interest, the interest itself grew from a desire to conform and be praised, not from a drive for aesthetic or spiritual blessings.

Similarly gaudy and unconvincing conversions visited a number of Frick's fellow robber barons, such as Jay Cooke, the "financier of the Civil War" and a notorious waterer of stock in an age when one had to be excessively venal to be noted for this sport. Cooke started out a Methodist. Before long his affinity for wealth and ceremony had turned his head to the Episcopal faith. He converted in a grandiose way—teaching Sunday school, organizing adult Bible classes, and filling his breathtaking mansion north of Philadelphia, Ogontz, with hordes of struggling young Episcopal clerics. He also built beautiful St. Paul's Church, which remains one of Philadelphia's most important and wealthy Episcopal congregations.*

Thanks largely to the many conversions among the business class, the Episcopal Church sustained growth of elephantine proportions during the end of the nineteenth century. It is no coincidence that this Victorian age was also the high-water mark of Anglo-Saxon self-confidence, of American business expansion, of a tide of xenophobic feelings as the great masses of immigrants arrived, and, simultaneously, of a rise in "sensibility," an aesthetic appreciation of Gothic forms of architecture (and, perhaps, thought), the calcification of the concept of the "gentleman" and of proper behavior, and the institution of the formal, idealistic prep schools, Ivy League colleges as places of nationwide social prestige, metropolitan men's clubs modeled on the English clubs, and country clubs reflecting a distinctly American preoccupation with sports and exclusivity.

---

* The impulse to build churches is one that afflicted the wealthy and powerful of every society since the West went Christian. Not far from Cooke's St. Paul's, in a suburb of Philadelphia called Ambler, stands grand and graceful Trinity Church—like St. Thomas's Fifth Avenue and St. Paul's, a product of the Episcopal boom of the late nineteenth century. Trinity was built by a local chemical manufacturer who in fact created the whole town of Ambler. The chemical factory has long disappeared. Today the church has an impossibly large maintenance bill, no endowment—and only 100 families to share the costs. In a clever attempt to keep the wolf from the door, the rector, Father John Schultz, has started a computerized survey service (with the snappy condensed name Nat Stat Dat) used by Episcopal dioceses around the country. For many other Episcopal parishes grounded by changing tides of population and wealth, there is frequently no such solution. Episcopal parishes close daily around the country.

Episcopalianism warped through all these social developments; its old-family clergymen encouraged by their words and
presence the development of these institutions of exclusivity
and involvement in them by the new-wealthy converts who
were flocking to the church. Sometimes, as with the prep schools,
the church founded and led these developments from the beginning.

For a church with a prejudice against missionary activity,
Episcopalianism's rate of growth in the late nineteenth century
was little short of incredible. It mushroomed from only 154,000
members in 1865 to 346,000 in 1880, more than doubled again
to 720,000 by 1900, and reached 1 million before 1915. In the
old eastern cities the conversions in the bluestocking neighborhoods became almost a rampage. One Easter during the 1870s
at New York's St. John's Chapel, there were sixty or seventy bap-
tisms; two priests administered the sacrament simultaneously.
A week later the bishop confirmed fifty-eight persons at Trinity
Chapel. On exclusive Rittenhouse Square in Philadelphia in
the 1860s, it was standing room only in Holy Trinity Church,
Sunday after Sunday. Whatever their social or political habits,
the cream of Victorian society in America was attracted to
churches like Trinity New York, because "the ideal was to ren-
der all services 'decently and in order,' with the beauty of color
and lights, but with the restraint of simplicity and good taste,"
according to a contemporary report. The Episcopal Church's
"ideal" had become the soul of the American upper class.

Boston's experience with conversion from the Puritanism,
then the Congregationalism and Unitarianism, that had served
the great merchant princes well in the early days shows the
sway that the refinement and stately, orthodox order of the
Episcopal Church exercised over the descendants of the wealthy
and aristocratic. In 1836 there were fifty-one churches in Boston—thirteen Unitarian and eleven Congregationalist, but only
six Episcopal. Lyman Beecher wrote, "All the literary men were
Unitarians; all the trustees of Harvard College were Unitarians; and all the elite of fashion and wealth crowded the Unitarian Churches."

Boston lived the depressing contradiction Henry Adams
painted: As the Age of the Dynamo crept over America, its
creators and beneficiaries turned back to the embroidered order

of medieval Europe. With Adams among them, Boston's elite abandoned the plainer Unitarianism of earlier years for the rich Anglo-Catholicism that swept first England and then America. Boston got its first Museum of Fine Arts in 1870, emblem of a new concern with visual ornamentation. Gothic architecture reigned supreme. Ralph Adams Cram, the Groton graduate who built St. Thomas's Fifth Avenue and other major Gothic-revival churches, came out of Boston to develop staunch high-church views and dream of a "Medieval Academy of America."

Even socialites like Mrs. Jack Gardner, whose amorous exploits and sensational bare-necked, pearl-waisted portrait by John Singer Sargent painted her name scarlet for a generation, crawled up and down the steps of Boston's Church of the Advent with a scrub brush in hand before services on Good Friday. She also sent out black-bordered invitations to Holy Communion. (Mrs. Gardner had begun her ultraeccentric career by deciding to become a Buddhist.) As a symbol of the dismissal of the plain, hard-bitten religion of the past, Boston's greatest church, Trinity Copley Square, was rebuilt in 1877, after a fire, in the style of the Episcocratic-aesthetic revival. The cream of Boston society followed its sense of fashion to hear tall, distinguished, proper Phillips Brooks, one of the great preachers of the Episcocratic age, advocate the new Catholicism and order from Trinity's pulpit.

Bishop Lawrence wrote:

. . . The Puritans were dogmatic and mystic, of deep religious experience. Their descendants, weakening on the spiritual side, had broken into two parties, both over-rationalistic, one dogmatic [the Congregationalists], the other discarding all dogma [the Unitarians]. The people were yearning for spiritual food, but husks were plenty. In the simpler creed and spiritual traditions of the Episcopal Church was the foundation of a revival of faith, but the spiritual element for which the people hungered was often lacking.

. . . Reacting from the Puritan dogma of original sin, he [Brooks] preached that all men are the sons of God, redeemed by their grateful recognition of the life, sacrifice, and resurrection of Jesus Christ. Of course he, like all forerunners, was distrusted by the conservatives, and deemed a heretic by those who thought and talked in the ways of the fathers; but the people of his own generation, the young men and women, understood him, gathered about him, and followed him.

Undoubtedly the "simpler creed" of the Episcopal church was an important attraction. Bishop Lawrence's own beliefs, as waspishly summarized by Cleveland Amory, ran "along the line that God was good to Bishop Lawrence and Bishop Lawrence was, in turn, grateful to God." The bishop was proud to admit he was "no theologian." Endicott Peabody, the rector of Groton, was so notoriously nonverbal on religious subjects that later few of his old boys could remember receiving any religious inspiration from him.

The patent lack of theological sophistication within the church, at least among all but a few seminarians, was not missed by the sharper observers among its members. In Philadelphia, before he was called to Boston, Phillips Brooks was referred to as "an Episcopalian—with leanings towards Christianity." Up in Boston, Ralph Waldo Emerson defined Episcopalianism as the best diagonal line that could be drawn between the life of Jesus Christ and that of Boston merchant Abbot Lawrence. Considerably later on, in the 1920s, the journalist T. S. Matthews, whose father was an independently wealthy Episcopal clergyman (later bishop of New Jersey) and who was sent away to St. Paul's like his father before him, came to the conclusion that there was something "ludicrous in equating a social sect like the Episcopal Church with its near-antithesis, the Christian faith."

Clarence Day concisely captured the magnetism of Episcopalianism for an aristocracy that cared little for theological questions:

My father's ideas of religion seemed straightforward and simple. He had noticed when he was a boy that there were buildings called churches; he had accepted them as a natural part of the surroundings in which he had been born. He would never have invented such things himself. Nevertheless they were here. As he grew up he regarded them as unquestionably as he did banks. They were substantial old structures, they were respectable, decent and venerable. They were frequented by the right sort of people. Well, that was enough.

As to creeds, he knew nothing about them, and cared nothing, either; yet he seemed to know which sect he belonged with. It had to be a sect with a minimum of nonsense about it; no total immersion, no exhorters, no holy confession. Since he was a respectable New Yorker, he belonged to the Episcopal Church.

The urge to join the Episcopal Church was encouraged by the air its clergymen had of belonging to an American as well as a divine aristocracy. "The social as well as apostolic succession was unbroken through such bishops of blue blood as William Ongreham Kip, Mark Anthony De Wolfe Howe, and William Heathcote De Lancey," wrote social chronicler Dixon Wecter. By the high-Victorian age Episcopal clergymen were intimately involved in setting the standards of their parishioners and fellow members of the upper class. The Reverend Henry Nichols of New York in the early years of the twentieth century published a book entitled *The Ultra-Fashionable Peerage in America*, in which he gave this advice to would-be aristocrats: "The Episcopal Church and the Catholic Church are the churches of beautiful manners, and if your birth has placed you under the social ban of being a dissenter, cultivate Episcopal emotions and shuffle off the mortal coil of Presbyterianism on as short notice as possible."

High-Victorian bishops such as William Lawrence, descendant of a wealthy and proper merchant family and cousin of all Boston's elite, not only were fine dinner partners for the likes of Theodore Roosevelt and J. P. Morgan but also pushed the creation of institutions that anchored the new upper class.

Lawrence's family gave the land on which the great church school Groton was founded. The bishop himself was one of the earliest settlers to build "cottages" at the rapidly growing upper-class resort of Bar Harbor. Among Lawrence, Bishop Doane, and Bishop Greer of New York, Mount Desert Island supported a greater per capita population of Episcopal clerical heavy-weights than any other square miles in the country. It early

St. Thomas's Fifth Avenue at 53rd Street during the 1890s, when it saw such weddings as that of Consuelo Vanderbilt and the Duke of Marlborough.

Grace Church, an earlier center of fashion, where August Belmont and William Randolph Hearst had their wedding ceremonies.

MUSEUM OF THE CITY OF NEW YORK

"Mother of Churches," Trinity New York in 1856. Location at Wall Street is significant for this wealthiest of all American congregations.

became the practice for Groton's founding spirit, Endicott Peabody, and St. Paul's great modern headmaster, Samuel Drury, also to spend summers watching over their young charges at their Maine retreat.

The small, strictly Episcopal prep schools that these men founded were a critical part of the Episcocratic boom that captured the imagination of the upper classes in the late nineteenth century.

The association of Episcopal clergymen with prep schools, long aristocratic lines, and a place in American society has come down to the present day. The Kinsolvings have continued to sprout clergymen from their roots in Baltimore and their place in the *Social Register* and on Fisher's Island with the likes of the Du Ponts. Former Dean Sayre of the Washington Cathedral could not have provided a more direct link to American power than his grandfather, Woodrow Wilson. When Alanson Houghton, Corning Glass heir-executive and son of the former ambassador to France and England, desired an alternative occupation, he chose the Episcopal ministry and the post of rector at an upper-class New York congregation, the Church of the Heavenly Rest on Fifth Avenue.

Presiding bishops, the highest rank in the church, frequently come from long lines of Episcopal clergymen, such as Henry St. George Tucker (1938–44) and Henry Knox Sherrill (1947–58). Recently there has been a takeover of the national organization by southern bishops; Bishop John E. Hines hailed from Texas, and his successor, current Presiding Bishop John M. Allin, directed the diocese of Mississippi before he went national. But the most prominent Episcopal clergyman of the present day, hero of the radical-chic, New York–oriented types who are the spiritual descendants of the social Episcocrats of the late nineteenth century, is the personally wealthy and socially impeccable Bostonian Paul Moore, Jr.

In the social geography of the new-rich Americans of the eastern cities, Episcopal churches shone like beacons to light the way to proper society. In New York, churches of fashion shifted from decade to decade, marching uptown with the silk-stocking neighborhoods: First Trinity Wall Street before the Revolution was the "proper" church, then St. George's, St. Mark's,* Grace Church, and eventually the grand midtown Victorian-era palaces of St. Thomas's and St. Bartholomew's. These churches nurtured the peculiar New York tradition of a déclassé but persistent and suave young man who becomes the social arbiter of the city, determining its mores and fashions and "important" families. Isaac Hall Brown, an ex-carpenter from upper New York State, became the first such arbiter before the Civil War.

Brown's social power was rooted in the post he held for thirty-five years—sexton at Grace Church, which a contemporaneous diarist extolled for its "pomp and vanities" and which Brown himself modestly conceded was "the most fashionable and exclusive of our metropolitan 'courts of Heaven.'" Brown's phrase for churches has the sophisticated sound of the medieval

---

* An indignity suffered by St. Marks-in-the-Bouwerie shows that even grave robbers knew where wealthy churches could be found. The missing body belonged to A. T. Stewart, creator of the first department store in America, who died in 1876. Stewart's posthumous troubles apparently arose because he foreclosed a loan to a group that had used the money to build a church, and in the process converted the church into a stable and dumped the graveyard remains into a pit. A ransom was set at $20,000, but Mrs. Stewart could not pay it for more than two years, despite her $38-million estate, because several sets of Stewart's remains turned up. More foresighted Episcocrats declined to use the graveyards of Episcopal churches; the Vanderbilts maintained a carefully guarded mausoleum on Staten Island.

"courts of love," which also flourished in a polished society that practiced an extremely earthy and social religion. Brown did his arbitrary best to eradicate the distinction between the Episcopal Church and society altogether; he used his sexton's role in weddings and funerals as the cornerstones of his suggestions about whom to invite and what to serve once they got there.

"The Lenten Season," he once noted, "is a horridly dull season, but we manage to make our funerals as entertaining as possible." This was at the same time that Philadelphians were noting, distressfully, that the growth of the Anglican population was shutting down social life entirely in the Lenten season.

As the society of the late nineteenth century grew simultaneously richer and more Episcopalian, the church seemed more and more, from inside and out, the proper accompaniment to a wealthy life. From the outside, a magazine of a different denomination denoted it "the Church of wealth, culture, and aristocratic lineage." From the inside, J. P. Morgan threatened to resign from his St. George's Church—and Admiral Alfred Thayer Mahan, the great theoretician of sea power in world history, did resign—when the rector of the church wanted to add "a workingman" to the vestry (the governing body).

"The rector [W. S. Rainsford] wants to democratize the church," said Senior Warden J. P. Morgan, "and we agree with him and will help him as far as we can. But I do not want the vestry democratized. I want it to remain a body of gentlemen whom I can ask to meet me in my study." This was no idle chatter from Morgan. He was accustomed to carrying out his promises; he actually had asked such vestrymen as August Belmont to meet him in the study of his massive marble temple on Madison Avenue. Morgan indicated that he felt the decision-making body of the church should be composed of aristocrats, people born and bred to rule—not people who worked with their hands and used their brains primarily to comprehend orders.

By the high-Victorian age, then, the rapidly Episcopalianizing business elite was ready for a gentleman-priest to mold and symbolize their aspirations—and they found him. Bishop Henry Codman Potter was generally considered the "first citizen" of New York at the turn of the century, and he loved that title. He gloried in the observation of English visitors that he was "a typical mid-Victorian bishop"—that is, an American version of the Englishman who holds a position in the church entitling him to sit in the House of Lords.

Son of a bishop of Pennsylvania, brother of the president of Episcopal Hobart College, nephew of the bishop of New York, whom he succeeded, Potter "was called, indeed, to be the pastor of the rich," his biographer wrote. "In Boston and New York he was brought into intimate relations with the most privileged people. Wherever he went, he entered naturally, as by right, into the best society. It was as a matter of course that at Baden-Baden he walked with the Prince of Wales, and that in London, even while he was a parish minister, content with 'humble lodgings,' he was sought out by the Archbishop of Canterbury."*

It was Potter who presided over the event in 1895 that was possibly the most lavish expression of American Business Aristocracy pretension that gaudy age ever saw—the consecration of the union between the impoverished ninth duke of Marlborough and the rich, unwilling Consuelo Vanderbilt, sacrificed on the altar of her mother's sociogenealogical ambition. The altar belonged to St. Thomas's Church on Fifth Avenue. The marriage symbolized the incredible power of the church's marital bonds in forming the modern American aristocracy—and the ultimate futility and emptiness of the achievement.

Marriage served to weld together the very old, largely Episcopalian, and frequently empty-coffered families of Boston, New York, and Philadelphia with the low-Protestant master barons of American industrial wealth. The children of such unions were naturally brought up in the Episcopal Church, educated at church schools, and turned into the mold of the Episcocratic professions of law, banking, and government—creating a unified upper class in America, whose products and institutions would dominate the country in the twentieth century.

---

* Following the fashion of the day, the grandson and namesake of Henry Codman Potter went to Hollywood, where he was a well-thought-of director during the 1930s. Lillian Hellman recalled in her autobiographical *Pentimento* that the Hollywood publicity factory had churned out Potter's picture on matchbox covers, as it did with movie stars, because he was so handsome. She and a coconspirator once spent two weeks figuring out how to stamp condoms with the message "Compliments of Henry C. Potter," which they then intended to roll into the matchboxes. After finally succeeding, they distributed the matchboxes as favors at a cocktail party.

As the biggest, wealthiest, brashest, and most "social" city in the country, New York was naturally the marriage capital. The city had its old Knickerbocker elite—the Livingstons, Jays, Van Rensselaers, Roosevelts who had long since turned Episcopalian—and the first aim for the rich outlanders who flocked to the city was to ally themselves by marriage with those families. Many did just that and thus made their own social careers.

The Astors were rich but not respectable until Caroline Webster Schermerhorn of the old gentry married William Astor and made the family name resonate more than any other name in American high society. The children of Richard T. Wilson, a salesman from Loudon, Tennessee, made such fabulous marriages in New York society—allying themselves with the moneyed Episcocratic lines of Vanderbilt, Astor, and Goelet—that a popular turn-of-the-century joke had it that the Diamond Match Company would go out of business "because Mrs. Richard T. Wilson beat them at making matches." Ogden Mills inherited a mining fortune from California and married a Livingston. Other California mining families had the same instinct, although more frequently they met their social levelers among the Episcocrats of Washington. "Slippery Jim" Fair married one daughter off to "Willie K." Vanderbilt, an unhappy but socially productive match. Fair's other daughter landed Hermann Oelrichs, wealthy son of a German immigrant, who had managed to accumulate immense shipping wealth and some social cachet; the daughter became a great Newport hostess and, in the tradition, a forlorn wife. Hearst, a nominal Episcopalian, married Phoebe Apperson, a more respectable (but Presbyterian) midwesterner, and the results of that marriage were the founding of the National Cathedral School for Girls by Mrs. Hearst and the education of son William Randolph Hearst at St. Paul's School. The daughter of Republican boss Mark Hanna married Medill McCormick, scion of the great Episcocratic Chicago newspaper family and son of the ambassador to Russia.

Henry B. Payne whitewashed memory of his purchased Senate seat by marrying *his* daughter to the immensely wealthy and increasingly social William C. Whitney. Then the process continued, solidifying the old family–new money connections under the benevolent gaze of the Episcopal Church. One son of the Whitney marriage, Harry Payne Whitney, married Gertrude Vanderbilt, by that time the fourth generation of wealthy Vanderbilts and a distinguished sculptress and arts patron (she founded New York's Whitney Museum of Modern Art) in her own right; they met in the classic manner through her brother, who was his roommate at Yale. "Just plain" Payne, the other son, married Helen Hay, daughter of John Hay, secretary of state in the Episcocratic administration of Theodore Roosevelt and once the private secretary of President Lincoln, who in *her* turn made much of another Episcocratic preoccupation, horse racing. (Descendants into this generation include John Hay ["Jock"] Whitney, who has been ambassador to England and owned the *New York Herald Tribune*, and the late Joan Whitney Payson, chief fan and owner of the New York Mets, as well as horse breeder and arts patron.) And so the intermarriages went on and on.

The Rockefellers, produced by the richest and most devoutly low-Protestant capitalist of the nineteenth century, proved geniuses at infiltrating Episcocratic society through intermarriage. The most financially and politically satisfying Rockefeller match was made by John D. Rockefeller, Jr., who married Abigail Aldrich. She was the daughter of the Rhode Island senator Nelson Aldrich, a rich ($30 million), self-made man like the elder Rockefeller, who had already achieved the respectability conferred by a seat in the U.S. Senate. John D. Jr. had begun gentling the family money by attending St. Paul's, but it remained for Abby to cultivate Episcopal emotions, introduce the mores of a leisure class. Early in their marriage, when her new husband asked her to keep account books, she replied simply, "I won't." She also had a habit of debunking Rockefeller parsimony by answering no to the question "Do you know how much this will cost?"

John D. Rockefeller's new in-law was even more helpful in the Senate than bought-and-paid-for allies like Harry Payne, involving himself in a continuing effort to defeat such radical proposals as the income tax and countering by creating the Federal Reserve Board. He sponsored the bill that removed customs duty from the art that J. P. Morgan, Mrs. Gardner, the Potter Palmers of Chicago, and other Episcocratic art patrons needed to bring in from Europe to adorn their new society.

One of John D. Jr.'s sisters married a McCormick. William Rockefeller, John D.'s brother and partner, in turn married two

of his sons to two daughters of his friend and banker James Stillman, founder of First National City Bank, which the Rockefellers came to control. (Another of Episcocrat Stillman's daughters
married Edward Stephen Harkness, whose father had become
one of the richest men in America, thanks to his father's $70,000
loan to John D. Rockefeller.) This branch of the family not
only sent its children to St. Paul's but actually converted to
Episcopalianism, which it has retained to this day. All this
had the double utility of providing the Rockefellers' ever-ex-
panding financial influence—moving their money from volatile
oil to solid banking—while it enhanced their social standing.
And it needed much enhancing. The old Episcocratic families
always had a prejudice against money that hadn't been inherited, as well as against non-Episcopalian midwesterners. Even
in the middle of this century, Mrs. David Lion Gardiner, *grande
dame* of the noble family whose name is commemorated by
Gardiner's Island in Long Island Sound, forbade her grandchild
to play with the Rockefellers of Nelson's generation by saying,
"No Gardiner will ever play with the grandchild of a gangster."

The children of these marriages between old blood and new
money grew up in the same sections of New York, vacationed
in Newport or Mount Desert Island with each other, and attended the same schools at the same times—Rockefellers and
Vanderbilts and Hearsts (including William Randolph) at St.
Paul's; Whitneys and Morgans and McCormicks and Crockers
at Groton; the Rhode Island elite of Aldriches, Pells, and Browns
at St. George's School, Newport. They grew up believing in the
same things and belonging to the same church. They became
the American counterpart of the English gentry, with a church
as firmly connected with their feelings and manners, if not their
government, as the Anglican Church in England.

This description of Cornelius Vanderbilt, chairman of the
New York Central Railroad, by his son and namesake summar-
izes the self-perception of the Episcocratic leaders: "Father was
a Vanderbilt. He had been reared by his parents in the firm belief that they were America's aristocracy, embodying in their
lives and actions all that was fine, honorable, and Christian.
Theirs was a sacred, God-given trust to maintain these standards."

"Dear, poor Marie Antoinette," Vanderbilt's wife, the great

hostess Grace, once reflected. "I feel so sorry for her. If the revolution ever came to this country, I should be the first to go."

The American preoccupation with the fashionability of "family" dates from the high Episcocratic age. The born aristocrats and the new-rich, from J. P. Morgan on down, sought out publicists to find their connection to Charlemagne, William the Conqueror, or equally unlikely royal forebears. The clumsy attempts by house genealogists to come up with aristocratic families as ancestors for the new-rich frequently produced a backlash. For example, when William Waldorf Astor was ambassador to Italy, he unveiled a respectable but unspectacular family tree, only to have a newspaper article claim that its own study had traced him back to Isaac Astorg, a Jewish doctor. But such attacks did not discourage the merchant princes. Wall Street broker Henry Clews's description of the Vanderbilts who were grandchildren of the Commodore is indicative of the Episcocrats' view of themselves. "In other countries," Clews said, "it takes many generations to develop such men as the present Vanderbilts. In this country three generations in this instance have produced some of the best examples of nature's nobility, which is superior in every respect to the vainglorious production which emanates from the succession of a hundred earls in England, or even a greater number of barons, princes, and kings on the continent of Europe." Not that such superiority prevented the Vanderbilts, given the chance, from forcefully grafting the House of Marlborough onto their family tree.

CHAPTER
6

The Business Aristocracy

In the autumn of 1910 a train platform in Jersey City was the unlikely gathering place for four of the most important financial men in the country—New York banker Frank A. Vanderlip, J. P. Morgan's executive officer Henry P. Davison, Assistant Secretary of the Treasury Abram Piatt Andrew, and Paul M. Warburg of the Jewish-upper-class banking firm of Kuhn Loeb (and, incidentally, grandfather of the yet-unborn third wife of Franklin D. Roosevelt, Jr.).

After a short time on the cheerless platform, they were joined by the man who had called them there—Nelson W. Aldrich, the most powerful man in the Senate and father-in-law of John D. Rockefeller, Jr. Swearing them to secrecy and demanding that only first names be used, Aldrich herded his select group onto a private railroad car in which they rode to, of all places, Georgia. Conveyed to the end of the line in Georgia, the men were led to a pier and rowed out to Jekyll Island. Here, in ten days with only one day off for shooting, the five men drew up the plans that would later become the Federal Reserve System —the "guarantee" that it would never take another titan like J. P. Morgan single-handedly to prevent the banks from shutting down and demolishing the nation's economy.

Jekyll Island was one of the most important of the hideaway retreats developed by the Episcocratic business elite to return to the land and to discuss, informally and privately, the deals that would shape the country. In 1883, a group of strong-minded businessmen, including J. P. Morgan, Cyrus McCormick, William Rockefeller, William K. Vanderbilt, and George F. Baker, got together to find themselves just such a retreat, which would not merely symbolize but guarantee the exclusivity and like-mindedness that would run their business enterprises. They hired two doctors from Johns Hopkins who scoured France, Italy, Egypt, and virtually the entire United States before deciding that the Georgia coast would be the healthiest, pleasantest, and most private place to retreat to. St. Simon's Island, where President Carter now retreats, was not on the market; but the group did kick in $125,000 to buy Jekyll, next door to it, and in 1888, as the Business Aristocracy's sway over American industry was hitting its peak, the Jekyll Island Club was born. At its height, it was said, no doubt with some exaggeration, that one-sixth of America's wealth unwound there. "For sixty years," one member observed, "no unwanted foot ever walked on Jekyll soil."

For sixty years also, it might have been said, no unwanted foot ever walked into the rooms in which most of the important business decisions of the Episcocratic age were made. Much as Morgan insisted that he wanted the governing body of the church to meet him in his study—and know how to behave there—so he held meetings for the reorganization of the New York Central Railroad, for example, aboard his yacht *Corsair* as it plied the Hudson River. "You can do business with anyone, but you can only sail with a gentleman," Morgan insisted, but the fact remained that when it came time for very high business, most of the participants were "gentlemen" in the Episcocratic mold. Cornelius Vanderbilt, Jr. (he would have been IV if they had numbered from the Commodore consecutively), recalled that his father

was an economic royalist of the old school in that, in his day, investments were a matter for private discussion among a group of very wealthy men. I used to see him and his old cronies [including such Episcocrats as "the Harriman boys," August Belmont, and William Rhinelander Stewart, Jr.], many of them men of wealth far surpassing his, sit around discussing the formation of new companies, their launching, the methods of enticing the public to invest, and then the methods by which they would eventually cash in. In those days it was not so much the general public which was doing the investing. Groups of men, or what they called syndicates, got together and decided to back something or not to back it. It was a game they played with each other, rich men against rich men.

Father and his friends would gather in our library in the Fifth Avenue house or on the *North Star*, or later in the beautiful green-brocaded library at Beaulieu in Newport, or perhaps on the *Winchester*, Father's very fast diesel-powered yacht, or in the New York Yacht Club. However, Charles M. Schwab, who was one of the group, couldn't join them in the Yacht Club because he was Jewish. And my father, who could have had something to say about the club rules, was one of those people who didn't care at all for Jews—including the Rothschilds, Otto H. Kahn, and Mortimer Schiff. But in business deals my father and Mr. Schwab got along very well together.

Cornelius Vanderbilt was not the only Episcocratic titan who managed to get along with Charles Schwab when occasion demanded. J. P. Morgan went so far as to invite him to a private dinner at the University Club on the night of December 12, 1900. The occasion was the final planning for the United States Steel Company, the most gigantic monopoly the country had seen up to that time. Schwab became its first president the following year and went on to make the highest salary in the country.

The Episcopal Church was more than an institution to which all these men belonged; it was also a relatively important part of their business life. Trinity Church Wall Street was even instrumental in the creation of America's first truly huge fortune, John Jacob Astor's. In 1767 Trinity shortsightedly gave a ninety-nine-year lease on twenty-six acres of land that it had been given in lower Manhattan. In the succeeding century the land changed from farmland to America's densest clutter of warehouses and factories and tenements, the area now called SoHo.

John Jacob shrewdly obtained the lease shortly after the Revolution and was happy enough to pay $200 a year for land that eventually yielded himself and his heirs $100,000 and more annually, enabling him to earn enough to remark, "A man who has a million dollars is as well off as if he were rich." As a partial recompense, the Astors later gave Trinity Church a fabulous set of reredos.

Trinity also dealt with Commodore Vanderbilt, the family founder, selling him a beautiful residential garden spot called St. John's Park in 1867 for $1 million, allowing the buccaneer railroader to turn the scene into a gruesome three-story freight terminal with his own bronze likeness towering above it.

Considerably more important to Episcocratic business culture was the philosophical support for the status quo afforded by Episcocratic leaders. Not that the church praised Mammon outright; that would have been vulgar. The church's attitude toward money reflected that of its old aristocratic members: It is wonderful to have, but debasing to make.

Leave it to the flinty, evangelistic barons of the grubby Gilded Age to attribute their wealth directly to divine intervention. "God gave me my money" was not something most Episcopalians would have said; it was Ohio Baptist John D. Rockefeller's unsubtle analysis of why his throat cutting and outright thievery made him the richest man in the country. "Pious John" Wanamaker, who founded Philadelphia's biggest department store and later bought A. T. Stewart's in New York, came from a Baptist and Methodist family and was active in the Presbyterian Sunday school movement, and it was this stuffy fundamentalist, not some third-generation aristocrat, whom Harvard business professor N. S. B. Gras used as the classical example of Max Weber's link between the "Protestant ethic" and stupendous business success. "We need all the Jay Cookes we have and a thousand more" was written, in 1873, not by one of Cooke's fellow Episcopalians but by the *Baptist Quarterly*.

It is true that one of the more infamous statements of God's preference for capitalism came from a proper Episcocratic businessman, George F. Baer, president of the Philadelphia & Reading Coal Company, who thundered during a bitter strike in the coalfields in 1901, "The rights and interests of the laboring man will be protected and cared for—not by the labor

The original John Jacob Astor, whose fortune sprang in part from a favorable lease from Trinity Parish.

J. P. Morgan, the greatest Episcocrat of all.

Morgan's namesake son and heir Jack Morgan (at left) at a round of government hearings into the business aristocracy's business, with partner George Whitney (center) and lawyer John W. Davis (right).

Leland Stanford, one of the uncouth California barons disdained by Eastern Episcocrats.

With wife, E. H. Harriman, son of an Episcopal priest and founder of a railroad empire.

Chauncey M. Depew, "the Vanderbilt prime minister," later senator from New York.

George F. Baker, one of Bishop Lawrence's most productive fund-raising targets.

Pierre S. du Pont, creator of the modern ammunition-chemical empire, opponent of Franklin Roosevelt, grandson of the current governor of Delaware.

agitators, but men to whom God in His infinite wisdom has given the control of the property interests of the country, and upon the successful management of which so much depends." But Baer was promptly denounced not only by Episcopal and other clergymen but by an infinitely higher-class Episcopal authority. President Theodore Roosevelt, who was Baer's audience, said later, "If it wasn't for the high office I hold, I would have taken him by the seat of the breeches and the nape of the neck, and chucked him out the window."

So the lines were drawn: the vulgar low Protestants who bragged about their money on the one hand; the genteel Episcocrats on the other. It was the purpose of Episcopalianism not to deify money, but to legitimize it. Analyses of society by leading Episcopalians of the high-Victorian era were subtle statements of superiority based on long-held truths, affirmations of the status quo with seldom much overt mention of one man's money.

"Material prosperity is helping to make the national character sweeter, more joyous, more unselfish, more Christ-like," Bishop Lawrence assured his listeners. The Episcopal general convention of 1877 asserted that any committee it created to consider "the social movements of the age . . . must be composed in large part of those who hold in trust the mighty forces of wealth and culture and social position." Bishop Robert L. Paddock, preaching in New York City's Christ Church (not one of the overtly fashionable churches) in January 1907, made probably the most extreme Episcopal defense of capitalistic wealth as an expression of God's will. Speaking of his divine master, Paddock asserted, "He calls some men to make money, a million it may be in one case, a thousand in another. Whatever the difference may be between the men who make these sums is God-given, and the million men should realize that fact and live accordingly."

That sort of aggressive assertion of divine right to wealth, and to the control of other men, did not usually issue from Episcopal clergymen, but rather from the more insensitive socialites among their parishioners.

Perhaps what one can best say about Brooks, about Endicott Peabody, Bishop Lawrence, and the leading laymen of the Business Aristocracy, like J. P. Morgan, is not that they either despised or approved of poverty; they were neutral on it. Everyone could become rich, they believed; they had done it even before they were old enough to worry about it. Everyone *should* become rich. No doubt the Apocalypse would provide a sort of spiritual equivalent of universal wealth, a celestial Gilded Age where no beggars need wait outside the gates.

The great Episcocrats were too high-minded to feel the physical grind of poverty, to realize what "want" meant. Not only did they grow up with the comforting assurance that the grand facts of interest and dividend would automatically take care of them all their lives—that assurance is available now, too; but there was something more precious available to the turn-of-the-century upper class: physical distance from poverty. Upper-class neighborhoods were still in the center of cities toward the end of the 1800s, so no one had to drive through slums to get to work. There was no television or film to show the grimier aspects of life to people who didn't want to see them and none of the freedom later brought by the automobile, which allowed the poorer folk to travel into the richer folk's neighborhoods.

It was not until the last two decades of the nineteenth century that the pressure of immigration bore down on aristocratic inner-city neighborhoods; great town houses were abandoned to slum apartments, and the gentry removed themselves to their suburban enclaves. Attending schools with each other, attending Episcopal churches together, going to colleges that only halfway through the twentieth century started approaching a demographic egality, and hobnobbing at country clubs and metropolitan clubs, the upper class grew up wrapped in the cocoon of its conservative, pleasant, optimistic philosophy. A great Philadelphia gentleman and Episcopal lay leader, law baron George Wharton Pepper, wrote in his autobiography in 1944:

In the past I have repeatedly tried to imagine what it is like to be cold and hungry and harassed by debts but I have always ended by admitting the inadequacy of mere imagination. Rolling along in a comfortable car, spending my days in congenial work, going back at nightfall to a happy home without fear of landlord or sheriff, I simply could not imagine what it is like to be an elevator boy or a taxi driver or a share cropper or a coal miner or a veteran too old to be employed or a man with a sick wife or child and unable to afford medical care or nursing comforts or a white-collar worker conscious of inherent capacity but up against a dead end with no chance of promotion.

The official church position—and the private impulse of the truly devout and socially aware—has been that those who did happen to find themselves on the top of the pyramid ought to use their wealth to benefit those under the pyramid. The enlightened view that came out of the great aristocracies and orthodox traditions of the church was expressed in 1887 by a prominent New York Episcopalian, William Reed Huntington: "If a government by wealth be inevitable (and perhaps it is), let us at least do what we can to spread the maxim that *richesse* as well as *noblesse oblige*."

Following Huntington's advice, the church took an active hand in a society in which *richesse* and *noblesse* were rapidly becoming one under its tutelage, in the fiscal education of its parishioners. In the more seasoned descendants of the self-made men who first converted to Episcopalianism, the obligation to give, help, and support was inbred—though shrewd attention to the details of the giving was also ordained.

Bishop Lawrence noted that he once addressed a group of Boston debutantes and recalled their "delight as I said, 'If I had your father here, I would tell him to give you a larger allowance than you can reasonably spend,' a delight mitigated by the next remark, 'under the condition that you give away a certain proportion, and keep exact accounts.'"

In the great families of the aristocracy that emphasis on the responsibilities of great wealth, on the quasi-religious stewardship Episcocrats commanded on behalf of their underlings, was handed out with the great wealth itself—often with certain quirks. John Hay ("Jock") Whitney, the one-time *Herald Tribune* owner, ambassador to Britain, and CIA front, recalls the advice he got from his father, Payne Whitney:

When I was about to go to college [Yale], my father and I had a talk. He told me that his father [William Whitney, founder of the family fortune], who was a rich man, had given him about half the allowance other boys of his age group received. My grandfather did this in order to teach my father the value of money and to make sure he didn't throw his weight around. The result, as my father described it, was that he could never do his share. My father told me that he was going to give me more than the other boys got, because he wanted me to do more than my share. Then he said, "The test is going to be whether any of your friends know you are doing more than your share. The first time I learn that they know you are doing more, I'll cut your allowance."

The advice not to let anyone know was ignored by other members of the Whitney family, as attested by the hospitals and museums they gave their names to. It did, however, represent the best of Episcocratic social virtues—unobtrusive, self-abnegating service out of the fullness of one's heart. It has been responsible for some of the great schools, museums, and libraries of the country. In the best of Episcocratic structures, where financial noblesse oblige has been observed with quasi-religious seriousness, the Episcopal gentry has alone supported most of the country's great libraries, museums, schools, hospitals, and other public accommodations. The near-visionary respect for their own money that marked the best of the Episcocratic titans of business was expressed by the Reverend David Greer, rector of St. Batholomew's and future bishop of New York, in his eulogy for Cornelius Vanderbilt II, grandson of the roughhewn Commodore who had made and passed along a fortune of $100 million: "The man was more than his money. His wealth was regarded by him, not simply as something personal, but as a great and sacred trust which it was his duty to administer, not with a lavish carelessness, but with a wise and discriminating consciousness, for the benefit of his fellow-men."

One of the fellowmen Vanderbilt benefited was the Reverend Mr. Greer himself, who emerged $50,000 richer thanks to his service in St. Bartholomew's—itself such an object of Vanderbilt's openhandedness that it became known as "the Vanderbilt church."

Harvard and Yale are great educational institutions because of the major aristocrats' generosity, encouraged by churchmen–fund raisers like Bishop Lawrence and hothoused by the family traditions among alumni. The scope of their support can be partly illustrated by a letter from the pen of Henry Lee Higginson, one of Boston's major Episcocrats, in support of Harvard's fund raising:

> Dear ———:
> Nobody knows his duties better than yourself—therefore I presume to admonish you. I want you, as the oldest and richest member of your family and mine, to give the College $100,000, to be used in any way which seems best to you.
>
> My reasons are that you, a public-spirited and educated gentleman, owe it to yourself, to your country, and to the Republic. How else are we to save our country if not by education in all ways and on all sides? What can we do so useful to the human race in every aspect? It is wasting your time to read such platitudes.
>
> Democracy has got fast hold of the world, and *will* rule. Let use see that she does it more wisely and more humanely than the kings and nobles have done! Our chance is *now*—before the country is full and the struggle for bread becomes intense and bitter.
>
> Educate, and save ourselves and our families and our money from mobs!

Exactly how Harvard's $100,000 would benefit the minds of the immigrants who were swarming into the country even as the Episcocrats took firm hold of the college and the country is a little hard to imagine. But the intent, the class feeling, the attempt to engender noblesse oblige are evident. Even today, in the largest private fund-raising drive ever undertaken, Yale is trying to raise an incredible $370 million (with only modest success) by appealing to this sense of stewardship, the quasi-religious impulse to preserve the future of mankind. (There is no public suggestion that Yale is trying to save upper-class money from "mobs.") The campaign is being led by John Danforth, Ralston Purina cereal and dog food heir, U.S. senator—and Episcopal priest.

Danforth's presence at the head of Yale's campaign resurrects visions of Bishop Lawrence, perhaps the single greatest fund raiser of all time. Lawrence raised money for Harvard's Hasty Pudding Club, for Massachusetts General Hospital (one of the best hospitals in the world), $1 million for the Cambridge Theological School, much for Wellesley College, Groton, and St. Mark's, untold millions in what seemed a never-ending campaign for Harvard, and, finally, almost $9 million for the Episcopal Church Pension Fund.

One seamy and paradoxical underside to the grand theological structure that supported the Victorian aristocracy was the shabby, sometimes desperate straits of retired clergymen who had assured their parishioners for so long of their right to their money. Priesting did not pay well then. Retiring from the priesthood didn't pay at all. As Bishop Lawrence noted, the church "naturally" treated its servants the same way as its rich members did their servants: by abandoning them to the tender mercies of the charitable. Frequently those mercies really were tender, but they were seldom adequate. "The common sentiment was that they ought to have saved enough out of their salaries and wages for 'rainy days' or their old age, and if they did not it was their own fault," recalled Lawrence, whose rich grandfather Apppleton had taken care of *his* old age before he was born. But Lawrence succeeded in establishing a pension fund, which survives to this day.

To hear Lawrence tell it, fund raising in those golden, homogeneous days was a matter of reminding wealthy men of the glorious experiences all members of their class shared, then carting away the proceeds in a wheelbarrow. "Looking up Murray Crane in the Senate, I told him the story [of Harvard's need], and in his quaint and nasal voice he said, 'Those Harvard people have been good to me: you can have twenty-five thousand dollars,'" Bishop Lawrence noted cheerfully. But Senator Crane was a piker compared with William K. Vanderbilt, from whom, Lawrence recorded in his notebook, he "got $100,000 in five minutes."

Lawrence's method, the tried and proved route of the Episcocratic fund raiser, depended on personal contact, the purveying of relevant facts, figures, and reasons for helping—and no pressure. No pictures of starving children. "My rule is never to allow a person to sign a pledge in my presence," the bishop asserted. "If I should get it by personal pressure, I should never succeed with that man a second time." He would not allow the names of his subscribers to be generally known, going only so far, later in his career, as to show balky prospects lists containing the names of their relatives and friends who *had* kicked in.

This can be an effective approach in the right community, surrounded by a tightly enough drawn circle of public-minded Episcopalians. It was the peer-group pressure from such a circle that must have led to the extraordinary gifts of Sylvia Green Wilks that were contained in the will opened after her death in 1951. The leading beneficiaries were the Kent School, $3 million; Groton and St. Paul's, $2.5 million each; and Trinity Church Newport (apparently because Mrs. Wilks once enjoyed a moonlight stroll through its graveyard), nearly $650,000. Certainly Mrs. Wilks was of the right class; she was the daughter of Hetty Green, the tight-fisted old New England lady reputed to be the richest woman in the world at the turn of the century.

Mrs. Wilks married a grandson of John Jacob Astor. But Hetty Green never allowed Sylvia to visit any of the institutions of her class; instead, she was brought up in poverty by her strange, rich mother, and lived most of her life in total seclusion. The family was not Episcopalian until Hetty Green, born a Quaker, converted with a view to being buried in the same Episcopal graveyard in Bellows Falls, Vermont, that contained her husband's remains. After Mrs. Wilks's sad, stilted life, the primary impulse that came to light through her posthumous wishes was the drive to enhance Episcocratic institutions.

George Baker provided Lawrence with the same sort of surprise. In his usual manner, Lawrence approached the grizzled, forbidding banker on Jekyll Island one evening in 1923—dropping conversation about how wonderful the planned Harvard Business School would be. Then he asked straightforwardly, "Mr. Baker, how would you like to give a million dollars?"

"I would not," Baker shot back. "I would not like to give a million dollars, and I would not like to give even half a million dollars."

While Lawrence was for once nonplussed, Baker gave him a taste of his own medicine by describing in Lawrentian terms the bridge that Baker would like to see built where the George Washington Bridge now crosses the Hudson. "I like the idea of my children and grandchildren driving over the George F. Baker Bridge," he said, making Lawrence even more uncomfortable. "It may not be the right kind of pride, but it appeals to me."

Then, suddenly, Baker stared at his victim and asked, "Bishop, if I give up my bridge, do you think that Harvard will let me give five million dollars and have the privilege of building the whole Business School?" Harvard let him; the world's best-known business school stands as testimony to Baker's philanthropy.

To some extent, today's Episcopalians conduct their money affairs in the same eccentric, but canny, way. When the National Cathedral got a call not long ago from a New York lawyer mentioning "high six figures" in a bequest, nobody could remember the donor. Finally, a search of the cathedral's records and mailing lists revealed that the attorney's client, one Sarah Bartram, had bought Christmas cards from the cathedral bookshop for years and had apparently been impressed. "I call that covering all the angles," former treasurer Robert Amory says with a smile. "Frank Sayre, on the other hand, calls it the will of God."

Another example of the quirky and free-enterprise ways of the Episcocratic moneyed class, especially in this age, is a lady named Olive King, whose tastes run to tennis shoes and the installations of presiding bishops. She was watching such a ceremony in June 1974. The chief primate of the Canadian national church, the archbishop of Sudbury, commended Dean Sayre on the magnificence the taxpayers had achieved in their national church.

"No, the taxpayers do not contribute," Sayre said.

"Well, Sir Dean," replied the cultured archbishop, "all the rich members of your wonderful national church, of course, had no trouble handling the cost anyway."

"No, they're not all that rich, and the rich ones haven't given that much," Sayre demurred.

"But, Sir Dean," said the surprised archbishop, "who has

paid for this cathedral, to allow lovely ladies like that to worship in such splendor?"

"That little lady is Olive King, Archbishop, and she gave a little over a million dollars." A sort of latter-day Astor, Mrs. King had given her farm, in the corridor of Baltimore-Washington development, to the cathedral.

CHAPTER
7

The Refined Reactionaries

The world was changing—that seemed obvious enough to Cornelius Vanderbilt, Jr. He was in uniform, ready to head off for France to fight the World War in 1918. The country was mobilizing, and he with it; so, for that matter, was his father, General Cornelius Vanderbilt. The son went to visit the giant Fifth Avenue home of his parents for a last time before being shipped overseas.

The huge square block of a house had seventy rooms, "most of them huge," thirty-three bathrooms, more miles of telephone wire than the Biltmore Hotel, thirty-five servants living on the fifth and sixth floors, a dining room that could seat sixty, and one of the largest private ballrooms in the world, exactly replicating Versailles. His mother, Grace Vanderbilt, would sometimes invite 1000 people to a single ball.

When she received him, an event that was infrequent and short because of her claustrophobic social schedule, the new Private Vanderbilt saw her aglow: "She was wearing a silver lamé gown with perfect cascades of diamonds over her bosom and at her waist, four or five diamond bracelets on her arms, her long pear-shaped diamond earrings, and a band of the same gems in her white hair." At that last, sad dinner before the departure which Grace Vanderbilt had tried hard to bluff and buy young Neily out of, she was preoccupied as always with writing little notes to herself about ways to improve her house, her hostessing, and the comfort of her guests.

That night and later, in letters to him in France, Grace complained about the hardship of not being able to travel to Europe and of the men absent from her parties, but she was happy to report that "the mob" at Newport was "still flourishing," and she detailed for her son her elaborate plans for his sister Grace's debut, which the general prejudice against debuts in 1918 had not affected. "It was with a kind of chill disbelief," Neil Vanderbilt wrote later, "that I became aware that not even the stunning impact of a world war could dislodge her from her purely social preoccupations."

Mrs. Vanderbilt's attitude was emblematic, if somewhat extreme, of the feelings among the great bulk of Episcocrats, who, after the turn of the century and accelerating into the Depression and the New Deal, turned more and more into themselves as they felt the America their class had built slipping away from them. The Episcocratic Victorian age produced, especially in the children and grandchildren and functionaries of the Business Aristocracy, a large group of Refined Reactionaries—people not directly involved in the great industries, in whom the liberal, noblesse oblige tendencies of Episcopalianism could not stem an increasing tide of staunch conservatism, xenophobia in general and anti-Semitism in ugly particular. These were the people who, if they did not exactly believe in God, believed nevertheless that their money and position were ordained, that capital was sacred, that Republicanism was automatic, proper, and undeniable.

It was in the political arena that the influence of the Refined Reactionaries was most noticeable and strongly felt; the Refined Reactionaries were largely a political arm of the Business Aristocracy. Nelson Aldrich was the foremost example of the Senate's spokesmen for big business and small income taxes. He was joined by numerous others with firm connections to the Episcocratic business elite: Elihu Root, for example, Teddy Roosevelt's secretary of war and later his challenger at the Republican convention in 1904. Root had gained his prominence by working for Thomas Fortune Ryan. According to the railroad magnate E. H. Harriman, who was in a position to know, "Ryan's success in all his manipulations, traction deals, tobacco combinations [the American Tobacco Company], manipulation of the State Trust Company into the Morton Trust Company, the Western National Bank, and then again into the Bank of Commerce—thus covering up his tracks—has been done by the adroit mind of Elihu Root."

The Senate was a "Millionaires' Club" in interest as well as in personal wealth. Harriman was later to employ railroad attorney John C. Spooner after he served in the Senate. Chauncey M. Depew, "prime minister" to Vanderbilts, became a senator from New York after graduating from the presidency of the Vanderbilts' New York Central. These men were linked, as we have seen, by marriage as well as by philosophical and political bent to each other and to the vast owners of capital in America.

The theory and practice of Refined Reaction were cultivated most purely in Pennsylvania, a state that had in Philadelphia the oldest, most Episcopalian, and most pliant aristocracy in the nation and that had also developed a large share of the country's new industrial wealth from coal, iron, and railroads. The roll call of Pennsylvania senators from the nineteenth century to the present is a striking list of outright Episcocrats of personal honesty but political big-business favoritism combined with corrupt political opportunists who merely served industry for pay.

From Simon Cameron to Matthew Quay to Boies Penrose to David Reed to George Wharton Pepper to Hugh Scott and pickle heir H. John ("57 varieties") Heinz III—Episcopalians all—Pennsylvania's senators loved money and closely held power as much as they loved themselves. Cameron, Quay, and Penrose were architects of what George Thayer, in *Who Shakes the Money Tree?*, called "America's Golden Age of Boodle"—that is, the fifty years after the election of 1876.

Not that freewheeling practices had been unknown before; Washington himself, in a 1757 race for the Virginia House of Burgesses, provided the 391 voters in his district with twenty-eight gallons of rum, fifty gallons of rum punch, thirty-four gallons of wine, forty-six gallons of beer, and two gallons of cider royal. With Pennsylvania's Big Three, the systematization of big-business investment in the political process reached its most refined form. Matt Quay, absolute boss of the state for fifteen years before his death in 1904, is credited with perfecting the technique of "shaking the plum tree." The enterprising politician "shakes" by putting state money into favored banks in return for good loan rates or investment tips, valuable as campaign contributions and personal income. Leading the fight against the income tax in 1894 (the tax passed the Senate but was voided by the Supreme Court), Senator Quay offered $250,000 outright to Senator Richard Pettigrew of South Dakota for a negative vote—but didn't get it. More successful was Boies Penrose, Quay's protégé, who, not to be outdone, once spent half a million dollars on the Pennsylvania legislature—and apparently made it stick. It remained for Simon Cameron to immortalize the lesson thus learned: "An honest politician is one who, when he is bought, stays bought."

Penrose, born to a relatively distinguished Philadelphia family and graduated from Episcopal Academy and Harvard, began political life as a protégé of that high-minded Episcocrat Teddy Roosevelt. But he quickly turned to refined reaction, spent two decades in the Senate helping the business aristocracy, and left $260,000 in cash sitting in a Washington safe deposit box when he died in 1921.

Remarkably, as Cordelia Biddle Duke noted—she was a descendant of Nicholas Biddle, sister of one ambassador and mother of another—while the rest of the country considered Penrose a barefaced crook, he was welcome to Philadelphia's Episcocratic elite as a big, strong, cultivated aristocrat and leading Episcopal layman. Stealing is not necessarily an upper-class sin, if done in good taste.

George Wharton Pepper, the corporation lawyer who could not imagine being "cold and hungry and harassed by debts," was even more acceptable to Episcocratic Philadelphia than his predecessor, Penrose. Pepper accepted appointment to the Senate despite an upper-class lack of an "itch for public office" and proved a happy fellow traveler of the business aristocracy.

Pepper was elected to his own term in the Senate in 1922 but lost the next election, because, as he admitted, he couldn't be bothered to campaign. The grit of practical politics persuaded many Refined Reactionaries, the ones who had no need or desire for further financial gain, to retire to their suburban homes and city clubs. The shock of the hardball politics at the turn of the century hit Cornelius Vanderbilt, for example, when he inquired about the possibility of a political career for himself at the Republican convention of 1900. He was finally invited to meet with some politicians, including Chauncey Depew, who had been his father's factotum at the New York Central before moving on to the U.S. Senate. (Vanderbilt *père* and *fils* were feuding, so Depew was in no hurry to help young Cornelius.) With Depew watching quietly, one of the pols took a cigar out of his mouth and told Vanderbilt he could go to the state legislature for $100,000.

Vanderbilt, getting angry but controlling himself, asked, "And how much to go to Congress?"

"Oh, I guess about three hundred thousand."

"Three hundred thousand dollars!" Vanderbilt repeated.

"To become a member of the lower house," his middleman added hastily.

"And the United States Senate?"

"Half a million."

Vanderbilt was so upset by that quotation that he walked silently up and down the room and finally blurted, "Look, my name happens to be Vanderbilt, but I'm not a Rockefeller, you know."

The bosses roared with laughter.

Not all Refined Reactionaries were so squeamish.

David A. Reed was a similarly Episcocratic Senate colleague of Penrose and Pepper. He sprang from the other center of power in the state, Pittsburgh, where his father had been Carnegie's lawyer and a founding board member of U.S. Steel. Reed was a Princeton graduate and member of the Duquesne Club, Pittsburgh's Business Aristocracy center, and his chief interest in the Senate was to pass legislation preventing the excessive "mongrelization" of the United States by restricting immigration from Europe. Passage of that measure in 1924 was an indication that the decade would see the flood tide of xenophobic reaction by Refined Reactionaries against Jews, Catholics, and "hyphenated Americans," a tide strong enough to staunch big business's previous desire for a cheap pool of malleable labor. By the 1930s Reed had swung even farther to the right, asserting on the floor of the Senate, "I do not often envy other countries their governments, but I say that if this country ever needed a dictator it needs one now."

The tradition of rich Republican Episcopalian senators has continued to the present in Pennsylvania, in the persons of former Senate Minority Leader Hugh Scott and current junior Senator H. John Heinz III. In their own ways both men represent other Pennsylvania political traditions as well. Heinz, a child of the ketchup family, if not quite of the ancient lineage of the Biddles or George Wharton Pepper or other famous old-Philadelphia families, certainly qualifies as an important part of the social structure of Pittsburgh, the structure that also produced Mellons and Phippses. Grandson of a low-Protestant peddler, Heinz is a firm Episcopalian. So is Scott, from Philadelphia's exclusive Chestnut Hill. Scott was a corporate lawyer and a notable power broker who finally left office in 1977 under the cloud of a number of scandals, including questionable campaign contributions from Gulf Oil and apparent interference in a federal building contract on behalf of a friend. Heinz was mentioned in Gulf contribution scandals, though why a man should be tempted to take a few thousand dollars when he spent millions of his own money to get elected in 1976 was never explained.

Still another strain of Refined Reaction grew up in the federal government at the beginning of the twentieth century. The foreign service took young men with superb background but a distaste for the boredom and bourgeois aspects of a business life and offered them an Episcocratic role in the wide world. Like Boies Penrose, this tiny but influential group took inspiration from seminal Episcocrat Teddy Roosevelt. Like him, they also turned from Roosevelt's own Public-minded Patrician attitude toward a backward-looking aristocratic ideal.

"In those days," recalled Jay Pierrepont Moffat of the foreign service he entered fresh from Harvard in 1919, "the Department was still like a club: the outsider was regarded with a faint air of suspicion, but a member, even a junior, was treated with absolute trust." Moffat's first post, Warsaw, was beloved of this first generation of Episcocratic foreign service officers because is was so aristocratic; they also found congenial its disdain of underlings in general and Jews in particular. The American legation took most meals at the Club des Chasseurs, which one member called "a very exclusive aristocratic club where one meets the members of the famous old Polish families who pride themselves on their lineage."

The principal criteria for belonging to this most refined circle were personal wealth (for the diplomat's salary would not allow one to live well enough), friendship with the right people, and education at the church schools and Harvard or Yale. Some fifteen years before Moffat joined it, the modern foreign service was established by men like Joseph Grew and William Phillips. Both had grown up in Back Bay Boston, attended Peabody's Groton and Harvard, then satisfied their aristocratic taste for adventure by calling on family friends to sponsor their diplomatic careers. Three quarters of the men recruited for the foreign service between 1914 and 1922 had attended prep schools, most of them St. Paul's or Groton—a percentage probably similar to the CIA's in its early years. The State Department discouraged those without private incomes from applying; it was felt they did not have the tone or resources to keep up with the nobility they would have to deal with overseas. So the foreign service became the equivalent of a European country's hereditary aristocracy, and took care to ensure that it attracted and accepted only men who could live up to that high standard.

Reed's despair over the American experiment as it seemed to threaten the ultimate power of the Business Aristocracy and the Refined Reactionaries was shared by a large segment of the Episcocratic class. Much of the upper class shifted from Refined Reactionaries at the turn of the century into Rabid Reactionaries by the time of the New Deal. What made the turn to the right, indeed to brooding self-isolation, so bitter for the Rabid Reactionaries was the presence at the head of the faceless hordes of Franklin D. Roosevelt, old-family Episcocratic New Yorker, "traitor to his class."

Coming from the tradition of Teddy Roosevelt—the Public-minded Patrician motivated by noblesse and muscular Christianity—Roosevelt was perceived as a threat to the very fabric of Episcocratic life. His own mother, the crusty Sara, disagreed frequently and publicly with his stands. One of his sons supported an opponent during one of his campaigns. Another married Ethel du Pont, from the largest and most influential Rabid Reactionary family in the country. Franklin's cousin Nicholas was a leader of the Du Pont–funded Liberty League, an instrument with which desperate millionaire Episcocrats by the dozen tried to demolish the "leftist" tendencies of the New

Deal. Outside his own family, the pressure on Roosevelt from the reactionaries in his own class was intense, as George Wolfskill noted in a history of the league:

> In their thesaurus of hate, Roosevelt was a "renegade Democrat," an "extravagant," "destructive," "vacillating," "unprincipled charlatan." A "cripple," an "invalid" lacking physical stamina, a captive psychologically who was morally "weak," intellectually "shallow," unbelievably "gullible," a "dupe" (surrounded by "radicals," "crackpots," "quarterbacks," and "foreign-thinking brain-trusters, some of whom were better known in Russia than in the United States").
>
> Nor was this the worst of it. From Newport to Miami, from Wall Street to Park Avenue, in country club locker rooms, the cathedral-like hush of bank offices, in board rooms and carpeted law offices, in hotel suites and cabin cruisers the broad stories passed: Roosevelt was an inveterate liar, immoral (hadn't you heard about his affair with Frances Perkins?),* a syphilitic, a tool of Negroes and Jews, a madman given to unbroken gales of immoderate laughter, an alcoholic, a megalomaniac dreaming his dreams of dictatorship.

Digby Baltzell concludes in *The Protestant Establishment* that the increasingly fervid revulsion to Roosevelt among the members of the upper class was rooted in a feeling of caste exclusivity—that is, a sense of superiority rooted in birth, breeding, and "what ought to be"—and frequently found expression in ethnic and racial slurs directed at "That Man, Rosenfelt" and his "nigger-loving" wife Eleanor. They were said to sit around the White House and sing to themselves:

> You kiss the Negroes,
> I'll kiss the Jews,
> We'll stay in the White House
> As long as we choose.

---

* Apparently they *hadn't* heard about his affairs with his secretaries Missy Le Hand and Lucy Rutherford Mercer, and would have to wait until his son Elliott wrote a book about it.

Threatened by changes in the modern world, the two traditions of Episcocrats battled among themselves—one group insisting that its birth and breeding should preserve its place forever, the other group calmly confident that it could master the tides of American society.

The institutions of the Episcopal Church itself were intimately mixed with the Depression-induced crisis of the calcifying Business Aristocracy. In the Episcopal New England boarding school the children of the elite—offspring of both Episcocratic strands, Rabid Reactionaries and Public-minded Patricians—faced the question of their class's future domination from the age of puberty. Franklin D. Roosevelt, Jr., was at Groton while his father was president, and the president visited Groton at the time—but not much to the pleasure of most of the students. For the prep schools were instruments of the Rabid Reactionary phobia during the 1930s. At St. Mark's, Groton's traditional rival and virtual twin in social solidity, the student body voted this way in a 1932 straw poll: Hoover 163, Roosevelt 14, and Norman Thomas an iconoclastic 5. By 1940 German atrocities had managed to swing only about 30 votes to Roosevelt.

Despite the tender ages of many of the students, there seemed little confusion about the facts of life; they knew already they were Episcocrats of the Reactionary strain. As a recent headmaster of St. Mark's, Edward Tuck Hall, suggested in his history of the school, "Conceivably they had heard their fathers talk about Franklin Roosevelt."

In 1936, the St. Mark's student magazine presented articles entitled "An Indictment of President Roosevelt and the New Deal," "Democracy: A Failure," and "The Freedom of the Slaves: A Threat to Society." The articles apparently produced no criticism except for a lone protest to the first one by a sixth-former whose father was in Washington with the government. In 1940 a second-former wrote to his family: "Last night we had a movie called 'Foreign Correspondent,' which was very good but it contained quite a bit of anti-Nazi propaganda."

Socially, Episcocratic culture was turning from the basic simplicity of such Public-minded Patrician institutions as Groton and clean-living Northeast Harbor, Maine, to the gaudiness and ultimate vapidness of the Fifth Avenue and Newport social whirl. For surprisingly many women like Grace Vanderbilt, running a thirty-five-servant house in the city and a forty-servant Newport "cottage" was a full-time occupation and more. Abandoning all work was taken seriously as an aristocratic ideal.

"Our hard-pressed English butler often complained that our family lived with more pomp and circumstance than many of the crowned heads of Europe," Neil Vanderbilt recalled.

Mrs. Vanderbilt used to think nothing of spending $1000 for a lunch for twenty-four. During the First World War she gave away $10,000 worth of gold cigarette cases and fans as favors at Gertrude Vanderbilt's debut. She built herself The Breakers in Newport for $5 million in 1895; it could hold a party of 200 without extra help. That was not as much as Alva Vanderbilt, later Mrs. O. H. P. Belmont and Grace's bitter rival as a social arbiter, spent on *her* Newport "cottage," Marble House, which cost $11 million and included a Japanese teahouse and a miniature railroad for the servants to ride to it. Seven-figure cottages in Newport or Bar Harbor not only were not rare but were expected by the 1890s, and they were not as big as the Fifth Avenue gilt-encrusted, marble-inlaid, tapestried palaces of the great Episcocrats.

Even the true dedication to social one-upmanship practiced by the two Mrs. Vanderbilts, along with *the* Mrs. Astor, Mrs. Hermann Oelrichs, and other social empresses, had a certain wholeheartedness that gave it legitimacy. What was eventually far more corrosive to the Episcocratic society, especially from the outside, was the tasteless (and finally self-mocking) drive for bigger and more lavish and more stimulating pleasures that finally appalled the saner members of the Episcocratic class. The great families crumbled under too much liquor, sex, and freedom, too little reason to live.

"Inherited wealth is a real handicap to happiness," observed the sad William K. Vanderbilt, victim of his first wife Alva's drive for social preeminence. "It is as certain death to ambition as cocaine is to morality."

His class, however, did not give its money away—not exactly. It spent it on increasingly bizarre parties. Consider the Bradley-

Martins, who decided in 1896, a depression year, to give "an impetus to trade" by throwing a party at the Waldorf. For $369,-000, Mrs. Bradley-Martin put together a costume party that featured herself as Mary, Queen of Scots; young Miss Anne Morgan, J.P.'s daughter, as Pocahontas; and a swarm of Fishes, Cuttings, Astors, Van Cortlandts, and others of the Four Hundred in historical costumes well embroidered with jewels. The host's own brother later wrote, "The power of wealth with its refinement and vulgarity was everywhere," and the public reaction against such unseemly extravagance in the midst of suffering drove the Bradley-Martins permanently into exile.

The same fate visited James Hazen Hyde after his $200,000 dinner at Sherry's in 1905, though Hyde's fancy accounting at his Equitable Life Assurance Company contributed to his downfall. Sherry's was also the scene of a famous "Horseback Dinner" hosted by C. K. G. Billings, a gas-company heir from Chicago. Billings's own horses were taken to Sherry's rear entrance and, after being carried on the elevators to the huge ballroom on the fourth floor, were decked out with tables anchored to their flanks and with two champagne-filled saddle-bags slung from their shoulders.

When the guests arrived, in riding costume, at the ballroom that had been transformed by real sod and real birds singing in the shrubbery, the guests munched course after course in the saddle and washed it down with sips through a tube that ran down to the champagne.

Animals were a favorite preoccupation as the party givers began to run out of new notions. The giant debutante ball made its debut, not very auspiciously, in Philadelphia in 1906, when James Paul, a nonpracticing doctor whose sole claim to fame was importation of the biggest consignment of French novels to enter the country up to his time, gave a "Butterfly Ball" for his daughter, Mary Astor Paul. Ten thousand rare tropical butterflies were imported from Brazil for the occasion and released from a large balloon at the height of the party—only to fall in a ghastly shower, dead from the heat of the ballroom.

The most illustrious of the society hostesses in the turn-of-the-century decadence was Mrs. Stuyvesant Fish. Though her husband, descendant of the noble old New York family that still offers Congressman Hamilton Fish as a public figure, was presi-

Harrison Grey Fiske dinner, 1900. Fiske is seated on right of white-bearded gentleman.

C.K.G. Billings's famous "horseback dinner" at Sherry's, 1903.

Mr. and Mrs. Potter Palmer, Chicago's social leaders and art collectors. Shown Mrs. Palmer's gold service for fifty, Boston's Mrs. Jack Gardner asked what she did for a "a large dinner party."

E. H. Harriman with daughters at James Hazen Hyde's $200,000 ball that turned Sherry's into "Versailles" and led to investigation of his Equitable Life Assurance Co.

Anne Morgan, daughter of the financier, as Pocahontas at the ball given by the Bradley Martins in 1896 as "an impetus to trade."

W. C. Whitney throws the first cotillion of the century, January 4, 1901, in the Fifth Avenue palace redecorated for him by Stanford White. The streetcar king is at center in pince-nez.

Mrs. Stuyvesant Fish turned Newport society upside down.

Alva Vanderbilt dragged the Vanderbilts into society.

dent of the Illinois Central—"the Society Railroad"—for twenty years, Mrs. Fish showed again that being a hostess in the Episcocratic age was a more preoccupying and celebrated occupation than being a major businessman. Mrs. Fish certainly had no trouble keeping up with the other Newporters in financial splash, though she once protested, "We're not rich: We have only a few million."

Her cottage, "Crossways," was less elaborate than the Vanderbilt villas "Marble House" and "The Breakers." It did contain a second ballroom Mrs. Fish built when she found the first, covering the entire first floor, was not large enough. And once, when she began coughing and her husband asked if he could get anything for her throat, she answered, "That diamond and pearl necklace I saw today at Tiffany's."

The reply was typical of Mrs. Fish's breezy, mocking style. Her forte as a hostess was to mock her own society's pretensions and to insult its stars to their faces. *Grande dames* in the classical tradition, like Grace Vanderbilt, held her personally responsible for the decline the old Episcocratic society suffered during her day.

The guest of honor at Mrs. Fish's famous Newport "Monkey Dinner" was a primate in full dress, named the "Prince del Drago" to satirize the visiting-nobleman fad, that climaxed the evening by getting drunk on champagne, climbing a chandelier, and pelting the guests with light bulbs.

Equally amusing was the "Dogs' Dinner" that Mrs. Fish gave with Harry Lehr, the man who succeeded Ward McAllister as social ringleader of the Four Hundred and worked closely with Mrs. Fish on her outrageous projects in Newport. Lehr took a regular dinner table off its foundation and placed it on the veranda of his cottage, "Ardleigh," and the 100 invited canine guests, most of them in fancy dress, enjoyed stewed liver and rice, fricassee of bones, and shredded dog biscuit served by human waiters.

Dogs being nearly as accepted a symbol of the country gentry's life as horses, they seemed in the twentieth century to become a preoccupation of latter-day Episcopalians. The rich and troubled Ailsa Mellon managed to outstrip equally wealthy brother Paul in only one field of art collecting—dog portraiture. And Mrs. George L. K. Morris, born into the political Frelinghuysens of New Jersey, twitted the august *Social Register* in 1936 by including the name of her Pekingese, Rose, as part of her family. And Rose wasn't even pedigreed.

Along with the fad for animals came an increased preoccupation, during the "Café Society" days after World War I, with drinking and sex. The problem had begun in the 1890s, when righteous Episcocrats who also wanted to be social were forced tacitly to approve the multiple adulteries of Edward, the lecherous Prince of Wales and leader of the international smart set. As future head of the Church of England, Edward thus set a problematic example for Episcopalians. It began to be expected that women as well as men would have a few encounters on the side from time to time. The elaborate round of social occasions which frequently required spouses to separate and the immense mobility of private train cars and yachts made it relatively simple to conduct an affair.

A little journal called *Town Topics*, which chronicled the gossip among the rich Episcocrats in New York's Gilded Age, made it particularly chic to dally. The publisher, Colonel William D'Alton Mann, would note with considerable glee, for example, that "a Philadelphia clubman" should watch out for his wife, whose "social freedom with certain society youths in and about the Bryn Mawr Hotel a couple of summers ago would lead to the belief that her husband is mistaken when he says she is as cold as she is fair." But Colonel Mann went too far even for the increasingly relaxed society of the day. In 1905 he said that when Teddy Roosevelt's daughter, Princess Alice, came to New York, she would probably conform to the ambitious drinking standards of the Ogden Mills family, with whom she was staying. That brought a libel suit.

On the witness stand, Colonel Mann admitted that he had blackmailed William K. Vanderbilt for $25,000, had got $10,-000 from William C. Whitney, $5000 from Collis P. Huntington, and $2500 from J. Pierpont Morgan. The implication, naturally, was that they had something, or things, to hide.

Further along in the century, the likes of the "poor little rich girls" Doris Duke and Barbara Hutton, with their multiple marriages to adventurers, their schizophrenia about publicity, their pills and liquor and loneliness, symbolized the final breakdown of the Episcocratic reactionary class.

The end of the Episcocrats' dominant age was signaled by the events of the night of June 25, 1906. Stanford White, the great old-family architect, great-grandson of an Episcopal clergyman, designer of the Century and the Metropolitan Club, was shot to death in the roof garden of another of his creations, the old Madison Square Garden. The assassin was decadent Harry K. Thaw of Pittsburgh. The focus was chorus girl Evelyn Nesbit, Thaw's wife. The cause, as it developed at the trial, was the extensive detail with which Miss Nesbit described her three years with Stanford White. White, it turned out, was a refined sybarite in the Edwardian mold who delighted in the underground novels with which the more adventurous gentlemen kept themselves amused at night. The most notable scene in Miss Nesbit's account involved a red velvet swing, the chorus girl, and no clothes. Whatever Thaw had heard, he made a desperate effort to imitate, and to surpass. Finally, perhaps in despair over the high standard set by White, he flew into a jealous rage and shot the architect. For many, as the lurid and celebrated trial dragged on for two years, this was the first and the last they wanted to hear about Episcocratic manners and morals.

Twilight of decadence: Stanford White, architect of the Business Aristocracy; Evelyn Nesbit, chorus girl and White's onetime lover; Harry K. Thaw, Pittsburgh "idler," dining in jail after shooting White in 1906 on the roof of Madison Square Garden (which he had designed) in a fit of jealousy over Miss Nesbit, whom he had married.

CHAPTER
8

Public-minded Patricians: The Roosevelts

"As for society people," thundered Roughrider Theodore Roosevelt, "the Four Hundred, the men and women who at this moment find their most typical expression at Newport—they lead lives which vary from rotten frivolity to rotten vice. . . . [They] are not serious people even when they are not immoral, and thanks to the yellow press, and indeed to newspapers generally, they exercise a very unwholesome influence on the community at large by the false and unworthy standards which they set up."

Roosevelt was speaking with an intriguingly mixed motive, distinctly Episcocratic: On the one hand, he wanted his daughter, Alice, to stay away from the "spiritually mud" Newport and Bar Harbor crowds; on the other, he was engaged in a bitter political battle with the "malefactors of great wealth" and their functionaries in the Senate. He could see well enough the attraction society held, for his own daughter felt compelled, at least before her marriage to Nicholas Longworth, the Episcocratic future Speaker of the House, to wait on her "tribal friends . . . the only people with big houses and big dances."

In Alice's own family, such things did not take place, at least not regularly. Service to God, to country, and to family was more important. For the Roosevelts were perhaps the leading American family of Public-minded Patricians, the small branch of Episcocrats that has had perhaps the greatest effect on the country through its involvement in the nation's government.

It is sometimes forgotten how firmly Theodore Roosevelt was planted in the soil of American aristocracy. The family goes back to patroon days in New York—1644, to be exact—and like the other old Dutch families, it adopted Anglicanism by the time of the Revolution. The Roosevelts were farmers, shopkeepers, soldiers, inventors, politicians, bankers, and doctors. By the time Theodore was growing up in Oyster Bay they were extremely wealthy, extremely aware of their position and of the responsibility that came with it. Growing up wealthy in Knickerbocker New York, uninfected in those years by the flood of new money and newer ideas of decadence, the young TR naturally went to Harvard, a simpler school in pre-Gold Coast days. There he was a member of Porcellian, frequently considered Harvard's best club. Theodore's classmate, Leverett Saltonstall, scion of the political aristocratic family of Boston, and father of the senator and governor of Massachusetts of the same name, introduced him to Alice Hathaway Lee, Saltonstall's next-door neighbor in Chestnut Hill and the daughter of George Cabot Lee, of the banking house Lee Higginson & Company.

Boston had nurtured as old, proud, and firmly moral an old-family structure as Knickerbocker New York, and TR's early inculcation in that milieu turned him naturally into the Episcocratic mold. A weak heart that needed to be strengthened encouraged him to spend time in the out-of-doors, an Episcocratic love, and he had a true noble's devotion to action and war. But his basic character was inherited from his father, Theodore, and the son's description of that man is a succinct introduction to all that is best in Episcocratic values of the Public-minded Patrician variety:

> He combined strength and courage with gentleness, tenderness and great unselfishness. He would not tolerate in us children selfishness or cruelty, idleness, cowardice or untruthfulness. As we grew older he made us understand that the same standard of clean living was demanded for

the boys as for the girls; that what was wrong in a woman could not be right in a man. With great love and patience, and the most understanding sympathy and consideration, he combined insistence and discipline. He never physically punished me but once, but he was the only man of whom I was ever really afraid. I do not mean that it was a wrong fear, for he was entirely just, and we children adored him.

That early training was bound, along with his own indomitable spirit, to raise Theodore above the rut of his Episcocratic class, above his just-out-of-college classmates, "fellows of excellent family and faultless breeding," he wrote, "with a fine old country-place, four-in-hands, tandems, a yacht, and so on; but, oh, the decorous hopelessness of their lives!" And his aggressive, rugged, ready-for-adventure life—the mere fact that he could consider going into politics in the first place—made him a fountainhead of the tradition of Public-minded Patricians among twentieth-century Episcocrats.

In office, TR was a rather confusing amalgam of policies and beliefs—another Episcocratic trait, the patrician trusting his instinct and distrusting dogma. He was perceived as a friend of the little fellow, and compared with Nelson Aldrich and his cronies in the Senate, he certainly was; but his decisions were also indissolubly rooted in the values and friendships of his class. He explained to the kaiser of Germany, of all people, why his future son-in-law Nicholas Longworth was acceptable: "We're both members of the Porc [Porcellian], you know." And TR's decisions depended on the character of the men he dealt with, more than on an abstract sense of what to do.

When he decided to prosecute J. P. Morgan under the Sherman Antitrust Act for making the former competitors James J. Hill and E. H. Harriman too comfortable in the Morgan Securities Company, Morgan got nowhere by sending the message "If we have done anything wrong, send your man to my man and they can fix it up." Morgan's mistake was in not realizing that TR was looking back to an older, purer idea of aristocracy, a feeling of the leading Episcocratic bishops that money should make life sweet, not dominate it. He despised the "tyranny of mere wealth, the tyranny of plutocracy."

Roosevelt, on the other hand, was long accustomed to conducting high affairs on the basis of personality. It can be no surprise that a quarter of a century later, when Franklin Roosevelt was looking around to get the country ready for war—ready to fulfill the Public-minded Patrician's mission of looking out to Europe—he would find the chief advocate of preparedness in his cousin Theodore's old friend Henry L. Stimson and make him secretary of war, too. For Franklin, like TR, like Stimson, was decidedly in the mold of an Episcocrat who loved power and public service—not to make himself money, but to be a leader in his own best instincts, to give back something the country had given. In government, the mantle was between the generations in Stimson. The mantle in thought, belief, and Public-minded Patrician attitude had been passsed to Franklin in the very air he breathed as a young man—though not through Franklin's own parents.

Becoming president "was the last thing I should ever have imagined for him," his mother, Sara Delano, asserted in the Refined Reactionary tradition, "or that he should be in public life of any sort." According to Joseph Lash, her ideal was the simple one of the country squire: "that he grow up to be a fine, upright man like his father and like her own father, a beloved member of his family and a useful and respected citizen of his community just as they were, living quietly and happily along the Hudson as they had."

Two institutions of Episcocratic noblesse oblige, turned into the public-service mold, more than countered for Franklin Roosevelt the status quo desires of his parents. First was the Groton School, still new when Franklin entered it in 1896, but already an extraordinarily forceful institution in the Episcocratic order that was coming to dominate America. And under Endicott Peabody, the school ran, as one Grotonian put it, on "an urgency which tended to push boys a little farther along the road to success than they would have got under their own steam." While this attitude was rather undirected, producing far more brokers and Wall Street lawyers than Public-minded Patricians, there was another upper-class institution that turned some boys' minds to public service. Its name was Theodore Roosevelt, and Franklin was especially close to him.

TR entered the presidency in 1901, shortly after Franklin entered Harvard, and Franklin's cousin was the greatest, perhaps the only, force contending with the blatant upper-class indifference and dissipation that pervaded Harvard's Gold

Coast dormitories in those days. Theodore had come to Groton once when Franklin was there; the talk had something to do with not taking champagne and butlers to the Adirondacks for camping, which sounds a little foolish now but was probably downright revolutionary in those Newporty days of huge, luxurious "camps" in the upstate New York alps. Franklin called the talk "splendid" and promptly accepted Theodore's invitation to Theodore's home at Oyster Bay, rather against his mother's inclination.

Theodore was a majestic example for the young Franklin, who was a dandified, somewhat unpopular college man showing interest in the public arena. He was struggling with his aristocratic heritage. He was always fascinated by his own family's genealogy, remained a lifelong vestryman of St. James Church Hyde Park, and became a founder and leader of the Dutchess County Historical Society. All those preferences—as well as a predilection for well-educated, well-bred men and women— would remain with him into the presidency, as they had with Theodore: not as prejudice, but as a matter of taste and fundamental belief in superiority. In a sophomore essay at Harvard FDR tried to come to terms with his heritage in distinctly aristocratic terms:

> Some of the famous Dutch families in New York have today nothing left but their name—they are few in numbers, they lack progressiveness and a true democratic spirit. One reason—perhaps the chief—for the virility of the Roosevelts is this very democratic spirit. They have never felt that because they were born in a good position they could put their hands in their pockets and succeed. They have felt, rather, that being born in a good position, there was no excuse for them if they did not do their duty by the community, and it is because this idea was instilled into them from their birth that they have in nearly every case proved good citizens.

He had the attitude, notes his insightful biographer Joseph P. Lash, "that in order to survive America's aristocracy had to justify itself by its works and a willingness to accommodate to change. This was Eleanor's feeling, too. . . ."

Eleanor, as it happened, represented still another Episcocratic tradition, the upper-class clubwoman turned social reformer, a group that was to prove a significant force in the New Deal in such personages as Labor Secretary Frances Perkins and Mary Harriman Rumsey, Averell Harriman's sister. Eleanor was always much less a polished member of the upper class than Franklin; she attended the Allenswood School near London, whose headmistress was a freethinker who emphasized truthfulness to self; she changed her social habits and beliefs radically while Franklin's remained static; and she was genuinely disturbed when he did not go to church on Sundays.

Though Eleanor was unusual among Episcopalians in becoming both a deeply convinced reformer and a deeply religious person, it was not strange that the two should be related in her. Throughout its long history, the Episcopal Church has supported a distinct undercurrent of patrician reformist thought, in the English Whig tradition, based in religious convictions and a sense of the aristocratic.

In the hard winter of 1914, Frank Tannenbaum had had enough of the churches' attempts to preserve their own endowments while his men went hungry. An organizer for the radical International Workers of the World—"Wobblies"—Tannenbaum decided the starving men on the Bowery needed a dramatic gesture to publicize and perhaps actually to help their plight. The gesture he settled on was the same used so controversially and effectively by black leaders fifty years later. He demanded "reparations" from the churches. He planned to invade churches with his ragged band and sit in until they gave food and shelter.

In those less socially conscious days, most of the churches had no trouble barring the door, sometimes with the help of the police. St. Paul's Chapel, a satellite of Trinity, took a different tack. The vicar, Dr. William Geer, invited Tannenbaum's terrorists to come to the chapel parish house for a protest meeting and conference. On March 3, 200 of the protesters held a fiery meeting in Rutgers Square, then marched over to the church they had just been condemning and were greeted with sandwiches and coffee. Dr. Geer invited anyone without a roof over

Franklin Delano Roosevelt, the quintessential Episcocrat: the Grotonian, front row center (top left); the country squire at Hyde Park, with Eleanor, 1913 (top right); the sailor (above). Facing page: the churchman, with mother, Sara, at St. James Episcopal Church, Hyde Park, 1937 (top left); joking with legislators (top right); as President, motoring with Fala (center); the grand old man (bottom).

his head to sleep in the chapel, but there is no record of anyone's taking him up on it—or of much change for the better in the protesters' harsh conditions.

Geer's gesture is the gentle upper-class commiseration of an earlier time, the semireligious social concern of the true Episcocrat. In those laissez-faire days, when the business of government was business, not social welfare, this was better for the workers than no attention at all. It is only a seeming paradox that the richest and most influential denomination in America should have been the most liberal socially and economically. Though most of its clergy was either patronizing, like Geer, or out-and-out money-respecting, like Bishop Paddock—and the laity as a group was even more conservative—the Episcopal clergy also contained, earlier than any other denomination, a proportion of genuinely liberal and even (for the times) radical thinkers.

For example, the Episcopalian-founded and -led Church Association for the Advancement of the Interests of Labor (CAIL) was the only organization connected with any nineteenth-century church that worked effectively to enhance what *labor* perceived as its own interests, not necessarily what the church did. CAIL was founded in 1887 by Father James Otis Sargent Huntington, a Boston patrician but a member of the Knights of Labor, in direct response to the Haymarket tragedy in Chicago, in which "anarchist" workers from the McCormick harvester plant fought deadly battles with the police. The organization's efforts included such direct actions as persuading the diocese of New York to give church printing jobs only to firms that paid union rates.

No doubt the leadership of prestigious Episcopal clergymen, along with important laymen like economists Richard T. Ely and Seth Low, helped gradually to move public opinion within the churches and even the country as a whole toward greater sympathy for workingmen and the nascent unions. Dr. Rainsford managed to keep J. P. Morgan in St. George's even while he continued to tinker with such sacrosanct policies as the aristocratic vestry. Though Morgan obviously never agreed with Rainsford's Social Gospel predilections, he did take care of his rector for life with a legacy.

Many other socially formidable Episcopal clergymen managed to get backhanded support from their backward-looking parishioners for social policies that—from less respectable mouths—the parishioners would have considered treasonable. Bishop Frederick Dan Huntington, the convert from Unitarianism who became bishop of the new diocese of central New York, also became the first president of CAIL, founded by his son, James O. S. Huntington, and through the two Huntingtons more than forty Episcopal bishops eventually signed on as vice-presidents. And Bishop Potter, confidant of the rich and famous, friend of Morgan, wedder of Vanderbilts, and "first citizen of New York," was so thoroughly identified with moderate but unmistakable support of workingmen's rights that when he died in 1908 Samuel Gompers wrote for the American Federation of Labor: "A movement for the social betterment of all the people had no stauncher advocate nor more earnest worker than Bishop Potter. His every work, his every act, was an effort and an appeal for a higher and better life for all."

It caused no little wonder outside the Episcopal Church of the 1890s that "the Episcopal Church—the Church of wealth, culture, and aristocratic lineage—is leading the way" in social causes. But that no longer seems so puzzling. As Karl Marx was perhaps the most famous person to point out, the more aristocratic elements of society always tend to be sympathetic to the subbasement categories. So the average, moderately well-educated, moderately easygoing Episcopalian would naturally tend to support moderate reformism much more easily than could the more Calvinist, middle-class religions like Presbyterianism or Methodism.

More critical in this Episcocratic concern for people at the bottom of the social scale is an unusual characteristic of the Episcopal clergy: It has always included (and still does) an extremely large proportion of converts. It is almost as though anyone who grew up in the Episcopal Church could hardly take seriously the idea that priests ought to be leaders of the church and that an outsider, unaware of the ingrained placidity of the mass of Episcopalians, is needed to think it possible that life can be breathed into the liturgy.

Thus, the prominence of Phillips Brooks in particular and Boston in general in the revival during the late nineteenth century: The man and the city were newly coined Episcopalians, unaware that the religion was dying out. And so it did not. The growth of the church schools and the previously Calvinist universities as factories turning out Episcocrats was largely a Boston phenomenon. As Digby Baltzell points out, of the twenty presiding bishops of the church through Henry Knox Sherrill (that is, through 1958), no fewer than twelve were converts.

There has always been something strangely Janus-faced about an orthodox Anglo-Catholic religion that has cheerfully catered to a laity concerned primarily with the things of this world. In the 1960s the newly radicalized clergy made it stridently clear that it was no longer interested in parishioners who were preoccupied with wealth and social status. The result was, to a large extent, the spectacle of the institutional church leaving its laity. But that Episcocratic laity continues to exist, even if much of it seldom goes to church anymore or gives money to the diocese—and it exists with social and economic power denied the institutional church.

CHAPTER
9

"To Serve Is to Rule"

The time was the late 1930s, the worst of times. For nearly a decade the nation had been in the grip of the most severe depression that ever crippled the world. Fortunately some people remained unaffected except perhaps intellectually—people who could continue to conduct the business of the nation without feeling undue personal pressure from the god Mammon.

The cream of those leaders gathered one night in the opulent Union Club on New York's Park Avenue. They ate well, drank well, talked well, enjoyed themselves well. The dinner was given to celebrate the recovery from a long and serious illness of a still-vigorous man in his eighties. He was probably the only man these wealthy, wellborn rulers of the American economy would gather to honor—the one man, perhaps, they all respected. This was their old headmaster, Peabody of Groton, spiritual father of all Episcocrats.

Peabody spoke of what headmasters will speak of: the survival of civilization and the school. Civilization was clearly not in very good shape, but Groton, the wealthiest and perhaps the most exclusive prep school in the country, was doing its best to leaven the dreariness. Then Peabody, the Rector, as his wealthy crowd of old boys called him, did something that even his greatest admirer would not have thought possible. He defended another old boy who was not present that evening, President Franklin Roosevelt.

Father Endicott Peabody with his Eton-collared, surpliced flock at Groton.

Grandfather Peabody at Groton football game, 1940. His grandson Endicott became governor of Massachusetts in 1964.

King's College (now Columbia University) started out as adjunct of Trinity Church in 1754.

Almost to a man, the dinner guests hated Roosevelt. They believed he was tearing down the economic system that made them and the social-caste system that preserved them in their Anglican purity. Roosevelt was "That Man," the class traitor, and members of his own Episcocratic class hated him the more for not being able to understand how such a destroyer of values could have come out of his bloodlines and out of Groton, too. Peabody probably couldn't understand it either, but he spoke up for Roosevelt.

"Something has troubled me a good deal lately," the Rector said. "Personally I don't pretend to know much about politics or economics. But in national crises like the present one, we get pretty excited and perhaps we give vent to expressions that later on we are sorry for. I believe Franklin Roosevelt to be a gallant and courageous gentleman. I am happy to count him as my friend."

"Complete silence" greeted the Rector's remarks, according to George Biddle, who attended the dinner. The silence was partly just shock, Biddle speculates. Probably more important, it allowed the gathered Episcocrats to think for a moment: "Good old Rector! By Jove, he has nerve. And perhaps—after all—he may be partly right. Perhaps we should not *talk* the way we do. Not in public. Not of a fellow Grotonian."

The highest achievements of the Episcocratic civilization were in that clubroom that night—the great power and money and exclusivity, the great loyalty to the old class-forming institutions, the suspicion of abstractions like politics and economics, the stress on personal ties and values. All those are distinctly Episcocratic values that, through the prep school Peabody founded and the ones he influenced, have become part of the very tissue of American institutions.

Dominating all those values is the massive presence—he was a tall and broad-shouldered man—of Peabody himself. Nothing is more central to the Episcocratic character, to the way Episcocrats deal with the world around them, than the father figure. He is the quasi-divine figure who has traditionally driven them, instructed them, and ultimately reassured them that all they do will be blessed. He is responsible for the dominating sense of family in Episcocratic culture. And he has been the ultimate goal of the aspiring Episcocrat, the vision that drives men on to the seizure of absolute power and absolute self-certainty.

More than any other man, Peabody, headmaster of Groton for more than half a century, was responsible for the creation of the American private church boarding school. And he created it the way he and Episcocratic society wanted it: firm; churchy; pragmatic; austere; mannerly; conformist. Perhaps even more important, he established the tradition that the headmaster is the man who in a real sense *makes* the school, the force that creates the school as an extension of himself, the great father to whom all the "boys," of whatever age, owe homage and awe.

"They used to call him the Sun God in his youth," wrote Ellery Sedgwick, Groton '90, master and trustee of the school, in 1957 the oldest living graduate.

> He was the perfect autocrat with the power of life and what to small boys was much worse than death. On the playground you could do anything short of snowballing him. But in his vast study with room for the whole school in it, that was a different matter. To be alone there, on instant summons, with your heart open and no desires hid, was like cramming for the Last Day. I do not believe any boy, however crooked his tongue, however deep his sins below the surface, ever lied face to face with the Rector. There was an instinctive, comprehensive understanding about him. He never spied, but he always knew and you knew he knew. Out with it! There was no other way. Yet perhaps the most remarkable thing about him, the thing a boy could never guess and only the friendship of decades could discern, was the complete and disciplined humility of his spirit. Underneath, the schoolmaster was the priest. God was all in all; to serve Him was to rule.*

A description like that leaves little doubt that the boys under Peabody's sway considered him an "Old Testament God the Father," as Franklin Roosevelt's attorney general, Francis Biddle, put it in his autobiography. The combination of the father's overwhelming firmness with his tender concern—stories abound of the Rector's dedication to memorizing new boys' names, his

---

* That phrase is a translation of Groton's Latin motto, *Cui servire est regnare*, which others have translated more loosely and more cynically, without the reference to God, suggesting that Groton "serves" fellowmen by ruling them.

care for their homesickness and real sickness—made Peabody the archetype of the father-headmaster, the father as an extension of the boy's real father.

But Peabody was more than an extension; he was a perfection of it. The Rector was more paternal than a "regular" father, who worked each day to send his boy off to boarding school. Moreover, Peabody brought into the young boy's life the consciousness of the majesty of the Father in heaven, creating a combination possessed by most Episcopalians since—both an ease and a practicality toward God. Boys at Groton were like the Lodges; they had a chance to talk directly to God, though apparently, unlike the Lodges as enshrined in folklore, they did not talk to Him exclusively. The identification of the Rector with the almighty Godhead and center of the universe would obviously have a fantastic influence as the boys grew old enough to begin assessing their own position in the country's society. There *were* no higher orders.

The church boarding schools—St. Mark's, St. Paul's, Groton, St. George's and others—have been the training ground of the nation's Episcocratic elite since they were founded in the late nineteenth and early twentieth century. The attitudes toward money, power, and society vivified and enforced by Peabody's peers formed the consciousness of the American ruling class— even for those who only aspired to it. Grotonian values have formed American business, government, and life ever since.

To go with the father-headmaster was his wife—she was mother, the essence for the boys of all that was female (in fact, in those days, before the recent coeducation at all the schools, she was the only female they saw for long stretches of time). Mrs. Peabody kissed all the boys good-night. Mrs. Peabody and Mrs. Thayer, wife of the second and greatest headmaster of the nearby St. Mark's, hosted "parlor nights" at which boys were given healthy doses of food, tea, and motherly affection. In Mrs. Thayer's case it was her famous scrambled eggs—they were written of as if some exotic, yet nourishing, delicacy. And Choate's* founding father, the Reverend George St. John, saw clearly whence his school had sprung. He wrote of Judge and

---

* Choate is not officially affiliated with the Episcopal Church, as it firmly asserts. Alumni assume that it is, for it has the Episcocratic churchy feeling. Ted Ayres, head of the alumni association, called it a "secular Episcopal school."

Mrs. Choate, in the treacly-biblical style reserved for school givers:

> To William and Mary [the school's founders] no child was born. Were pictures running through Mary's mind of imaginary children there before the homestead's great fireplace? No son had been born to bear the Judge's name; might there not be born to them, yet, a school with many sons who could carry on the name of Choate forever? So might she, yet, bear the Judge children; and he there before the homestead fireplace, at dinners and parties (and, best of all, when the boys might just drop in to talk), could be, as it were, father to them.
>
> And her doctor brother, childless child-lover, he should now have children around him. There should be a school, and the school should be a family. "Choate was not *founded*: it was loved into life."

Peabody saw himself as a quasi-divine father-leader.* In his New Year's sermon in the school chapel one year he quoted approvingly, and with reference to himself, from Matthew Arnold's poem to his own father:

> Therefore to thee it was given
> Many to save with thyself:
> And, at the end of thy day,
> O faithful shepherd! to come,
> Bringing thy sheep in thy hand.

Two strands emerge: the insistent linking of the headmaster to a demiurgical father and the perception of himself in a servant role, that of the biblical shepherd, hard to dissociate from the "good shepherd" role, as Christ saw Himself. Peabody and Christ both felt themselves servants who became greater by serving and in that greatness felt able to lay down rules. *Cui servire est regnare.*

---

* A massive man, physically dominant like the other great Episcocrats of his time—J. P. Morgan, say, or Theodore Roosevelt—Peabody always hovered over the school and the society, as a friend observed, "like some splendid eleventh- or twelfth-century crusader; the militant Christian, half warrior, half priest." It was an age in which the Episcocrats won the world through might *and* right.

It was no accident, either, that Peabody selected for his preaching in Groton Chapel Arnold's poem, which is entitled "Rugby Chapel" and is about Matthew Arnold's father, Thomas Arnold—Arnold of Rugby. As headmaster of the Rugby School, Thomas Arnold was the most important force in the creation of the English public school system. (Public schools, of course, mean private schools in the American sense; the English schools were "public" as compared with the in-family tutors that had previously educated the British wealthy.)

Rugby and the rest of the English public schools—Eton and Harrow are the most famous—became, under Arnold's influence, the repositories of a massive characteristic that was eventually identified as muscular Christianity. In the context of the nineteenth century, Arnold was liberal, politically and theologically; he believed, like many of the other members of the sophisticated, well-educated Victorian gentry, in a worldly religion, one that would not make its practitioners overtly pious in crowds, as were members of various dissenting sects, usually culled from the lower and middle classes. Arnold's religion, in other words, was not incompatible with being a gentleman, an aristocrat. At the same time, both stations in life—gentleman and churchman—required adherence to the old Latin precept *Mens sana in corpore sano*—a sound mind in a sound body.

Brought up under the Arnold regime, boys early developed a healthy confidence that their position in the universe was secure; there was no need for insecurity, apology, or humility. One *knew* God was on one's side. The "muscular" part of the Christianity was taken seriously and literally. Nineteenth-century upper-middle-class England witnessed an incredible emphasis on sports, physical activity, and sexual self-denial, all to keep the body an entity pure enough to support a soul with a divine mission. Too much thinking was frowned upon, at least by the offshoots of Arnold, if not by the great man himself. The emphasis was on putting whatever theories might crop up into action. To get things done, to get on in the world were the great things.*

Groton was directly descended from the English public schools through its creator and inspirer, Endicott Peabody. Pea-

---

* Arnold's essays speak continually of the difference between the "pragmatic" British (Anglican) and the "theoretical" French (Roman Catholic).

body had attended one of those schools—Cheltenham. Peabody
was reared in England as the son of a partner in J. S. Morgan
and Company, J. P. Morgan's father's company. He fused the
English-school values of formal structure, strict discipline, haz-
ing, and austerity with the background of his race, the Salem
Puritans. (The Peabodys had been the leading aristocrats of
Salem, the town that burned witches. "Peabody or nobody"
was what you were in Salem.)

Under Peabody, Groton became more fevered, more messi-
anic, more of a city on a hill than Rugby, Eton, or Harrow
would ever be. The English schools were too civilized in a
worldly way, too old-world aristocratic. Peabody wanted to
create a moral aristocracy in the tradition of his Puritan ancestors, who considered themselves the pioneers of *New* England, vastly superior to the decadent citizens of *Old* England
(not to mention Frenchmen, Indians, and such). Not because
they had more money or power. Because they were assured of
God's glowing approval.

Something of that old Puritan superiority colored the surface
of Groton's masters only a few years after the founding of the
school in 1884. One of them remarked, on being taken to see
Eton during a visit to England, "Ah! The Groton of England, I
believe?"

Though none embodied the conveyance of the English system into the American stew so succinctly as Peabody's Groton
did, the other Episcopal prep schools were a product of the
same forces and eventually produced the same result: an American master class. They were not all founded as late in the
gilded nineteenth century as Groton was; St. Paul's dates to pre–
Civil War days, 1856; St. Mark's was founded in 1865. It was
something in the air, the founding of a prep school. "Every so
often the aristocracy would divide like an amoeba, and produce
a new school," one observer remarked. There was a feeling that
there ought to be a place for boys to go away to school and
meet one another—the young lords, that is to say, from the
various growing centers of wealth.

That need for a national "family" of upper-class Episcocrats
coincided with the assumption of final industrial, social, and
political power by the Episcocratic corporate barons of the
high Victorian age. "The following well-known schools, for

example," Digby Baltzell points out, "were founded within a decade, before or after, of the formation of the United States Steel Company in 1901: The Taft School in Watertown, Connecticut, was founded by Horace Dutton Taft, a brother of President Taft, in 1890; the Hotchkiss School, Lakeville, Connecticut, was founded and endowed by Maria Hotchkiss, widow of the inventor of the famous machine-gun, in 1892; St. George's School, Newport, Rhode Island, which has a million-dollar Gothic chapel built by John Nicholas Brown, was founded in 1896; in the same year, Choate School, whose benefactors and friends include such prominent businessmen as Andrew Mellon and Owen D. Young, was founded . . . ; while the elder Morgan was forming his steel company in New York and Pittsburgh in 1901, seven Proper Bostonians, including Francis Lowell, W. Cameron Forbes, and Henry Lee Higginson, were founding Middlesex School, near Concord, Massachusetts; Deerfield, which had been a local academy since 1797, was reorganized as a modern boarding school by its great headmaster, Frank L. Boydon, in 1902; and, finally, Father Sill of the [Episcopal] Order of the Holy Cross founded Kent School in 1906." All these schools are either formally associated with the Episcopal Church or have been connected to it through their headmasters and founders.

For institutions that quickly loomed so large on the American social scene, the beginnings of the church schools were amazingly small and intimate, a matter of decision by a few family-preoccupied headmasters urged on by a few influential and wealthy backers. Bishop William Lawrence, perhaps the grandest churchman of the Episcocracy, had met a certain William G. Thayer one day in the late 1880s through the modern-sounding device of picking up a young man hitchhiking into Newport, Rhode Island. Newport was then, of course, one of the chief watering holes of all that was grand in American aristocratic families.

When Peabody did come to visit Lawrence within a week or two, the bishop asked "this young man with the tennis racquet" to come and dine with the two. According to Lawrence, "They met, and this young man who was headed toward the Presbyterian ministry rather liked the looks of the two Episcopal ministers at the table, and he thought he would work his way toward the Episcopal church by becoming for a year or two years a master at Groton and sampling the church and school life. So Dr. Peabody took him, and he went to Groton."

From small acorns grow great oaks—and schools.

Shortly thereafter, in 1894, the trustees of the thirty-year-old St. Mark's were faced with a crisis when the headmaster, William E. Peck, resigned and, worse, founded the rival Episcopal boarding school Pomfret, which still exists. The trustees acquired Lawrence as their chairman. The bishop brought with him the new Grotonian methods. Relatives of his had donated the land for Groton; he was chairman of its board and his connections to Episcopal powers like J. P. Morgan were well known. Lawrence promptly pulled his young friend Thayer away from Groton to become the new headmaster of St. Mark's.

So St. Mark's was changed from a somewhat parochial and confused school to an institution on the model of Groton—a school to groom sons of the new aristocracy around the country. To groom them for Harvard or Yale, and for life. As in any family, rivalry was one of the most intense ways of expressing affection, and it has rankled St. Mark's to this day that its stability and stature were achieved through the intercession of Groton. Probably even more galling to St. Mark's, at least to judge from the tone of the school's official history, was the touchdown Thayer scored when he played for Groton in the football game of 1886.

It took no time for the budding American aristocrats to realize the importance of the new Episcopal schools. Francis Biddle, Roosevelt's attorney general from the old and distinguished Philadelphia family, wrote:

> When I was entered at Groton School on November 5, 1888, at the age of two and a half, the school was only two years older, although its fame had already begun to spread to our corner of the country. But before sending us Mother went up to take a look at the place and to meet the famous headmaster, the Reverend Endicott Peabody, the Rector as he was universally known, who had been favorably recommended to her by Miss Agnes Irwin.* Mother lunched

---

* Miss Irwin founded one of Philadelphia's poshest girl's schools along the Main Line.

Philadelphia gentlemen: (left) Nicholas Biddle, from 1822 to 1836 president of the ill-fated Bank of the United States; (below) Drexel Biddle, Jr., with family during his prime as ambassador to numerous European countries; (bottom) Francis Biddle as the New Deal attorney general.

with him and found him manly, a gentleman, and, above all, absolutely charming. His speech was cultivated, his voice rich and moving. He was obviously successful. He was hardly two or three years older than she, and the attraction was mutual.

She was persuaded to spend the night at the school, and her earlier impression was confirmed by the little boys in blue suits and Eton collars at supper, who looked the way she thought boys ought to look. She was interested to hear that the school coat of arms had been designed by Ralph Adams Cram, the eminent authority on ecclesiastical Gothic. Mr. Peabody told her that he believed in inculcating a sense of "tone"—neatness and form—from the beginning. In America form was greatly overlooked.

He smiled when he talked. He had light blue eyes and fine blond hair. He was tall, broad shouldered, courteous. He was aristocratic. He would have made a good soldier. She realized that this was what she was looking for, the proper discipline, which as a [widowed] woman she could not give her boys, who were getting a bit out of hand in the country, running wild. They needed a father, and that was a gap she could never fill. . . .

There was only one objection—the school was expensive, six hundred dollars a year for tuition and board, with laundry thirty dollars extra. But somehow she would manage.

The unimpeachable quality of the schools for those who would be aristocrats was conveyed unmistakably to young Cornelius Vanderbilt, Jr., early in the century by his governess, a sure test. Just before his father, who had gone to St. Paul's with John D. Rockefeller, Jr., put young CV on the special, private train to Concord, New Hampshire, Miss Coxhead, his old English nanny, said to him, "You will like St. Paul's, I fancy. Just like Eton and Harrow, they say it is. A real gentleman's school."

Matthew Taylor Mellon, who attended St. Paul's at the same time, noted, "The names of the boys in my class at St. Paul's read like a condensed volume of the Social Register. There was 'Ribbs' McAdoo, Bill du Pont, Cornelius Vanderbilt, Bobby

Strawbridge, Tony Biddle and Freddy Church, just to throw a few names around."

But like many other young Episcocrats, Vanderbilt and Mellon hated St. Paul's—or professed to. A few years after he graduated, Matthew Mellon described the boys at Eton as "a snobbish set of little rascals like the handpicked spawn of the American rich at St. Paul's." Vanderbilt faced constant embarrassment trying to explain that he couldn't afford ice-cream sodas for everyone (his father didn't give him enough allowance) and suffered from his peers' allusions to watered New York Central stock. "How can a decent fellow like St. Paul's?" he wrote in 1915. "I hate it more and more each day."

It was striking, nevertheless, how rapidly and effortlessly Peabody and his analogues filled a gap in the developing class of Americans who had made a substantial amount of money, or inherited enough to realize the nearly limitless things that could be done with it and the great intangibles it could free one to pursue. Intangibles like the "successful" and "aristocratic" bearing of Peabody—the clear suggestion that at Groton and the rest of the schools the boys were being formed into adults who would possess the full consciousness of what was "overlooked in America."

Of course, $600 tuition was considerably more than the total annual wage of the average American worker at the time, yet one didn't have to be a millionaire to join the elite. The true Episcocrat was then, and is now, willing to ignore a few bugs in the kitchen, omit a few new modish items of clothing, to ensure that the children are connected with the right institutions and become exposed to the proper tone. It's a compulsion; more, an assumption. It's a large part of what makes them America's aristocracy, not merely its moneyed upper middle class.

By no mere coincidence, the schools were founded by full-bred (or converted) Episcopalians, served by Episcopal boards that even managed sometimes to be "sniffers after heresy," and emphasized religion in their daily chapel. The schools reflected the great importance that belonging to the right church was taking on in an America that was increasingly developing a national society. America was developing an aristocracy distinctively its own, a society stratified along class and religious, not geographical, lines. It might be fine to be a Lutheran if you were a big wheel in Milwaukee, but if you wanted your son to go to Groton or St. Paul's, you had better recognize that Episcopalianism was the proper expression of your relationship with your God.

Henry Coit, St. Paul's first headmaster, recognized the keystone nature of the religious side of the schools very precisely. He was half horrified and half amused when a proper Boston lady told him once that her son was thinking seriously of converting to Presbyterianism. "Never forget, my dear," the rector remonstrated, "that in the life to come the Presbyterians will not be on the same plane as the Episcopalians."

In this life, boarding school boys resided on a plane different from anyone else. As George Biddle points out, "There were, in fact, numberless small tokens—each in itself most insignificant, but which in the aggregate very sharply defined a 'Grotty,' and marked him off from all other American schoolboys to the outsider, but more especially in our own self-esteem. To others we might seem a little different. We knew that we moved in a world apart—and always of course in a world above."

The distinguishing marks were distinctly English: dressing for supper; calling Peabody the Rector; playing "fives" instead of squash racquets; saying "hip-hip-hurrah" instead of a more standard cheer; making the classes "forms"; saying "hi" instead of "hello"; not talking dirty; playing football and baseball "no matter how thoroughly we disliked them." Some outward manifestations have changed, but the English-based habits survive today in the schools and in the executive suites they prepare a young man for.

Louis Auchincloss, '35, prolific and excellent author-lawyer from a family that continues to fill places at the school,* remarks that

> much later, in the unexpectedly small world to which one found oneself relegated after college, looking back over the shoulders of the sneering or of the envious at a curiously re-inflated institution, one discovered that the label "Grottie," so often considered an impediment, could be used to a snobbish advantage by the astute in dim grey

---

* *The Rector of Justin*, one of Auchincloss's best books, is about a school and a rector with frequent parallels to Groton and Peabody.

downtown business areas where that murky boys' god seemed to have enjoyed an undeserved reputation.

What is the stuff of being a "Grottie"—or a graduate of St. Paul's or St. Mark's or Kent? It is partly, without a doubt, the dawning realization that the school was a collection not merely of boys from the neighborhood, but of people who were the very cream of American society: political, economic, and social. The schools were even, as we shall see, very much the decisive instruments in developing in the sons of marriages between old blood and new money a class consciousness that extended in diminishing ripples from Boston and New York's first families to Philadelphia and Chicago and San Francisco and isolated members of prominent Episcocratic families elsewhere.

"Ninety-five percent of these boys came from what they considered the aristocracy of America," remarks George Biddle. "Their fathers belonged to the Somerset, the Knickerbocker, the Philadelphia, or the Baltimore Clubs.* Among them was a goodly slice of the wealth of the nation, little Morgans, Harrimans, Whitneys, Webbs, McCormicks, Crockers, Stillmans." These names still resonate with the sound of America's aristocracy.

Each year Groton and its competitors received another shipment of young boys from these wells of affluence. The families, by the act of sending their sons to Episcopal church schools in New England, indicated an interest in acquiring certain vaguely defined aristocratic qualities. How did the schools go about granting them?

---

* The Somerset was Boston's highest-ranking men's club; the Knickerbocker, one of the best in New York. The two other names explain their place in their respective cities.

Muscular Christianity

First they sent the boys out onto the playing field. Sports were a critical ingredient of school life, very much in the English public school tradition. Their significance harked back at least to Wellington's famous remark that the Battle of Waterloo was won on the playing fields of Eton. It is perhaps significant as well that many more people are aware that Rugby School invented rugby football than that it nurtured muscular Christianity. Certainly more people now play rugby than muscular Christianity. At any rate, it was not accidental that religion and football developed together.

At Groton, Peabody stood at least as firm on the unacceptability of physical weakness as on religious doubts. In the family school, it could be no other way, since, as Sedgwick remarks, "the Rector himself was the perfect example of the healthy-minded man. 'Sick souls' he imperfectly understood. And though he was tolerant toward ills of the flesh, it was evident that he did not think well of them. A boy with a cold felt under a stigma, and a leg twisted in football practice was little to be proud of. Born in the days when hopes of a perfected world seemed possible, never ill, with a wife lovely as she was beloved, knowing nothing but happiness, he looked on trouble as transitory and held it firmly underfoot. If ever in the freshness of his youth a man was born into eternal life, it was the Rector."

The unrelenting insistence that every boy succeed at athletics created, apparently, far more unhappiness than did either academic competitiveness or religious struggles among the developing boys. The reason was simple: At the church schools as they developed, muscles were as important, not only as Christianity, but as the cut of one's clothes. Success at football guaranteed social success at school. Ellery Sedgwick said Bayard Cutting was the "single instance of a boy who became the acknowledged head of the school wholly innocent of athletic supremacy and merely gifted with character and superlative intelligence."

For the most part, athletics *was* character and personality. These were times when football, in particular, was an upperclass game. Well into the 1920s and even later, Harvard and Yale had the best teams in the country, provided the bulk of the all-Americans, and fought for the championship of the world when they played.

The prep schools, Groton and St. Mark's and St. Paul's, provided a good part of the cannon fodder for these titanic clashes. The intense dedication of athletes to their team and their sport is common stuff now, but in the early years of the century there was something very properly and purely crusading about it, very much in the Christian tradition. Oliver La Farge, Groton '20, wrote of his schoolboy struggles:

> Football is violent. In its periods of action it is the use of everything you have to the limit of your capacity directly against the bodies of your opponents. For the linemen it is pure physical conflict, formalized, disciplined to serve an objective, but nonetheless violent, and it is comradeship. These are strong things, part of the juice of life, they reach into the very origins of man. Call them forth, add the pure singlemindedness of your schoolboy, and you get something between ecstasy and a crusade.*

---

* It was a near-poetic turn of events when the grandson and namesake of Endicott Peabody was named an all-American guard at Harvard in 1941, probably the last of a long series of Episcocrats honored that way. Peabody later followed another latter-day Episcocratic tradition, losing races for high office. He ran unsuccessfully for the governorship of Massachusetts in 1960 and 1964, just as John deK. Alsop lost in Connecticut in 1962 and Franklin D. Roosevelt, Jr., in New York in 1966. Peabody did win one two-year term in 1962; other recent Episcocratic governors include Christian Herter in Massachusetts and W. Averell Harriman in New York.

Peabody made it very clear, as did the headmasters of the other schools, that the boys played games that were "good," not "silly," like tennis. Football, hockey, and crew were the major approved sports. All, interestingly, were team sports, though the first two provide ample opportunity for individual glory as well. The twin goals of individual achievement and school solidarity were appropriate; they expressed what the schools as a whole were trying to drum into the unformed psyches of their young charges. The playing field has always been a microcosm of its society.

The Big Game, between traditional rivals like Groton and St. Mark's, was, for a New England prep school, the central event of the year and the grandest expression of school unity. Missing a game was committing a heretical act—even for the school's masters. They might as well have tried to seduce seventh-formers. When Arnold Whitridge wrote about William Amory Gardner, one of Groton's original masters, he reached a crescendo of praise over "Billy Wag's" remarkable difference from the prevailing athletic climate of the school:

> Outside of the football field and the classroom there was little chance for a boy to develop that happy sense of achievement which modern psychology has revealed to us as the only panacea for the pains of adolescence. There was nothing but Billy Wag, lounging in his canoe, smoking endless cigarettes, reading Russian novels and Greek tragedies, to remind us that there was a world elsewhere. He was one of the masters who never did calisthenics at morning recess, and who never joined in the triumphal parade after the St. Mark's game. While the stalwarts of the sixth form built the bonfire and fed the flames, the rest of us marched around the field shouting, "Right! Right! Groton's all right. Left! Left! St. Mark's got left." For some reason Mr. G. never joined in this orgy of victory. I am not sure he even went to the St. Mark's game, but no one ever criticized him for this amazing eccentricity. He was always a law unto himself.

The main point of football—pulling together—was a goal emphasized up and down the church schools. From the cold showers to the small, austere rooms to the harsh discipline led by the tyrannical strictures of a group of proud sixth-formers, the boys who attended a church school in the early part of the twentieth century were almost literally whipped into line. It is a suggestion of the Episcocratic code: The most privileged young men in the country were also among the most harshly dealt with. Early on, even in the considerably loosened prep schools of today, the privileged learn the lesson, through doing, that life is cruelly ordered, that you either dish it out or take it. There are few very "favored" children, in the sense of being pampered, in Episcocratic families. Theirs is a sterner code.

Early Groton, a graduate wrote, was "a cruel place; for neither wealth nor prominence availed to buy peace." Discipline in the schools was physical and public; its purpose clear: One played by the rules, as defined by the rigid hierarchy. At Peabody's Groton, the major penalty, pumping, consisted of ten seconds of drowning under a spigot, conducted after evening prayers while the whole school, including the Rector, sat quietly and watched.

In 1901, three weeks before Theodore Roosevelt was inaugurated as vice president, his fourteen-year-old son Teddy was pumped—"as the most typical of his form, the general tone of which we disapproved," George Biddle recalls. When young Roosevelt made the mistake of denying that he was fresh and swelled-headed, he was pumped again. At St. Mark's, the older students could make the younger ones do virtually anything they wanted—run errands, clean rooms—and the abolition of that order was vigorously protested by alumni in the 1920s and 30s.

Groton again. "Another season we pumped the Rector's son, Malcolm, just recently elected Bishop Coadjutor of New York," Biddle wrote, in an appalled tone, in 1939. "Nor had he committed any specific breach of the school code. We just didn't like his 'tone' either; and it was definitely important to keep the tone of the lower forms up to Groton standard. The Rector was splendid about it. He certainly could take it on the chin."

The willingness to inflict punishment even on his own son in the name of maintaining the general discipline was a characteristic cross between the Rector's English-school system of the older boys' domination of the school and the Old-Testament-God sternness of his Puritan roots. The school's hierarchical structure, in which the sixth-form head monitor (at Groton, the senior prefect) took power directly from God and the headmaster and administered it to the young, impressionable boys, was a fascinating system. It was, in fact, a democratic system within a preselected aristocracy of equals.

Once a boy was deposited in the school—removed from the outside world—and proved himself willing to live by and act on its code, he was recognized by his peers as a living part of that code. Of course, a system based on such peer pressure, one that overtly requires a boy to play the game before being allowed a position on the varsity team, produced results about as democratic as Mussolini's Italy.

Only the details, never the main direction, were at the discretion of the leaders of the sixth form. Peabody always held the final power—of expulsion, if necessary—which he was not loath to exercise. As little Averell Harriman, future statesman, said: "You know [Peabody] would be an awful bully if he weren't such a terrible Christian." The sixth form was allowed just enough power to vote in favor of the prevailing codes and mores of the school and to point out to the lower forms that well-marked path. It could not be otherwise in the fundamentally Christian world the church schools inhabited—the Christianity of the established order, in which society, studiously ignoring the Freudian and relativist energies that would eventually catch up with it, remained frozen in the inheritance from the classical and medieval thinkers.

There was no flux in the Rector's school; what had been done would continue to be done. For the boys who spent six adolescent years in the bosom of this static family, the lesson was unmistakable: The world must be faced with a stoic confidence, superiority, and conservatism. The best vote one could cast was "Yes, forever!"

The muscles of that Episcopalianism protruded continually. They shouldered every aspect of school life. Even today they are consciously, if somewhat shyly, acknowledged by most of the church schools. As George Biddle saw it, Peabody's Christianity was "an unshaken faith in his particular God and a fervent wish to keep physically fit, sexually clean, morally honest, and

—in every sense of the word—a gentleman. I fancy he dislikes a dirty collar as much as a dirty word, and is shocked by an East Side accent as well as by outspoken atheism." The schools were fundamentally Christian, then, practicing Christianity of a physical, English style—that is, Episcopalianism. And that worldly Christianity became the moral code of the country. Practiced by the privileged, imitated by the others.

Like many other schools, especially those with religious affiliations, the Episcopal boarding schools emphasized sexual purity to the eclipse of most other virtues. In George Biddle's time, dirty words were an anathema, socially as well as theologically, and were strongly discouraged by the student powers. As in many other areas, Peabody's attitudes drew from a deeply Victorian morality, a musty Puritanism. But what affected the boys was only the *antisocial* nature of swearing. Church schools have always been run by men of the cloth, but rarely produce future rectors.

As we have noted, Peabody was a vice-president of Boston's book-banning Watch and Ward Society. At school, Peabody's favorite sermon sprang from Tennyson's description of Galahad: "My strength is as the strength of ten,/Because my heart is pure."

In a combination of the schools' muscular Christianity and the Episcocratic love of the outdoors, there even sprang up a specifically entitled "Galahad movement" in the church, which sponsored a summer camp in East Sebago, Maine, for some 200 aspiring Christians. Through frequent self-examination and healthy living, the boys would achieve spiritual and physical strength of an even higher order than the schools could offer. The boys would progress in five steps of spiritual health until finally they reached Knight Counselor and were ready to convey their spiritual power to others. One participant, Stephen Howe, now chancellor of the diocese of Boston, recalls that the camp induced in him and others a spiritual scrupulousness unusual in the easygoing world of religious Episcopalianism. Howe, his brother, and William Hull, a friend from Harvard, waited years beyond the normal age to undergo confirmation, such doubts did the camp induce. It still exists under the grandson of the original founder, though reduced to about 150 boys.

Francis Biddle speculates:

> Why was it that school teachers of this time [the early part of the century] were so incessantly concerned with purity? L. E. Jones, in his charming *Victorian Boyhood*—he was my contemporary—was struck by his teachers' obsession with impurity at Eton. He never heard a word about other immoralities—the sin of unkindness, the sin of cruelty: it was always the evil of impurity, expressed in admonitions not to talk filth. The Rector preached directly at us when he talked about impurity, and though he never said what he meant, he looked into our eyes as he towered above us from the chapel pulpit, beautifully white and clean and healthy and manly, searching out our hidden secrets. To children of twelve or thirteen "impurity," denounced in that suggestive yet fulminating manner, could hardly be understood to refer to harlots, as the Bible called them, for at that time we had not even begun to speculate on the possibility of a Groton boy "going with women," as the phrase was, at Harvard or Yale or Princeton. Those discussions did not really begin until the fifth or sixth, and by then some of us admitted the possibility. . . . The Rector's words were rather puzzling at first, but it did not take us long to discover his meaning. Although he never came at it directly, it was clear what he was driving at when he told us that a boy could never be a true Grotonian—i.e., make the football team—if he did that sort of thing, or thought those sorts of thoughts. Such exhortations were nicely calculated to create a secret sense of guilt. He equated failure with what he called impurity.

This confusing mass of "morality" separated Episcocratic schoolboys from the unwashed and unsaved of American society. First were the people who would attend the prep schools. Then were all the others, who, by their actions of "impurity" —more social than religious—separated themselves from that golden, crusading crowd of Galahads.

The preoccupation with morality has survived, in gentler form, in the church schools to this day. A well-situated lawyer in his mid-thirties tells legendary tales of the absolutely baroque conceptions that were nurtured, if not created, by the atmosphere at St. Paul's. Those fantasies held two main components: masturbation and Christ's sufferings! Schoolboys continue to accuse the dinner on the night of a dance with a neighboring girl's school of having too much saltpeter, a chemical supposedly reductive of sexual capability.

That situation—indeed, the entire climate of sexual morality —has, of course, been radically altered by the acceptance of girls at nearly all the rich boys' schools. It may appear, someday, that coeducation was the greatest change in the prep school-college-Wall Street track that has allowed the Episcopal establishment to dominate far more than its share of the country's power.

Coeducation has certainly altered the social development of the young men of the St. Grottlesex schools, though sexual abstinence continues to be the recommended policy for the schools' young charges. Choate–Rosemary Hall, for example, warns even in its catalog against "certain degrees of sexual intimacy." There is a suggestion that a point exists beyond which one would not venture. How politely Episcopalian is the catalog's admonition! Too sophisticated to be outright condemning and Puritan. Too church-affiliated totally to forget the words of St. Paul.

The early prep schools balanced their preoccupation with things physical with a somewhat disdainful attitude toward things mental. Episcocratic society always looked down on "grinds," and the schools' fist inculcated the attitude. It was not, as all headmasters of the early twentieth century would have cheerfully admitted, a school's sole function to teach academic subjects. Academics were an area for competition like everything else. But they certainly held no revered place in a school's life. A somewhat inferior one, if anything.

It was a reflection of the fundamental class biases of the rectors and, to a greater or lesser extent, the boys' own parents. Then and now, Episcocrats have been concerned more with the concrete elements of this life than with "idle speculation," and since the early days, anti-intellectualism was accentuated by a roll-up-your-sleeves, God-helps-those-who-help-themselves morality. Whatever you do, do something; don't just sit there and think.

Peabody, "though head of a school . . . wasn't really interested in education of the mind," Walter S. Hinchman wrote.
"What he called 'mental discipline' was moral discipline. It was
good for you to master difficult subjects, such as Latin and
Greek, if you had no taste for them. Intellectual curiosity
simply did not interest him, and a boy, like George Martin or
Charlie Curtis, who had such curiosity in abundance, was almost suspect. Furthermore, he believed so ardently in team-
work that a shy youngster or an individualist sometimes was
stigmatized as a 'rank outsider.' "

The curious George Martin described the Rector's approach
this way: "Sophisticated persons know that it is not enough
to be right. In this world it is necessary to be successful also.
This is often resented by closet theorists—especially women—
but wise men accept the universe and get on with their knitting."
That well-rounded malcontent George Biddle, meanwhile,
concluded that Groton was "socially conservative rather
than actually hostile to scholarship," but the total "effect was
to stifle the creative impulse . . . and by and large, in many small
ways, it was intellectually dishonest."

It was hardly surprising in an era of WASP dominance based
on the gentle inheritance of position, rather than on the intellectual and material scrambling of the immigrant groups, that
a large helping of anti-intellectualism was dished out in the
prep schools. After all, their graduates were soon to go on to a
Harvard or Yale, where "grinds" were synonymous with "meatballs," and a Gentleman's C was a living institution, a standard.

The Groton that creative men found stifling was actually
more distinguished academically than any of the other church
schools, a distinction attributable to Peabody's proclivity to
appoint masters like the iconoclastic William Amory Gardner.
In sharp distinction to the rapidly changing nonsectarian prep
schools Andover and Exeter, St. Mark's and the other church
schools all but demanded an intellectual vacuum of their students. They were hardly ashamed of it. One alumnus wrote to
St. Mark's in 1924 that he regretted having been too much of a
bookworm in school.

"Colleges run, at present, too much along scholastic lines,
with rigid curricula which do not encourage a man to develop
himself along the line of his special abilities," he wrote. "I
think that St. Mark's is absolutely right in giving a solid, hard

grounding, without stressing intellectuality, and in seeing that the boys have enough hard exercise." And a St. Mark's faculty committee reported in 1936, "The general tendency seems to be in the direction of enlarging the group characterized by harmless mediocrity—the Gentleman's C." The committee noted, with more than a note of discouragement, that the "prevalent spirit of the boys is antagonistic to scholarship." By the twenties the schools were dismayed, not cheerful, about the weakness in academic areas.

Peabody, typically, had no qualms about what he was doing. "I am not sure I like boys to think too much," the Rector said. "A lot of people think a lot of things we could do without. Manifestly the world is full of evil that we all encounter as we go along. Nobody denies that. But why emphasize it as we go along?"

So overriding was the schools' sense of class importance that most of the students were constantly cognizant of it—which only made them strive harder.

"Everything about my classmates fed my shyness—their smart Brooks Brothers clothes, their self-assurance, a certain undefinable breath of the larger world about which I felt so ignorant," Francis Biddle wrote. Mixed in Biddle's comments are the twin inferiority complexes of a boy not faring well on the competitive battleground of the school and feeling the great bulk of a bustling, powerful outside world that some of the boys sprang from. Others, Franklin Roosevelt among them, felt both pangs as well. And Bronson Cutting, the senator from New Mexico who, like his brother Bayard before him, was a once-in-a-decade brilliant student as soon as he entered the school, had little confidence, as George Biddle relates:

A few months ago [i.e., in 1939] at a gathering at the Whitney Museum [the donation of a Groton family], being told that Mrs. W. Bayard Cutting was present, I introduced myself to her, telling her how little I had known her son but what a vast admiration I had for his liberal-mindedness, his valiant fight against reaction, and his deep intelligence. She told me that Bronson had also felt himself a failure at school, unable to compete in athletics, so delicate that he gave the impression of a cripple; but that when he was elected head editor of *The Grotonian* he had written her:

"You may not know it, but I believe today that I am the happiest human being in all America."

Partly—but only partly—as a result of growing up, prep school boys are tossed from depression to elation by the most minor expressions of the disapproval or approbation of the school as a whole. The school is their entire world. It magnifies each small triumph and tragedy. The razor edge the boys apparently feel is also intimately connected to the schools' mixed message. You are the elite of America, going to its best school. At the same time, you are a frail being saddled with massive moral and financial responsibilities. You have inherited success. Now you must pass it on.

The schools performed well their dual function of inculcating the manners and assumptions of an aristocracy while supplying strategic, if polite, spurs to great achievement. George Biddle knew what he was feeling. "I got through the next two years all right," he wrote of his final two forms at Groton. "Off and on I headed my form. I was an editor of *The Grotonian*. I rowed on the school four. I knew I was a failure. I was liked well enough. I was never entirely defeated. I knew Groton was the finest school in America; I knew that being a failure was my own fault. I knew that I was a happy fellow to be there. I was that low. Life had compensations."

The confusion in the students, while it helped create an ingrown, highly successful, and homogeneous aristocracy (for those who did not turn neurotic or alcoholic), also reflected the schools' basic confusion of purpose. The confusion is centered in the Episcopal character of the institutions. For the official religion of the upper class had a straitlaced, moral edge that the rectors and masters could not and did not want to ignore. But the boys, who had to return home to the world of real families—as opposed to the standard, homogenized family of the school—could very well ignore the Christian precepts that were to regulate parts of their upper-class behavior.

The first three decades of the twentieth century were notorious for their riotous college life. Drinking to sickness and dissipation were considered the highest forms of upper-class life, at least by the nation at large. Most likely this was a reaction to the pent-up, straitlaced life of the church prep school.

An even more acute split between Episcocratic theory and practice was nurtured in the prep schools and left a sore on just about every Episcopalian of today. This is the subject of money—getting it and spending it.

Peabody's thinking on money was unambiguous, and it was integrated into his thinking on sin. George Biddle made this entry into his diary: "Febuary 14. The Rector spoke about Gambling, drinking and Impurity. There are two ways of legitimately spending one's money. First, spending it and getting something for it. Then giving it away. Never tell an unclean story or allow one to be told in your presence. The reading for the week is . . ."

Unfortunately, while it was assumed that the possession of money was a great good—it naturally would be so considered by Peabody, son of a Morgan partner—the steps to acquire that money were something the Rector did not have to—in fact did not—deal with. He did not like Wall Street. No question about that.

He was both a refined upper-class gentleman and a minister of God, suspicious of worldly pursuits. He did not mind communicating these suspicions to the boys' parents, though he was extremely pleasant and impressive to them. Peabody aroused suspicion on more than one occasion that he did not think too highly of the way some of them got their money. "The trouble with your school, Mr. Peabody," a Boston mother complained to him, "is that it makes boys despise their parents." "No," Peabody replied haughtily, "it makes boys anxious about them."

Peabody had a Yankee distrust of big-city mores. He certainly did not choose to produce future corporate lawyers or bankers. The ministry and, secondarily, public service were the favored Episcocratic choices. (The professions, a sort of worthy third choice, were—with the exception of the law—beginning to fall out of favor with the upper class by the twenties.)

We see here a central contradiction of Peabody and of all Episcopalians: the battle between God and Mammon. The two are difficult to reconcile, and Peabody, both "the Rector" and close friend of J. P. Morgan, stands as a prime example of this knotty problem. On the one hand, he devoutly wanted "his boys" to eschew Wall Street success and to turn their thoughts (and careers) to God. On the other hand, he knew (as did Bishop Lawrence) that funds had to be raised to maintain the schools. The only way out of the difficulty, of course, was to inherit, not make, money. Happily, this was often possible for Episcopalians by the end of the nineteenth century, since many of them were second or third generation. But not always. As George Martin concludes, speaking of the school's force-fed success ethic, "This attitude is conducive to an urgency which tended to push boys a little farther along the road to success than they would have got under their own steam. Unfortunately it did not induce any increased discrimination in the selection of occupations, and the graduates took to finance as eagerly as to medicine." Martin added:

> The Rector saw this very clearly; but his only weapon of opposition was exhortation. He urged the boys to go into the professions and keep away from Wall Street. He lectured on vocations in Sacred Studies: and they asked him how an Army officer could possibly send his son to Groton. He had not thought of it. His whole school project required a large income for its customers. When he urged the boys to be true to themselves and drop out of their parents' income class, they simply did not hear him. They were going to make money enough to be able to send their sons to Groton. That was the first and greatest commandment.*
>
> This business of money and vocation was fantastic, and the Rector got no help on it. Everybody from Jacob Riis to Booker Washington undertook to give talks to the boys and advise them. In the very early years of the century Gifford Pinchot, who was then a forester, came up to lecture on forestry. The lecture is long forgotten; but, at its close, he looked at the boys meaningly, almost menacingly, and said: "Fortunate is the man so rich he does not have to work, but twice fortunate is the rich man who works hard though he does not have to."

---

* Since the first (and greatest) commandment is actually to love the Lord your God with your whole heart, graduates of Groton cannot resist poking fun at the obvious discrepancy between the high Christian values of the school and the moneymaking Episcocratic tendencies of its boys.

He might have saved his breath. When the annual product grew up, rich and poor alike fell to the task of making money and getting power with a fury which astounded their classmates in college.

Martin reported on TR's trip to Groton and the president's admonition "not to take champagne or butlers with them on camping trips in the Adirondacks." He commented: "Honestly, that is what he said. It sounded awfully *pukka* at the time; but long afterward many wondered what it was all about."

What it was all about was the confusion of an upper class attempting to meld its two disparate elements—old gentility and new, fabulous wealth—into a single moral code. Inevitably the two elements clashed, though not enough to disturb the fundamental message of the schools: self-assurance.

No real conflict arose among the graduates over what they would do after school; with the exception of a few artistic or religious fanatics, the graduates went into occupations promising money and power. By 1925 the St. Mark's class of '20, only a year out of college, was already well embedded in upper-class occupations increasingly led by the prep school grads. Of the nineteen members of the class, ten were part of the money occupations—four in banking or brokerage, four in "business," and two in law school. Four were doing postgraduate work (some, no doubt, in business), and the five others were distributed among theology school, medical school, journalism, and "literature."

At St. Mark's, as among the rest of the prep schools, there was a curious dual attitude toward wealth and social prestige: a perception that it was necessary for the school's continued existence, at least on its current level, and a suspicion that it might not be exactly what a secondary school ought to be doing. "The greatest handicap a boy at St. Mark's has to overcome is the handicap of prosperity," suggested Frederic Carrol Baldy, a master from the early part of the century.

That was certainly true from the viewpoint of educational motivation. Episcocrats have never placed a high premium on studying. By the 1920s, their high-water mark, St. Mark's and the other Episcopal church schools had become little more than the first strong link in a chain that stretched from birth through college and clubs and jobs and neighborhoods directly into a heaven of Episcocratic men and women. By this time the schools had become massive institutions; that is, they had acquired the burden of a group of alumni who wanted for their sons exactly what they had themselves. Dependent, as all schools are, on their alumni for contributions and tuition payments, the schools fell victim to the narrow philosophy of self-perpetuation and success through well-loved channels that the schools had helped inculcate in their first generation.

By the twenties the public symbol of the church schools' exclusivity was their antediluvian admissions policy. A prime Boston snob could hardly have developed a better plan for keeping the aristocrats mixing with other aristocrats if he spent a year by himself in a Henry James drawing room. Recent St. Mark's headmaster Edward Tuck Hall grows uncharacteristically wide-eyed over the process:

> The system in use was so ridiculous as to seem grotesque today. Except for a handful [seven in 1927] of competitive places, priority of application governed likelihood of acceptance. Getting into St. Mark's in the 1920s was a little like getting into the Somerset Club of Boston [which many of the successful applicants would eventually join]: a boy's name was put down within hours or days of his birth if he was to have a chance of acceptance.
>
> Dr. Thayer wrote in 1930, acknowledging his failure to improve the process: ". . . The present situation is that we have from 145 to 165 applicants for every year up to 1941; even for the year 1942, twelve years ahead, there are 70 applicants [to a school which in 1927 had 35 in the sixth form and only 190 boys in the entire school]. . . . For the last few years we have been taking five boys on the competitive list without regard to the priority of application and further we have been taking the sons of graduates even though their names were not reached on the priority list.* . . . The school has cumbersome lists of boys that

---

* The acceptance of alumni sons, while offered as a relatively radical step toward reform, provided at least as much and probably more homogeneity among the student body as allowing boys to be signed up at birth. Of the 191 students in 1930, 57 were alumni sons, and another 33 had some family connection with St. Mark's. Either procedure obviously tends to create a school that breeds out differences among its students from generation to generation.

cannot possibly get in; it has little to say about what boys it wants as long as they pass the qualifying examination."

But the headmaster's concern was not merely with the system itself: he worried about its effects. Of 190 boys in the 1928 student body, 93 were from New York City and vicinity. Dr. Thayer . . . was dealing with a problem that has continued to plague St. Mark's and schools of its kind: drawing for its earliest student body upon families of adequate means within reasonable reach, the school subsequently discovered that these alumni tended to settle in the same general areas, send their sons and encourage their sons' friends, and unwittingly perpetuate the very geographical constriction that every St. Mark's headmaster from 1924 to the present has struggled to overcome. . . .

Certainly the homogeneity of the school's student body was not due to any chauvinism or narrowness of view on the part of the trustees themselves. The Board was thoroughly in sympathy with Dr. Thayer's view that a broader base of enrollment should be sought. But St. Mark's was still somewhat in debt, had a small endowment, and very little to spend on scholarships.

The endowment was at least as great a problem for the newer prep schools as it was for St. Mark's, since the better-known schools—St. Paul's, with twice St. Mark's endowment in 1939, and Groton, which had twice St. Paul's—largely monopolized the Episcopal school donation dollar. Even with the greater amount of money available to them, St. Paul's and Groton were limited in their diversity by the same geographical treadmill as St. Mark's. The prep schools of the 1930s were like the prep schools of the 1900s—only more so. Even in the liberal 1970s, the student bodies are clotted with Episcocratic children of alumni, flecked with a few students of the new-rich who aspire to the Episcocratic label.

By the twenties and thirties the church schools had fully assumed the position they were destined to occupy all along—that of first and most important arbiter of who would occupy the highest position in the American aristocratic hierarchy. The student bodies of the important Ivy colleges, fed largely by graduates of the church schools, were becoming more and more heavily Episcopalian. By 1926 Bishop Lawrence could note that Harvard, which for two centuries had been an overtly Puritan-Unitarian institution, had dropped its religious affiliations and had the largest proportion of undergraduate Episcopalians in the country.

Around this time and after, a Yale alumnus noted, the Yale Bowl was one-quarter Episcopalian when full. Seats of power and membership in the Episcopal Church had become one.

More important, the social standards of Harvard and Yale were very decidedly set by the Episcocrats. The relatively new boarding schools rapidly replaced the older institutions like the Phillips academies at Andover and Exeter and Roxbury Latin as the sine qua non at Harvard. "Only the top-ranking émigrés of New England's elite Episcopal Church schools—Groton, St. Mark's, St. Paul's, St. George's and Middlesex—can be positive from the start that they are club material with no questions asked," wrote Cleveland Amory in 1947. "Even these, the 'St. Grottlesexers' as they have been called, find themselves in the position of waiting anxiously for the call to Harvard clubdom at the same time knowing that more than a third of them, as sophomores, will never make it."

The clubs at Harvard, Yale and Princeton have been even more determined sifters of aristocratic material than the church schools. The preference for church school graduates in the clubs means that a vast proportion of the clubmen will be Episcocrats. The novelist Owen Wister, of one of the proudest of old Philadelphia Quaker-turned-Episcopal families, declared to a reporter in 1936 that belonging to the Porcellian, Harvard's most social club, created a bond that could be "felt but not analyzed." And when his daughter, Alice, was engaged to Nicholas Longworth, President Theodore Roosevelt's acceptance of his son-in-law as another member of the Porc is equally suggestive of that ineffable connection. Around 1945, a graduate of St. Mark's who had moved to the traditional upper-class town of Tuxedo Park, described his school as "the best club I belong to."

The proper college—especially the proper club in college—has traditionally led directly to the top in the American Business Aristocracy, which, as we have seen, tends to be the ultimate goal implanted in the hearts of the young church school

Episcocrats. It is in getting that first job after college that the "old school tie"—and the church schools do have an actual necktie—can be a critical factor.

School diplomas are much better than the old system of letters of introduction from one's father's friends—more standardized, easier to recognize, more universally applicable. The best way to get a job right out of school, of course, is to inherit a business—in the manner of, for example, the Houghton family, which sends its sons to St. Paul's and then employs them, upon graduation from Harvard, in the family's Corning Glass works. Given the increasing centralization of business, it has become more and more likely that the young Porcellian member will be showing up for an interview with an older grad at Morgan Guaranty Trust, say, than just reporting to work at Dad's firm.

Investment banking firms, a 1976 survey by *Fortune* magazine shows, are led by an Episcopal chief executive officer in fully one-third of all cases. The law, too, has been a classic pipeline for graduates of the right prep schools, the right colleges, and the right clubs. In New York, law firms by early in the century had moved away from strictly family recommendations (nepotism laws took hold) and depended largely on the recommendations of school-college-club-law school. The firms were even ranked (unofficially) in order of preference of the proper "family" credentials. Cravath Swaine was at one end of the spectrum, in terms of emphasis on merit; Davis Polk, probably at the other, being the most "white shoe" of the New York firms. It all worked very smoothly.

An almost too neat example was Richard Whitney, who moved effortlessly from Groton to Harvard and Porcellian. He married the daughter of the president of the Union League Club, worked at Kidder, Peabody in Boston and Morgan in New York, joined all the important New York clubs and achieved the presidency of the Essex Fox Hounds (in the Somerset hills country) and the treasurership of the New York Yacht Club. He promised to bar forever from the Knickerbocker Club several drunken Grotonians who had defaced the school's chapel. Laundered by these proper institutions and by his own family wealth, Whitney was the shining-clean figure of the New York Stock Exchange president, disdainfully rejecting the slightest attempt by the federal government to regulate an institution which had helped cause the Depression.

Whitney was soon the one who needed to be regulated. He was tried and convicted for embezzling funds not only from the exchange but, perhaps worse in his Episcocratic milieu, from the Yacht Club as well. By the end of the thirties he was in Sing Sing, where he received visits from Peabody. His final prejail photograph showed his gold Porcellian pig prominently displayed on his watch chain.

Family is a vital consideration in sending a son to the proper prep school, from which he goes on to the proper college, where he joins the proper club. Innumerable times women from one important family have married their brother's prep school or college roommate—Theodore Roosevelt set the style. At Harvard, the clubs became a simple and easy-to-use substitute for a formal invitation list when proper Boston mothers sought to provide their debutante daughters with proper escorts. The same is true for the considerably larger number of prep school boys and clubmates who lived in and around New York.

That was the church school of the 1920s: an institution so homogeneous and ingrown as to make the Episcopal House of Bishops look like the League of Nations. It was a fully blossomed flower to be plucked by each graduate and worn as a sign of acceptance in circles that never hesitated to call themselves the best—a substitute family that brought a boy into the proper path with much greater success than even most rich parents had a chance of doing. It was a consuming experience, in short, that spit out nearly identical boys with nearly identical goals and a minimum of vulnerability. They knew they were meant to rule, and they ruled. A stanza in the Grotonian Song Book made a virtue of their conformity:

> Some come from Boston and some from New York,
> As much two extremes as Cadiz and Cork.
> There are thin ones and fat ones and short ones and tall,
> But they speedily change to Grotonians all.

At St. Mark's, too, conformity was the watchword. Edward Tuck Hall notes in his centennial history of St. Mark's:

There was the occasional non-conformist, the rebel, the anarchist, the atheist, the socialist, the religious mystic. But if a stereotype were to be fashioned of the typical St. Marker as he lived his life in the Parkman years [1930–42], he might be described thus: he liked the school but did did not love it as his father did; he saw more and knew more of the world outside; he was something of a material-ist who wanted what was coming to him. He was a con-servative in most matters; he had not thought deeply enough to become a rebel. He valued acceptance, tangible achievement, and recognition. He cultivated a sense of humor but abhorred sentiment. He prided himself on dress-ing well and appearing to advantage in public. He had been touched by his friendships at St. Mark's, and as he prepared to graduate he realized that he had been touched by some other things as well. Intellectually he had only begun to live, and spiritually he had yet to be born inde-pendently. He was going to college well trained in the fundamentals of learning, but only partly prepared to make self-reliant use of them.

The Right People

The 1920s saw the beginning of the end of the stranglehold (though not the importance) of the prep schools on the worlds of college and career. It was a very specific event, though at the time it was not noticed. Edward Tuck Hall calls it "a cloud no bigger than a man's hand."

In 1924 the colleges announced for the first time that they would no longer accept everyone with the correct preparations who could pass the entrance examinations. In the next few years competition began—though for a while it was no contest at all for the church schools. Their graduates were very much the type of person Harvard and Yale wanted. And it was not the prep school grad, but the increasing numbers of aspirants from the public schools, who suffered from the first slight closing of the gates. Though previously there had been no need for them, the colleges now found it necessary to institute the infamous Jewish quotas as a regular and frequently enforced policy.

With little change, the situation continued right up to the Second World War. The Ivy colleges, which provided the massively disproportionate bulk of leadership in politics, law, and business, continued to be heavily Episcocratic institutions led by those who had been trained for that role at the church schools. It was a very simple and very satisfactory system for St. Grottlesex.

Only after the war—a war, by the way, that many of the preppies, no doubt reflecting their fathers' ill-disguised Nazi sympathies and perhaps a more subtle feeling that such a war could end Anglo dominance, did not much favor—did the colleges begin the shift from being predominantly private school institutions to increasingly public school ones. The Ivy colleges grew larger, thus diluting the proportion of private-schoolers. But to a large degree the new balance shifted against the church schools because fewer and fewer of their graduates were getting in. No doubt the percentage of Grotties who get into Harvard is considerably higher than at a public high school on Long Island. But compared to the prewar years, when almost every church school graduate got into whatever college he wanted, the competition became, as Hall puts it, "nightmarish." By the 1970s only one or two St. Markers went to Harvard each year.

Internally, the church schools have been changing, belatedly catching up with a twentieth century that was getting a little bored with them. It became impossible not to change—communication was too easy, the masters themselves, once Peabody left, too open-eyed to society at large. Kenneth Auchincloss, now managing editor of *Newsweek*, catalogs some of the changes of the fifties:

> In 1950 I came to a Groton whose old order was still being gently ushered out. The Thanksgiving vacation was a new and welcome treat, comfortable seats and dual projectors in the Hall made entertainment less spartan a pleasure, and new boys believed Mr. Abry for only about a week when he told them that they must take cold showers every morning. Dance weekend's traditional monopoly on term-time encounters with girls was broken by small dances with Concord Academy subtly inserted into the fall and spring schedules. And, perhaps most dramatic of all, the first Negro entered Groton in 1952.*
>
> To people who had long been associated with the school, most of these changes probably seemed only tidbits, but I remember that all of them were important to me. For, taken together, they highlighted a liberal trend which helped to reassure me that Groton had moved out of what

---

* St. Mark's, however, did not enroll its first black student until 1964, the high point of student unrest and social activism.

seemed a Neanderthal Age. This reassurance was necessary because of Groton's forbidding aspect to outsiders and prospective new boys, who tend to associate Groton with snobbishness, tin-wash-basin asceticism, and the stern figure of Mr. Peabody. The good that the school does may live on in its graduates, but not in the national press or idiom. When I went home for vacations and told people where I went to school, I remember that I was always careful to add apologetically, "But Groton has changed a lot since the war."

The changes, which continue, were partly forced on the schools by outside events; partly they were the schools' own response to those events and the justified anticipation that they would continue. Frequently the headmasters and faculty, broadened by their education, were considerably ahead of the background-absorbed students in seeing the handwriting on the wall. When Francis Parkman resigned as St. Mark's headmaster in 1942, he told a chapelful of students that in the world then being born "a man will need more than a comfortable set of Republican principles and a proper school and background to meet the stresses and strains of the next ten or twenty years."

Parkman warned, "I've seen too many boys go out to college with the attitude that the world is their oyster; that they and other graduates of similar schools are the 'right people' and the rest are 'meatballs.' The world will not admire them until they have shown something worth admiring." Recognizing that public disdain for the rich boys' schools would probably be a greater factor after the war, he added that "the gilded youth won't get very far in the world you're going into, nor will he get much sympathy from the world for his failures." The perceptions of Parkman and his fellow headmasters liberalized their institutions only minutely; in 1960 a student straw poll at St. Paul's elected Nixon over Kennedy, even while the masters went heavily for the graduate of a fellow private school, Choate.

The changes in the world around them, especially the broadening experience of a mass-levied army, created at the schools in the fifties a low-profile, my-country-right-or-wrong attitude that had not existed in the somewhat more dandified and individualized days when one could expect the postschool world to be as exclusive as St. George's. As the schools grew older and the original muscular-Christianity traditions lapsed into obsolescence—nobody could figure out how to apply them to a nuclear age—the schools began producing even more conformists and fewer distinct leaders. Kenneth Auchincloss wrote in 1960:

> Another striking and controversial aspect of Groton is the lack of serious self-criticism that goes on within its walls. . . .
> . . . It would be going too far to say that Groton stifles individualism and originality, but the school molds a certain unquestioning acceptance of The Way It Has Always Been Done which is surely not a good thing.

Another postwar alum, John Train, founder of the *Paris Review* and later investment banker, noted succinctly:

> One achievement of the school is that it sets up a struggle in the mind of the boy between what he feels is common sense and what he finds himself doing. . . . Not to mince words, Groton pushed many a boy to become something of a hypocrite; or perhaps we should say, to acquire a certain protective coloration. . . .
> The boy learns early to be a small Christian gentleman, but he also learns to go along with the higher-ups, to play ball, to "fit in," to conform. In six years he may lose the desire to think for himself. . . . It is dangerous to become addicted to obvious success. Real values are more likely to go with apparent failure. "Success" at Groton, "success" on the campus, "success" on Madison Avenue.

Madison Avenue and Wall Street were the primary beneficiaries of the mass production of men in gray flannel suits, the prep schools' most obvious postwar legacy. Another great depository for the graduates was service in the federal government, primarily in its aristocracy, the CIA and foreign service. It is hard to tell exactly how many graduates ended up in Washington, but there is no doubt it has been a remarkable proportion of the nation's leaders in war and peace. Attempting to refute charges that its boys generally became "dog show judges" when they grew up, an alumnus said in 1961 that no less than 12 percent of all St. Mark's graduates went into governmental or diplomatic careers. Among them were two U.S. senators, four congressmen, six officers of cabinet or subcabinet rank, eight senior foreign service officers, and numerous political figures on the state or local level. Groton, St. Paul's and Choate have similarly impressive representations among the top leaders of the country.

While Groton did officially urge its students to serve their country and their fellowmen through government service, and a significant minority always did, it was the Second World War and the subsequent cold war, led by Grotonians Franklin Roosevelt and Dean Acheson, that made federal service especially inviting. The heavily patrician CIA that grew from the equally well-selected wartime OSS showed the church-schoolers that the New Deal had not turned all of Washington into a classless society.

The enemy was well defined: first Germany, then Russia, both countries that opposed the church schools' official inspirations, God and England. All these encouraging messages were brought back to the schools, and the colleges they commonly fed into, by perceptive grads like McGeorge Bundy, who realized the sort of intelligent followers they could recruit from the schools. And so the students marched off to Washington. John Train noted that they were pushed toward government service "whether suited for it or not."

George Cabot Lodge, '45, a former assistant secretary of labor, described the schools' attitude in 1960:

> Groton is an outstanding trainer of men. Increasingly it is becoming a trainer of outstanding men as the opportunity increases for scholarships and thus entrance to the school regardless of economic status. Groton thus has in its charge for a critical four, five, or six years a group of men from among whom is likely to come a relatively high percentage of national leaders. It is only realistic to suppose that part of the obligation for the continued safety of the world and the well-being of humanity will probably fall on a number of Groton boys.

What training and ideals are imparted to these Groton boys, McGeorge Bundy and his successors, who hold the fate of the world in their hands? One assessment of the Episcocratic attitudes and goals instilled by Groton in the cold war era comes from a graduate named Christopher T. E. Rand. Rand, a foreign correspondent for *The New Yorker* who was graduated in 1930 and has since sent three sons to the school, distinguished between Groton and the Negroes, the Jews, the Roman Catholics—who can be further subdivided—and the various Low-Church Protestant communities:

> It seems to me it is the Anglican or Anglophile style that Groton represents and that Roosevelt chiefly represented, though he was a big enough leader to speak for many others too. With frank partisanship I would say it is the richest and most civilized style for the country to follow, and the one best able to harmonize us with the world at large.

At Groton, a 1969 graduate recalls, one of his closest friends was a son of John De Koven Alsop. The Alsops are an old American (twelve generations stretching back to prerevolutionary times) and Groton (columnist brothers Stewart and Joseph went there, too) family, but you wouldn't know it from the way young Alsop walked around in a shredded shirt and print ties. There will always, of course, be a Groton way of dressing; it merely changes with the times. It became chic for the upper class to look ratty, but there was always an inner order to the rattiness, like a Brooks label in the torn shirt and a certain jauntiness to the canvas pants on the children of old-line families.

For Groton, even now, does not draw on a very wide background. It is a place for descendants of the families that have made it what it is. Friends of young Alsop, for example, could meet his father, president of a Hartford insurance company and unsuccessful Republican candidate for governor in 1962. They could meet the son of Cyrus Vance, now secretary of state, then a Wall Street lawyer. They could meet Rodman Bundy, Mac's nephew. They could meet Biddles from the prolific family that has kept Groton, as well as political and artistic ranks generally, supplied with itself for centuries. It was not your average public high school.

On the other hand, diversity had arrived. "There were more blacks at Groton than at my local high school back home," reports our '69 grad; more than 10 percent of the student body of 203 was black. Certain things one did not talk about, in the sense that not talking about how important you are is one sign of how important you are. Clothes competition is frowned upon. A little of the stiff old formality is left, but the round of ordinary life goes on quietly. Lunch after chapel is the biggest event of the day. To a casual visitor it is all very humdrum— no tremors of sprouting aristocracy.

The smaller signs, vestiges of the great elaborate-simple days, remain. "It gave me martial kinds of feelings," says the 1969 graduate. "It was highly organized, somewhat Spartan." Rooms were not rooms but "The Cubicle"—little more than a stall with a curtain on it. No pampering. Chapel *every day*. Still the old school tie, a rather dowdy striped knit affair, and the school blazer that only seniors are allowed to wear. Students still must wear coat and tie for seated dinners, although other meals are informal. Boys no longer defer to seniors by getting off the path into the snow, but a feeling of position remains and implies, "Don't get too familiar, buddy, I'm a senior." Still the familiar nicknames for the masters one saw every day: The headmaster was "Black Jack" Crocker at the time.

But these are largely remnants of an abandoned tradition. They are no longer the definitive grounding in upper-class mores that leads to inevitable power in America. Better than most of the prep schools, Groton managed to respond to trends in American society, from the sublime to the ridiculous, that would otherwise have left the school on a little-traveled road outside Boston, ignored by everyone. The changes have inevitably changed the old Groton. The women. The first and second forms (seventh and eighth grades) are gone. Day students are now admitted, making the school considerably more open financially. All these are changes of the 1970s—indications that a church school is no longer the bastion of privileges it was even through the fifties and into the sixties. It no longer sets the tone for all society. For the most part, Groton and the other church schools now look more like slightly younger college campuses than anything else, with the same lacrosse sticks, Frisbees, and shorts.

The biggest change of all: Church school graduates no longer inherit Harvard and Yale as naturally as they inherit their trust funds and their benign God. Graduates of Groton, it is true, are still far the most likely of any students in the country to go to Harvard; of 224 graduates in the five years ending in 1976, 43, or more than 20 percent, went to Harvard, and another 25 (more than 10 percent) entered Yale. Penn, Princeton, Dartmouth, and Amherst, all traditionally Episcocratic colleges, were represented by substantial numbers as well. It is still much easier for an average Groton student to go to the college he wants than for the average graduate of, say, Poughkeepsie High School.

The other church schools have not had even Groton's declining success in admission to the top universities; many of the smaller ones, like Salisbury and Pomfret, are lucky if half their grads get into Ivy colleges, and acceptances by the really selective schools, the Big Three in particular, are becoming as rare an event around Episcopal schools as they are at the better public high schools.

St. Alban's, for example, is a relatively well-known school, but only eight of its fifty-three graduates in 1976 entered the Big Three, and while the rest still lean toward the Ivies, they are spread around twenty-nine different colleges. The increasing academic standing (and wealth) of student bodies at the public suburban high schools and the gradual dilution of alumni pulling power point to continually declining Ivy presence from the church schools.

It doesn't take much reading between lines to see how worried some of them have become. "You will need considerable help from many quarters if you are to be successful in your quest" for college admission, warns the St. Mark's catalog. ". . . Recent experience has shown that you must be aggressive, persistent, and organized in your efforts in addition to being able to submit an impressive list of accomplishments both academic and extra-curricular. Therefore, the fall trimester of your senior year will no doubt include college application, which will demand the time and energy of another course." For a school where the only qualification for college used to be social and financial, not academic and extracurricular, those are extreme statements.

With the exception of the stronger church schools, Groton and St. Paul's, the admission of students has become increasingly *less* competitive. Higher costs and greater uncertainty about the value of a church school education have made it more and more difficult to recruit students; there are reports that without alumni sons the survival of many of the schools would be in serious question. Going coed has been one stopgap measure.

With the increasingly questionable value of a church school education, their exclusiveness has changed from a proudly guarded characteristic to an undesirable, but inevitable, burden. Today not many schools can turn away anyone who wants to come and can also afford to pay $4000 or $5000 annually for a high school education. For most of the schools, a continuing and probably increasing homogeneity is ordained. At Kent, for example, about one-fourth of the 500 students have some family connection to a Kent graduate. The homogeneity is geographical and social, too. A check of the student bodies listed in the 1976–77 catalogs of St. Paul's, St. Mark's, Kent, and Salisbury reveals that 100 percent of the students from the Philadelphia area are listed in the *Social Register*. Those four, plus Groton, draw at least half their students from the five traditional eastern states: New York, New Jersey, Massachusetts, Connecticut, and Pennsylvania. At St. Mark's, forty-four of the eighty-three students in the class of 1976 came from a single state, Massachusetts.

Groton is probably the most successful at maintaining vitality in a changing world. Partly because of its appeal to the "best" of the American aristocracy—the Brahmin reformer types, interested in politics and education—and partly because of its massive endowment (the largest per capita of any school in the country), Groton has been able to maintain a kind of upper-class domination, though it is no longer an automatically *Social Register* domination.*

---

* Groton was the only church school checked against the Philadelphia *Social Register* which didn't have 100 percent correlation.

The immediate postschool careers of some of the 1969 graduates show how things have changed and how, in a deeper way, they have remained the same. Young Alsop dropped out of Yale after a month. A Gannett, descendant of the newspaper-chain family and one of the class's brightest stars, set up a day care center in Birmingham, England. Rodman Bundy dropped out of Yale to go to India, then came back to finish Yale and go on to the University of Virginia Law School. The class's senior prefect, Hugh Auchincloss III, was graduated summa cum laude from Harvard and went on to Harvard Medical School. (In the class of 1976, John Winthrop Auchincloss II won prizes in history, literature, modern language, and debating. The last prize was given by W. Averell Harriman, '09, in memory of Franklin D. Roosevelt, '00.)

The lockstep of previous days is broken: College is not necessarily the inevitable next step after prep school; skiing or world travel is as likely. The graduates seem much more interested in seizing whatever advantages accrue to their inherited wealth and circle of acquaintances than in preserving their isolation from the world. While graduation from Groton and membership in Porcellian, say, still confer distinct prestige in New York's legal and financial circles, they are no longer sine qua nons the way they used to be. And the circles they control dominate a smaller percentage of American wealth and power than they used to.

The recent history of St. Mark's, always one of the two or three most socially acceptable names when its graduates got to the Harvard club system, is a somber reminder of what has happened. St. Mark's troubles were not only symbolized but directly connected with coeducation. In the late 1960s a plan was drawn up with St. Margaret's School, which educated young women in Waterbury, Connecticut, to move its complete plant to Southborough, Massachusetts, home of St. Mark's, and work toward complete integration. Just as plans had been completed, Connecticut's legislature vetoed plans for a local junior college to buy the school's old plant; this effectively scuttled the transfer.

St. Margaret's headmaster took many of the students and faculty and journeyed to Southborough anyway and, thanks to the unexpected gift of a St. Mark's grad, built a small school there. Plans went ahead for *those* schools to merge. But, according to George Kidder, the pleasant, silver-haired Boston lawyer and great-grandson of the founder who is now president of St. Mark's board, "we were transmitting an inconsistent signal on coeducation, and that hurt our applications with both boys and girls." Kidder's three sons still go to St. Mark's, as he did and his father before him, but those hereditary places are no longer enough to fill even a small school like St. Mark's.

The uncertainty over coeducation was only one factor contributing to declining applications. Whispering campaigns were racing through New York and Boston Episcocratic circles about scandals, some apparently true and some not, allegedly involving St. Mark's figures. Kidder says he was told by a Groton master, "Ten years ago, St. Mark's was the best school of its size in the country." That was, increasingly, not true when Kidder took over the board from old William A. Coolidge a few years ago. A new headmaster arrived, the Reverend Robert ("Red") Hansel. According to Coolidge, he is successfully integrating a change from the old prep school manner of rote teaching to a more modern, progressive system.

So now, says Kidder in his corner office in downtown Boston, St. Mark's is struggling to "get a better class of student." It is not really that St. Mark's or its graduates are doing anything new; they are doing their old thing less successfully. "We still have our dilettante crowd," Kidder admits—that old bugaboo of serious prep school masters. And a survey of recent graduates ten years out shows them, as always, leaning heavily to corporate law and business, with the usual minority in the Episcopal ministry. No longer can St. Mark's get all its students into the good colleges—only five into Harvard in 1977, and that was the best in a long time.

Perhaps most significant is the feeling of no longer being all that important—a sad realization for a school that remembers, as Kidder does, "the lush times when they were beating the doors down."

Groton and St. Paul's remain significant forces in American life, in the sense that they train a few hundred young men and women who will rise to disproportionately high positions in American society. To some extent this is true because these two schools have a stronger tradition of achievement and drive, a long-standing lack of interest in the Gentleman's C and—to a degree—an ability to ignore social considerations in their students' life. Partly, no doubt, this is true because St. Paul's and Groton do provide a superior education. And the superior education, in turn, is provided by a faculty that respects tradition and the salaries the schools can afford to pay.

Here, perhaps, is an even more significant selector of the great schools. For Groton and St. Paul's are much the most heavily endowed of the church schools, each with per student endowments of $100,000 or more. The income from such a financial glacier can buy a lot more equipment and a lot brighter Ivy League graduates as teachers than the few thousand per student of the poorer church schools. The suburban school districts that now compete with the church schools have the relatively unlimited funding capacity of property taxes, which (unlike endowment and tuition) rise inevitably.

To the class of people most likely to send their children to prep schools, the value received per tuition dollar means as much as it ever did. Moreover, Groton and St. Paul's are able to provide scholarships for bright, compatible students who can spur on the paying crowd and provide an intellectual ferment to the mix. The difference was summed up by our 1969 Groton graduate: "At St. Mark's, the admissions guy was shabby, smoking a cigar, and the lab was old and dirty. Basically, it had the look of the last of a long line. At Groton, everything was more polite, crisp, formal, more colorful and alive."

It may, after all, be money, which their graduates long had the reputation of making at will, that will eventually wipe out many of the great old church schools. It will also be money that keeps Groton and St. Paul's the most important schools in the country.

Bonds

"The man was taking a photograph of me," explained Franklin D. Roosevelt, Jr., in 1934, "and I don't like to have my photograph taken."

For the big (six feet four inches) Grotonian son of the president, that was plenty of reason to make a flying tackle at a cameraman for a Philadelphia newspaper and smash his camera. The other person in the photograph may also have had something to do with Franklin's pique. It was Ethel du Pont. Aside from the fact that Franklin was going somewhat steadier with another young lady at the time, the personal attraction of the two young lovers, both still in boarding school was caught in the bitter squabble that had divided their nation and particularly the great clan of Episcocrats to which both belonged.

FDR, Jr., was an active supporter of his father (he was a future Democratic congressman from New York). Ethel was the daughter of Eugene du Pont of the guns and chemicals company. Like most of the other Du Pont cousins, he belonged to the Liberty League, the collection of wealthy reactionaries who found Franklin Roosevelt's ideas all the more distasteful for being spouted by a man who came from the same Episcocratic background as they did. FDR, Jr., then, came from a line of Public-minded-Patricians; Ethel du Pont's family, the unchallenged lords of the state of Delaware, had gained the top rank of America's Rabid Reactionaries.

The newspapers called them Romeo and Juliet because of their apparently star-crossed backgrounds. As much as their families epitomized the clash of American classes and values during the Great Depression, the young people continued the tradition of privileged youth that dominated the public's perception of "college kids" during the years of WASP hegemony after World War I. Franklin Jr. had done his best to live up to the two-fisted drinking and brawling tradition of the Episcocratic gentleman. As soon as he got to Harvard, he touched off a rowdy balcony beer party that broke up the annual theatrical night which debutantes put on for Boston's fancy woman's club, the Vincent. This was an excess even by the standards of Harvard's Fly Club, which he had joined in his illustrious father's footsteps.

Franklin's courtship of Ethel, which seemed to have the effect of toning down his hair-raising energy, was an equally perfect illustration of how the upper classes were supposed to live. After meeting at a Groton school dance—she returned the favor by inviting him to her Ethel Walker School in Simsbury, Connecticut—the teen-aged sweethearts made the rounds of coming-out parties together, including Ethel's own event, which took place shortly after Franklin took a dislike to the photographer at a wrestling match.

Ethel's debut was celebrated at the familial manse, Owls Nest, in the Château Country around Wilmington, where her father tended $10 million in Du Pont stock. The romance developed in the Du Pont summer home on the Episcocratic coast of North Harbor, Maine, and in the winter home in Boca Grande, Florida. Serious illnesses left Romeo attending Juliet's bedside, and vice versa. And when Ethel returned from a trip to Europe in March 1936, young Franklin dashed out to meet her in the middle of New York Harbor aboard a Coast Guard cutter, every inch the young prince with his father's army at his command. Ethel, the long, lean horsewoman, displayed the same regal air as present-day Princess Anne.

The wedding was a staggering event. Organized by Philadelphia social arbiter Mrs. Edward J. MacMullan and publicized by a full-time news bureau in Wilmington's Hotel du Pont, the wedding turned into something of an industry of its own before the 300 guests finally crowded into little Christ Church Christiana Hundred. Wilmington paved some of its streets for the occasion. Cabinet officials, socialites, and servants shared the happy event. FDR, Sr., arrived as inconspicuously as possible; he had conferred with cabinet ministers about how he should behave in enemy territory and was told by Eleanor not to steal the show as Cousin Theodore had stolen theirs. FDR and Eugene du Pont greeted each other civilly, with the understated restraint that marks personal relations between Episcocrats even in the times of their most bitter philosophical disagreement.

And so the two leading families of the Patrician and Reactionary strains of the Episcocratic elite were joined on a sunny July day in 1937. Concelebrating the ceremony was the grand old man Endicott Peabody, marrier of generations of Grotties, the man who had blessed the 1905 union that FDR, Jr., sprang from. Once again, Peabody served to reconcile the disparate strains of the Episcocratic class that he had educated, bringing the Roosevelts back to the class they had been "traitors" to. To the music of society bandleader Meyer Davis, an even 1000 reception guests welcomed the new couple to the fold under a spacious striped awning on the lawn of Owls Nest. "If the lighthearted scenario continues as it has begun," chortled *Time* magazine, a chronicler of Episcocratic doings for the masses, "they should live happily ever afterward."

For a country in the midst of unprecedented depression and social change, the sight of the children of the Episcocratic classes marrying one another was a throwback to the past. Franklin Jr. and Ethel had the biggest, most famous Episcocratic nuptials since 1926 saw the staggering opulence and refinement of the National Cathedral wedding of Ailsa Mellon to David K. E. Bruce. The bride was the daughter of Andrew W. Mellon, the immensely wealthy treasury secretary, and of the English-born-and-bred Nora McMullen. It was from her mother that Ailsa learned to speak with a British accent. Bruce was the son of a distinguished senator from Maryland, and, to add to the British flavor of the nuptials, the future ambassador to the Court of St. James's—a post for which he was perfectly suited.

Mellon escorted his daughter to the altar; with traditional

Episcocratic simplicity, she wore a string of pearls around her neck as her only ornament, though the string was reported to be worth $100,000. Less understated were the gifts and the parties afterward, which required Mellon to lease an extra apartment in his Massachusetts Avenue building, despite the ample number of rooms he already occupied.

Led by Secretary of State and Mrs. Frank Billings Kellogg, the Episcocratic social and political elite witnessed the joining of the two wealthy, pedigreed houses. The entire cabinet, the full Supreme Court, and the U.S. Marine Band were on hand. Gladys Vanderbilt had come back, now as the wife of the Hungarian ambassador; Senator James W. Wadsworth, Jr., was there, whose daughter Eve would also marry a senator, W. Stuart Symington; Senator George Wharton Pepper was in the cathedral he had helped to build; so were Senator and Mrs. Hiram Bingham, whose children would continue to join the government and make upper-class marriages, down to Jonathan, the current congressman. In that company even the ushers stood out: Ailsa's brother Paul, the future angel of the National Gallery, and cousin Richard King, the biggest banker in Pittsburgh.

The most important Washington wedding before *that* was another Roosevelt event—the joining of "Princess Alice" to Nicholas Longworth, the future Speaker of the House, in the White House by Episcopal Bishop Henry Yates Satterlee of Washington. Theodore Roosevelt's and Nicholas Longworth's Porcellian brothers came down to the White House for the occasion, an opportunity for TR to exercise upper-class fairness by ordering the Porc's black steward to be in charge of the champagne and be allowed full run of the house.

The White House overflowed with gifts and guests and Episcocratic government officials. Like the Mellon-Bruce nuptials, Alice's wedding was front-page news in every paper in the country. (The 1926 Mellon wedding was so newsworthy that the *Washington Post* troubled to scoop everyone by sneaking a reporter into the choir; he bribed a singer to hand over his robes.)

The wedding of Eleanor and Franklin Roosevelt, by contrast, was a relatively intimate affair in New York in 1905— although no event attended by President Theodore Roosevelt

Thanks to the greatest of the Episco-cratic-European alliances, Consuelo Van-derbilt wears coronet of her husband's house of Marlborough to coronation of Edward VII of England, 1901.

"Princess Alice" Roosevelt in her father Theodore's White House. Her wedding to Nicholas Longworth, future speaker of the House, was the event of Washington's 1906 season.

Payne Whitney married Helen Hay, daughter of the secretary of state in the Theodore Roosevelt era. His brother Harry Payne married Gertrude Vanderbilt.

Six days after Consuelo Vanderbilt's transatlantic wedding, W. C. Whitney's Fifth Avenue mansion hosts marriage of Whitney's daughter Pauline to Sir Almeric Hugh Paget, Baron of Queensborough.

UNITED PRESS INTERNATIONAL

"Poor little rich girl" Barbara Hutton with fifth husband, Dominican playboy–prince Carmine Porfirio Rubirosa, 1970.

UNITED PRESS INTERNATIONAL

Tobacco heiress Doris Duke also found Rubirosa an attractive husband.

and Endicott Peabody could really be considered small. The Peabody presence testified to the Episcocratic tradition; less so, but still interesting, was TR's congratulations on Eleanor's not having to change her name. (As Franklin's cousin, she grew up a Roosevelt, too.) Eleanor also showed her Episcocratic mettle; halfway through the ceremony, when Peabody stumbled in the service, she prompted him, showing that she knew the Book of Common Prayer order by heart.

Frankin Jr. and Ethel could not retain the golden-days feeling that their wedding had given, briefly, back to the country.

They lived together for twelve years and two sons, then got divorced. Franklin married Suzanne Perrin six months later; she was the daughter of Lee J. Perrin, a Wall Street lawyer who, in the Episcocratic tradition, had expanded beyond law to become chairman of the Ciba Pharmaceutical Products Corporation. That marriage lasted longer—twenty-one years and two daughters—but it, too, crumbled before the increasing acceptability of divorce, a hazard to Episcocratic family continuity that would never have arisen in the old days.

The reason for Roosevelt's marital troubles became obvious two days after his Juárez divorce. The reason's name was Felicia Warburg Sarnoff. Roosevelt's marriage to the daughter of Paul Warburg, the banker from the Jewish upper class of New York, pointed up a minor key of Episcocratic marriages much as his banns with Ethel du Pont had exemplified the major key. Through business and marriage, the Warburgs had long been connected with the Episcocratic world of banking and industry which they sometimes fought with, sometimes cooperated with.

Paul Warburg had been one of the architects of the Federal Reserve System at Nelson Aldrich's secret meeting in 1910 on Morgan-owned Jekyll Island. And his banking house of Kuhn Loeb, like the other big Jewish investment firms, worked with the great gentile bankers. Warburg's circle of Jewish relations was already intermarried with the gentile elite. His partner in Kuhn Loeb and relative by marriage, John Schiff, married the granddaughter of banker George F. Baker.

In the Jewish banking elite tales of conversion to Episcopalianism were relatively commonplace. Simon and Olga Guggenheim converted outright, joining socially impeccable St. Thomas's Fifth Avenue. Bernard Baruch baptized his daughters in the church.

So intense was the wish to associate with the Episcocratic upper class that Felicia Warburg's family was decidedly more upset at her first marriage, in 1950, than at her second. The first choice of this very Episcocratic-acting woman—she was educated at Brearey and Bennington, presented at the Court of St. James's as a young woman, involved herself in charity work, and dressed in the elegant, understated long lines of a fashion-conscious Episcocrat—had been Robert W. Sarnoff.

Though he was to become president and board chairman of RCA, an achievement most Jewish mothers would acclaim in a son-in-law, Felicia's distinguished family sniffed that her husband was "the son of that Russian radio man." It was their way of referring to General David Sarnoff, founder of RCA and possibly the most illustrious name in electronics. Felicia's first marriage lasted almost exactly as long as Franklin's second, some two decades; she was divorced precisely six months before she married Franklin.

It is not recorded what the Warburgs thought of the second wedding, to a gentile who had been divorced for only two days, at that, but none of them was present when Felicia, Franklin, and a wedding party of close friends pulled up in a single limousine to the Supreme Court Building in Manhattan on July 1, 1970. None of his four children or her two was on hand either, as the *New York Times* pointedly noted. The supporting players were Mrs. Warburg's old friend Mrs. Emil Mosbacher, wife of President Nixon's protocol chief, the yachting champion, and Richard Miles, a friend and business associate of Roosevelt's. (The president's son imports Jaguars and Fiats—that internationalist trend in Episcocrats—since his political ventures, such as being appointed undersecretary of commerce by President Kennedy and running for governor of New York on the Liberal ticket in 1966, came to naught.) The only member of either family present was John A. Roosevelt, brother of the groom, with his wife, Irene; John ignored politics and went right into business, rising to become senior vice-president of the Jewish-elite investment house of Bache and Company.

The wedding party, somewhat flustered when unexpectedly ambushed by a gang of press photographers in the court building, dispatched its business cheerfully enough in a quick civil ceremony. The new Mrs. Roosevelt came out of the ceremony glowing that her Franklin was "just the most sensational man alive," which is a lot more public adulation than Franklin got from either of his previous brides.

The party retired to Roosevelt's East Side offices for a quick reception, then to a well-groomed French restaurant for lunch. The happy couple's plans included a month-long cruise to Europe on the liner *France*. One projected stop was a few days with another celebrated couple of diverse (and even wealthier) backgrounds, Mr. and Mrs. Aristotle Onassis.

Seven years later, on a sunny September afternoon, Nancy Suzanne Roosevelt walked up a grassy aisle in an ivory dress, her hair covered by the classic lace veil that Eleanor Roosevelt had worn when she married Nancy's grandfather in 1905.

If Franklin Roosevelt, Jr.'s, marriage to Mrs. Sarnoff was a small, hasty affair of the previously married—the sort of thing that threatens to confuse people about the solidity of the Episcocratic upper class—Nancy's wedding gave reassuring promise that Roosevelts still lived the best of Episcocratic lives. The ceremony, orchestrated by FDR, Jr., at his country home— Cove Creek Farm, far up along the Hudson in patroon country—was followed by a buffet lunch in a pink-and-white-striped tent on the lawn that seated 400 guests. The ceremony was conducted by the Reverend Gordon L. Kidd, rector emeritus of St. James Hyde Park, where FDR, Sr., had been a vestryman. Tradition was enhanced by the strong familial connections among the bridal party: Nancy's sister was maid of honor, her attendants were the wives of her half brothers by her father's Du Pont marriage, and the rest of the supporting cast was made up of classmates from Vassar.

Only the Roosevelt glory eclipsed the groom's own familial position in the Episcocratic business elite. Thomas Ellis Ireland was a descendant of one of the premier families of the Middle West. His grandfather, R. Livingston Ireland, an usher at the wedding, was retired chairman of the executive board of the Consolidated Coal Company of Pittsburgh (now a division of Continental Oil) and also of the M. A. Hanna Company of Cleveland (now Hanna Mining), source of wealth for the

Episcocratic political kingmaker Mark Hanna of Theodore Roosevelt's day. The groom's father, R. L. Ireland III, who served as best man at the wedding, had taken a traditional route of the cultured sons of powerful men, becoming a partner in the investment banking firm Brown Brothers Harriman.

All of which distinguished genealogy might daunt a man without benefit of young Ireland's thoroughgoing education in the ways of a young gentleman. After the Buckley School—the alma mater of his new father-in-law—the bridegroom attended Phillips Andover, spent a year at England's lordly Harrow School, and was graduated from Yale in 1974. In between, Ireland served in the Marines, including a tour of duty in Vietnam. (Even after the strong antimilitary feeling among most young people in the sixties, a stint in the service has remained a fairly desirable thing for many proper young Episcocrats.) At the time of his marriage, Ireland was an account officer in the agribusiness department of Citibank, where his superiors no doubt have their eye on him. He had the presence, after all, to marry a Roosevelt, and in a wedding that showed a proper respect for families on both sides and for tradition.

In a well-constructed Episcocratic marriage, the family network radiates waves of self-assurance throughout the national family of upper-class peers. Ireland and the former Miss Roosevelt, by the way they were married—and by their choice of partners—sent messages to people they never met about their knowledge of position and power, things that would be impolite to say out loud.

Forty years after Ethel married Franklin Jr., the Du Ponts, having survived three American wars (handsomely, since they make ammunition) and unprecedented calls for the eradication of privilege in the United States, still held most of the effective power in a piece of ground called Delaware. For the first time in history a member of the dynasty had even won the governor's chair. Pierre S. du Pont, Harvard graduate, yachtsman, millionaire, walked into a state government that presented him with a problem he had never encountered before: It didn't have any money.

"Pete" du Pont responded by taking up the challenge in

words that rang with a Public-minded Patrician's conviction. "How could you ever explain to your grandchildren that you had the chance to be governor and straighten things out—then turned it down?" he asked. Presumably that question never occurred to his own grandfather and namesake, the head of the Liberty League who fought Roosevelt so furiously. As governor, Pete made the public-relations mistake of calling the average citizen "Joe Six-pack," which his opponents matched by dubbing him "Champagne Pete."

The nickname is apt. Today the Du Ponts are, with the Mellons, the richest family in America. They are also the most prolific, with an estimated 2000 members and 100 new Du Ponts each year.*

The focal point of this incredible familial network has been Christ Church in Christiana Hundred, the exclusive section outside Wilmington where Du Ponts have returned for generations to be married. The tradition of Christ Church as an agent for injecting new blood into the Du Pont empire survives with vigor today. In November 1976, for example, Antonia du Pont Bayard walked up the aisle of Christ Church trailing a pedigree that celebrated the success of Du Pont intermarriage. No fewer than six U.S. senators were her direct ancestors, including her grandfather Thomas Bayard, her great-grandfather, her great-great-grandfather, her great-great-granduncle, her great-great-great grandfather, and her great-great-great-great-grandfather. The great-grandfather, Thomas Francis Bayard, was also secretary of state and ambassador to Britain. The bridegroom who joined Antonia du Pont Bayard before Christ

---

* A dynasty came to a close when at the end of May 1978, Irénée du Pont, Jr., great-great-grandson of the founder of the Du Pont Co., retired from the executive committee. For the first time in 177 years, the vast textile and munitions firm did not have a Du Pont family member in its hierarchy.

That did not mean that the family's estimated $5 billion wealth would stop producing the income that the company's dividends had maintained for centuries. As firmly as anyone in the company, Irénée du Pont was behind the earthquake that made Irving Shapiro, a Jewish lawyer from Minneapolis, chief executive of the country's most family-controlled business.

The abdicating prince was as low-keyed in talking about the era he was ending as he was in discussing the new one that had just dawned. Being named Du Pont, he conceded, "must have been an enormous advantage to me. I must have gotten many promotions that would not have been open to me through any other route. . . . I did the best I could. But it would be highly unusual for a B.S. chemical engineer to reach the level I did other than by pull."

It is not Episcocratic to be ashamed of the position bestowed by one's family.

Church's altar that November day was Milford Lewis II of Median, New York, also of distinguished business heritage. His father was president of the Phinney Tool and Die Company in that town. The bridegroom's grandfather had been a vice-president of the concern—as was young Mr. Phinney. As they celebrated the couple's nuptials afterward at the Greenville Country Club nearby, the many members of the Du Pont clan could relax in the knowledge that another business enterprise had been brought under their umbrella by marriage.

So it has always been for Du Ponts. Marquis James, who told their story, wrote:

> Down the generations, it is almost uncanny the brains that Du Pont has been able to pluck from its own family tree. A Du Pont by birth not being available, one by marriage was usually on hand with the qualifications required. . . . Since the first generation in America, marriages with young men who could be of use in the firm have kept the family vital, and consanguinate marriages have kept it tightly knit.

Probably the most useful marriage in American social history took place in 1848 in New York's exclusive Grace Church, the one that Sexton Isaac Brown had made his headquarters as social arbiter of New York society. It was the gala wedding of August Belmont, and it completed one of the first and most successful climbs to the top of American society that ever bewildered traditionalists. Only thirty-two years before, Belmont had been born in Germany to Jewish parents named Schönberg. Gallicizing his name, young Belmont started working without pay for the Rothschilds at the age of thirteen, came to the United States (by way of Naples and Cuba) when he was twenty-one, and within three years, thanks to the Rothschilds' financial backing and prestige, had become one of the leading bankers in the country.

Despite—or maybe because of—a manner that made women feel they were being undressed, Belmont also became a social leader in early New York. He introduced the still-uncouth Americans to a number of important social customs, including arriving late for dinner, serving gourmet food at home, and building gigantic ballrooms in private marble mansions on Fifth Avenue. Though he did not invent it, Belmont certainly raised "marrying up" to the status of a fine art.

The clever financier knew he would have to make a decisive move when he got married, because he had been unable to scale the final heights of New York's first, oldest, and most Episcocratic social group, the old Dutch-colonial Knickerbocker aristocracy. The Van Rensselaers told ugly stories about him, and the Astors, who were building the country's biggest fortune on fur trading and on Trinity Church's wonderful ninety-nine-year contract for Manhattan real estate, were no friends either. In 1848, the year before Belmont married, John Jacob Astor had died, leaving $20 million and a vast funeral conducted by a half-dozen Episcopal clergyman—red flag to Belmont's bull.

Finally, Belmont won the social wars. Even before the Astor funeral, he had proposed to Episcocratic Caroline Slidell Perry. She was only modestly wealthy and a prototype of the mindless but beautiful blonde. But more important to Belmont, she was the daughter of Mexican War naval hero Commodore Matthew Perry and niece of War of 1812 naval hero Oliver Hazard Perry. Instinctively, Belmont had combined his own nouveau wealth with the military and social heft of the Perrys. He topped his confection with a grand Episcopal wedding in Grace Church and a reception attended by Goelets, Winthrops, Vanderbilts, Morrises, even a few Astors.

Thanks to his new hostess, his new religion, and his new ballroom, used only one day per year for his annual ball, Belmont led fashionable New York for the next thirty or forty years. Society writer Dixon Wecter indicated how important the right marriage in the right religion was to Belmont and all who would imitate him:

Since the first August Belmont set foot in America, no member of that family has ever married a Jewess, but invariably a Gentile of social standing. In this way, plus an exchange of the synagogue for Episcopal communion, a constant association with non-Jews, and the adaptability of Nature which has given Belmonts scarcely any Semitic cast of feature except in their patriarchal age, a complete break with their Old World background has been successfully effected. In social acceptance no later Jewish family can compare with them.

Exclusion from social acceptance has been the fault not of the Jewish families that arrived in America later than Belmont, but mainly of the xenophobia and anti-Semitism that burst into poisonous bloom among the Episcocrats of the 1870s—and have thrived to some degree to more recent times. When June Rossbach, Jewish aristocrat, married Jonathan Bingham, Episcocrat, in 1939, they received a flood of hate mail from both sides. The persistence of such sentiments is largely why marriage became, and remains, a tool not for assimilation of a complete stranger but for the consolidation of the Episcocratic business elite and the solidification of its wealth and prestige.

Marjorie Merriweather Post was a midwesterner, not a Jew. Yet she too, with the money accumulated by her cereal-king father C. W. Post, had to "marry up." She chose an Episcopalian easterner to gentle herself and her money. In 1905 she married Edward Bennet Close in a fashionable wedding which, like Belmont's, was celebrated at Grace Church. The Manhattan land on which the church stood had been given to the parish by Close's great-great-grandfather. The self-possessed but déclassée Miss Post was deeply stung as she was coming down the aisle to hear a Close uncle mutter, "She's a pretty little thing, considering who she is and where she's from."

Two years earlier William Randolph Hearst, who thought of himself as an Episcopalian though he never went to church, chose the same Grace Church as the scene of his wedding to Millicent Willson. The omnipresent Bishop Henry Codman Potter blessed the union, and Phoebe Apperson Hearst gave her new daughter-in-law, whom she did not much like, a set of emeralds. Indulging an Episcocratic predilection for privacy, the press baron refused to allow his own photographers into the church and ducked out so quickly that they got only one blurred print.*

* Three quarters of a century later, after newspaper heiress Patty Hearst had gone through the harrowing experiences of kidnapping, guerrilla warfare, and prison, she returned for solace to the active practice of her family's Episcopal religion.

A perfect match took place on the same day in September 1977 that saw the nuptials of Nancy Roosevelt and Thomas Ireland along the Hudson River. Not very far away, in the Berkshire town of Stockbridge, Massachusetts, retired Bishop Anson Phelps Stokes helped join his niece Adaline H. Frelinghuysen to a young banker, William Blair Meyer, Jr. There was a sense of completion to the alliance of these offspring of noble families: a great-great-grandfather of each had been secretary of state during the post-Civil-War growth of the American elite.

Little St. Paul's Church was filled with a confusing but dazzling collection of families—not all in person, but there in name and consciousness. Miss Frelinghuysen sprang from the family that had produced three U.S. senators besides the secretary of state; her father, Peter H. B. Frelinghuysen, had been for twenty-two years the congressional envoy of the exclusive hunt country in central New Jersey that includes Bernardsville and Princeton.

Bankers also were well represented in the family. Through her paternal grandmother, for whom she was named, Miss Frelinghuysen is descended also from Henry O. Havemeyer, creator of the giant (and Episcocratic) American Sugar Refining Company. The Anson Phelps Stokes connection linked her to the Stokeses and Auchinclosses and *their* vast web of Episcocratic intermarriage.*

Young Mr. Meyer had nothing to be ashamed of, genealogically speaking. His link to Great-great-grandad John Hay, the secretary of state, ran through the late Joan Whitney Payson, New York Mets owner and Whitney heiress. In the male line, Blair Meyer came from an old St. Paul's family and several generations of presidents of the Cord Meyer Company. The bridegroom's father was secretary-treasurer of the Cord Meyer Real Estate Development Company. The family government connection on the male side was Uncle Cord Meyer, Jr., a former

---

* The Berkshires, site of the wedding, was an upper-class resort area at the turn of the century. Bishop Stokes's father, Canon Anson Phelps Stokes, grew up in the most elephantine "cottage" in the Berkshires, Shadowbrook. In 1896 the senior Stokes wired his mother from Yale, ARRIVING THIS EVENING WITH CROWD OF NINETY-SIX MEN, and got back: MANY GUESTS ALREADY HERE. HAVE ONLY ROOM FOR FIFTY.

top CIA official—through whom Blair was also related maritally to the descendants of Gifford Pinchot, the Pennsylvania governor in the Episcocratic age, and to *Washington Post* executive editor Ben Bradlee.

Altogether, they will make a nice couple.

Nor were they the only nice couple enhancing the Frelinghuysen clan into the next generation; in that respect, the Episcocratic New Jersey bankers and politicians were as aggressive as their Du Pont counterparts in Delaware. Four months after Adaline recited her vows, her first cousin George L. K. Frelinghuysen became engaged to Alice Cooney, a young graduate of the Kent School and Princeton. (A generation before, when both schools were all-male, that would have had a scandalous ring to it.)

Frelinghuysen, whose parents, Mr. and Mrs. Henry O. Havemeyer Frelinghuysen, also live in the Jersey hunt country (Far Hills), had gone to St. Mark's, the family's school for generations. Armed with a Princeton B.A. and a Columbia M.B.A., he joined Wood, Struthers & Winthrop as a portfolio manager, conceivably in preparation for the day when his father would no longer spend his time managing the family investments, as he does now.

Miss Cooney's father, Daniel, who lives in the well-groomed Connecticut exurb Darien, is also a portfolio manager for a New York investment firm, Lord, Abbett. While the men go into the gray, but lucrative, business world, the new Mrs. Frelinghuysen is enrolled in the Winterthur Museum Program of Early American Culture in preparation for an art-related career. As befits a museum in Delaware, the Winterthur Museum was once a Du Pont mansion and is now the Henry Francis du Pont Museum. It is unique in the country.

Probably the most obviously social marriage ever arranged, as well as one of the cruelest ever executed, took place in the cold Gothic splendor of St. Thomas's Fifth Avenue in 1895. Consuelo Vanderbilt was married to the ninth duke of Marlborough —but just barely.

Consuelo's marriage became the late nineteenth century's star exhibit of social climbing through marriage—as well as the most audacious attempt to create an international Victorian elite—thanks to the social ambitions of her mother, Alva, Mrs. William K. Vanderbilt. When Alva steamed out of Mobile, Alabama, with thoughts of lavish gaiety, herself the center of attention, the Vanderbilts did not rate in New York society. The old Commodore, William K.'s grandfather, was scorned as an unscrupulous waterer of railroad stock, uncouth personally, morally, and aesthetically, and William H. Vanderbilt's only notable statement of thought was "The public be damned." Fortunately for his descendants down to the present, the old Commodore left such a vast fortune that Alva was able, in a very few years, to arrange social parity with such massive figures as *the* Mrs. Astor and Mrs. Stuyvesant Fish.

In 1883 she threw a fancy-dress party in her new $3-million French château on Fifth Avenue. The cost of costumes alone, to be worn once, was estimated at $156,000 for the 1200 lucky guests. Mrs. Astor, who had never deigned to visit the *arriviste* Vanderbilts, did not receive an invitation to the mock-Versailles party; but Alva spread word of such details as the $11,000 worth of long-stemmed roses and orchids, and Mrs. Astor's daughter literally begged her mother not to be so snobbish. Mrs. Astor gave in. From then on the Vanderbilts were fully accepted members of the first circle of Episcocratic *haut monde*.

But Alva Vanderbilt's ambitions were not merely to be accepted; she wanted to be first. A clergyman at the time estimated the collective jewelry of New York society was worth something in the range of $170 million, and Alva made sure she had her million dollars' worth. She helped instigate construction of the Metropolitan Opera House to obviate the snobbery of the Knickerbocker families who tightly held all the boxes at the old Academy of Music. The thirty-five boxes of the Diamond Horseshoe at the Met went for $60,000 each in 1892; the hall at Thirty-ninth Street and Broadway was terrible for music but perfect for its main function, the display of the personages who had built the house in the first place. On her own— literally on her own, for she divorced William, though not his money (and eventually married the son of August Belmont)— Alva Vanderbilt constructed "Marble House" in Newport, then in the height of its glory as a summer playground for the lighthearted rich. The house itself was a bargain at $2 million, compared with the furnishings, which cost $9 million more.

In Newport, in the summer of 1895, the most vicious phrase was: "A marble palace is the right place for a woman with a marble heart." For Alva Vanderbilt's plans included the use of her own daughter as the ultimate weapon in her struggle for social immortality. The target was the grandest of British noble houses, the Marlboroughs. These were the very Marlboroughs who had provided the first great catch for an American heiress in the era of international marriages—Jennie Jerome of Baltimore, who married Randolph Churchill in 1874 and soon became the mother of Winston Churchill. Consuelo Vanderbilt had another target—Winthrop Rutherford, the rich, distinguished, bright, and fabulously good-looking heir of one of New York's very good Knickerbocker families. That was not enough for Alva. She invited Marlborough for a visit; he had none of Rutherford's good points and many bad ones of his own, but he had an older and—catnip in those slavishly Anglophiliac days—a British line behind him.

Marlborough, it was said, first proposed to Gertrude Vanderbilt (future bride of Harry Payne Whitney), who had a larger fortune than Consuelo through her mother, Alice, Alva's sister-in-law and bitter enemy. When the duke did finally turn to Consuelo on the last day of his visit, Alva tore her from Rutherford and forced her into the doomed marriage.

"I forced my daughter to marry the Duke," Alva said later. "I have always had absolute power over my children. . . . When I issued an order, nobody discussed it. I therefore did not beg, but ordered her to marry the Duke." Alva told Consuelo her insistence on choosing her own lover was ruining her mother's health and hastening her death. When that proved ineffective, Alva threatened to hasten Rutherford's death by her own hand, telling poor Consuelo that she would therefore be responsible for her mother's hanging. The night before the wedding, fearing Consuelo's resistance might not be completely demolished, Alva put a guard at her door to keep away any potentially seditious visitors.

The wedding on November 6, 1895, was the lead story in the *New York Times*. "Thousands of yards of smilax and holly" garnished elegant St. Thomas's. The church was overrun by people who went so far as to stand on the pews to catch sight of a jewel-encrusted gown. Consuelo looked pale and troubled and could barely manage a brave smile as she left after the ceremony was performed by Henry Codman Potter, "pastor of the rich." She was, onlookers noted, half a head taller than her husband.

The duke bore that indignity, among others, for the simple reason that the Vanderbilts had settled on him $2.5 million in Beech Creek Railway Company stock. He used it to fix up Blenheim Palace, built by the first duke and named after the battle that had made him England's hero. Before it was over, the marriage had cost the Vanderbilts an estimated $10 million, but they felt they had nothing better to invest it in.

The marriage ended in divorce, like many of the transatlantic marriages that sprouted in the Gilded Age. "This arrogance of his character created in me a sentiment of hostility," Consuelo testified in her divorce proceedings. "He seemed to despise everything that was not British and my pride was therefore hurt." After thirteen weary years Consuelo separated from Marlborough, and she ended her life as the obscure but presumably peaceful wife of a French former army officer, and a Catholic to boot.

Consuelo was somewhat larger of scale than many of the daughters of America's Episcocratic elite of Victorian times, but she was typical of a trend that turned into a torrent—marrying nobility. The custom became a human version of collecting art. American money could buy anything. Titles were unstintingly purchased by such notable families as the Whitneys, Goulds, and Huntingtons. Even the granddaughter of President Ulysses Grant and daughter of Vice President Levi P. Morton were exported to impoverished European castles. In the international marriage era, between Jennie Jerome's catch in 1874 and 1909, some 500 American heiresses were given to titled Europeans, together with an estimated $220 million in American industrial wealth.

The money-title fever that permeated society nearly overwhelmed—though it also delighted—such privileged young ladies as May Goelet, a cousin of Consuelo's who served as a bridesmaid at her wedding and so had a firsthand idea of the possibilities for obtaining a title. In the winter of 1902 the twenty-four-year-old Miss Goelet, a real estate heiress on her father's side to go with her Vanderbilt wealth, ran into a solid line of proposals in London, including, in rapid fire, Lord Shaftesbury, the duke of Roxburgh, Captain Holford ("unfortunately," May wrote, "the poor man has no title"), and George Cornwallis-West, the brother of Princess Pless. (The duke of Roxburgh won her hand the following year.)

In the end, it became a mark of gaucherie among the more solid Episcocrats to marry a foreigner. Henry Cabot Lodge, Sr., the distinguished senator from Massachusetts and father of another distinguished senator of the same name, wrote disdainfully, "Every pork-baron will buy a European title because he comprehends that the title has value as a trade-mark, and a trade-mark he understands." And when Gertrude Vanderbilt married Harry Payne Whitney, a real American aristocrat, at the Vanderbilt cottage The Breakers in 1906, the bandleader took it upon himself to play as her wedding music "The Star-Spangled Banner."

The tradition of international marriage fell into disrepute during the years after World War I, thanks largely to the "poor little rich girls" Barbara Hutton and Doris Duke. Miss Duke came into some $70 million from her father's tobacco empire when she was thirteen. Miss Hutton became a teen-age millionaire from her grandfather, Frank W. Woolworth, the five-and-dime man, and became a progressively larger millionaire through the rest of her life. Both ran through a seemingly endless succession of oddly matched husbands, domestic and imported. Porfirio Rubirosa, once son-in-law of the Dominican dictator, married them both. Barbara also married Alexis Mdivani, her first love, who with his brother formed half of the "Marrying Mdivanis" and pretended to be a prince from Russian Georgia.

"I didn't realize the worst thing I could possibly do was to marry a titled foreigner," Miss Hutton said just before she divorced Mdivani.

Despite such excesses, the Episcocratic marriage lives on in its most serviceable form, as a device for joining the offspring of America's business and political elite. Sometimes, as in the Roosevelt-Du Pont nuptials of 1937, the marriage is made to bear a heavier social freight than it can support. More recently Episcopal priests have been puzzled, though usually accommodating, when asked to join the descendants of their respectable parishioners in such nontraditional arenas as meadows and mountaintops. Even that phase seems to have passed, like the splashy international marriage and the political fence mender. Today the Episcocratic marriage in families like the Roosevelts, Frelinghuysens, and Meyers is doing the job it has always done. It is preserving, and revivifying, the American aristocracy.

To the extent that the Episcocratic class has lost some of its luster, the disintegration of the marital tradition is largely to blame. Not simply marrying outside the class. Episcocrats have always been able to assimilate outsiders. Getting divorced. It was very different in the old days.

In 1916, when Eleanor Roosevelt found her husband's love letters from Lucy Mercer, Alice Longworth discussed the matter with the Roosevelts' Aunt Corrinne, who told her, "Yes, there was a family conference and they talked it over and finally they decided it affected the children and there was Lucy Mercer, a Catholic, and so it [the divorce] was called off."

FDR's son Elliott wrote:

> Mother would have preferred a divorce. That was her first thought, and her tactic was to offer it. She had grounds in the state of New York, which recognized only adultery. The letters were her proof. But Granny held ironclad views about her class and broken homes. If divorce were the answer, she would cut off Father's money as punishment for his offense. . . . And to be divorced for adultery would mean political suicide for a man who was already being talked about by a handful of people as a future President.

At the foundation of the Episcocratic establishment, the concept of divorce was taboo. Of all the Protestant sects, Episcopalianism, the religion of the upper class, has had the firmest religious ban on it. Socially, getting divorced meant immediate expulsion from the Assemblies in Philadelphia and Charleston, South Carolina, the two most stringently aristocratic cities in early America. The religious and social taboos served to guarantee the purity of bloodlines, as well as the unencumbered in-

heritance of money; Granny Roosevelt's tactics of referring
to cash as well as to noblesse oblige are telling. Layered on top
of that primordially aristocratic revulsion to divorce was the
prudery of the Episcocratic, high-Victorian age. It was expected that one would put up with whatever small personal
embarrassments might develop between husband and wife.
Cornelius Vanderbilt put it elegantly when it became clear
that his wife Grace's partying and his sailing did not mix:
"People in our position do not get divorces."

The sharpest tongues wagged, reinforced by blatant public
pressure from clergymen, to keep wayward Episcocrats within
their marital bonds. When Alva Vanderbilt divorced William K.
Vanderbilt in 1895—she didn't mind that the only ground in
New York was adultery—it was an act of bravado for her to
show up at Trinity Church Newport with her daughter, Consuelo, and the duke of Marlborough. As late as the 1920s Bishop
Potter was so dismayed at her "immorality" in divorce that he
tried to remove her from the board of one of her favorite
charities—one she had founded. Eventually a casual attitude
developed toward adultery, abetted by the obvious practices
of international celebrities like the Prince of Wales, that tended
to allow married couples to go their own relaxed ways. Not long
ago an Ingersoll from Philadelphia told his mother he was getting along poorly with his wife. She answered, "Then I think
you should take a mistress, dear."

The barriers to the breakup of proper family lines, and with
it some of the Episcocratic tradition, meant little in the face of
the determined onslaught of several generations of remarriers.
The children of the tone-setting Roosevelts and Vanderbilts,
whose original marriages were so determinedly preserved, made
a practice more than an exception of divorce. When FDR, Jr.,
was running through his first two marriages and his siblings
were marrying young and unsuccessfully, parents Eleanor and
Franklin did not interfere. Cornelius Vanderbilt, Jr., ran through
six marriages in rapid succession, a record that led him to compare himself to founding Episcocrat Henry VIII, with no
apparent attention from his parents.

The marital determination of latter-day Astors and Whitneys
was similarly fleeting—to say nothing of Barbara Hutton, Doris
Duke, and a string of glamour girls.

The Mellons provided the country with one of its most

spectacular divorces. The young English wife of Treasury Secretary Andrew W. Mellon, Nora McMullen, began having an
obvious affair and, so her husband thought, poisoning the minds
of children Paul and Ailsa against him. There were celebrated
kidnappings back and forth. At one point, in 1910, Andrew
reneged on a promise to deliver the children to his wife as she
was departing for Europe. Nora, sensing what had happened,
abandoned her servants and jumped overboard to pursue him.
In the midst of the sensational divorce case that followed, re-
plete with detailed testimony about which Mellon had what size
sexual organs, the Pennsylvania legislature, at the banker's
behest, unanimously passed a change in the divorce law that
provided for private divorce hearings without a jury. "The
Mellon law" finally separated the two.

The children of those horrific episodes had their problems
with marriage too. Ailsa grew up a sad person, and her fabulous
National Cathedral wedding was the high point of her life with
David Bruce. She insisted on living far beyond his diplomat's
salary. He divorced her in 1945, marrying Evangeline Bell three
days later; and the Mellons, including Bruce's National Gallery
colleague Paul, went out of their way to demonstrate that they
thought he was the reasonable one. Ailsa died in 1969, leaving
three New York apartments, two houses in Greenwich, a magnificent estate in Syosset, Long Island, still another residence in
Palm Beach, and $570 million.

Paul Mellon did not engage in divorce himself, but both his
wives were divorcées. His second, Bunny, had gone to Foxcroft
and married a proper Philadelphian, and led Paul into a more
social world, which included, eventually, Jacqueline Kennedy.
For by the 1960s, divorce no longer carried a trace of a stigma
in proper society. Nelson Rockefeller proved once and for all
that divorce and remarriage no longer rule out a political career
for Public-minded Patricians. The *Social Register* no longer
drops divorcées either (except in exceptional cases, such as
former Secretary of the Navy John Warner's remarriage to
Elizabeth Taylor).

Following the trend toward divorce came a predilection for
remarriage within the same Episcocratic circle, which confused
the genealogical lines even further. John Hay ("Jock") Whitney, the *Herald Tribune* owner, took Betsey Cushing as a wife

shortly after she was divorced from James Roosevelt. Meanwhile, Jock's brother "Sonny"—Cornelius Vanderbilt Whitney —underwent a brief marriage with Marie Norton. She went on to become Mrs. Averell Harriman and enjoy the pleasures of Sun Valley, the ski resort that Harriman built just for her.

As far as Cornelius Vanderbilt, Jr., could tell, multiple marriages for men of his class were almost inevitable: first, because there were so few girls from the same class to marry who might be like his mother; secondly, because "the women who married me . . . were beglamoured by my mother, in that they themselves wanted to become 'Mrs. Vee,' enthroned in society, living in luxury, entertaining crowned heads, and enjoying the background I had left behind." Finally, CV, Jr., located his troubles in his own sea change of ideas, one the previous generation of Episcocrats could never have agreed with: "I've always thought it a lot more 'decent' to be married often than to marry only once or twice and keep women on the side." That is why there will never be another personage like Mrs. Vee. Rather, there could be so many of them that none can claim preeminence. Only in the Business Aristocracy, not the "society" of the Refined Reactionaries and their descendants, is marriage still a valuable Episcocratic tool.

Where the Elite Meet

Many strange things happen in New York, perpetrated by fringe groups that the majority has long given up hope of understanding, perhaps none more peculiar than the piping, strutting, pirouetting band that marches down Park Avenue to the strains of "St. Julien" one fine spring Sunday every year.

Obviously a ceremonial, military occasion—the rifles, swords, and flags can hardly be mistaken—it is somewhat disconcerting because any adult viewing the parade from one side of Park Avenue can stare into the eyes of even the smallest adult on the other side of the avenue. For the marchers, some 100 in all, despite their snappy gray tunics trimmed above and below in white, are all under sixteen. That is the mandatory retirement age from the Knickerbocker Greys, the most exclusive "children's club" in the country.

While the Greys are a training ground for young men, something like the Boy Scouts in their aims, the Greys are to the Boy Scouts what New York's Links Club is to the Kiwanis. The Greys drill twice weekly in the Park Avenue armory of the Seventh (Society) Regiment of the New York National Guard. They give a Christmas tea dance. Their destination, as they march downtown with precision, is the most lavish of New York's Episcopal churches, St. Bartholomew's Park Avenue.

There, traditionally, they hold a massing of the colors on the church's great steps, and are traditionally told by Dr. Terence

J. Finlay, St. Bart's revered rector, that their goal in these years should be to plant foundations as deep as the skyscrapers constantly rising around the church, so that someday they may rise as high as those monuments to money and achievement.

For most of the young marchers, this is their first organized group outside the nuclear family, the first club in their Episcocratic lives. The Knickerbocker Greys do not tap the best marchers or the boys who promise to be the best soldiers. Averell Harriman was a Grey before he went off to Groton, railroads, and globe-trotting diplomacy. So was Major General Pierpont Morgan Hamilton, great-grandson of Alexander Hamilton and a man who, by his Congressional Medal of Honor, shows that the Greys are serious if they are also social.

The ranks of the Greys have long been filled with chips off the Roosevelt, Vanderbilt, Morgan, Dodge, Fish, and Gould blocks. They find it natural to march to St. Bartholomew's, where many of them attend church anyway. (There are also such surprising graduates as Mel Ferrer, Bob Considine, and Douglas Fairbanks, Jr., demonstrating that Episcocrats like to succeed at whatever they're doing.) Sometimes the Greys have to serve purposes probably never thought of by the founders. When Winthrop P. Rockefeller and Laurance Rockefeller both joined the Greys one year, it became clear that, though they were first cousins, they had never met because of intrafamilial feuding. The Greys' commandant, Colonel William Warrick, introduced the two scions.

Though many of them do not know it—the older ones surely suspect—joining the Greys is the first step a wellborn young man will take in establishing a lifetime of connections, extending through prep schools, college clubs, and men's clubs. Once he has reached the age of eight and the height of forty-eight inches, the young man must fill in an application and undergo a personal interview at tea with his own nervous mother and a few ladies from the membership committee. Though the Greys are no longer "overwhelmed" with applicants as they were even a few years ago, according to Mrs. Frederick Wahlers, the Greys' 1978 president, the membership committee still decides whether a boy is in or out according to criteria known only to them. "Most of the boys come simply because their friends come," notes Mrs. Wahlers.

Acceptance or rejection on the subtle bases of friendship and

New York's Century Association, 1890. Its membership tends more toward achievers than gentlemen.

The library of the Philadelphia Club.

The Union League Club, 1893.

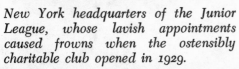

New York headquarters of the Junior League, whose lavish appointments caused frowns when the ostensibly charitable club opened in 1929.

The New York Athletic Club winning tug-of-war, 1904.

The Colony Club, New York's best for women.

Dining room of the Metropolitan Club in New York.

The lounge of the New York Yacht Club.

A bachelor dinner at the Yale Club, 1904.

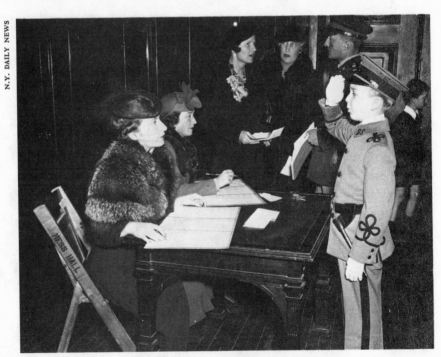

The mothers' committee examines a young Knickerbocker Grey, 1938. The young gentlemen still march every spring.

Theodore Roosevelt with fellow members of the Porcellian Club.

TR explains acceptability of his son-in-law, Nicholas Longworth: "Nick and I are both members of the Porc, you know."

Richard Whitney going to jail for embezzlement as president of the New York Stock Exchange. Porcellian pig is visible on his vest.

The annual dinner of the New York Yacht Club: "You can only sail with a gentleman."

intangible criteria for approval is a process that the young Grey will become more and more familiar with as he graduates to prep school, college, and the business world. Another by-product the successful young Grey becomes familiar with is the envy of the left-out; at New York's private schools, the non-Greys jeer that the initials "K.G." on the uniforms stand for "kitchen grease."

The Knickerbocker Greys, like so many other exclusive Episcocratic institutions, sprang from the seemingly endless energy of the Episcocratic consolidation in the late nineteenth century. One Mrs. Edward Curtis decided that her sons were turning into dangers to themselves and everyone around them at their nonmilitary school, so she gathered a few friends whose children also required shaping up and formed the drill-conscious Greys. Neither then nor now do the boys do any shooting; they do receive physical training and cultivate a taste for regimentation and proper form. The military connection is important. Episcocrats have long been the most important segment of the upper ranks of the armed forces. Harry H. Lucker of the Warnock Uniform Company, which until the early 1950s had a franchise for the Greys' uniforms, used to research and construct the elaborate uniforms earned and enjoyed by Admiral Alan G. Kirk (Ret.), McGeorge Bundy's old family friend and now the ambassador to Somalia. For some graduates of the Greys, the army or navy becomes the biggest club of all, one they can belong to for the rest of their lives.

Not getting into the Porcellian Club, Franklin D. Roosevelt wrote to a relative, was "the greatest disappointment" in his life. Roosevelt was rich, wellborn, well bred, Groton-educated, smart, personally charming—and still not good enough. No one really knows why Roosevelt was not good enough for the Porcellian, but his rejection is the best evidence available that at the top of the Episcocratic ladder the social criteria are so strict they rule out even those who seem, from below, to be perfect.

Even in the Episcocratic world of Harvard, the Porc, as it is called, is unique. No other college club—no club of any kind, for that matter—comes close to matching the tightness of the

Porcellian's bonds, which connect over space and time the men of such august Episcocratic clans as Cabot, Cuyler, Lowell, Lyman, Gardner, Sears, and Alsop. Francis Biddle, Roosevelt's attorney general, who could not make the club either, tells of a Porc member who informed a young man, hesitating over which club to apply to, "that in the United States, membership in the 'Pork' was equivalent to a peerage in England—that was the clearest way he could put it." What made Franklin's hurt all the keener was the fact that his cousin Theodore had made the Porcellian during his undergraduate days—a reminder that the Oyster Bay Roosevelts had an indefinable social edge over the Hyde Park Roosevelts.

Yet for most Americans, the Porcellian Club is no more real than, say, the smallest star in the constellation Orion. No more Americans, certainly, know the name of it than know the name of that star. Partly, this is because of the changing times. A few decades ago, both Al Smith and Dwight D. Eisenhower went out of their way to persuade their upper-class Boston friend Grenville Clark to show them the inside of this fabulous association that represented, to both of them, the inner sanctum of Episcocratic society in America. What they saw was nothing special: several unspectacular rooms over a cafeteria on Massachusetts Avenue, in which members could have suffered tear gas inhalation during the riots of the sixties. Grenville Clark got nothing out of the visits either; he was reprimanded for having had more visitors than anyone in Porcellian history.

At Harvard, still the most exclusive and most Episcocratic of the nation's universities, the Porcellian is only the top of an elaborate club system that sorts the acceptable from the ill-born, clumsy, Jewish, ugly, and Methodist. Following Porcellian in social clout are A.D., Fly, Spee, Delphic (or Gas), and a host more, until they trail off into Rotten Boroughs, where the clubs become so nonexclusive it may be better not to belong at all. If the great majority of Harvard's students do not participate in the heartbreak and glory of joining a club—most students sneer at "preppies," in public at least—that does not make the strict club system less important to the Episcocratic circles that do participate.

The clubs do not seek a high public profile. Their attitude is symbolized by the one-way mirror through which Porcellian men may look down on the mortals along Massachusetts Avenue without being observed.

Up to the early nineteenth century all Harvard was one big club; entering students were ranked according to social cachet, difficult and troublesome as that choice was. The "heart's desire" of Harvard President Josiah Quincy (1829-45) "was to make the College a nursery of high-minded, high-principled, well-taught, well-conducted, well-bred gentlemen." When those days of exclusivity ended as Harvard inevitably became a national institution and a real university, the clubs became conduits for exclusivity and good breeding, leading from the Greys and the prep school to the world of business and men's clubs. As the college became bigger, the clubs became stronger and the Episcopal faith took over the higher echelons of Harvard.

Yale and Princeton, the other colleges which Episcocrats have traditionally attended when they got out of St. Paul's or Middlesex, developed their own methods to separate the few from the many. At Yale the annual selection of twelve or fifteen new members by the two major secret societies, Skull and Bones and Scroll and Key, is—at least to those who think they have a chance—a matter of immense importance. Membership is thought to influence the course of a man's life beyond the ability of science to account for.

Bones accepts members from a rather wide range of students, including various kinds of campus leaders. A while ago it became the first club to elect a black. The honored man, football great Levi Jackson, punctured the self-congratulatory air that seeped from Bones on that occasion by remarking, with obvious truth, "If my name had been Jackson Levi, I'd never have made it." Keys would hardly descend that far; its membership is more distinctly old-family and social. But by insisting strenuously that Bones is the better club, members of Keys somehow manage to convey the impression that it perhaps tries a little too hard and that *they* might be better after all.

This backhanded snobbery tends to creep into Episcocrats' actions. Skull and Bones has claimed such activist-cum-good-breeding members as Averell Harriman, Robert A. Taft, and McGeorge Bundy, Episcocrats all. Scroll and Key favors the likes of John Hay Whitney, Rockefellers, Browns, Delanos, Auchinclosses, and Dean Acheson, certainly not a negligible group. From the outside the two societies exhibit far more similarities than differences. One similarity is the tomblike quality of their clubhouses. Another is the strict secrecy in which they are operated. A Bones man, for example, is supposed to leave the room immediately if an "outsider" sullies the name of the club by saying it.

Princeton has maintained a reputation of splashier fashion-ableness than its elder brothers in New England. Its "eating clubs," though also younger than the Harvard and Yale clubs, concede nothing to them in the way of toniness. Like Harvard and Yale, Princeton after the middle of the nineteenth century had no significant presence of the national fraternities that swept the rest of the nation. Ivy exclusivity was of a higher order; the eastern colleges declined to associate through national fraternities with poor-relation colleges in the Midwest.

Princeton's first and most distinguished eating club, Ivy, was founded in 1877. At first only an alternative to the wretched food in the college and the village restaurants, the Ivy Club was soon swept up in the wave of Episcocratic class formation. Aided by the presence among its first officers of such figures as Blair Lee, a future U.S. senator, and endowments from J. S. Morgan, Cuylers, Van Rensselaers, McCormicks, and Winants, Ivy became a tower of exclusivity and began spinning off imitations like Cottage, Cap and Gown, and others.

How exalted a place Ivy held in its sons' hearts was demonstrated by George Kerr Edwards, Princeton '89, who responded to an incurable disease by returning to the club. He bequeathed it his worldly goods, attended its last dinner of the year, and died on its premises during Commencement Week. "Let me be so bold," Edwards wrote to the Board of Governors, "as to urge upon each Ivy man, past, present, and those to come, to earnestly and continually strive to push onward and expand our present prestige by word and deed, so that amongst Princeton men, to say 'I am an Ivy man' shall correspond to the proud declaration of the ancient Roman, 'I am a Roman citizen.' "

Princeton's clubs expanded rapidly enough to include a much greater percentage of the junior and senior classes than at Harvard and Yale—about two-thirds early in the twentieth century—but increasing the number of clubs did not diminish the social pressure to get in. Quite the reverse. Woodrow Wilson pointed out when he became president of Princeton in 1902:

It would be difficult to exaggerate the importance in the life of the undergraduate of the question whether at the end of his Sophomore year he is going to be taken in to one of the upper-class clubs. . . . About one-third are left out in the elections; and their lot is little less than deplorable. . . . It often happens that men who fail of election into one of the clubs at the end of the Sophomore year leave the University and go to some other college or abandon altogether the idea of completing their university course.

Some still think the battle Wilson fought with the dining clubs at Princeton was more important than his struggle to join the League of Nations. He lost both. William C. Procter, the wealthy soap manufacturer (Procter & Gamble) whose descendants married into the family of an Episcopal bishop, withdrew a tentative half-million-dollar gift when informed of Wilson's plans to do away with the eating clubs. When Wilson quit to run for governor of New Jersey in 1910, the Presbyterian democrat had made no dent in the ways of Episcocratic patricians who flourished in the Ivy Club. They still do today, if not with quite the same far-reaching impact on college careers.

Wilson's career was to have a further disturbing effect on the Episcocratic caste he battled at Princeton. When the old-family representatives Theodore Roosevelt and Robert Taft could not agree among themselves and left the 1912 election to the Democrat's plucking, Mrs. Cornelius Vanderbilt wrote to Cornelius Jr. at St. Paul's, "How strange to have a President we do not know!" Those words came back to haunt Mrs. Vanderbilt and fellow Episcocrats when a president they did know, Franklin Roosevelt, took "Bolshevism," as they would have called it, farther than Wilson ever found possible. In the meantime, TR and Taft first shook hands again, after their bitter dispute, at one of Mrs. Vanderbilt's famous parties.

Graduating from college to business means graduating from one club to another, although, once in Porcellian and Ivy, one remains always in these clubs. Nowhere is this transition smoother than in Boston, where graduating from college meant little more for an Episcocrat than moving "from armchair at the Porcellian to armchair at the Somerset." That mordant assessment came from a man whose son had failed to make the Porc. In reality, the place of men's clubs in the Episcocratic scheme is relatively complicated.

George Kerr Edwards's men's club counterpart belonged to New York's Union Club, although in this case the action was more humorous. In 1936, when this "mother of clubs" was celebrating its hundredth anniversary, this longtime member participated with such dedication in one of the clubroom's most important activities—the cocktail hour—that he disappeared. After a while the other distinguished members missed their colleague and began searching the many nooks of the clubhouse. He was found stretched out on a bed in an upstairs bedroom, white tie and tails still flawlessly pressed.

Clubmen frequently being unable to resist a little fun, the distinguished member's friends took the masses of flowers they had received on the club's anniversary, piled them under and around his bed, and established a guard system. Within a few hours the guard called them. Silently the clubmen filed in and stood around the bed, heads bowed, hands clasped, tears, where possible, rolling.

After some stirring and mumbling, the sleeping gentleman opened his eyes. Quickly he shut them. He blinked several times. His eyes widening visibly, he took in the laudatory flowers, the grieving friends, and then, with a hint of smile, the tasteful, well-polished parameters of the bedroom that had so often served him as a home-away-from-home. Sighing, he lay back, shut his eyes, and the other members heard his surprised but overjoyed comment: "I never knew it would be like this."

The great men's clubs in their day could easily be accepted as an earthly approximation of the Episcocrat's heaven. The similarity was enhanced by the frequent presence of Episcopal clergymen, especially bishops, who were considered fine fellows when their background made it likely that they would not be overly theological. One could eat, drink, sleep, read, and live in the clubs, without the presence of undesirables—that is, in the pithy phrasing of the Union Club, "no women, no dogs, no Democrats, no reporters." Episcocratic society often tended to express its ideals in the negative.

Chief among the positive elements, as the club members saw them, was the availability of the clubs as a gathering place for deal-minded Episcocratic businessmen—more convenient and quieter than stock exchange floors. In New York a hierarchy evolved for talking business. R. Stuyvesant Pierrepont, Jr., whose name indicates his descent from a blur of Episcocratic ancestors, remarked in 1959: "At the Metropolitan or the Union League or the University, you might do a $10,000 deal, but you'd use the Knickerbocker or the Union or the Racquet for $100,000 and then, for $1,000,000 you move on to the Brook or the Links."

The Links is probably the most distinguished club in New York today, its Episcocratic members at the apex of the business-government connection—men like C. Douglas Dillon, Roy Chapin, Joseph Alsop, Winthrop Aldrich, and the late David K. E. Bruce. Joining them as nonresident members in the Links are the leaders of business from across the country—a Mellon from Pittsburgh, a Field from Chicago, a Du Pont from Wilmington, a Cabot from Boston, and a Bechtel from San Francisco. Many of the New Yorkers in the Links Club, to return Mellon's favor, acquire nonresident status at Pittsburgh's top-of-the-heap Duquesne Club, where John Heinz, father of the present senator, ate lunch every day along with top executives of U.S. Steel and Alcoa and Admiral Ben Moreel, former chairman of Jones & Laughlin Steel, who regularly lunched with the Episcopal bishop.

San Francisco's Pacific Union Club, one of the country's oldest, despite the city's relative youth, brings Hearsts and Crockers together with their Episcocratic brethren from out of town. The Bohemian Club sponsors an encampment once a year in its wooded setting outside the city that is probably the nation's greatest gathering of leaders of business and government. A single "camp," Mandalay, attracts Episcocratic businessmen Thomas S. Gates, Jr. (former chairman of Morgan Guaranty Trust and former secretary of defense), Amory Houghton (former chairman of Corning Glass), and Peter M. Flanigan (a Dillon, Read partner and an aide in the Nixon White House). Here the powerful meet to unwind, to enjoy "High Jinks" and "Low Jinks," after a ceremonial "Cremation of Care" opens the festivities. They have listened to entertainers like Bing Crosby and politicians like Nixon and Ronald Reagan; at the Bohemian encampment in July 1967, Reagan promised to leave Nixon an open field to the presidential nomination unless he faltered.

The club for gentlemen is a tradition going back to eighteenth-century Britain, where gatherings at coffeehouses of the type made famous by Dr. Johnson and Boswell gradually put down roots, built a clubhouse, acquired slippered servants and slightly worn overstuffed chairs, and began building the exclusivity that is half the pleasure of belonging to a club: an institution for "gentlemen" whose tastes and habits were ideally known to (and approved by) one another, men without axes to grind, who enjoyed the company of other men without the petty squabbles of family life—and without, at least in the beginning, the press of business allowed to intrude. Clubs were places for the "best men" to unwind with serious fun, whist and gambling games and newspapers and cocktails; monuments to the notion that neither family (except relationships to other members) nor work was more important than relaxed intercourse between a homogeneous group of males; oases that perpetuated themselves by selecting the best young men to join them.

The oldest surviving American clubs are in Philadelphia, which has not acquired its reputation for stodginess and conservatism for nothing. The Fishing Company of the State in Schuylkill claims that its founding date, 1732, makes it the oldest club not only in the United States but in the world. Through quaint traditions, like the assertion that the club is an independent state of the Republic (an assertion, though never formally recognized by Washington, that came in especially handy during Prohibition, which State in Schuylkill rejected as an infringement of states' rights) and its Fish House Punch of legendary puissance, the State in Schuylkill, or Fish House, has preserved its extremely select membership of about thirty. It is perhaps the most exclusive organization of any kind in the country. Over the years, important government officials visiting Philadelphia—the socially acceptable ones—frequently found themselves entertained at the surprisingly modest encampment of the brave little band on the Delaware River.

The country's oldest men's club with a downtown clubhouse

is also in Philadelphia and is called, appropriately, the Philadelphia Club. Most members of the Fish House also belong to the Philadelphia Club. The Philadelphia Club, in turn, is practically interchangeable with the Philadelphia Assemblies, the annual dance that started before the Revolution and whose roster is a convenient list of who is upper-class in Philadelphia. "Bounded by these three sides of a triangle lies probably the most compact and inviolable little group of aristocrats in America," observed Dixon Wecter. Almost without exception, the members of these three institutions are Episcopalians, and clergymen from socially august families are fixtures in the staid old Philadelphia Club.

Like all gentlemen's clubs, the oldest of them all abounds in tales of the crusty bonhomie of its members. John Gibson, a nineteenth-century chief justice of Pennsylvania, dedicated equally to the exigencies of club whiskey and talk and to his early-morning decisions, always ordered the boy who waked him to rush in "Coffee, hot as hell and strong as the wrath of God." A man named William Fisher Read opposed converting the former coatroom in the club's building into a tearoom; outvoted, he registered his protest for the full thirteen years before his death by, whenever he entered the club, aggressively depositing his hat and coat on a chair in the new tearoom.

Slightly younger than the Philadelphia Club, but considerably more important in the eventual history of Episcocrats, was New York's Union Club, which gathered itself together in 1836 with enough social latitude at the time to include an invitation to James Gordon Bennett, who had just founded the *New York Herald*. Bennett had second thoughts about signing on—not, as he told his readers, because of the club's social exclusivity, but rather because no women were to be allowed. "What is the use of any social system in which women do not participate?" Bennett asked. "In which their petticoat is not seen—where glossy ringlets cannot enter and make it Paradise?" Finally, Bennett rejected the Union Club and concluded, "Down with all clubs say we." Five years later a newspaper publisher like Bennett could not buy into the club at any price, for it rapidly became a bastion of Episcocratic exclusivity and remained that way into the twentieth century.

The Union Club became so exclusive that nobody could get

into it even from the class that already belonged. When the Union instituted a ten-year waiting list, it became too much for some of the more hot-blooded of its younger members, and the Episcocratic likes of Alexander Hamilton, John Jacob Astor, and Philip Schuyler went out and founded the Knickerbocker Club in 1871. Even before the Knickerbocker, a group of members split from the Union Club to form the Union League Club in 1863 because their demand to expel Judah B. Benjamin had been rejected. In view of the post–Civil War unanimity of anti-Semitism in the clubs, it is interesting that the secessionists did not object to Benjamin's presence because he was Jewish, but because he had become the financial brains of the Confederacy. A similar split in Philadelphia also produced a Union League there in 1862. Both politically motivated clubs have always been less acceptable socially than other men's clubs, membership running to Presbyterian insurance men more than to Episcocratic bankers and brokers.

For various reasons, the Union Club continued to beget younger, rival clubs, though most of them eventually returned to the fold enough to allow the high-Victorian tradition of the "clubman"—a member of fifteen or twenty organizations—to flourish. The somewhat younger and swanker Brook Club was founded in 1903, legend holds, by two high-spirited young gentlemen who were expelled from the Union for the rather distasteful prank of putting a poached egg on the smooth head of its most revered patriarch. Other clubs were started to encourage particular activities among members—like the sports clubs (Racquet, for example, and Links, though both, especially the latter, expanded far beyond their original purposes).

Then there are the clubs of artists, preferably wellborn, distinguished artists. The original and most famous of these, and probably the most vigorous of any of the clubs today, is New York's Century Association. "Wellborn" and "artist" have not always been compatible, as Francis Henry Taylor, the very Episcocratic director of the Metropolitan Museum, once observed. Viewing the Century's exhibit of a member's works, Taylor inquired, "Just how the hell bad an artist does one have to be to get into this club?" Swarming with the world's foremost experts in a range of subjects, Century members are fond of telling stories about correcting one another; Austin Strong, for example, is supposed to have one-upped Charles Evans Hughes, chief justice of the United States, by correcting him on a point of law.

Still another of New York's great exclusive clubs, the Metropolitan, came into being in 1891 because J. P. Morgan, the most vibrant can-do man ever, was angered over the blackballing of a business associate and single-handedly hatched what came to be known as the "Millionaires' Club." It was not the first club Morgan founded. That honor belongs to Harvard's Delphic Club, which Morgan created two years before the Metropolitan in partial recompense for slights he had suffered at Harvard.

Those two examples are often cited by defenders of voluntary associations when they decide to blackball those they find uncongenial. If a man is determined enough, so the argument goes, he can go outside the system and found his own club. The case of Morgan is supposed to indicate that clubs have no final social power. (Morgan, however, did not maintain his vendetta; by the time of his death he belonged to nineteen different clubs in New York and London.)

But if the tight club system could be surmounted by a baron like J. P. Morgan, it held considerably more sway over Franklin Roosevelt.

When Roosevelt became, because of his policies, a "traitor to his class," the great Episcocratic clubs fought back. The Rabbit Club, a virtual twin in size and exclusivity to the Fish House, pointedly omitted its traditional toast "To the President of the United States" when Roosevelt was chief of state.

Similar determined slights invaded nearly every clubroom in the country. One member of the membership committee at the Union Club in New York was ready to cast his blackball against the candidacy of another member of the Roosevelt clan when he was reminded that this was an Oyster Bay Roosevelt, better than a Hyde Park Roosevelt and not directly related to That Man. It made no difference. "Goddamn all Roosevelts," the member said.

The Harvard Club of New York was bitterly divided after FDR's death over whether his name should appear on the War

Memorial, and his portrait was removed from the main hall to behind the buffet table in the dining room.

Roosevelt has often been interpreted as the personification of the aristocrat driven by noblesse oblige to help the lower orders, with whom he would also mix personally and socially. Among his most quoted words have been: "Remember always, that all of us, and you and I especially, are descended from immigrants and revolutionists."

Yet Franklin, the product of the exclusive, self-consciously privileged worlds of the ancestral Hudson Valley estate and Peabody's Groton, came to Harvard the typical product of the Gold Coast mentality. He lived in one of the posh dormitories along Mount Auburn Street and promptly threw himself into the self-contained social whirl which existed largely to introduce Boston women to their future husbands and their future husbands to their future business and club colleagues.

"Last week," young Franklin wrote home excitedly soon after he arrived in Cambridge, "I dined at the Quincy's, the Amory's & the Thayer's, three as high-life places as are to be found in blue-blooded, blue-stocking and bean-eating Boston!" A little later he "ushered & had great fun" at "the Bigelow's ball at the Somerset," Boston's premier men's club.

Even when he had become the scourge of the clubmen and their class, Franklin deeply enjoyed such aristocratic preoccupations as tracing his own family's genealogy (it was so complicated that someone once remarked that James Roosevelt, Franklin's son, was his own sixth cousin once removed) and yachting—especially on the luxurious craft of his distant relative by marriage Vincent Astor—a sport and a name that correctly made his advisers fear image problems during a depression. And Franklin enjoyed his exclusive clubs all his life: the Knickerbocker in New York; the Metropolitan, Washington's best; and the exclusive Chevy Chase Club with its golf course.

Not as well known is a skeleton in his club closet: Franklin was deeply and perhaps crucially wounded by the machinery of the Episcocratic society into which he was born. As we noted, he did not always, as he appeared to in his later days, look down with blithe unconcern on the distrust of his upper-class peers. Though he liked Groton, he never felt successful there—he missed being a good athlete and was not elected a prefect—and when he was rejected by Porcellian at Harvard, it was a bitter blow. He did join the Fly Club, which was good, but it was not Porc. When he became president, FDR's Republican relatives, meaning most of them, always ascribed his attacks on Wall Street and his hostility to bankers like Morgan and Whitney to the deep wound of rejection by the Porc. "He was getting back at them," they said.

Joseph Lash's biography of Eleanor points out another result of the snub: "He had been disappointed, Eleanor agreed, and even developed something of an inferiority complex as a result; but the blow to his self-esteem at Harvard, like his loneliness at Groton, had widened his sympathies." Little did the self-consumed members of the Porcellian suspect how great an influence they were exercising on the social and political futures of their children!

If Franklin Roosevelt gained his sympathy for the underdog from personal acquaintance with the cruelties of the Episcocratic establishment, that code of behavior can also claim to share in his values and theories. While a certain amount of rebellion was necessary to turn into a Public-minded Patrician, Roosevelt was also solidly and consciously grounded in his own milieu. When he and Eleanor first went to Washington for Franklin to man the Episcocratic post of assistant secretary of the navy, they naturally gravitated to their Episcocratic peers, mostly Republican—the Nicholas Longworths, the Henry Cabot Lodges, and the William Phillipses (he was assistant secretary of state, and she, an old friend of Eleanor's, was a granddaughter of *the* Mrs. Astor).

Even more striking, the early-Washington Roosevelt was aggressively trying to make up for not making the Porcellian. Lash writes:

> The Metropolitan and the Chevy Chase country clubs were the gathering places of the socially acceptable and politically powerful; businessmen were not admitted—neither were Jews, nor, of course, Negroes. (One reason Washington high society suspected Woodrow Wilson of social radicalism was his refusal to accept honorary membership in the Chevy Chase Club.) Franklin spent a great

deal of time at both. Their acceptance mattered to him. They were the people who counted, and their recognition eased the pain of his exclusion from Porcellian. Eleanor later said that it was Louis Howe, who had come to Washington as Franklin's aide, who saved Franklin from the snobbishness and total dedication to pleasure-seeking represented by the Metropolitan Club.

The Metropolitan Club was (and is) the leading men's club in Washington, just as Union is in New York, Philadelphia in Philadelphia, Somerset in Boston, Chicago in Chicago, and Pacific Union in San Francisco. Because the Metropolitan is in the nation's capital, it retained vigor from the influx of important lawyers and government officials. A number of rules have changed, particularly the exclusion of businessmen. The Metropolitan is a gathering place for the important partners of the big Washington law firms, and business is more than occasionally mentioned among them.

What has not changed is the exclusive, predominantly Episcocratic air of the club. It became such a symbol of WASP dominance that when John F. Kennedy became president in 1961, his brother Robert, the attorney general, made a point— and a big splash—by resigning from it to protest the exclusion of blacks. Kennedy was joined at the exit door by such redoubtable Episcocrats as Angier Biddle Duke and George Cabot Lodge. Their exits did not end the Metropolitan's exclusivity, possibly because of the retention of membership by such bellwether "liberals" as McGeorge Bundy.

The Metropolitan is an attractive Washington club for out-of-town businessmen like AT&T's John D. de Butts. The important Washington law firms remain clustered in the downtown caverns near its H Street location. Here the capital's most powerful law firm, Covington & Burling—operational base of national-rank Episcocrats like the late Dean Acheson and his son-in-law, William P. Bundy—holds its "partners' luncheons" and listens to well-heeled speakers like Maryland's Episcocratic Republican senator, Charles McC. Mathias. Though it does not command the old-family base of the men's clubs in other eastern cities, the Metropolitan has managed to remain nearly as Episcocratic as most of its fellow clubs—thanks largely, no doubt, to the tendency of Episcopalians to monopolize high posts in the federal government.

As recently as the mid-1960s, after the big flap, all fourteen vestrymen at St. John's Episcopal Church, "the Church of the Presidents" across from the White House, were members of the Metropolitan Club. The Metropolitan remained as discriminatory as its old-city colleagues, too. Again, despite the 1961 controversy, it was not until 1972 that the Metropolitan finally accepted its first black member. He was John Walker, then suffragan bishop, more recently bishop of the Episcopal diocese of Washington. He was sponsored by Phillip Watts, a brokerage executive who is also a member of the St. John's Lafayette Square vestry.

The vigor of Washington's Metropolitan Club is the envy of many of the "better" men's clubs around the country, which are facing some membership problems. No greater symbol exists of the change in the solid front of the Episcocratic elite than the troubles facing the clubs. Not that the Episcocratic elite has lost its importance; its younger members, however, are no longer working only through institutions of strict exclusivity like the clubs. Pragmatism has a lot to do with it. Cleveland Amory found one member of the Century and Harvard clubs in New York who recently resigned from Union because "I want a club where I can take a couple of friends without producing a birth certificate, a marriage license and a blood test." The Second World War was the great watershed; many of the dedicated clubmen of another era could no longer find time or energy to maintain multiple club memberships, and there seem to be extremely few younger men, even sons of club members, who are interested in joining—or at any rate, admitting they have joined—the exclusive clubs.

Everyone noticed the decline. "Bah," said Alexander Hamilton Rice before he died in 1954, "it's just a plain damn revolution." Rice honored forty-three societies and twenty-seven clubs with his membership when he hit his stride; by the end of his life he had only twelve left. The late Grotonian Undersecretary of State Sumner Welles dropped down to two clubs before *his* death and muttered, "There is no such thing as club life any-

more. They can't even keep in the men they used to keep out."
Banker-ambassador Winthrop Aldrich and his wife eliminated
seven of their eighteen clubs between 1950 and 1967. Virtually
every well-known Episcocrat has followed the same trend. If it
hadn't been for Welles, Rice, and Aldrich, who agreed to have
its bonded indebtedness settled for ten cents on the dollar, their
Knickerbocker Club would have disappeared entirely in 1954,
back into the fold of its parent, the Union Club. The Knickerbocker also owes its continued existence to Nelson Rockefeller,
Aldrich's nephew, who bought the clubhouse at Fifth Avenue
and Sixty-second Street and permitted the club to remain there
for the next twenty years rent-free. And even with the saving of
the Knickerbocker, there are no "clubmen" coming along of the
stature of Aldrich, Welles, Harold Vanderbilt, or Vincent Astor.
The very word *clubman* seems to be disappearing from the
language.

Considerable prestige has shifted to suburban country clubs,
which became in the 1920s and 1930s the symbol of the exclusivity, snobbishness, and anti-Semitism of the dominant
Episcocratic culture. It followed the shift from city houses to
country houses; from indoor activity to outdoor sports; from
all-consuming interest in business and business colleagues to
a certain tolerance for family activities.

The country club was ever associated with the leadership of
Episcocrats. At the very first one in Brookline, Massachusetts
—called ever since its 1882 founding, with typical self-assurance, The Country Club—a historic tennis racket graces the
wall. It was supposedly used by Bishop William Lawrence to
play the first game of tennis ever in this country. Shortly after
that signal event, in the winter of 1885–86, Pierre Lorillard III
of the tobacco family laid out a golf course and built a lavish
clubhouse at Tuxedo in upstate New York, a resort whose name
would soon become synonymous with all that was swank.

Among the early contributors to its reputation were William
Waldorf Astor and Mrs. James Brown Potter; the latter, who
married a nephew of the ubiquitous Bishop Henry Codman
Potter, began a theatrical career at Tuxedo that was to shock
presidents and lead her to a life on the London stage that was

then deemed risqué; she became the great example of what could befall society girls who went on stage.

Tuxedo Park became almost a caricature of the Episcocrat's drive for country pleasures—somewhat like the aristocratic "back-to-nature" impulse practiced at the court of Louis XIV— with its three artificial lakes and miles of newly installed riding trails. For many years its autumn ball kicked off the New York social season. The implicit aristocratic distinction of the Tuxedo Park complex, as opposed to the nearby village of natives, can be deduced from a speech by the distinguished former congresswoman from the area, Katherine St. George, who once addressed the "ladies of the Park" and then referred separately to the "women of the Village." Tuxedo has, of course, left its name on the jacket of formal dining; only when it was invented, the "tuxedo" was the "country" style of dressing, as opposed to truly formal dinner jackets, which had tails.

Even more aristocratic were the less accessible clubs for hunting, the sport par excellence of the English lord. Long Island's Creek Club, for example, was founded by the ne plus ultra of the Episcocratic community, Vincent Astor, Marshall Field, Harry Payne Whitney, and their likes. Barely a mile away from the Creek Club in Long Island's wealthy Locust Valley section on the North Shore sprawls the similarly prestigious Piping Rock Club, where the driveway alone runs through trackless forest for more than a mile from the main road before it reaches the clubhouse.

From Boston's North Shore to New Jersey's Far Hills section to the backcountry of Maryland, gently rolling country has always had a particular charm to the Episcocrat. Hunting and riding have always been popular ways to see that country, too. Breeding the horses to ride on has also been a distinguished pastime, as shown by Episcocratic country folk like "Jock" Whitney and his late sister, Joan Whitney Payson.

CHAPTER
14

Over the Bounding Main

The most ennobling of Episcocratic sports has always been yachting. "You can do business with anybody," J. P. Morgan memorably put it, "but you can only sail with a gentleman." Morgan's *Corsair* was one of the great oceangoing yachts of the high Episcocratic period; the only other ones in its class were Cornelius Vanderbilt's *North Star* and the royal yachts of England and Germany.

Even the term *yachting* does not quite do justice to the fashion in which, say, Cornelius Vanderbilt III lived on his boat during the years before the First World War (which demolished this style of sailing, literally; Vanderbilt gave his boat to the British navy). The *North Star* was 233 feet long and 30 feet wide, which dimensions allowed such regal inside proportions as a dining room 30 feet long. There were quarters for a crew of forty, each wearing the Vanderbilt crest of crossed Vs or Cornelius Vanderbilt's personal CV mark. The ship carried two sets of china, one with 29 teacups and 37 coffee cups; the formal dinner set came with 108 dinner plates. There were 107 Irish linen sheets for use under the silk-bound French blankets.

The galleys bore eight kinds of crystal glasses for champagne, wine, and liquors. Waiting to fill them in the yacht's wine room were cases of Grand Vin d'Ay '89, claret, Grand Marnier, and the best of scotch and Irish whiskeys. Vanderbilt, at least early

Yachts of the American aristocracy were as large as the European royal families': Cornelius Vanderbilt's North Star *(above) and J. P. Morgan's* Corsair II *(below), both scenes of major business pacts.*

At anchor, the seagoing home of "Colonel" John Jacob Astor (IV), who went down with the Titanic.

on, drank only beer—from a tall silver tankard with a glass bottom, emblazoned with still another crest, from the New York Yacht Club. Even the English sailor hats worn by the young Vanderbilt heirs who were forced, not much to their liking, to sail along, were inscribed in gold letters "S.Y. North Star."

By the time the stock market crashed and Vanderbilt was on his next yacht, the expenses of such a style of living made a dent in even his seemingly bottomless pocket; it ran $7000 a month to keep the craft drydocked, twice as much on cruises. Perhaps as a rationale, perhaps not, Grace Vanderbilt, Cornelius's wife, used to tell the children that the money was not entirely frivolously spent; by sailing to Europe and becoming personal friends of the monarchs, their father would be in a much better position to influence the sales of his railroad inventions and patents to their subjects. "The royalty payments and patent sales from the inventions my father sold in England, Germany, Spain, and other European countries more than compensated for the cost of the upkeep of the *North Star*," Cornelius Vanderbilt IV claimed.

Morgan, meanwhile, traded up to bigger and bigger yachts —four in a row, all christened *Corsair*, a name that his enemies endowed with considerable significance. In 1899 he settled on a magnificent craft more than 300 feet in length. He also outdid Cornelius Vanderbilt in the extensive business he conducted aboard the yacht. The *Corsair* was the setting in which Secretary of War Elihu Root delivered Theodore Roosevelt's plea to Morgan for help in the bitter coal strike of 1902 in which George Baer, Morgan's mine-boss ally, distinguished himself by alluding to God's silent partnership in Baer's ownership of the Philadelphia and Reading Railroad.

Six years before, Morgan had put his imprimatur on the candidacy of Roosevelt's predecessor, William McKinley, during a shipboard conference with that other Episcocratic kingmaker Mark Hanna. In an 1885 summit that was perhaps even more important, Morgan met with Chauncey Depew, the Vanderbilt "prime minister" and future senator from New York, and with Pennsylvania Railroad president George B. Roberts to iron out a complicated stock transaction that ended a murderous rate war and set the stage for the boundless railroad affluence of the latter nineteenth century. Morgan won his day largely by inviting his opponents aboard for an all-day cruise up the Hudson to West Point and back down again, declining to lower the gangplank till they finally settled.

Yachting bred exclusivity and isolation from the baronial wealth these financial rulers needed to maintain their yachts as a place of business. There was also the elaborate ritual of yachting, distinctly English and upper-class in its formality, inherent in Morgan's remark about the gentleman who sails. The gentleman's ritual of sailing existed long before the plutocracy of the industrial barons (and has survived it). Long before *arriviste* New Yorkers sailed their ample boats up to marbled Newport, older Episcocrats from Boston and Philadelphia found it more aristocratic to sail their own small sloops from their vacation haunts on the rocky and considerably less "soft" coast of Maine. The Morgans and Vanderbilts usurped the old yachting ritual as they had usurped the prevailing fashions in marriage, education, and religion. The ritual blended smoothly into the prevailing government of the American economy by a small group of staggeringly wealthy, predominantly Episcocratic men.

Two generations later not much had changed. Sidney Weinberg of the brokerage house Goldman Sachs was one of the great Wall Street figures of the twentieth century, as well as one of its great rags-to-riches stories. To all appearances, his rise from Brooklyn's P.S. 13 to the summit of the American business world was accompanied by his rising interest in all that was best of the predominant Episcocratic culture. Weinberg lived modestly for decades with his wife in Scarsdale, served on the boards of worthy charities like the Presbyterian Hospital, raised funds for Franklin Roosevelt and then Dwight D. Eisenhower, sent his two sons to Deerfield and Princeton.

In even more personal and deeply symbolic ways, Weinberg proved himself all but part of the Episcocratic establishment that so bestrode the financial world in which he thrived. One of the financier's sons married the daughter of Amory Houghton, not only the prominent chairman (now retired) of family-owned Corning Glass and formerly ambassador to both England and France, but a profoundly religious Episcopalian with an interest in helping the church—not least by producing a son, Alanson, who became rector of a Fifth Avenue parish.

Weinberg consistently engaged in yachting. His constant partners during adventures off the Maine coast were Paul Cabot, prominent banker and until recently treasurer of Harvard, and Episcocratic Philadelphians Charles Dickey (a senior partner of J. P. Morgan) and Charles Cheston. Weinberg was, *Fortune* magazine wrote, "not after superficial contacts or cultivation, but was apparently more sought after than seeking." The gentleman of the club ideal.

Still, Weinberg never could join any meaningful clubs. He was Jewish. The consistent, nearly inviolable longtime exclusion of Jews (not to mention blacks and sometimes Catholics) from the club life of high Episcocratic civilization was at the same time a strangely logical and ultimately self-defeating policy. It was logical because the emphasis on things English and aristocratic was only too clearly not shared by the Jews, who began arriving in large numbers in the country in 1878, precisely at the peak growth periods of the institutions of Episcocratic domination. Almost inevitably, those institutions—from college to country club—absorbed anti-Semitism as a fundamental principle.

The depth of anti-Semitic feeling among the Episcocratic class frequently came as a surprise to members who tried to break down the barriers or perhaps were liberated enough not to notice them in the first place. Francis Biddle, the New Deal attorney general and a member of the high-minded clan that rose above the class instincts of its Philadelphia milieu, had a telling experience after he graduated from Harvard:

> When Franklin Roosevelt, a member of the Fly, resigned as Assistant Secretary of the Navy in 1920, Guy Murchie, who was running the graduate dinners, asked me to be toastmaster at a banquet given in Franklin's honor. Murchie had secured two or three speakers, and wanted me to get one more. I was fortunate enough to persuade Felix Frankfurter, then a professor of the Harvard Law School, to fill the bill. As chairman of the War Labor Policies Board during the First World War, he had come to know Roosevelt well. When several of the members of the club would not go to the dinner, and one refused to speak to me because I had asked Frankfurter to speak, I realized

how strongly anti-Semitic feeling permeated Harvard clubs. I felt deeply humiliated that this could have happened.

Both anti-Semitism and the country club bloomed vigorously during the 1920s, one fertilizing the other. It was the high-water mark of the xenophobia of the Anglo-Saxons in America—their moments of most public power and also of greatest fear. When FDR did start making inroads into their power, at least as they perceived it, he and Eleanor, the "Rosenfelts," were sneered at by their fellow Episcocrats more for their love of Jews and "niggers" than for their economic policies. There remained a suspicion among Jews and other ethnic groups in the United States that the high-minded internationalism of even the Public-minded Patricians concealed a continuing disdain for people without power or, worse, pedigrees.

Intermittent incidents suggest to the ears of many Jews that a subliminal anti-Semitism persists among Episcocrats. Francis Sayre, Jr., compiled a strikingly liberal record as dean of the Washington Cathedral for two decades, taking outspoken positions in controversies from McCarthy to Vietnam, but by the time he retired in 1977 his accomplishments had been wiped out, in the eyes of many Jews who had previously supported him, by his hard-hitting criticism of Israeli "oppression" and his implied support of the terrorist Palestine Liberation Organization.

Nor has outright discrimination disappeared from the country clubs, which have nourished it all along. From the outside, one could hardly imagine a grander Episcocrat than C. Douglas Dillon, who moved in a straight refined path from Groton to chairman of his father's investment house to an ambassadorship to a cabinet post to chairmanship of the Metropolitan Museum of Art. He is Republican and Episcopalian, and his family is worth more than $200 million.

To the Chevy Chase Club, which looks deeper than the surface, those seeming qualifications for membership hardly outweighed the fact that Dillon's grandfather was named Sam Lapowski—and he was half Jewish. When, in 1962, Treasury Secretary Dillon applied for membership in the Chevy Chase Club, that ancestry was examined carefully and long. Finally,

One of the longest, most lavish lines of society Episcocrats: "Commodore" Cornelius Vanderbilt, the crusty Dutchman who amassed a fortune of $100 million in ships and railroads (above, left); his grandson Cornelius II's ornate château at 608 Fifth Avenue (above, right); Willie K. Vanderbilt (below, left), Cornelius's nephew, behind the wheel of a German sports car, one of many new autos he helped popularize; Grace Vanderbilt (below, right), still the grande dame at the opening of the Metropolitan Opera, 1948.

Dillon was allowed in—on his friends' solemn assurance that he was no more than 25 percent Jewish.*

Anti-Semitism is no longer a necessary part of the scenery whenever Episcocrats join a country club or go sailing, but the conservative upper-class nature of those activities has persisted. All through the 1930s Franklin Roosevelt, a devoted yachtsman like most of his family, retreated for solace to the yacht of his good friend (though later political opponent) and distant relative Vincent Astor. The idea of Roosevelt basking and fishing aboard Astor's regal ship *Nourmahal* was not one that pleased the pragmatists on the Episcocratic Democrat's staff.

Roosevelt continued to use his rich old-family friends and their distinctly Episcocratic sport as an outlet. He even managed to conduct some busines with Rabid Reactionaries whom he happened to meet on the water. One spring, as he was watching the Harvard-Yale boat races off Newport from the stern of Astor's yacht, a wind shift brought his perch bumping against the *Winchester* of Cornelius and Grace Vanderbilt. Roosevelt, ever the politician, invited the Vanderbilts aboard. Cornelius Vanderbilt, ever the Rabid Reactionary and self-conscious aristocrat, hedged because the president had not extended his invitation in the proper language of yachting.

"Well, I waive all those customs," Roosevelt called across to the Vanderbilts in his patrician tones.

That put Cornelius Vanderbilt in a spot. He had no intention of letting either yachting or Republicanism down. On the other hand, he could hardly be rude to the president of the United States.

World-class hostess Grace Vanderbilt could. "I don't like you, Mr. President," she called from the rail. "I don't like you at all."

Roosevelt, used to this sort of thing from his Episcocratic fellows, smiled and replied, "Well, Mrs. Vanderbilt, lots of people don't like me. You are in good company."

That sporting reply suggested to the Vanderbilts that, while

---

* These instances of anti-Semitism should not obscure the fact that many Episcocrats—the Public-minded Patricians in particular—have been more accepting of Jews personally and professionally than most other Americans. Having Jewish friends has actually carried a certain social cachet in many Episcocratic circles. And the Episcocratic eras in Washington have usually been auspicious for Jews in government.

Roosevelt was betraying his Episcocratic background by his national policies, he had not abandoned the politesse and good humor expected from members of their class. So they went aboard Astor's yacht and enjoyed themselves. In a nice Episcocratic compromise, Grace Vanderbilt promised before she left that, while she could never vote for Roosevelt because of his policies, she would never vote against him because he was a fighter and a gentleman.

(Vincent Astor, though, let the "socialism" of "Cousin Franklin" get to him. He not only stopped inviting FDR aboard his yacht, but as majority stockholder of *Newsweek* in the late 1930s campaigned publicly against him.)

The relationship between yachting and Episcocratic men of power has continued to this day. President Harry Truman, though he was born an Episcopalian and met his future wife at an Episcopal church, succeeded Roosevelt, the ultimate old boy, as an outsider, a midwesterner, and once a little-thought-of man. One way he attempted to remedy that state of affairs was by engaging in the tradition of yachting—inviting colleagues like Secretary of Commerce Averell Harriman and Senator Stuart Symington on board the presidential yacht *Williamsburg* to lend their Episcocratic tone to weekend bourbon-and-card parties.

Perhaps the most memorable bond between newsman and president of recent years was forged between John Kennedy and Ben Bradlee, then *Newsweek's* Washington bureau chief, now executive editor of the *Washington Post* and the newspaper's charismatic strategist in the Watergate Scandals, a performance memorialized by Jason Robards in the film *All the President's Men.* The main photographic residue of Bradlee's warm friendship with Kennedy is a picture of the two men stretched out in a small boat off Hyannis Port together—the Choate graduate and the St. Mark's graduate, away from jobs and women, communing with each other and the sea.

Yachts and the New York Yacht Club life sailed in different directions as the price of world-class sailing burgeoned far beyond the capabilities of any taxed income to support easily. Now syndicates buy boats that require preparations worth

many millions to have even a chance in the races. Almost inevitably the people who now struggle and win in this greatest
of Episcocratic competitions are not necessarily the sort of
people who always used to. Like Emil ("Bus") Mosbacher. A
State Department chief of protocol during the 1960s, husband
of the oldest and dearest friend of FDR, Jr.'s, third wife, Mosbacher won the 1962 America's Cup as skipper of the yacht
Weatherly. He would seem perfect material for the traditional
next step—acceptance by the New York Yacht Club.

But Mosbacher was Jewish. Once he would have been simply
ignored; in 1962, in face of the fact that winning skippers have
always been taken in, Mosbacher became the crusty old Yacht's
first Jew. It was not something club members were happy to do
at the time and not something they talk much about now. With
most of the prestige clubs, like the Yacht Club, the admission
of Jews changed status during the 1960s from impossible to
highly unlikely.

CHAPTER

15

Making a Business of Leisure

———⌐———

Late one evening in 1900 Miss Mary Harriman found herself unhappy. Outwardly there seemed little reason for her to feel that way; most young women of her age would have been happy to have all of Daddy E. H. Harriman's railroad money to spend that they needed and could easily have enjoyed the deliciously tired feeling of dancing all night at a debutante ball.

Miss Harriman's thoughts were on sadder topics this evening. She was thinking of the profusion of bouquets, more than she could ever love individually, that had been given her by the beaux who swarmed around her (also more numerous than she could ever enjoy individually). The thought that all those flowers were sitting in a ballroom by themselves, fading already, moved her to tears. A young lady already demonstrating that she was a woman of action—she would later be an important figure in the New Deal, along with her brother Averell— Miss Harriman acted on her somber thoughts the next morning by calling together several debutante friends to help her distribute the fading flowers to local hospitals. As frequently occurred among the Episcocratic elite at the turn of the century, the wish of a major figure became an institution. In this case it was the Junior League, the most widespread network of upper-class American women.

Though by now it requires no social cachet to join, the Junior League started with a flourish, thanks to the social prominence of the eighty or so debutantes that Miss Harriman called upon to join in her charitable work. "They were smart," said Countess Szechenyi, born Gladys Vanderbilt some time before the club was founded, "and they made it smart."

Spreading around the country, the Junior League became, with the country club, one of the great institutions of Episcocratic domination by the xenophobic decade of the 1920s. The league reached its social apogee, appropriately, in 1929, when ground was broken for its lavish new New York headquarters. Eventually the building cost more than a million preinflation dollars. It included fifty offices and bedrooms, a swimming pool, squash courts, a hair salon, a formal ballroom, two dining rooms, and two bars, one for snacks and one for cocktails.

Such lavish appointments in an organization founded ostensibly for the promotion of voluntary charitable work among its members bespoke the place of Episcocratic women in the frequently conflicting worlds of society and "nobility." In their responses, the women divided up neatly into categories as clear as the Public-minded Patricians and the Refined Reactionaries that their fathers and husbands became. One classic option at the height of the Episcocratic age was to become a hostess on the order of the various Mrs. Astors or Vanderbilts, spending one's husband's practically limitless money for the exhausting and rather fascinating (if ultimately fatuous) game of finer and finer social distinctions, in which the ultimate goal was to exhaust oneself having fun.

This was a doomed route, as Cornelius Vanderbilt IV suggested when he met with his mother, the famous salonkeeper Grace Vanderbilt, shortly after he joined the army during World War I. He saw with "chill disbelief," as we noted, that Mrs. Vanderbilt's main objection to the war was that it had prevented her from yachting abroad to visit her royal friends since 1914.

The older generation of social Episcopal clergymen helped reinforce the determined nostalgia of the countesses of the Episcocratic age. When Bishop Potter became aware of the strong momentum behind the suffrage movement generally provided by Episcocratic women, he said with a sigh, "Once woman was my superior. Now, alas, she is only equal."

For many Episcocratic women, especially by the increasingly modern 1920s, a new feeling of self-sufficiency blossomed forth —nurtured by increasing freedom, money, and education, inevitable by-products of the second and third generations of wealth. One of the most famous suffragists pushing for the right to vote was Alva Smith Vanderbilt Belmont, the same woman who had charged out of Mobile, Alabama, in the 1880s to marry two of the most powerful Episcocrats of the time, struggle viciously with her sister-in-law Grace Vanderbilt for the social crown left by the passing of *the* Mrs. Astor, and forcefully join her daughter to the short, scheming duke of Marlborough.

When one of her fellow suffragists was to be sent to jail for pouring carbolic acid into mailboxes, Alva fortified her with the famous advice "Don't cry, my dear. Pray to God, and *She* will help you."

The suffrage movement did not create the Junior League, although the league was certainly a product of a new independence among women. The league grew from an older attitude condemned by suffragists—the urge to use the wealth and power of men in the family for the gentling and amelioration of social injustice. Perhaps the most straightforward statement of this subservient, if shrewd and generous, attitude was voiced at the New York Junior League's groundbreaking in 1929 by Mrs. B. Tappen Fairchild, the chapter's president.

"Someone—father, mother, husband—has provided us with our homes, our clothes, our education, and has released us from the necessity of doing those things for ourselves," Mrs. Fairchild noted. "We in turn have the privilege of making a business of leisure, and in this leisure applying ourselves to the study of the needs of our communty and of fitting ourselves to carry forward the future of all that is essential in the civic and economic advancement of our country and our generation."

Those words have survived with considerable vitality among Episcocratic women, as any scanning of most old-family women's activities—hospital benefits, horse shows, and flower sales, all for good causes—will demonstrate. But the Junior

League now contains neither a real drive for important influence in society nor an especially Episcocratic membership.
Thanks to its New York palace, it did retain a distinctly debutante air through the 1930s. But the unfavorable publicity at-
tendant on members getting manicures while outside people's
hands froze for lack of gloves proved too much for the clubby
atmosphere. After World War II the league sold the grandiose
clubhouse—to the Catholic archdiocese, appropriately—and
began reading and listening to its own public relations booklet,
disarmingly titled "How to Get Off the Society Page." It succeeded. Today the 50,000 or so Junior Leaguers have a reputation that, while still WASPy, leans more toward the midwestern sorority-girl type than the Episcocratic debutante.

It may say something about Episcocrats in general, and Episcocratic women in particular, that while the Junior League
wandered off into a wasteland of insurance salesmen's daughters
and boxed-candy sales, women's clubs with no purpose other
than to compete with men's clubs in privacy and exclusivity have
remained among the strongest of Episcocratic institutions. The
women's city clubs came out of the same social milieu as the
Junior League. Three years after the Junior League was begun,
New York's Colony Club, then (and now) the most prestigious
of all women's clubs, sprang up through the efforts of not one
but two Harriman women—Mrs. J. Borden Harriman (E.H.'s
sister-in-law) and Anne Harriman Vanderbilt (wife of William
K. the younger). They were ably supported in their efforts by
such notables as Anne Morgan, Elsie de Wolfe (later Lady
Mendl), Mrs. John Jacob Astor III, and Mrs. W. S. Rainsford,
wife of the rector of J. P. Morgan's St. George's Church.

While the Colony became the social equal (and then some)
of the Union and Knickerbocker clubs in New York, there were
skeptics. Mrs. Harriman's husband told her, "Daisy, I don't
think you can make it pay." The Princeton Club expressed the
opinion of the corporate body of Episcocratic men by postpon-
ing plans for a new clubhouse in anticipation of the early and
cheap sale of the clubhouse of a bankrupt Colony.

The dire male prophecies were more wishful thinking than
hard business judgment. Frequently it was precisely their men's
suspicions that persuaded women to join the Colony and its
imitators in other cities. They felt the time had come to do to

their men what their men had done to them for so long: enjoy the pleasure of privacy. Husbands apparently suspected that the women's clubs might follow the men's in becoming a convenient depot for billets-doux.

"And they were jolly well right," remarked Margaret Emerson, who inherited a Bromo-Seltzer fortune and was once (like, it seemed, most other Colony members) married to a Vanderbilt. "Anyway, I know that's where I got mine." When old Grover Cleveland warned that a woman's "best and safest club is her home," he was surely helping the Colony more than he hurt it.

Up in Boston, the women who at about this same time started the Chilton Club ran into the same troublesome, yet enjoyable, suspicion. (Even earlier, in 1899, the first woman's club in the country, Philadelphia's Acorn—still a relaxing and bibulous rendezvous for Episcocratic women in town for the Academy of Music or to meet their husbands—began life at the behest of two women named, almost inevitably, Biddle.) The Chilton Club began when younger women, dissatisfied with the staid ways of the leftover Mayflower Club, told Mayflower president Mrs. Barrett Wendell that they "wanted a club like the Acorn where they could play bridge, have cocktails and invite their fathers, husbands and sons." At that point a Mayflower fixture, Mrs. Jane Mottey, rose wrathfully to exclaim, "To think that Boston women wanted a place where they could drink, gamble and have assignations with men!"

Though Mrs. Mottey was promptly denounced into silence, she or someone else passed along the shameless truth to a locally famous Baptist preacher, who lost no time devoting a Sunday sermon to the wickedness of Boston society women. The first Episcocratic instinct was to sue him for libel, but that was impossible, it was soon realized, because it would require an unpalatably public court appearance. Finally, the Chilton Club decided to get back at the preacher by blackballing any Baptist who applied for membership. Thus was the club kept Episcocratic *and* informal in matters of drink and monogamy.

Given such piquant publicity, the new women's clubs soon had all the applicants they could turn away. Possibly because their clubs were founded more recently, the women have been far more successful at preserving vigorous clubs than have their sons and lovers. To be sure, old-timers complain that the clubs don't preserve their former exclusivity and general desirability. "They've spoiled it completely," Mrs. Harriman complained decades after she founded the Colony. Its membership has been held up as old and stuffy, and Mrs. Joseph Choate, Jr., complained that they have been "just letting men absolutely *everywhere.*"

In common with their male club counterparts, however, the women of the Colony haven't been letting Jews everywhere. The Colony's admissions policy is no more open than in the 1930s, when Eleanor Roosevelt quit—without noticeable effect —because her friend Elinor Morgenthau, wife of the secretary of the treasury, was excluded on grounds of religion.

Such values are no longer so easy for Episcocrats to hold (or at least to admit publicly). Clubs founded on them have lost some of their power. A more serious erosion arose from the extension to city clubs of the sporting and coed features of the country clubs—as in New York's River Club, founded by Kermit Roosevelt, TR's son.

Perhaps even more seismic is the slow, but seemingly irreversible, trend, among both men's and women's clubs, to allow members of the opposite gender to creep gradually farther up the clubhouse stairs, like water. The eventual result could be a flood of unisexuality. In Philadelphia in 1978, women applied what may be the coup de grâce to the policies of exclusivity by sex. They persuaded the Philadelphia Bar Association, heavily composed of male members of the private clubs, to announce that no more lunches would be held in the old Episcocratic institutions until they opened their doors freely to women members. Economic pressure may well succeed in breaking down the proud traditions of the Philadelphia, Rittenhouse, and Racquet clubs—long fixtures of the city's strict and Episcocratic society—as well as of the leading Jewish downtown club, the Locust Club.

The handwriting may have appeared on the wall when the first women priests were ordained into the Episcopal Church, shattering the male monopoly of the oldest, most elaborately ritualistic Episcocratic brotherhood of all. If man can put aside what God seemed to have ordered, how can woman be kept out of heavens founded by Morgans and Roosevelts?

CHAPTER
16

The Sporting Resorts

Bobby and Teddy Kennedy decided, one day at the end of summer in the mid-sixties, to crash a party.

Normally, that wouldn't have been much of a problem, since the Kennedys were fun-loving, powerful, exciting, and generally irresistible.

It was not certain they would be welcome, however, given the place they were aiming to visit. This was North Haven, one of the little islands along the coast of Maine where, originally, wealthy Bostoners, then the rest of America's Episcocrats, escaped the heat and rush of the city. North Haven never became the posh resort with elaborate "cottages" that Bar Harbor did; it remained relatively rugged, pure, undisturbed by outside fetishes, dedicated to the timeless verities of unostentatious wealth and well-preserved background.

John D. Rockefeller summered on North Haven. So do a whole number of Cabots, enough to set up their own compound, "Cabotville"; the Irving Pratts of Standard Oil wealth; and other redoubtable families from Boston and elsewhere—enough to give the island the reputation as "the richest square mile in the world."

The Kennedys tore up from Hyannis Port in a thick fog to join this exclusive company. Somewhere below the island, they passed a Maine fisherman, one of the near-proverbial figures prominent in jokes of the Episcocrats who made their resorts along the old-Yankee coast.

"Where's North Haven?" called out one of the clan.

"Thataway," replied the State of Mainer, rather amazed at their panache, "but go slo-o-ow."

The Kennedys were extremely proud of their sailing. The sport's reputation as a test of exclusivity and manhood no doubt had a lot to do with it. They sailed jauntily into the port of North Haven and promptly made it clear that they wanted to be included in the end-of-summer festivities. On North Haven, as in most Episcocratic resorts, simple, comfortable ceremonies mark the passing of another summer of good fellowship among old friends and families. One of these is the transfer of the little North Haven church from its summer role as an Episcopal chapel back to its native drab habit of a Baptist church. Another is the end-of-summer yacht race.

Yacht is a little grand for the North Haven boats, actually. Residents are proud of the fact that they sail the oldest type of racing-class boat in continuous use—for 100 years. A world of self-assurance and background rides on that fact. The Kennedys had heard of these old boats. With their usual cockiness they determined not only could they conquer the sea with any weapon, but they would best these family-proud Bostonians, national leaders when the Kennedy forebears were bartenders or less, at their own game.

The boats were a lot easier to contemplate from Hyannis Port than they were to sail in the pitching waters off North Haven. First across the finish line was Senator Leverett Saltonstall, the grand old man of Massachusetts, then well over seventy years of age. To the best recollection of a participant, Bobby Kennedy finished eighteenth out of thirty boats. Teddy was twenty-seventh—"and many of the ones ahead of them," the old-family observer pointed out, "were being sailed by nine-year-olds."

With Episcocrats, there are thousands of ways to try but fail to keep up.

All along the Maine coast during the summer, Episcocrats of varying shapes, sizes, and family backgrounds relax in the

Algerian marble and solid bronze furniture in the dining room of Alva Vanderbilt's Newport "cottage," Marble House.

The young sport of lawn tennis at the Newport Casino in its heyday.

Cottages along Ochre Point and the Cliff Walk, Newport. Grace Vanderbilt's The Breakers is a half-hidden presence in the center background.

Entering Marble House.

Rocky Point, built at Newport by Frederick W. Vanderbilt and later bought by the mother of Doris Duke.

"Little do I care for riches," proclaimed Cornelius Vanderbilt's library mantel-piece in The Breakers.

The Malvern Hotel in turn-of-the-century Bar Harbor. The showy resort disappeared, but Episcocratic Northeast Harbor thrives on the other side of Mt. Desert Island.

rugged, piny splendor they seem to appreciate, perhaps as a reflection of their ideal: strength refined into handsomeness. For as long as anyone can remember—which is to say since the beginning of the nineteenth century—well-bred Bostonians have pitched their tents along the glacial ruggedness of Maine.

The late G. Peabody Gardner, for example—staunch old St. Marker, prominent Episcopalian member of half the boards of Boston, and sailing companion of Cabots and Chestons on legendary cruises—lived with his family on a tiny island which a distant ancestor had bought as timberland in 1825. Other families had similarly out-of-the-way pleasure spots, including, of course, Franklin Roosevelt on Campobello Island, so far into Maine that it was Canada.

Not until the end of the nineteenth century, the same period that saw the growth of so many Episcocratic institutions, did the Maine coast become one of the grandest—and the only continuing—summer playgrounds of the upper class. The presence of the key figures of the Episcocratic consolidation was critical to Maine's success. Almost inevitably, Bishop Lawrence was first on the scene; in 1870 he visited Mount Desert Island, later noting that "there were only farms and forests where the hotels and cottages of North-East and Seal Harbor now [i.e., 1926] stand." Thanks partly to Lawrence, those two towns and Bar Harbor almost overnight gained singular fascination for the intellectuals and Public-minded Patricians of the day.

James Russell Lowell "enjoyed the talk of the village people," Lawrence noted, while historian Francis Parkman, Harvard president Charles William Eliot, Columbia's Seth Low, Pennsylvania Railroad president A. J. Cassatt, Theodore Roosevelt the father of President TR, and Captain (later Admiral) Alfred Thayer Mahan were among the big names that turned the sleepy Maine island into the summer social center of the United States. Lawrence had a personal hand in introducing an important Philadelphia physician, Dr. Weir Mitchell, to the island; Mitchell liked the simplicity and beauty compared with already-gaudy Newport and soon was joined by a good number of his Episcocratic friends.

The Episcopal Church helped the tone. When Lawrence first puffed into the harbor, greeted by seventy-five or so artists and nature lovers who had already discovered the place, he noticed that "the white spire of the Union Church was conspicuous."

The Church of St. Mary's was built in Northeast Harbor under the care of Bishop Doane. Doane was a man of such Anglican bearing that he once got carried away and signed his first name and his parish in the English manner: "William of Albany." Whereupon William David Walker, the bishop of Buffalo who was with him, grabbed up the pen and wrote "Buffalo Bill."

St. Mary's was later joined at Northeast Harbor by St. Christopher's-by-the-Sea, a rustic wood structure. St. Saviour was built across Mount Desert Island, in the rapidly growing village of Bar Harbor, and soon was so overcrowded with newly arriving Episcocrats that it had to be doubled in size. The rector, Christopher Starr Leffingwell, showed typically Episcocratic consideration for the feelings of his parishioners, especially in the lonely months of the winter when the State of Mainers were his only (and infrequent) duties. The Reverend Mr. Leffingwell was once so grateful to be called to see "one of the wickedest men in the village" as he lay dying that, he explained later, "considering his open hostility to religion, I did not think it tactful to mention that subject."

As breathtakingly quickly as Groton and St. Paul's took over the upper class's children during the winter, Mount Desert absorbed them during the summer. Francis Biddle, the future attorney general, recalled the great triumph of young Episcocratic love: getting one's girl to write to one's boarding school from her boarding school. Biddle wrote that at the end of one summer he sat overlooking the beautiful island with a beautiful young lady, bitterly accusing her of treacherous plans. The boy he accused her of favoring was Norman Armour, Chicago's Episcocratic meat heir who would begin his ambassadorial career a few years before Biddle was attorney general.

After a brief period of simplicity as a place where good Episcocrats went to commune with nature and each other, Bar Harbor turned into a cliché of the upper-class resorts which fascinated American newspaper readers at the turn of the century and afterward. Beginning early in the 1890s, Bar Harborites built "cottages" that began to defy description. The resorters came up with such innovations as private electric power plants, hanging gardens, marble elevators, and motorized dining-room tables, rather to the dismay of the more upright Bostonians who had founded the place.

It took two self-made Philadelphians, the Morgan partner

E. T. Stotesbury and radio manufacturer A. Atwater Kent, really to refine old traditions to the point of absurdity. Stotesbury—whose 145-room Philadelphia mansion, now falling prey to vandals and junkies, once prompted the first Henry Ford to remark, "It's a great experience to see how the rich live"—never read a book and was determined to have a good time. His preoccupation was revealed one night in 1929, shortly before the crash, when acquaintances at the Bar Harbor Club were called to hear the announcement "I have today received a letter from my financial adviser telling me that I am worth a hundred million dollars."

Atwater Kent, a ruthless and tiny character, was a stereotype of the man who thinks he can buy everything. He owned nine "cottages" on Mount Desert at the same time. In the Depression year 1932, he threw a party with three bands playing until dawn—in the house, by the swimming pool, and on the yacht—while beflowered boats shuttled guests in between. Showing a predilection for the morbid fantasies that set in just before World War II ended old-fashioned high jinks at places like Bar Harbor and Jekyll Island, Kent threw a Bad Dream Ball in 1938, at which the women guests materialized as prostitutes, young mothers, and brides.

Newport, as we have noted, was the grandest expression of Episcocratic opulence ever seen in this country or probably in any other. Grace Vanderbilt, among many, was not content merely to spend 5 millions of 1900 dollars to build her "cottage" with its landscaped lawn running down to the beach; she closed a Broadway show of the time, *The Wild Rose*, and brought the entire company up to Rhode Island for a single private performance at Beaulieu. Her sister-in-law Alva, competing, put $9 million in furniture alone into Marble House.

Episcopal worship was merely another and (since it was in the sight of God) greater performance. At Newport's Trinity Church—the second oldest Episcopal church still standing, dating back to 1726, the resort's fishing-village days—the box pews were thoughtfully outfitted in the same color plush as the liveries of the families that held them. The best-equipped of these pews, that of Mr. and Mrs. Edwin Morgan, was known colloquially as the Morgan Parlor Car. It held two large armchairs upholstered in crimson damask and—so the children wouldn't get bored during the service—three identically trimmed swivel chairs. Trinity was also the site at which Mrs. Alva Vanderbilt, the future Mrs. O. H. P. Belmont, threw down the gauntlet to her sister-in-law Grace and to all Newport society—first by appearing publicly despite her very public divorce, secondly by showing up with her daughter, Consuelo, and the duke of Marlborough, the premier social match of all time.

Income taxes and a feeling of surfeit became too much for the lush lawns and manners of the Episcocratic age in Newport. Signs of the times came to Le Roy King in his unique vantage point as senior warden of Trinity, which his father, grandfather, and uncle had been before him. "Nowadays," he told Cleveland Amory, "they're even making change from the plate, but I just look the other way."

Bar Harbor endured the same bitter fate, crumbling under the weight of its social pretension and the upkeep of the "cottages" that proved intolerable for latter-day Episcocratic fortunes. In 1947 a huge fire burned down several of the "cottages." It was more than an omen. It was an opportunity for some of the resort's chief citizens to collect their insurance and get out.

The decline at Newport was perhaps even more steep than, if not as abrupt as, that in Bar Harbor because the lavishness of luxury had been so immense in the beginning. By the end of World War II the great "cottages" had become insupportable. Cornelius Vanderbilt, Jr., noted that his mother Grace's attempts to maintain the style to which she and her thousands of guests had become accustomed resulted in even the fabulous Vanderbilt income's being overspent by $125,000 a year.

Money may or may not have been relevant, but many of Newport's most ostentatious hostesses finally lost their minds, from *the* Mrs. Astor, "Queen of the Four Hundred," on down. Mrs. Hermann Oelrichs, who had started out as the daughter of Comstock Lode millionaire "Slippery Jim" Fair, became an aggressive and highly famed hostess. In her last years, when almost nobody came around anymore, Mrs. Oelrichs could not stop herself from wandering through the hushed marble rooms of her copy of the Villa Trianon, reseating imaginary guests again and again, pressing on them more imaginary ice, just one more champagne before they left.

Skiing, like tennis, the Maine coast, and Jekyll Island, gives the appearance of being an Episcocratic tradition but was actually created by very specific people in very specific times precisely for vacation purposes. Skiing in America was the product of Averell Harriman, and he did it all for his wife, Marie Norton.

In the early 1930s Harriman, when he took time off from the chairmanship of his father's Union Pacific Railroad and his concerns in Washington, was considered (with Marie and his sister, Mary Harriman Rumsey) an exotic type. He and Marie proved it by becoming fascinated with skiing, a sport at that time practiced almost exclusively in Europe.

Marie wanted a stateside ski resort. Averell simply agreed to give her one. In the tradition of the Morgan syndicate's sending out scouts for the perfect island resort, Harriman hired an Austrian ski expert, Count Felix Schaffgotsch, to find the perfect ski resort in the Rockies. For months the count roamed the West. Always there was something wrong. Finally, near Ketchum, Idaho, he found the place, later named Sun Valley. Ten days afterward Harriman arrived in his private Union Pacific car. In 1935, $3 million later, the world's first ski lift having been invented for the occasion, Sun Valley opened as a nearly inaccessible and thoroughly upper-class resort. Mellons, Goulds, Pierreponts skied there and built houses there, and their children lived together much as other Episcocrats did on Mount Desert Island.

Much the same fate befell Sun Valley as Newport and Bar Harbor: Nobody could afford it anymore or be bothered to try. Skiing became a mass sport. Ski resorts became much closer and more convenient than Sun Valley, which fell into desuetude. Then something happened that never did at Bar Harbor: Sun Valley was reborn. The telling stroke was an invitation to the Kennedys, all the Kennedys, to ski there free. In their wake came the celebrities, and Sun Valley lived again in a post-Episcocratic incarnation.

Unlike the playgrounds of the Episcocrats of the Refined Reactionary class—Bar Harbor and Newport, later Sun Valley—

the old-time back-to-nature artist-colony resorts went through a cycle that leaves them as basically Episcocratic, if not as lavish or well known, as during the Episcocratic golden age. Mount Desert and the nearby coast of Maine survived especially well.

Across Frenchman Bay from Mount Desert—which is pronounced like the last dinner course, not the wasteland—stands a home called Frenchman Bay Lodge. This imposing structure in the Episcocratic resort of Winter Harbor was built in 1894 by a partner of Jay Gould's. After the boom-and-bust period of Mount Desert, the "cottage" was turned into a commercial venture in 1950 and survived until 1970 as a hotel. In that year it was turned back into a private residence. It cost only $25,000 and is being used as is. Episcocratic simplicity has returned to the Maine islands, as tourists in increasing numbers swarm over the public portions of Mount Desert, which the early Episcocratic founders and John D. Rockefeller, Jr., encouraged by building up the glorious Acadia National Park. As a sign of the times, John D. Rockefeller, Jr.'s, son Nelson, the former vice-president, put his Mt. Desert Island house up for sale in the summer of 1978, asking an even $1 million for the four-acre estate of The Anchorage, with its breathtaking sea views from its private promontory and its swimming pool carved into solid granite. For Rockefeller's Northeast Harbor neighbor, former Secretary of Defense Thomas Gates, the breakup of the power concentration must have been a sad day. (Only a year before, Rockefeller sold his mansion in another Episcocratic redoubt, Washington's Foxhall Road neighborhood.)

The glitter of resort life has shifted to Southampton, once exclusive socially but now only financially, and to Palm Beach, which always had a reputation as a place a proper Episcocrat would find a little much. The great Endicott Peabody, dismissing his charges for Easter vacation, gave the same speech for years: Beginning with a wish for pleasant times, he built to his thunderous finale. *"But do not go to Palm Beach—that den of iniquity,"* he rumbled ominously. (Even Harry K. Thaw was appalled. When he saw Marjorie Merriweather Post's ostentatious Palm Beach mansion, he muttered, "I shot the wrong architect.")

The unofficial mayor of Winter Harbor, a town across Frenchman Bay from Mount Desert, is also its best-known citizen. Fitz

Eugene Dixon combines the best of the old and the new: old money, as an heir to the Elkins and Widener fortunes in Philadelphia, and new money and power where it counts. Dixon owns the Philadelphia 76ers. It was a warning of how he would operate when he paid $6 million cash outright for Julius Erving, the ballplayer. Dixon once acknowledged the change from the old order of Episcocratic money by remarking, "All my players drive Mercedes." He added, "Sometimes I have to show up in my Rolls just to indicate who's the boss."

Dixon's style of living somewhat calms those who believe there is no longer any real money or real class, or the combination thereof. His estate outside Philadelphia, Erdenheim Farms, has its private racetrack—Dixon's other passion is raising horses —and contains $1 million worth of flowers.

At Winter Harbor, Dixon shuns such display and concentrates on injecting life into the upper-crust sports—yachting, tennis, and golf. As the generally acknowledged first citizen and commodore of the Yacht Club, Fitz Dixon's ideas usually become facts, whether his notion is interfering in undesirable real estate sales or building a new commissary to relieve the rigors of the wilds somewhat by importing novelties such as yogurt and fine wines. He is also dedicated to keeping up the standards of a place where, as one longtime resident put it, "you know who you are." Unfortunately for Dr. Benjamin Spock, Fitz Dixon knew that the famed pediatrician had turned into a political activist, then a presidential candidate, during the 1960s. Except for the occasional Public-minded Patrician, the Episcocrat does not appreciate either activism or candidacy for positions outside exclusive clubs. Fitz Dixon liked the cut of Spock's jib so little that in 1969, though the doctor had been vacationing at Frenchman Bay Lodge for years, Dixon denied him the privilege of the Yacht Club's slip. The head Episcocrat told friends later that he didn't want "pinkos" cluttering up the Maine shore. Spock, showing his activism, cruised up close to the shore, anchored, and threw over a dinghy.

The doctor was in good company. As summer adjuncts of Rabid Reactionary society—proper Philadelphia Episcocrats refer to the Maine coastline as "Philadelphia on the Rocks"— Episcocratic resorts long kept their heads turned to the distant past when it came to social and political trends.

Probably the most impressive resort club is the Pot and Kettle at Bar Harbor. Founded in 1899 by six members of Philadelphia's small and select Rabbit Club, it produced the same Episcocratic bonhomie that the Rabbit and the State in Schuylkill maintained for centuries—primarily the tradition of good conversation with all the distinguished members rotating the cooking chores. The Pot and Kettle's toasts have always been considered a central portion of its ritual. Two toasts are drunk at every dinner, one to the Pot and Kettle and one to the president. But when Franklin Roosevelt came to the club's dinner, the fifth president to do so, he was snubbed there as elsewhere. The toast was drunk to the Constitution instead of the president.

Even at play, certain principles will be upheld by Episcocrats. They bow their heads before no one who meets with their disapproval, from the president on down.

CHAPTER

17

To Reign Always

In 1905 Sara Roosevelt received what she recorded in her diary as "quite a startling announcement"—her son, Franklin, still at Harvard, wanted to marry his cousin Eleanor Roosevelt. (He had proposed when Eleanor came up to Boston and the couple visited Groton.) Eleanor was, to Sara's mind, no prize catch, and down through her son's New Deal, Sara never shied from telling him what was on her mind. If it did not conform to her ideal of the life of an Episcocratic Hudson River gentleman, it was something to tell Franklin, and that applied as much to Eleanor as to the New Deal.

Eleanor was of the right family (Sara's late husband, James, had been her distant cousin, too), and she was relatively wealthy. Too bad she was an ugly-duckling type, high-strung, skittish, yet possessed of a disconcertingly serious and idealistic streak. A woman of action, Sara immediately tried to sidetrack Franklin's plans. She took her son with her to Washington. There they visited Joseph Hodges Choate, a ranking Episcocrat, Sara's old friend, and Cousin Theodore's ambassador to England. He happened to be back in the capital to confer about the Russo-Japanese War and was the perfect man to spirit Franklin away from Eleanor. Sara lost no time in making her pitch: Would Choate take her son back to England with him as secretary? Sorry, Choate replied, in his early twenties he was too young. So it was marriage for Franklin and not, for the moment, government.

A government job: It was Sara Roosevelt's first impulse. For a century now, government has been dominated at its highest levels by Episcocrats, thanks to the old-family lines that ease entry and the education that gives them desire and equipment to perform public service jobs. Nevertheless, Episcocrats have long carried on a love-hate relationship with the government. The Public-minded Patricians were spurred by the example of the Roosevelt dynasties and their network of similar-minded friends to look on Washington as their place of natural habitation. There has also been a strong undertow of Refined Reactionaries in government, even Rabid Reactionaries, who assail it bitterly from within. Both these latter groups believe government's chief job is to preserve and enhance the house that Episcocratic dollars built. The policies of the second Roosevelt combined with "betrayal" of his background drove most Refined Reactionaries out of politics altogether, mumbling half-manic threats against "That Man" and forming the core of the upper-class flat-earth conservatism that survives in some boardrooms and hunting clubs. Since Franklin Roosevelt's presidency, the dominant trend of Episcocratic public servants has been away from the "Millionaires' Club" of TR's day and toward a church-school liberalism in the classic mold. In government, idealistic Public-minded Patricians won the day, leading a government that usually tries to be high-minded, if not necessarily effective or right. In running the government, they are fulfilling, sometimes implicitly but often consciously, the great function of a hereditary nobility.

Antibourgeois, internationalist, and especially pro-British, comfortable primarily with upper-class manners and with graduates of the prestige schools and colleges, these Episcocrats have been the major force in directing foreign and domestic power since the New Deal. So strong has the Public-minded Patrician element become among Episcocrats that it has even altered intrafamily politics radically.

A case in point is Congressman Hamilton Fish of the 1930s. A reactionary of the most compulsive sort, he was utterly disgusted at every move of Franklin Roosevelt, who hailed from the same Knickerbocker Episcocratic circle in New York but lampooned the Fish brand of politics so unmercifully that the congressman's very name became something of a joke.

Fish's son, also Hamilton and a current member of Congress from upstate New York, is conservative, but without his father's rabid tinge, reflecting the milder times. *His* son, in turn—yet another Hamilton—has in his twenties used the wealth and connections of his Episcocratic heritage to purchase *The Nation,* a magazine known for leftist tendencies. Though an administrator and businessman in good Episcopal fashion, young Fish is a committed liberal Democrat. Floating with the tide, influencing its course, the Episcocrats maintained their hold.

In 1936, in the depth of a depression that Franklin Roosevelt's class-threatening policies had not yet ended, Cornelius Vanderbilt, Jr., was aware that the mass of Episcocrats with governmental interests had by no means swung to the Public-minded side. Entering the Hotel Barclay in New York for a dinner one evening, he found the place full of Episcocrats, most of them plotting against Roosevelt.

Winthrop Aldrich, the Episcocratic banker from the family of Rockefeller in-laws, was lecturing Clarence Dillon, the Wall Street wizard, that he disliked Roosevelt for the Episcocratic reason that he lacked financial principle. (Dillon, however, was a Roosevelt backer; his son, C. Douglas, is one of the great government business-and-art Episcocrats of our day.) Also at the Barclay, Vanderbilt found an acquaintance of his, Lady Granard, warning, vaguely but ominously, that her brother, Ogden Mills, together with Andrew Mellon—both former secretaries of the treasury—was formulating plans to tie "That Man's" hands.

Vanderbilt, who worked closely with the president as a pollster and semiofficial international agent, felt the sharp political and social divisions among Episcocrats very keenly; so did Roosevelt. The future political landscape was covered with Public-minded Patricians that Vanderbilt could hardly help knowing: Christian Herter,* later the secretary of state, had

* Intriguingly, Herter substituted the Browning School in New York for St. Paul's when he provided the editors of *Who's Who* with his eductional back-

gone to St. Paul's with him, and Allen W. Dulles, future CIA director and brother of a secretary of state, married a young lady, Fanny Billings, whom Vanderbilt had once been engaged to.

Among Vanderbilt's circle of friends, the political tendencies still ran very far to the right during the New Deal. He felt a special fondness for Tony Biddle of the Philadelphia family, Vanderbilt recalled, not merely because they both had gone to St. Paul's and had undergone several marital changes. "But there was an even greater bond between us," he wrote, "because Tony among all my friends, with the exception of two Newporters, Dudley Pierrepont Gilbert and Le Roy King [the senior warden of Trinity Newport], was the only Democrat I happened to know who came from my same walk of life."

One of the striking features of FDR's administration was a strong tendency to choose for important government positions people who had strolled down the same gilded walk of life— even if they were Republicans. While nurturing Democratic tendencies, the men and women of Roosevelt's cabinet choices often came from Republican Episcocratic families, frequently remained card-carrying Republicans, and, above all, cherished an ideal of government as a matter more of high thinking and personal relations than politics or ideology. Shortly after his first inauguration, when he prayed for an end to the Depression in St. John's Lafayette Square,* Roosevelt made an appointment that typified the FDR bureaucrat: John Gilbert Winant.

Like many other New Dealers, Winant had firm class and family-friend connections to Roosevelt. His father-in-law had been the law partner of Eleanor Roosevelt's father in New York. Born into an old New York family, Winant pursued a career pattern common in early-twentieth century modern American government. He was educated at St. Paul's, then at Princeton. Like other Public-minded Patricians, Winant campaigned for Teddy Roosevelt in 1912. He returned to St. Paul's as a master and served in both houses of the New Hampshire legislature— New Hampshire is the home of St. Paul's. He led a political

---

ground; this is reminiscent of Mayor Lindsay downplaying the same school by referring to it as "my high school."

* FDR did not worship regularly there because of difficulties with his wheelchair.

revolt as a Republican Brahmin reformer, culminating in his election as the youngest governor in the United States at the time.

Convinced that Roosevelt's "common-man" policies were the path to national salvation, Winant surrendered personal ambition to help create the Social Security system. Later he accepted Roosevelt's appointment to the International Labor Organization, again without becoming a Democrat. He was named ambassador to England when Britain came close to falling, just before the United States entered the Second World War. The appointment was made without the traditional considerations (before and after that time) of campaign contributions in return for plum ambassadorships.* Instead, the Episcocratic statesmen relied on their knowledge of one another's background and values.

Francis Biddle, Roosevelt's National Labor Relations Board chairman and then his attorney general, followed a path very similar to Winant's and ended up even more powerful. Biddle was also an old, personal acquaintance of Roosevelt's. He first began to admire the future president as a first-form (seventh-grade) new boy at Episcocratic Groton, where Roosevelt was in the sixth (highest) form and a notable figure on campus.

Biddle started out after Groton, Harvard, and Harvard Law School much as one would expect a Biddle to do then, today, or 200 years ago. He became an important lawyer for a fashionable

---

* So, apparently, was that of Winant's successor, Averell Harriman. Both men, though, had another prerequisite traditionally associated with the post at the Court of St. James's: considerable personal wealth to pay for the style of entertaining expected of the American ambassador. Lately the English ambassadorship has reverted to the Episcocratic tradition, in the persons of the late David K. E. Bruce, Boston blueblood Elliot Richardson, and former Yale president Kingman Brewster. This after a considerable period in which the post was the province of basic quid pro quo. Such ambassadors as Joseph Kennedy, President Kennedy's father, and Walter Annenberg, the Philadelphia publisher whose father did time in jail for tax evasion, were neither part of the upper class—they were just dirt-rich—nor noticeably impressive ambassadors. The traditional association between proper breeding—including, especially for the English ambassador, membership in the Anglican Communion—and the nation's foreign service reasserted itself. Understated, cautious, and discreet minds produced by Episcocratic society do yeoman service when it comes to smoothing paths between this country and others—at least in the eyes of the well-polished, well-educated people who run the State Department.

Hamilton Fish, governor of New York, U.S. senator, and secretary of state (1869–77). His descendant and namesake is now congressman.

Frank Knox as secretary of the navy, 1943. Theodore Roosevelt said of him, "Just our type!"

McGeorge Bundy in 1955 as dean of Harvard. He became President Kennedy's assistant for national security affairs and is now president of the Ford Foundation.

TR, founder of the Public-minded Patricians, amidst his family in 1903.

Nelson W. Aldrich, whose daughter Abby married John D. Rockefeller, Jr., supported the Rockefellers and other business interests in his reign as the Senate's major power (1881–1911).

Senator Bois Penrose, Quay's successor as Pennsylvania boss.

Senator Matthew Quay, Pennsylvania's absolute boss, known as the "Big Chief," shortly before his death in 1904.

Senator George Wharton Pepper (at left), Episcocratic Pennsylvanian, with pickle man Henry J. Heinz. Heinz's heir, H. John Heinz III, spent millions to win senate seat in 1976.

John Hay, Lincoln's private secretary and TR's secretary of state. His daughter married into the Whitneys.

Mary Harriman Rumsey (1912), sister of Averell Harriman, founded the Junior League in the tradition of reform-minded upper-class women.

Senator and Mrs. Joseph S. Frelinghuysen (1922), of the family that has represented New Jersey in Congress almost continually since the Revolution.

John Gilbert Winant, St. Paul's master, later ambassador to Great Britain.

Franklin Delano Roosevelt reviews troops with his secretary of war, Henry L. Stimson.

James V. Forrestal, first secretary of defense after a career in Dillon banking, testifying before Congress.

David K. E. Bruce, heading for France as ambassador with his second wife. His first was heiress Ailsa Mellon.

Christian A. Herter of St. Paul's celebrates election as governor of Massachusetts. He was later secretary of state.

John W. Davis, ex-candidate for president, here as attorney for the steel industry.

Ellsworth Bunker, ambassador to Vietnam in 1971, began diplomatic career when Yale roommate Dean Acheson plucked him from American Sugar Refining Co.

Elliott Richardson, Boston blue blood and holder of many cabinet posts.

Admiral Alfred T. Mahan, advocate of sea power, who resigned from the vestry of St. George's Church in protest against acceptance of a workingman.

Claiborne Pell, from a long line of New Yorkers, represents Rhode Island in the Senate, where he is one of eighteen Episcopalians.

John Danforth, U.S. senator and Episcopal priest.

law firm, personally handling "The Railroad" account (the Pennsylvania Railroad being probably the most important foundation stone of Philadelphia's Protestant Republican establishment). Though it was unheard-of for a gentleman to be anything but a Republican at that time, Biddle, like many another New Dealer, nurtured Democratic sympathies through a long incubation period.

He worked for Theodore Roosevelt and the Bull Moose party against the Republican Taft in 1912. He pushed Al Smith in 1928. (More than a few proper Episcopalians favored Smith, largely because of their agreement with Smith that alcohol should be allowed in a man's castle.) Biddle reported that he was not temperamentally suited to other aspects of the society that Episcopalianism supported—the "formal dinner parties where the same faces appeared and reappeared each year, each season a little older, the cautious well-bred talk, the amiable and routine minds, not so much disillusioned as devoid of curiosity and passion." His connections from Groton, from his important Philadelphia friends, and from his early post-Harvard career—he was clerk to Supreme Court Justice Oliver Wendell Holmes, Jr.—all served him well when he wanted to get started in government.

Francis was not the first Biddle in New Deal Washington. That distinction went to his older brother, George, also a Groton grad. George arrived in the capital in 1935 to inaugurate the Federal Arts Project. The Biddles' predilection for official art survives to the present day in another branch of the family; Livingston Biddle, Jr., became head of the National Endowment for the Arts. His cousin James Biddle ran the National Trust for Historic Preservation. James Biddle shared Andalusia, the Greek Revival temple built by banker Nicholas, with his wife, Louisa, a sprig of the Du Pont dynasty.

The Harrimans were another example of the presence of the Episcopal upper class in New Deal Washington. Best known is W. Averell, son of robber baron railroad organizer and Morgan confidant Edward H. Harriman. Edward Harriman was the son of the rector of an Episcopal church on Long Island. Averell, a Groton and Yale graduate and old-time friend of Roosevelt's, became, almost effortlessly, governor of New York, ambassador to England, co-organizer of the influential Business Advisory Council, adviser to several presidents, an administrator of the NRA, and shining example of an aristocratic political tradition. Not to mention Harriman's life as banker, chairman of the Illinois Central—the "Society Railroad" his father had wrested from Stuyvesant Fish—and polo player.

More unusual was the presence in the New Deal constellation of Mary Harriman Rumsey, widow of the sculptor Charles Cary Rumsey and older sister of Averell. Like Averell, she rode and hunted—she had a farm near Middleburg, in Virginia's hunt country—and is thought to have been one of the major liberalizing influences on the future ambassador and governor of New York. But Mrs. Rumsey's life was no round of parties. After founding the Junior League, she became active in the Women's Trade Union League in New York. That work and her energy and generosity led her to found the Consumers' Advisory Board in Roosevelt's new NRA.

Her explanation of the growth of her social conscience represents the best of the second-generation Episcocrat. "When I was a young girl," she said, "I began to realize that competition was injuring some, and I dreamed of a time when there would be more cooperation." She was fully aware of her father as a railroad tycoon in the great industrial age: "His period was a building age, when competition was the order of the day. Today the need is not for a competitive but a cooperative economic system."

Before Mrs. Rumsey died tragically in a riding accident late in 1934, she shared a home with the formidable labor secretary Frances Perkins, who was cut from the same Brahmin-reformer cloth. A Boston patrician and proud of it, she had risen through the turn-of-the-century social-work apparatus developed by such other aristocratic young women as Jane Addams. She was "one of the boys" in the then-rising tradition of upper-class feminism. When asked if, as the new secretary of labor, she would find being a woman a handicap, Mrs. Perkins replied, "Only in climbing trees."

She retained the social-work side of her training when she turned to labor problems, tending to prefer doing chores for labor rather than help it organize to do things for itself. She was preferred more by the conservatives in Roosevelt's circle than liberals like Harold Ickes and Henry Morgenthau—and she was much appreciated by Roosevelt and his wife, Eleanor.

Eleanor, Mrs. Perkins, and Mrs. Rumsey were women who had developed social consciousness in a churchy childhood and applied it later to mitigate somewhat the miserable conditions that the new-rich—frequently their husbands or fathers-in-law—had inflicted on the immigrants and native-born paupers. It is the same "service" impulse that fills the charity balls of hospitals with Episcocratic women; in the New Deal, for the first time, that impulse was turned to government service.

The spectacle of capitalist Episcocrats helping labor struggle through the Depression also featured men like Robert Amory, Sr.—old-family Bostonian, high corporate executive in textiles, clubman, chairman of the board of Episcopal Theological Seminary—called upon by FDR to create the codes and legislation that helped revolutionize American economics. Amory applied the first NRA code to the textile industry. He was "no flaming liberal," as his son Robert Jr. points out, but he did work with Roosevelt in the spirit of an aristocrat helping to run the country. Like the Harrimans, his family provided, in the person of former CIA and present National Gallery official Robert Jr., Episcocrats to continue the link between governments of different generations.

A substantial number of New Dealers and later Roosevelt appointees came from an upper-class business background and Episcopal associations and schools. Two Brahmin reformers, Gardner ("Pat") Jackson and Josephine Roche, were descended from fathers of Colorado's business-power elite. A young lawyer, Archibald Cox, later to continue the great tradition of upper-class investigators of corruption in the Watergate caper, first made his appearance in Washington at this time. Chester Bowles, later undersecretary of state and governor of Connecticut, came out of Choate (where he met Adlai Stevenson) and his own Depression-era bonanza in advertising (Benton & Bowles) to come down to Washington to head the Office of Price Administration in 1943; when FDR tried to appoint him,

Bowles was "lost" for days on his oceangoing yacht. Another man who marched through an open door: Frederic A. Delano, Franklin Roosevelt's uncle, heir to a China trading business and a place in the New York social empire, was appointed a member of the National Planning Board.

The New Deal hierarchy included at least two men with family connections to the Episcopal clergy, a continuation of the influence and power possessed by men like J. P. Morgan's two favorite bishops, William Lawrence and Henry Codman Potter. Dean Acheson, who became undersecretary of the treasury despite little economic knowledge, was, as we have seen, the son of the Episcopal bishop of Connecticut and a graduate of Groton. Francis B. Sayre, an assistant secretary of state, was not the son of an Episcopal clergyman (he married the daughter of a president) but the father of one—Francis B. Sayre, Jr., retired dean of the Washington Cathedral and the man who nearly completed it.

One relatively minor New Deal figure, William C. Bullitt, is a good example of the close personal and class bonds that helped direct Roosevelt's government. Bullitt's ancestry was French, Jewish, and German Lutheran. The edges having been smoothed during the generations, Bullitt was brought up attending Philadelphia's most posh church of the late nine-teenth–early twentieth century, Holy Trinity Rittenhouse Square. He attended Yale, a certified member of the upper class. He married Aimee Ernesta Drinker, daughter of the president of Lehigh University, sister of biographer Catherine Drinker Bowen (she wrote about John Adams, Benjamin Franklin, and her own family) and a member of Philadelphia's old Quaker aristocracy.*

* A fascinating example of the key part the Episcopal Church plays in the emotional makeup of the upper class came at the time of Bullitt's death in 1967. Even then, religion remained an important enough social factor for a Philadelphia newspaper to run a headline: BULLITT BECAME CATHOLIC HOURS BEFORE HE DIED. The second intriguing fact is that Orville Bullitt, Willliam's brother and later his editor, was appalled at the story and rushed out to contradict it. He told the *Philadelphia Bulletin,* no scandal sheet, that he had been with Bill in the hospital in Paris at the time of his death and the priest alleged to have given him the last rites was never in Paris at the time. Orville got the priest to issue a "formal denial." The next day, he notes happily, the headline

In the tradition of Episcocrats, like his contemporary Cornelius Vanderbilt, Jr., Bullitt was both well educated and well traveled. In 1932 he met Roosevelt, then running for president from the mansion of the New York governor. Roosevelt aide Louis Wehle, who had noticed Bullitt's wide contacts with statesmen in Europe, arranged the meeting and described it afterward: "In that first talk the two men became warm friends. There was a certain community of social background, as well as a temperamental congeniality heightened by the fact that both were brilliantly and boldly intuitional. . . . They made an ideal team."

It is hard to imagine Nixon or Carter selecting a secretary of state, say, this way (Nixon and Kissinger at best disliked each other). In Roosevelt's time political decisions often were rooted in the upper-class habit of man-to-man friendship, that habit cultivated in the church boarding schools. So strong was Bullitt's personal devotion to Roosevelt—and so powerful his religious training—that Bullitt once said ecstatically he could compare Roosevelt only to Christ.

Agitation to depose high-ranking officials also rested on personal influence colored by an Episcocratic sense of "what gentlemen do." In 1941 Bullitt initiated a three-sided tug-of-war among Episcocrats in the State Department: himself, Roosevelt, and Sumner Welles, the Grotonian undersecretary of state and clubman who coined the term *Good Neighbor Policy*. Besides his connection to Roosevelt and Acheson through Groton, Welles was connected by family to the bully days of Teddy Roosevelt, having married the former Mathilde Townsend. Miss Townsend had been a member of Alice Roosevelt's inner circle.

Personally, Welles had problems; at least that was Bullitt's opinion. Exactly what Welles did to Bullitt or to American policy is not very clear from the record. Welles appears to have been involved to some extent in a political mess that turned Bullitt's *pro forma* resignation as ambassador to France after Roosevelt's reelection in 1940 into a real ouster. Bullitt reported

---

read: PRIEST SAYS BULLITT STORY WAS INCORRECT. Even more happily he adds, "Bill was buried from Holy Trinity Episcopal Church in Philadelphia, which we had all attended in our youth."

a telephone call during which Roosevelt told him, "I wouldn't blame Welles entirely."

At any rate, Bullitt was a free-lance elder statesman when he went to see Roosevelt in April 1941 to warn him about Welles. Bullitt showed up dramatically with a document he said had been given him by Judge R. Walton Moore, a former acting secretary of state and a close personal friend, on the latter's deathbed, together with the mission to deliver it personally to the president. Roosevelt read over the document and said that he had had a full report on "the allegations" about Welles and that they were true.

Bullitt informed the president, according to his own account, "that Judge Moore had felt the maintenance of Welles in public office was a menace to the country since he was subject to blackmail by foreign powers and that foreign powers had used crimes of this kind to get men in their power; and that the Judge was also convinced that this matter was one of the utmost danger to the President personally . . . and a terrible public scandal might arise at any time which would undermine the confidence of the country in him, the President."

Roosevelt, not happy to be told to fire somebody he wanted to keep, informed Bullitt that no newspaper would publish the information because it was "too scandalous." He was one step ahead of Bullitt, anyway. He was having Welles watched by a chaperon in the guise of a bodyguard so "Welles would never be able to behave in that way again." To which Bullitt, moralizing, replied it was a question not of future avoidance of transgressions but of criminal prosecution for past crimes, which would be a scandal affecting Roosevelt as well.

Bullitt's attack on Welles's personality continued: "I added that morale in the Department of State and the Foreign Service was being ruined by the knowledge that a man of the character of Welles was in control of all appointments and transfers. I repeated that blackmail of high government officials guilty of crimes of this nature had been used often by different persons to oblige such men to act as traitors. . . ."

Bullitt's move backfired. Instead of Welles, Bullitt was the man cut off by Roosevelt. The president took offense at Bullitt's aggressive lobbying and resolved the question by ignoring him. "I had observed that the President had resented my remarks and that his attitude toward me had changed from that time on, and that our intimate friendship had ended." The end of intimate friendship also meant the end of Bullitt's government career.

Welles, having survived the ultimate horror of a widely known exposure of some secret sin—its nature has never been revealed—now faced a second crisis. This was his inability to follow orders, to know his place in the State Department. As early as the beginning of 1942, Secretary of State Cordell Hull, now buried in the Washington Cathedral, was objecting to Welles's practice of making speeches without consulting superiors. After some apologies, Welles fell back into his old ways, and in the summer of 1942 Hull finally persuaded Roosevelt to let him go. It was apparently only the longtime friendship of the two former Grotonians that kept Welles in government as long as he was.

To judge from Bullitt's account, at any rate, FDR's administration was run primarily on how much personal trust the president had in each particular man and very little, if at all, on the ideology of the government officials. It was a continuation of the network of personal reference through which Cousin Theodore had run *his* administration, a network dependent on loyalty and on the belief of well-bred men in a common system of values.

Bullitt's national career was at an end, except for a personal mission to North Africa for Roosevelt—during which, Roosevelt acknowledged to him, Welles tried to "stab me in the back." Bullitt eventually ran for mayor of Philadelphia through the intercession of Roosevelt, who was persuaded to persuade Bullitt to run by Francis Biddle, that other old-family Philadelphian high in the New Deal. One problem with Bullitt's candidacy, as Biddle wrote Roosevelt: "The [Catholic] Archbishop [of Philadelphia] has intimated that he will oppose Bill as he has been twice divorced, and has written a dirty book!" (Bullitt's only novel, *It's Not Done,* concerned what was and wasn't proper in Episcocratic Philadelphia.) It was not yet time for a reforming Brahmin as mayor in Philadelphia—like Richardson Dilworth, a St. Mark's graduate, in the 1950s—and Bullitt went down to defeat at the hands of the Republican ward machine in 1943.

Shortly after the trouble began between Bullitt and Roosevelt over Welles, Bullitt wrote the president the only note in which he addressed him by his first name:

> Dear Franklin:
> When I saw you at the service in St. John's Church this morning, I wanted deeply to shake your hand and say, God bless you.
> Since I could not, I do it now.
> May God be with you.
> Bill

St. John's Lafayette Square was being used, as so frequently, for personal and national politicking as well as for divine service.

Bullitt's son, like Amory's, continued the family's Episcocratic interest in national government and foreign affairs. After being graduated from Harvard, young John Christian Bullitt went to work for Episcocratic Shearman & Sterling, New York's largest law firm (211 attorneys) which gets much of its income from its representation of Citibank, the Stillman-Rockefeller creation. In time-honored fashion, he took a sabbatical in Washington, working for the Treasury Department in 1961, then eventually putting in some time with his father's old stamping ground, the State Department, before returning to the cash-green pastures of Wall Street law.

The Roosevelts carried on America's premier Episcocratic dynasty. James Roosevelt and FDR, Jr., became congressmen, James from California and Franklin from New York. Both also headed companies named after themselves, and James is a former president of IOS Management Company. John A. Roosevelt, another son, is a senior vice-president of Bache and Company, the big brokerage house. Their distant cousin Kermit, TR's grandson, combined business with politics as Mideast consultant for the Northrop Corporation, the giant defense contractor.

A former CIA operator who helped restore his personal friend the shah to the throne of Iran in the 1950s, Kermit was reportedly responsible for close to $1 billion in contracts for Northrop over seven or eight years. Northrop documents were said to portray this Episcocrat as the classic insider, "moving among top Saudi and Iranian officials, and officials in the Pentagon, State Department and CIA—gathering intelligence for Northrop and pushing its products at the same time." On the other side of the political fence, Theodore Roosevelt IV, a New York investment banker, unexpectedly backed the treaty to give away the Panama Canal his grandfather had worked so hard to build.

The second Roosevelt president's namesake made the most public mark on the post–New Deal scene. Besides marrying the former wife of RCA chairman Robert Sarnoff—continuing the family tradition of famous second marriages begun by brother James, who shared Betsey Cushing with "Jock" Whitney— FDR, Jr., tried to exercise the power of dynastic succession by an active and nearly famous political career. President Kennedy appointed him undersecretary of commerce, another indication that JFK, the Choate–Boston Irish aristocrat, was not immune to Episcocratic presidential traditions. According to Benjamin C. Bradlee, Kennedy once told his wife, Jackie, that FDR, Jr., had been a strong contender for his handpicked successor in 1968 if only Franklin and Jackie had not given him a political black eye by bouncing about Aristotle Onassis's luxury yacht. In 1966, FDR, Jr., ran unsuccessfully for governor of New York. The dynasty was played out, a victim of fading political talents in the third generation.

Even more thoroughly than such family dynasties, the Episcocratic extended family of prep school grads continued its influence of the federal government, especially the Senate and the foreign policy establishment, down to the present.

Groton's class of 1955 began its sixth-form year in June 1954, in Washington, D.C. New Jersey Congressman James C. Auchincloss, Groton '04, one of the seemingly endless stream of Auchinclosses who attended Groton, sponsored the trip. After the school's blazers made the rounds of Washington institutions, the boys settled down for a dinner at the Capitol Hill Club. There, the class historian related,

we were offered after-dinner cigars and oratory of several St. Grottlesex congressmen.

One notable absence among these lawmakers was Representative F. D. Roosevelt, Jr., 1933, whose absence was explained when one congressman gravely assured us that Roosevelt was in favor of the demise of institutions like Groton.

With this horrible thought in our minds throughout the summer, it was with joy and relief that we returned the next fall to find that Groton, in spite of the increasing chances of a Democratic victory in the coming elections, was still gloriously intact and unspotted.

The young gentleman need not have worried. There would be no significant Democratic victories until 1960, with status quo Republican Dwight D. Eisenhower guiding the country along its conformist way. The irony of the situation was that Eisenhower had come out of very low-Protestant Kansas and had broken a 200-year string of Episcocrats by becoming the first non-Episcopalian president of Columbia University.*

Eisenhower's two-time opponent Adlai Stevenson, on the other hand, was the product of an old New England family and, though a Unitarian, a graduate of Episcopal-oriented Choate. Stevenson was perceived as a threat by the young Episcocrats visiting Washington. Again, it is the clash between the Reactionaries—Refined in the quiet fifties—and the Public-minded Patricians like Stevenson, who increasingly tended to be more liberal and Democratic than their low-class fellow politicians.

These were also the happy times of an institution that, as much as any other, was an Episcocratic outpost—the CIA. Requiring the perfect blend of brains and guts, the CIA from the beginning was an Ivy League group of gentlemen soldiers. It grew from the daredevil intelligence operations of the Second World War, in which so many future Episcocratic government officials helped think America to victory.

"You had to draw guys who you knew had the background to do the job," says Robert Amory, Jr., who rose to be No. 3 in the agency. "Al McCormick from Cravath Swaine, who was on the code-breaking side of G2 [Army intelligence], had a flat rule: he would take anybody who was on law review."

*Eisenhower's brother Milton, who had also been a college president—Kansas State, Penn State, and Johns Hopkins—listed himself as an Episcopalian in *Who's Who*.

Given the social composition of law school in those days, the CIA became as Episcocratic an organization as Davis, Polk & Wardwell or any other Wall Street law firm. Amory was recruited for the agency after the war by Loftus Becker, his personal friend and law school classmate at Harvard. During the 1950s, while classes of young Republican Episcocrats from Groton were touring Washington, Amory remembered sitting at meetings of the eight top men of the CIA and noting that half had gone to Harvard, the rest to Yale, Williams, or Amherst. Looking around at his CIA during the 1950s, Amory could note such Episcocratic friends and relatives as George Kidder, a Boston lawyer who married a cousin; and Cord Meyer, Jr., relative of Frelinghuysens, Stokeses, Havemeyers, and other families who marry each other. Inevitably, 5 or 10 percent of mid-fifties Groton classes would find themselves subtly and easily recruited into the spy agency. They would be recruited as smoothly and promisingly as Ellsworth Bunker, who was chairman of the Havemeyers' American Sugar Refining Company before his Yale classmate Secretary of State Dean Acheson tapped him as an ambassador.

Had the young gentlemen from Groton noticed, there was a spirit abroad which, while they might consider themselves Refined Reactionaries withdrawn from politics, would lump them together with the Patricians as objects of hatred. The spirit was named Joseph McCarthy, and perhaps more than anything else, his appeal lay in his attack on the Episcocratic establishment. He represented midwesterners fed up with the slick East, Catholics fed up with slick Protestants, as much as he represented conservatives fed up with Communists. He represented mass America against the high-minded, oft-blinded gentlemen who had guided its course with their quasi-religious assurance for so long. He represented public and Catholic school graduates. That, at least, is how McCarthy was perceived by one Grotonian, foreign correspondent Christopher Rand:

Then a few years after VJ Day the isolationist movement rose again, in the form of McCarthyism, and one of its main targets was another Grotonian, Dean Acheson. I claim it is beyond question that McCarthy acted the bigoted Philistine in this case, and that Acheson, so far as he could, was upholding chivalry, tolerance, and civilization.

Those three are certainly the virtues one would trust the well-educated, well-connected son of an Episcopal bishop with. At any rate, it is clear from McCarthy's characterization of Acheson, by then secretary of state—"a pompous diplomat in striped pants, with a phony British accent"—that the demagogue was appealing as much to a resentment of an Anglophiliac aristocracy as he was to anti-Communist sentiment. In "the state department," McCarthy charged, "the bright young men who are born with silver spoon [sic] in their mouths are the ones who have been worse [sic]."

As Digby Baltzell points out, "What was new about McCarthyism . . . was that it was a calculated attack on the loyalty of members of the Anglo-Saxon establishment rather than members of minority communities." Roy Cohn and David Schine, two of McCarthy's closest associates, were Jewish—and it was their group that in previous "populist" surges of resentment would normally have been the targets of a conspiracy theory. Joseph P. Kennedy and even his son Robert were among the large proportion of "hyphenated Americans" who found McCarthy's crusade justified.

The Refined Reactionaries were disgusted enough with their fellow Episcocrats after the Roosevelt years to give at least tacit support to McCarthy's attack on their class. Senator Robert A. Taft, the Senate's grand old man and a living symbol of the continuity of the bedrock conservative old-family force in Republican politics, not only failed to support Dean Acheson, with whom he shared a seat on the Yale Corporation, when the secretary of state was under attack but suggested McCarthy should "keep on talking and if one case doesn't work out he should proceed with another." (Were ethical and logical standards higher at the Episcopal boarding school that bears the Taft family name?)

The Public-minded Patrician branch of the Episcocratic elite was among the first groups to notice the danger of McCarthy, primarily because they were the people most directly attacked.

Dean Francis B. Sayre, Jr., of the National Cathedral, described his opposition to McCarthy as one of the most important battles of his life. Sayre had political as well as religious connections to the Episcocracy as the son of a New Dealer and grandson of Woodrow Wilson.

"Joe McCarthy was attacking the rule of law and suborning our basic form of democracy, government and integrity," Sayre said when he retired. "I am proud of the fact that I was able to use the cathedral as an instrument of first breaking that thing open. The first attacks on McCarthy were made right there [at the cathedral] by [Episcopal Bishop James] Pike and [Methodist Bishop G. Bromley] Oxnam" and by Sayre. From the great cathedral, the Episcocratic elite defended itself against irrationality and lawlessness.

Whatever McCarthy's motives, many of his followers acted out of a feeling of generalized resentment against the dyed-in-the-wool political influence exercised by the Sayres and other old families, with their British accents and Anglican religion. Specifically, the establishmentarians were suspected of too much influence over American conduct in world affairs. After the Second World War the Brahmin, Anglican internationalists —the Patrician branch of Episcocrats—did turn their attention more and more to foreign affairs and the CIA. That preoccupation is no accident; State is the department of government most demanding of specialized knowledge, refined manners, special educational equipment like foreign travel, and special connections to the conduits of school and family that traditionally lead to higher department posts.

Foreign policy became almost as exclusively Episcocratic as in Teddy Roosevelt's day. These Patricians were trained in the Roosevelt years, and their influence carried over into the fifties and sixties. They were Episcocratic men—like Averell Harriman, the railroad heir; Thomas S. Gates, Jr., of Morgan Guaranty; C. Douglas Dillon, of the family banking house Dillon, Read, secretary of the treasury, ambassador to France; Robert B. Anderson, head of his own finance company, secretary of the navy and later of the treasury; the combination of Ellsworth Bunker, sugar company chairman and ambassador to Vietnam, plus McGeorge Bundy, Harvard dean and national security adviser; and down to the present, Cyrus Vance, Wall Street lawyer and secretary of state.

Through the long interregnum of the Eisenhower years these men waited until their time would come—retreating, as always, into their private institutions of power, the banking houses and law firms that produced them. Finally, they found the man to bring them out of the wilderness. Incredibly, he was not one of them. Irish Catholic out of Choate and Harvard, with Episcocratic ways, aspiring to more, he had all their ambition and sense of power—but not their depth of family, their ineffable roots. For the deep-rooted power, he needed them.

CHAPTER
18

Episcocrats in Camelot

It would be called Camelot, a kingdom of the young, but the Kennedy administration took inspiration and advice directly from the Roosevelt triumphs. Kennedy's striving for vigorous manliness, combined with refinement and proper education, was a Public-minded Patrician's ideal. The man Kennedy met in the cold preinauguration December 1960 in Georgetown, amid the quaint houses and fancy shops and several historic Episcopal churches, was, in effect, an emissary from the Episcocratic kingdom. Joseph P. Kennedy had recommended him, as he had recommended Choate and Harvard and other Episcocratic tools of power. The senior Kennedy felt he was the best of that old-line, Wall-Street-Washington-right-schools connection. The man, Robert A. Lovett, was not an Episcopalian either—he was a Presbyterian, the next step down—but that would be even more useful to Kennedy in a way, since he had observed the mores and methods of the Episcocrats from the outside.

Lovett came from Texas, yet his connections to the Episcocratic community were intense and continuing. His career had been guided by their rules. They had made his family and himself. Robert Lovett was born to a lawyer for E. H. Harriman's Union Pacific Railroad. Being legal counsel to that railroad was a position of majestic power and position in the late nineteenth century. Eventually Robert Scott Lovett became a judge, then a member of the Union Pacific board of directors, finally president of the railroad.

Young Bob Lovett went east to school and college—the Episcocratic-modeled Hill School and Yale, where he belonged to the ultraexclusive Skull and Bones. Lovett was patriotic, fashionable in those days; he was instrumental in forming a Yale unit of pilots for World War I and commanded the first U.S. Naval Air Squadron. It is a tribute to the Episcopalians' power to shape American society that Catholics and Presbyterians, hungering after power, imitated their ways.

The two decisive steps in Lovett's life came next. He married the beautiful Adele Brown, daughter of James Brown, the senior partner of the private banking firm of Brown Brothers. Lovett went to work for Brown Brothers, rising effortlessly. Then he performed another perfect marriage: He arranged the merger of Brown with the Harriman banking interests to form the banking house that still stands for privacy and influential wealth among the investment bankers: Brown Brothers Harriman and Company. Something about how Lovett got to where he was—the family connections and the private behind-the-scenes power of money, nobody but the banker knowing whose—was to have an undetermined but major influence on the kinds of people Kennedy selected.

Lovett was meeting with Kennedy to determine who would be in Kennedy's cabinet—who, in particular, would be the men of his foreign affairs brain trust. The most significant difference between Kennedy and Roosevelt was religious, signaling a profound cultural gap. Old Joe Kennedy had done all he could to bridge that gap, including becoming ambassador to England, but he did not abandon Catholicism. The time had come in American politics when the sociopolitical advantages of converting to Episcopalianism would not get the votes for Kennedy that he could get from Catholics.

JFK had no few connections with aristocracy. His wife came from the Catholic wealth of the Bouviers. Her stepfather, an Auchincloss, and JFK's brother-in-law Sargent Shriver, of the old Baltimore family, connected him to old-line stock. In a more profound, for the country a much more fateful way, Kennedy was, through this meeting with Lovett, going out of his way to plug himself into the Episcocratic establishment. The emphasis on foreign affairs during his campaign was a signal of a return to the Episcocratic internationalism of the Roosevelt years. Kennedy was comfortable with Episcocrats. The Episcopalians of the Roosevelt era had accepted Jews and Catholics better— not only better than their cousins the Refined Reactionaries, but profound, for the country a much more fateful, way, Kennedy manners and attitudes were Episcocratic, eastern, private school, Ivy League. He was Episcocratic in attitude. The opposition, as he saw it, was not Roosevelt and Lovett, but Nixon and Eisenhower. And to be sure, McCarthy and his silent, resentful hopefully less-than-majority.

Kennedy, like FDR, was hurt by the Episcocratic superstructure. He loved to have his Boston Brahmin friend Ben Bradlee tell how even recommendations from Mrs. Borden Harriman and Mrs. Gifford Pinchot couldn't get Bradlee's daughter Nancy into an exclusive dancing class. Bradlee recalled: "In Boston, he said, people like the Bradlees had kept people like the Kennedys out of many more significant institutions than dancing classes." And when Teddy Kennedy's Harvard cheating scandal became public, the president remarked viciously, "It won't go over with the WASPs. They take a very dim view of looking over your shoulder at someone else's exam paper. They go in more for stealing from stockholders and banks."

Nevertheless, Kennedy was attracted to people like Ben Bradlee and his wife, Tony. Tony, he said, was his ideal woman. Once the president went far out of his way to Milford, Pennsylvania, for a one-day visit to Ruth Pinchot, Tony's mother and the sister of Governor Gifford Pinchot, the towering figure in TR's Bull Moose party.

The combination of attraction and hurt Kennedy handled through sheer toughness that gave a hard edge to his Episcocratic administration.

Kennedy in private was, by all accounts, considerably different from his public *persona*. Behind closed doors he was elitist while publicly he was the essence of democracy; privately, a tough guy, a hardball player, where publicly he was frequently a bleeding heart. Above all, he was, as it turned out, a cynic in his thoughts, not the idealist of his public self. "He looked into the abyss and saw an abyss," notes Harris Wofford, an adviser from the 1960 campaign. There was always something peculiar and unconvincing about his public statements, especially in public affairs. What was *ich bin ein Berliner* supposed to mean anyway? That he *wanted* to be oppressed by the Communists?

Kennedy, at any rate, had a sympathetic vibration with Lovett, the private power broker, the old Episcocratic fellow traveler, that he could not achieve with the more thoroughgoing of the "eggheads," a Chester Bowles, an Adlai Stevenson. Bowles and Stevenson, both Choate alumni like Kennedy, represented the purer strain of Public-minded Patrician that descended from the Roosevelt years. A non-Protestant, a second-generation *arriviste*, Kennedy tried too hard to put all Episcocratic aspirations together. The result was something *beyond* the Public-minded Patrician.

There was too much personal ambition in himself and his selections, too little experience in real life. It had been one of the virtues of the older Episcocrats, perhaps, that they frowned on too much study, too little practice of business and law. These were the pragmatists, the men who seemed more solid because they refused to be "idealistic," because they assumed that everyone was playing their game of hardball with the same rules. Intriguing reflections of their attitudes came from the lighter moments in the grand Georgetown drawing rooms, the Harrimans', for example, when they would tell their Stevenson jokes: Stevenson, about to give a speech, asks, "Do I have time to go to the bathroom?" Told that there is time, Stevenson follows up: "Do I want to go to the bathroom?"

One fatal flaw: Kennedy himself and the men he selected had too little experience in the world that gave the old Episcocratic elite their pragmatism. His men were professional politicians or students or bureaucrats; even Robert McNamara, the Ford boss, had been an academic first, saw problems in terms of theories and numbers. A backlash faced by these would-be pragmatists was their preoccupation with proving their solidity, their manhood. "Isn't it marvelous!" exclaimed Joseph Alsop, who built a journalistic career on associations from the oldest of Episcocratic New England families, when Kennedy was about to lead the country to Episcocratic heaven. "A Stevenson with balls."

Kennedy's administration possessed the arrogance of the Episcocrats without their experience and the relative lack of personal ambition that restrained men from excesses because they had already arrived. Gone was the previous disdain of the businessman for professors of any sort; even Franklin Roosevelt, though he certainly numbered some bright people among his friends and ran State and War departments filled with well-educated young people, had no confidence in intellectualism per se.

The new administration adored the right degree; Eisenhower-era Episcocrats like Thomas Gates and Douglas Dillon came from banking and business, while McGeorge Bundy, age forty-two, came right out of his Harvard deanship. Bundy's Grotonian muscular Christianity produced an Episcocratic self-assurance peculiarly inappropriate for dealing with the foreign policy tragedy that began under Kennedy—the terrible tar baby, Vietnam.

It was Robert Lovett who mentioned to Kennedy McGeorge Bundy, dean of Harvard College, son of Lovett's fellow assistant secretary of state during World War II, Harvey Bundy.

Mac Bundy became not only the most aristocratic of Kennedy advisers and the most arrogantly mistaken, but also, probably, the most powerful. A man with a continuing talent for landing on his feet in very high places—not many posts are as influential as the presidency of the Ford Foundation—Bundy came from as far up on the American social ladder as there are rungs.

His mother was a Lowell, and the Lowells are like nobody else in Boston, though Cabots and Lodges got a lot of press. Perhaps first among Harvard's many distinguished clans, a family renowned for the production of world-famous poets (Amy) and astronomers (Percival), as well as a more conventional constellation of businessmen, lawyers, and educators, the Lowells had long been wealthy enough to do what they wanted and secure enough to know what they wanted.

Mac's sister, wife of Boston lawyer G. Andelot Belin, told an interviewer about their mother, Kay Lawrence Putnam, "Mother never forgot for a minute that she was a Lowell. She was one of those people who believed that there are three classes in society —upper, middle, and lower—and you know which one she belonged to. We sometimes kidded her about it, but it was

assumed in the family that none of us would want to become
bus drivers. Mother took this position that you have this tradition, so why not use it, and I suppose we did.

"We were a noisy family," Mrs. Belin continued, "and mother
was the noisiest among us. For her, things were black and white.
It's an outlook that descends directly from the Puritans, and we
all have it. But Mac has it more than the rest of us."

The sense of superiority that presumes to separate right from
wrong may have descended directly from the Puritans, but in
the process it had been transmogrified—domesticated, yet perhaps sharpened all the more, by the rich and tapestried formality of the Episcopal Church. The church had been adopted
by Bundy's ancestors, as it was by the ancestors of so many
proper Bostonians, sometime by the late nineteenth century.
Puritan righteousness and Anglican mannerliness were blended
to perfection in that quintessential New England institution
where Bundy began his meteoric career: Groton.

The school gave him its usual polish, its patented sense of
easy superiority. Bundy gave it one of its more remarkable
academic careers. He won the FDR Debating Prize three times.
Once, unprepared for an assignment, he created an excellent
"essay" about the duke of Marlborough on the spot and read it
from a blank piece of paper. Louis Auchincloss, the lawyer-
writer, said Bundy was ready to be dean of the school at age
twelve.

At Yale it was more of the same—sure, inevitable brilliance,
combined with easy access to anybody he wanted access to.
Bundy became a legend; the Yale yearbook for 1940 cracked,
"The week passed without Mahatma Bundy making a speech."
He was an incisive and widely informed student of government,
with firm opinions already very close to the standard Episcocratic internationalism of the men whose political, social, and
religious background he shared, including Roosevelt and his
own father, the assistant secretary of state. In 1940, in a book
in which young writers looked at the international scene,
Bundy reflected the sureness of his background and his beliefs
in one sentence: "I believe in the dignity of the individual, in
government by law, in respect for the truth, and in a good God;
these beliefs are worth my life and more; they are not shared by
Adolf Hitler."

Bundy's roots in the foreign affairs establishment of the Roosevelt years were more than philosophical. His father, Harvey, had moved to Washington power after first sinking his roots into his Lowell wife's background as a lawyer for the trust funds Episcocratic Bostonians set up for their offspring. Young Bundy was an extremely accomplished junior fellow at Harvard, but it helped, when Secretary of State Henry L. Stimson was seeking a coauthor for his memoirs, that McGeorge's father had been Stimson's assistant. Stimson had been a close aide to the first Roosevelt and secretary of state for the second.

Bundy's second book was a collection of the speeches of Dean Acheson, father-in-law of older brother William. Bill Bundy had entered the CIA during the 1950s and spun a substantial government career for himself; he was always a little peeved, after Mac became the powerful national security adviser, to be thought "Mac's younger brother."*

The family connections through his father and through Admiral Alan Kirk, who was later repaid for his early sponsorship by good jobs for himself and two relatives, were useful to Bundy. But his own ambition and self-assurance were crucial.

Bundy did proper establishment-intellectual chores after World War II—he worked a little on the Marshall Plan, did a little political analysis for the heavily Episcocratic Council on Foreign Relations, did a little speechwriting for John Foster Dulles when he ran for senator from New York. Eventually Bundy ended up at Harvard as a lecturer in government. There he performed another very Episcocratic service: recruiting students from his background for the CIA—not at all surprising given Bill's membership in the spy club and the fact that Allen Dulles, the head of the CIA, was a good friend of the Bundy family. Bundy was a great success at Harvard, beloved by almost all, accessible to all, and for a time he was considered for the presidency of the university at age thirty-four. (He did not get it, leading classicist John Finley to quip, "Sic transit gloria Bundy.")

His star still very much on the rise, Bundy became a friend and adviser to Kennedy, who asked Bundy—on Lovett's

---

* The eldest brother, Harvey, is executive vice-president of a food company near Boston, where he belongs to the Somerset Club and the Myopia Hunt Club on the North Shore.

recommendation—to come to Washington as special assistant to the president for national security affairs. From ·that post Bundy became a smash social success in Washington with his patrician friendliness, his casual, yet sharp, wit. During office hours he, possibly more than anyone, led the country headlong into the Vietnam quagmire.

David Halberstam described the quasi-religious self-assurance and confidence in background, intelligence, hard work, and manhood that produced Bundy:

> He carried with himself not so much an intellectual tradition as a blood-intellectual tradition, a self-confirming belief in his origins and thus himself, all of this above partisanship. "I was brought up in a home where the American Secretary of State is not the subject of debate," he once said during the McCarthy period when Acheson was under attack. It was the Establishment's conviction that it knew what was right and what was wrong for the country. In Bundy this was a particularly strong strain, as if his own talent and the nation's talent were all wrapped up together, producing a curious amalgam of public interest, his destiny and the nation's destiny; a strong conscious moral sense of propriety, which he was not adverse to flashing at others, and a driving, almost naked thrust for power all at once. Partly as a result he had what one friend called a "pugnacious morality."* McGeorge Bundy, then, was the finest example of a certain elite, a certain breed of men whose continuity is among themselves. They are linked to one another rather than to the country; in their minds they become responsible for the country but are not responsive to it.

Other aspects of Mac Bundy were also rooted in his upper-class background and his Episcopal Church school education. He was a man of extreme pragmatism, of action rather than excessive intellect. The subsurface anti-intellectualism and suspicion of thought, of "philosophy," was also a traditional Episcopal trait. During the great Vietnam debates he called

---

* Or, one might say, he believed in muscular Christianity.

Undersecretary of State George W. Ball, a man of more reflection, "the theologian" because he didn't want to move as fast
as Bundy did. Previously the Public-minded Patrician had supported an ideal of Americans helping achieve freedom overseas; when Bundy reacted that way to the Viet Cong, it was
disaster.

Family, education, and continuing easy success combined to
make Bundy a driven man confident that anything he wanted
to do was best for the country. He was there at all the critical
decisions that drove America into the Bay of Pigs and the burn-
ing swamp of Vietnam. He railroaded the Tonkin Gulf Resolution, in which Congress gave President Johnson the right to do
what he liked in Vietnam, through the presidential staff. Halberstam tells an instructive story about Bundy's explaining why,
for domestic political reasons, the president had to move right
away. Douglass Cater, a White House adviser on domestic
issues, spoke up to ask if the move wasn't somewhat precipi-
tous.

"The President has decided, and that's what we're doing,"
Bundy snapped.

Cater, new in the White House, persisted: "Gee, Mac, I
haven't really thought it through."

Bundy replied with his small, tight smile, "Don't."

Bundy also undertook one of the most critical trips of the
war, during which he wrote one of the conflict's most influential
memos, early in 1965. Johnson, glorying in his landslide victory
over Goldwater, was toying with massive escalation. Bundy was
still undecided. Because he was considered the apolitical prag-
matist, he was sent to Vietnam to make a decisive recommendation on the war's course.

While he was there, the Viet Cong made a small mortar attack
on the American base of Pleiku. It was a deliberate provocation,
Bundy decided. The challenge stirred his Christian sense of
fair play, and a visit to an American army hospital stirred his
Christian sense of pity for American casualties. More, the
attack seemed to be directed at him. It was too much. Bundy
called Washington and suggested immediate retaliatory air
strikes, stepping up the scale of the war irreversibly and later
writing a memo that would establish the fully logical, but dis-
astrously false, pattern of retaliating when the VC attacked,
"rewarding" them by laying off if they did.

It would have worked on a roommate at Groton; it did not work in Vietnam. The order was received in Washington by Cyrus Vance, the powerful New York lawyer with strong Episcocratic connections who had come out of West Virginia to attend the Kent School, then Yale and Yale Law School, and was now general counsel to the Department of Defense and rapidly becoming a trusted deputy to Robert Strange McNamara, secretary of defense.

Mac Bundy was not the only man making decisions about Vietnam, but he was probably the most important one besides the president. Not that his background made him notably a warmonger. There were plenty of those in government, including his brother William, "that other Bundy" as Johnson called him. "That other Bundy" was thought by Johnson to be a little gutsier, readier to do what had to be done, than the relatively squeamish Mac. (Johnson delighted in making Mac Bundy hand him reports while he was squatting on the presidential toilet. It was, to Johnson, a wonderful put-down of the eastern type in the half-rimmed glasses, who stood for the oppressive Episcocratic establishment Johnson had fought all his life, even though Lady Bird, who gave him money and connections to begin with, was Episcopalian, and an important vestrywoman at that. Still, she was not eastern; not a true Episcocrat.)

It never crossed Bundy's mind that the Asians who were causing all the trouble wouldn't understand the muscular Christianity he practiced. When one has conquered Groton, the world should respond to one's fiat. In his overwhelming comfort with force, Bundy had plenty of support from like-minded theorists in the Kennedy-Johnson government. David Riesman, the Harvard sociologist, had lunch in 1961 with two of the superconfident young social scientists who believed that Americans had the option, probably the obligation, to wage "limited war," to conduct "counterinsurgency" in Vietnam.

Riesman got steadily more upset. Finally, in desperation, he asked if they had ever been to Utah. Puzzled, they said no, of course not. Riesman had not been there either, but he had read a lot about the Mormons. He suggested that his friends' advanced concepts had no application whatever to the Mormons or the masses of other evangelical, inward-turned people who inhabited the America they presumed to speak of so confidently. "You all think you can manage limited wars and that you're dealing with an elite society which is just waiting for your leadership. It's not that way at all," Riesman said. "It's not an eastern elite society run for Harvard and the Council on Foreign Relations."

Ah, the Council on Foreign Relations. Beginning with Franklin Roosevelt, the Rockefeller-funded, New York-based organization stabled many of the horses for the foreign policy establishment in particular and the government in general. *Newsweek* called it a "Who's Who of the Eastern Establishment elite." It was the ultimate club.

The council is decidedly Episcocratic in religious and social preference, reflecting the general preference of the foreign policy establishment, from *Foreign Affairs* editor William Bundy on down. It also has the important role of selecting and certifying non-Episcocrats who have demonstrated they cannot be left out of decisions.

Henry Kissinger, not only Jewish but an immigrant, came out of the CFR, and he is probably the preeminent secretary of state at least since John Foster Dulles and possibly since the turn of the century. Very much in the establishment, but not of it, he fitted perfectly into the plans of Richard Nixon. Nixon was as paranoid as Johnson about the accomplishments of the eastern elite, but without Johnson's redeeming sense of his own achievements in the face of it. Since the time of his vice presidency under the arch-midwesterner Dwight Eisenhower, even going back to his first campaign for Congress with its unconscionable Red-baiting and a "trust fund" accumulated from poker winnings in the navy, Nixon had centered his whole career on appealing to the nagging envy of the masses toward those they perceived as better born and more advantaged.

The infamous "silent majority" was an expression for the great Protestant hordes positioned economically and socially between the haut monde of the Public-minded Patricians and the demimonde of the Patricians's allies, the urban ethnics and blacks; positioned geographically between the rich, teeming, suspect coasts; positioned religiously in a belief in an irrational, fundamental God. Nixon rose on the same Episcocrat envy that had propelled McCarthy.

Both basically nonestablishment, Nixon and Kissinger complemented each other well; but Kissinger derived a sense of balance from the establishment rather than from shrill envy. This led him to private disdain for Nixon and an honored rather than disgraced retirement. It was Nixon's low Protestantism that made the haut-Episcopal establishment—at least its Public-minded wing—swing to the previously unacceptable alternative of a Catholic, John Kennedy.

Remember: At St. Paul's in 1960, while the student body still followed its old Republican blood and voted for Nixon in a straw poll, the faculty chose Kennedy. By the late sixties, with a new youth solidarity and the obvious disgrace of the war effort—cheerfully assumed by Nixon—the student bodies at even the rich boys' church schools had become substantially anti-Republican; even antiestablishment.

The eclipse of the self-consciously Episcocratic government establishment continued with the defeat of Gerald Ford, who combined a Babbitty midwestern background with membership in the Episcopal Church and a Yale law degree. Perhaps because the country was not sure whether Ford was a Public-minded Patrician or a Refined Reactionary, it then elected another odd combination, a southern liberal fundamentalist Baptist big businessman.

Much like the Thomas Gateses and Robert Andersons of the Eisenhower years after the Roosevelt aristocracy, latter-day Episcocrats maintained important government influence by plying the network of connections built in long years of inter-marriage and interschooling among a relatively small group of important families. When Carter wanted to turn away from the aberrations of the Nixon years, these were the people of well-known stability. Even in an administration drawn from the South, numbering Baptists and some Presbyterians, the Episcocrats used the stabilizing network to land on their feet.

Vance was the quintessential feet lander. To start with, he had almost as many proper connections as Mac Bundy. The quaint place of birth—Clarksburg, West Virginia—is easily offset by the fact that Vance's mother came from Philadelphia's blueblooded Main Line; his father, a landowner by birth and a banker by vocation, moved his family to Bronxville, New York, shortly after Cyrus's birth. Even though the senior Vance died when the future secretary of state was five, "we never had to struggle . . . there was still money for education," Vance's attorney brother John explained. Vance did all the proper things at Kent—he was senior prefect, commander in chief of librarians, waiters, and sacristans at chapel, and a member of the noted Kent crew that reached the Henley Regatta in England. His old school crew coach, T. Dixon Walker, gave him the nonpareil accolade: "Very aggressive, but a perfect sport and gentleman."

Vance continued his gentlemanly ways at Yale: He played the prep school game, hockey; attended the Episcopal church every now and again, and was tapped by Scroll and Key at about the same time as Mac Bundy. About the only ungentlemanly thing he did was to make A's in economics instead of the Gentleman's C's. It was the crucial distinction between a future as an aristocratic statesman and one as a rich man deploring the decline of capitalism. It made him, that is, a Public-minded Patrician.

After college, the critical factor: family. There was good old "Uncle" John W. Davis—actually a cousin—who was happy to educate up-and-coming young Cyrus along the classic roads he had traveled personally: corporate lawyer, ambassador to England, Democratic candidate against Calvin Coolidge in 1924, and one of the people John Kenneth Galbraith has called "free-lance cliché statesmen."

It was natural that after being graduated from Yale and serving as a gunnery officer on destroyers in the Pacific, Vance should join Simpson Thacher & Bartlett, one of the important and socially correct Wall Street corporate law firms—and a traditional launching pad for government service. And John Davis, into whose mold he seemed ready to be poured, was not the only important family influence. Vance married Grace Sloane, heiress to the Sloane furniture fortune and to one of the proud names in New York society. She had gone to Bryn Mawr and could discuss affairs of state with him. It was perfect.

Through Grace Sloane, Vance the rising young attorney in 1952 joined another exclusive circle, the Episcocratic government-service crowd that inhabits the hunt country around

Bernardsville, a little pocket of political and social prominence in the Somerset hills of central New Jersey. Besides Vance, who lives on a thirty-acre "remnant" of his wife's family's former estate there, Bernardsville and nearby Far Hills and Peapack are amply stocked with current and former government leaders. C. Douglas Dillon, vineyard owner and chairman of the Metropolitan Museum, has an estate nearby; so does Nicholas Brady, who has combined a substantial inherited fortune with an investment banking career that has taken him to the chairmanship of his neighbor's firm, Dillon, Read.*

The late Sumner Welles, Dillon's fellow Grotonian, lived in Bernardsville. Bernardsville is the home, too, of Archibald S. Alexander, an Episcocrat who was undersecretary of the army in the Truman administration. Alexander, in turn, is the uncle of the area's congresswoman, crusty, pipe-smoking, independently wealthy Millicent Fenwick, who was educated at the heavily Episcocratic girls' boarding school Foxcroft. Mrs. Fenwick's predecessor in the Bernardsville-Princeton congressional seat was Peter H. B. Frelinghuysen.

Roderic L. O'Connor is another local dignitary; after St. Paul's and Yale, O'Connor followed a well-worn path from legislative assistant for an important senator (John Foster Dulles) to the State Department and rose to be undersecretary under Eisenhower. Norman Armour, heir to the Armour meat business, yet another church school product (Groton), rode his Chicago Episcocratic family to become ambassador to Guatemala, Chile, and Argentina from Roosevelt's time into Eisenhower's. A more local, but more socially impressive, name belongs to Hamilton Fish Kean; his first two names come from the family prominent in New York politics, his last from a family prominent in New Jersey politics. Malcolm Forbes, the active Episcopalian, balloonist, and publisher of *Forbes* magazine, has a Far Hills estate called Timberfields.

The "Mountain Colony," as the locals call the prominent folks, frequents the Essex Fox Hounds with the Dillons, the pharmaceutical Mercks—and Jacqueline Kennedy Onassis, a

---

* As an example of some of the rewards of shifting between business and government service, still another Dillon, Read executive, Peter M. Flanigan, helped swing the lucrative first issue of Postal Service bonds to Dillon, Read while he was in the Nixon White House. James V. Forrestal set the pattern for moving from the top of Dillon, Read to the top of the federal government by becoming the first secretary of defense in 1947.

Blessing pack and huntsmen before riding to hounds. Long Green, Maryland, 1941.

The Prince of Wales with grande dame Mrs. August Belmont at Belmont Park, 1924.

Thirty-five years earlier, August Belmont takes reins in style.

An 1892 engraving of coaching party leaving the Claremont Inn, on newly opened Riverside Drive.

A Currier and Ives etching of fast traffic on Harlem Lane, 1870. Cornelius Vanderbilt, "the Commodore" and family founder, drives in the foreground.

R. V. Reves awaits the start of a 1926 Essex Fox Hounds meet, where Douglas Dillon now rides.

Mrs. Amory S. Carhart, 1936, wife of the master of foxhounds of the Warrenton Pack in the Virginia horse country.

Charles Cary Rumsey, whose New Dealer wife, Mary Harriman, died in a fall from her horse.

woman of polyglot background and marriages, but with in-law relationship to the Episcocratic Auchinclosses. For inspiration, the hunt country Episcocrats attend St.-John's-on-the-Mountain Church in Bernardsville, one of the country's few important Episcopal churches in a rural area. All that power and glory are tucked away in the same type of rolling hillside that seems to grow tall Episcocratic timber on Boston's North Shore, Long Island's Locust Valley, the Philadelphia Main Line, and the Maryland and Virginia countryside around Washington.

Vance did not let perfection stagnate. If he had all the advantages, he could also get the job done; he made sure there was no question about that. Working for Kennedy, McNamara, Lyndon Johnson, first handling procurement and contracting for the Vietnam army and then serving as a chief peace negotiator in Paris, Vance was later tapped for ad hoc troubleshooting assignments as diverse as quelling black rioting in Detroit and Panamanian rioting in the Canal Zone—a classic Episcocratic generalist and insider. As secretary of state he was no Kissinger—no brilliant thinker, no grand designer, no charming and open host to reporters, no charismatic superman. He had the good Episcopal virtues, the strengths of the church schools: calm, persuasive, pragmatic, gentlemanly, nonideological, nonintellectual, a Man Who Gets Things Done.

Vance did not accomplish the sweeping deals of Kissinger partly because he did not try. Vance is much more the manager of the State Department than its superstar, with the department lending him logistical support. By all accounts, he has lifted esprit de corps in the State Department much higher than the self-promoting, nonretiring Kissinger ever could. He is their man, a man of their background and world view; no reader of thick tomes at Harvard, no self-made man, but a man of the system who came up the right way and knows how to treat his subordinates the right way as well. For the State Department, it has been a return to normality.

The foreign service and the CIA never did lose their attraction for ambitious young Episcocrats. Rooted in a national service ethic, spurred by the highbrow manipulations of the Office of Strategic Services during the Second World War, injected with new blood through recruitment by figures like McGeorge Bundy, the CIA and the foreign service continued as a haven for well-educated young men of birth.

During the cold war a trend toward a hard-nosed, tougher-than-thou stance was germinated by the McCarthyite suggestion of striped-pants softness. The Bundys and the Episcocrats they recruited for the CIA were forced to show the low-Protestant and Catholic generals that Ivy League Episcocrats could be tough, too. John Train viewed the CIA process from the point of view of his alma mater, Groton:

> Everybody was rather encouraged toward Washington, whether suited for it or not. It was felt that as a civil servant one could dash forward like St. George dispelling dragons, clearing away materialists and skeptics from the highway of Christian progress. Nobody presented the problem as a collision of imagination and perhaps conscience versus politics, routine and the need to "win." As a result, after the war dozens and probably hundreds of Grotties wandered into the C.I.A. and similar agencies, were trained at large trouble and expense, and after a few years, just as they were getting valuable, quit to go to law school, yielding their places to a more hard-boiled professional type. The postwar "white-shoe" contingent has now largely vanished from Washington, like snow in summer. Things were not as they expected. The ones that have survived are often the old school misfits, hardy characters who were disillusioned before they arrived.

This was published in 1960, so Train lacked the knowledge of the impending Kennedy aristocracy and the well-bred Episcocrats from the Ivy League playing hardball. McGeorge Bundy was surely no misfit; he was as born and bred to be a high diplomat as any American has ever been. He did represent the distillation of the outer qualities Train mentions: the unquestioning turn to Washington; the Christian muscles that cleared away doubters, skeptics, and materialists (including those dialectical Communist ones). Both Bundys survived well the challenge of political routine and the need to win, to say nothing of whatever moral questions might have confronted them.

Nor, perhaps, was Train aware of Episcocratic CIA leaders like Lyman B. Kirkpatrick, Jr., the Princeton-educated executive director whose role in dispensing false information overseas has been questioned. Between William Bundy, Robert Amory, Lyman Kirkpatrick, and other proud bearers of haut-Episcopal family names, the CIA never suffered seriously from the "white shoe" drought seen by Train. The prep schools did not teach "dirty tricks." They did teach success. When the choice came to being a gentleman or a success, the definition of *gentleman* could acquire flexibility.

When Nixon took over, the Episcocrats had to change their approach. The new president, suspicious of the eastern elite, wanted to reduce everything to a democratic equalizer—money. Fortunately many Episcocrats had plenty. Though Nixon did not know it, he was practicing the good old British tradition called place buying. Nixon sold more ambassadorships than anyone ever, naming no fewer than thirty-one known contributors, and the old Episcocratic gentry were among the most active participants. J. Fife Symington, Jr., of a haut-Episcopal family,* contributed a secret $100,000 through Nixon's former personal counsel Herbert Kalmbach and in return was named envoy to Trinidad and Tobago. The late Vincent de Roulet, who along with his late mother-in-law, Joan Whitney Payson, the sportswoman owner of the New York Mets, was a substantial contributor to the 1968 presidential campaign of Richard Nixon, became ambassador to Jamaica after Nixon won. The new ambassador agreed to give the Committee to Re-elect the President $100,000 in exchange for an ambassadorship in Europe, Kalmbach testified. Joan's cousin Cornelius Vanderbilt ("Sonny") Whitney, in and out of

---

* Other Symingtons in government recently included Stuart, Missouri senator until 1976 and a major force in the National Cathedral, and his son James, President Johnson's chief of protocol from 1966 to 1968, then three-term congressman from Missouri. Like another Episcocratic chief of protocol, Angier Biddle Duke, James Symington came from several long lines of Public-minded Patricians. When asked recently whether he would like the job back, he replied, "In the words of my great-grandfather, Secretary of State John Hay, no man ever takes the same job twice."

businesses all his life, decided to try for another. He secretly gave a quarter of a million dollars in the expectation of being posted to Madrid. He asked for (and got) a refund when the State Department, expecting even well-bred diplomats to bring aboard some foreign service experience, managed to persuade Nixon not to nominate him. It is a great mystery why the Groton-oriented Whitney family, full of money and position and intermarried with Vanderbilts and Hays and Paynes and Symingtons and Roosevelts, found it more difficult than descendants of other nineteenth-century barons to stay out of trouble in the twentieth century.

Yet another Whitney, Joan's brother "Jock," took the lead in a specialized branch of Episcocratic service to the country—acting as a CIA front. The grandson of Theodore Roosevelt's secretary of state, John Hay, Jock Whitney was the original owner of record of Forum World Features, a front created by the CIA in 1966 to supply newspapers and magazines around the world with right-minded information about politics and other subjects. His long, solid Episcocratic career made Whitney a good front; he had such solid credentials. He was replaced as the owner of record in early 1973 by Richard Mellon Scaife, an Episcocrat-connected trustee of Deerfield Academy, with major interests in his family's banking and oil holdings. He gave $1 million to Nixon's reelection campaign.

What of the rest of the government—the former "Millionaires' Club" of the Senate, for example? While the old-family Episcopalians lost the massive dominance they enjoyed during their cooperation with the big-business juggernaut in the early twentieth century, the number of Episcopalian senators in 1977—eighteen—was still nine times the 2 percent of the population at large who belong to the church. A substantial number of these men are the inheritors of the proud old-family Episcopal tradition in the Senate. Until he lost in the 1976 elections, there was Robert A. Taft, Jr., direct descendant of a family that dominated government to the extent of supplying a president and Supreme Court justice and dominated the Episcopal religion to the extent of founding the Taft School. The family of Harry C. Byrd goes far back into the ancient Virginia where the Anglican Church first and most completely took root in the otherwise nonconformist solid ground of America.

Payne's son John Hay "Jock" Whitney as ambassador to Great Britain, 1956.

Payne Whitney as squash player; his wife, Helen Hay Whitney, became queen of American horse racing.

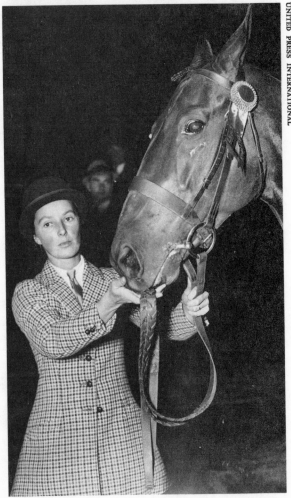

Jock Whitney's first wife, "Liz" Altemus Whitney, the most famous horsewoman of her day.

The young Jock Whitney is introduced to the sport of kings by mother Helen Hay Whitney.

Gertrude Vanderbilt Whitney, wife of Harry Payne Whitney (the brother of "plain" Payne), in her role as patroness of American art.

Probably the best current symbol of the continuation of an aristocratic Episcopal tradition in the Senate is Claiborne Pell, the Democratic senator from Rhode Island. His father, Herbert Claiborne Pell, was a neighbor of Franklin Roosevelt at Hyde Park on the patroon-dominated stretches of the upper Hudson River. The senior Pell was brought up among the idle-rich class that Theodore Roosevelt hated so much, drifting through Newport and Tuxedo Park. In response he developed attitudes much like TR's—a thoroughgoing and quasi-religious aristocratic disdain for the small-thinking self-preoccupation and vulgar excess that the Refined Reactionaries were showing an increasingly appalled nation.

"The destinies of the world were handed to them on a plate in 1920," he wrote. "Their piglike rush for immediate profits knocked over the whole feast in nine years. These are the people, with an ignorance equaled only by their impudence, who set themselves up as the proper leaders of the country." Pell took a rather dim view of human nature, considering both the bourgeois and aristocrat completely selfish, but he tended to favor the aristocrat, who at least thought of his grandsons while the bourgeois thought only of himself. Despite the continuation of this very Episcocratic combination of cynicism and superiority at Newport's St. George's School, young Claiborne Pell grew up to become a liberal Democratic senator beginning in Kennedy's Camelot.

Most of today's Episcopalian senators (twelve of the eighteen) are not Democrats. Many are not descendants of old-line families, but come—like Barry Goldwater—from families that converted largely for social reasons. Some are intriguing surprises. The Senate's only black member, Edward Brooke of Massachusetts, is one—making him even less representative of the black population than the white Episcopalians are of the whites. Spark Matsunaga of Hawaii is another, an illustration, perhaps, of the tendency of the upwardly mobile to associate with the Anglican Church. Wide-open Wyoming has the demographically unlikely distinction of being one of two states with two Episcopal senators. The most recently elected (1976), Malcolm Wallop, is not only an Episcopalian but the son of English immigrants. He had to do fancy talking during his campaign to convince natives that a New York–born, Yale-educated type was not a carpetbagger. That task was made easier by his resounding success in the ranching business since he arrived in Wyoming.

The other state with all-Episcopal Senate representation is Rhode Island, where John Hubbard Chafee was elected in 1976 to join Pell. Maryland had two Episcopalians. Extending back to Senator Bruce and the Episcocratic father-son team of Millard and Joseph Tydings, its Senate delegation has been markedly homogeneous. Then Senator Mathias's former colleague, J. Glenn Beall, Jr., lost to Paul Sarbanes, lawyer son of Greek immigrant parents, in 1976, signaling to some the changing of the guard in Maryland from old Waspocracy to newer ethnic politics, represented by former Vice President Spiro Agnew and former governor Marvin Mandel. The change has not demolished Maryland's susceptibility to control by a tight and none-too-scrupulous group of insiders, as the political careers—ending in court—of those two gentlemen show.

Maryland's remaining Episcopal senator, Mac Mathias, is the very embodiment of the pipe-smoking, wainscot-library, Anglophiliac gentleman. In Mathias's view, no trace of an old boys' network is left in government. "I don't see any validity to that idea," he remarks dismissively. "Why, the biggest old boy in town is Nelson Rockefeller, and he's a Baptist."

True. A Rockefeller can be whatever he wants; the Connecticut branch, for example, has followed its class and joined the Episcopal Church. It is also true that government in Washington is not run as in the bad old Aldrich-Penrose days, when building an Episcopal cathedral to the skies showed the limitless aspirations and confidence of the Episcocratic elite. But Episcopalians retained a larger chunk of political power on a national level than any other religious denomination—while they remain the smallest well-known religious group in America.

As the cream of society, even in the South, Episcopalians continued to make their way in the Carter administration. The country's two biggest and fastest-growing Episcopal parishes are now in the South—St. Michael's and All Angels in

Dallas and the Cathedral of St. Philip in Atlanta. And of the eighteen cabinet officers and other top executives appointed by Jimmy Carter, four were Episcopalians—more than any other denomination.

Take Hodding Carter III, spokesman for the State Department. This other Carter is a product of Exeter and Princeton, offspring of Faulknerian local gentry who send their sons away to Ivy League schools. Carter's father was Hodding, Jr., publisher of the *Delta Democrat-Times in* Greenville, Mississippi. The father was known around town as Big. Besides serving as a vestryman of St. James Episcopal Church and as a local honcho for the Boy Scouts, the Rotary Club, and all other power structures of a small town, Big wrote searing editorials against the remnants of the Huey Long crowd across the border in Louisiana and against the segregation-obsessed legislators and cutthroats of his own state, earning him widespread disdain and a Pulitzer Prize for editorials.

The staunch position of the Hodding Carters, their Public-minded Patrician attitude, led to this analysis in the *New York Times*: "For liberal Southerners, Hodding Carter 3d's decision to join the Jimmy Carter campaign staff was symbolically as important as the endorsement by Andrew Young—whose curious pronouncements the Mississippian is now obliged to interpret to the world." With Little Hodding, the Episcopalians continued in the forefront of understated reform. Given the centrist mood of a country that elected Carter, the Public-minded Patricians may well possess the political faith of the late seventies and beyond.

Things were changing in Washington, the city that sits beneath the grand but unfinished cathedral. The many Episcopalians were changing with them—and continuing to lead in the changing government.

"The Law in Its Majestic Equality"

The Seymours were on the spot. Uptown, in the government sector, Whitney North Seymour, Jr., United States attorney for the Southern District of New York, suddenly realized that an assistant, a longtime close colleague, had involved his office in a huge confrontation with General Motors. There was more than a little irony in this. In 1969, Seymour had been appointed by President Nixon as a "safe" Republican prosecutor. The understanding, if not the direct order, was that Seymour would not go after corporations prominently represented—if not always listed on the books—with the Nixon Finance Committee.

Downtown, in the private sector, the U.S. attorney's father, Whitney North Seymour, was being pressed by increasingly vocal peace activists within the New York Bar Association actively to use that organization, over which Seymour had presided for nearly twenty years, as a tool for agitating against the Vietnam War. Seymour wasn't having any. Being what a colleague called "the quintessential bar association lawyer," he would present formidable opposition.

Being a "bar association lawyer" implied a lot more about

a lawyer's background and connections—and therefore about his power—than most professional organizations did. Both Seymours, probably the country's best-known father-son lawyer team, were massive blocks of background and connections. They were quintessential Episcocratic lawyers, too. Their credentials were unmistakable. Both belonged to New York's Church Club, the old-line organization that allows members to contribute to Episcopal seminary students and to meet their social and professional peers. Socially, the Seymours come from an old Episcocratic family rooted in Anglophilia. When the American Bar Association, of which he was then president, held its 1971 convention in London, Seymour escorted Princess Margaret at a garden party (an indication of the social prestige of Wall Street lawyers). One visitor noted later, "The only lady who curtseyed to her was Lola [Mrs. Seymour] because Lola thinks she's English."

Seymour possessed the larger-than-life quality of the Victorian giants. "It's the funniest thing in the world," a colleague remarked, "when he's out of town on a case, at the end of the day, after dinner, to see him stride down the aisle of a burlesque house, bowler hat and Chesterfield and all, followed by Lola—who's very striking herself—followed by a retinue of a half dozen associates toting briefcases."

The retinue is appropriate to the elder Seymour's stature as a baron of the legal as well as the social world. He is the senior partner of Simpson Thacher & Bartlett, one of the large and socially prominent firms catering to the great business elite of Manhattan—and also one of the important suppliers of willing leaders for the machinery of government. Seymour stands in the direct line from the firm's founding during the turn-of-the-century era of Episcocratic consolidation: He was the chief protégé of founding partner Thomas Thacher.

The firm continued the tradition of helping ordain the high priests of each Episcocratic generation. Its currently most famous alumnus is Secretary of State Cyrus Vance. John W. Davis, Vance's "uncle" and his first guide to a proper establishment career, was a founding partner in another of the major Wall Street firms, Davis, Polk & Wardwell. By the time Vance was ready to begin making legal waves Davis was into his dotage, a period he climaxed by arguing the case against desegregation before the Supreme Court in 1953. Instead, Vance hitched his star to Edwin L. Weisl, Sr., a Simpson Thacher partner and President Johnson's Man in New York. When Johnson acceded to the purple, Vance's government career was laid out before him.

The father-son relationship that propelled Whitney North Seymour, Jr., into the U.S. attorney's office neatly illustrates how the Episcocratic network connects Wall Street law with government service. Whitney Jr.'s appointment was at least in part a recognition of Whitney Sr.'s support of the Nixon administration. That support was never more obvious than in 1969 when insurgent lawyers had gathered enough steam to request that the Lawyers' Committee to End the Vietnam War be allowed to meet in the bar association's meeting hall.

One of the antiwar committee's organizers said the time was right because Orville H. Schell, Jr., senior partner at prestigious Hughes, Hubbard & Reed, had just joined up. "You don't get a WASP Wall Street lawyer involved in these things every day," the organizer said.

Seymour made his opposition to the insurgents stick. But after the expansion of the war into Cambodia the next year, the president of the New York Bar Association, Boston Brahmin Francis T. P. Plimpton, name partner in Debevoise, Plimpton, Lyons & Gates—as giant an Episcocratic firm as Thacher Simpson—raised his voice on the other side. The Wall Street bar split down the middle. Plimpton pushed a quasi-official antiwar committee based in the bar association. Seymour pulled Weisl and other old-line bar members into a New York Committee to Support the President. Once again, Episcocrats split, with Refined Reactionaries and Public-minded Patricians leading opposite sides of a conflict.

The Episcocratic bar association's eventual swing to the antiwar side was crucial in turning the tide. That, at least, is what Plimpton's visit to Washington demonstrated. With about 1200 other properly credentialed New York lawyers, Plimpton descended on the capital in 1970. While the rest fanned out over Washington and saw various officials, Plimpton went straight to the top—to Solicitor General Erwin Griswold (later a partner with David Acheson in Jones, Day) and Undersecretary of State Elliot Richardson, who shared

with Plimpton their old New England ancestry and their connections from Harvard. While the government officials hardly
took everything Plimpton recommended to heart, the meeting
was another step in the gradual alienation of support for the
war among the Patrician members of the Nixon administration.

Uptown, while this was going on, Whitney North Seymour,
Jr., was as much on the spot as his father was downtown. His
father helped get him into the mess, in fact. Young Seymour's
executive assistant, John W. Burns III—who had previously
managed Seymour's successful campaign for the state Senate
and a losing drive for Congress—had pulled the U.S. attorney's
office into the prosecution of the country's biggest industry,
General Motors. Burns accused GM of dumping poisons into
the Hudson River from its Tarrytown Chevrolet plant. The
younger Seymour realized he was in a conflict-of-interest position; Simpson Thacher, the law firm he had joined following
his father, had occasionally represented the automaker. While
the case was pending, Ross Malone, GM's general counsel, was
arranging a testimonial dinner for Seymour Sr. Seymour Jr.
found himself compelled to withdraw from any association
with the case.

General Motors' attorney in fighting the pollution charges
was Lawrence E. Walsh, a Canadian-born lawyer and leading
litigator for Davis Polk—the upper-crust Wall Street firm of
former Mayor John Lindsay's late twin brother, David.* Walsh
was a former federal judge, deputy attorney general, and later
an ambassador to the Paris peace talks, giving him important
connections to the Episcocratic upper echelons of the federal
government.

In the General Motors case he did not hesitate to put those

---

* David Lindsay died in December 1977 at fifty-six, leaving behind a perfect
Episcocratic career. He attended the exclusive Buckley School in New York,
then St. Paul's and Yale, where he was tapped by Skull and Bones. Joining
Davis Polk out of Yale Law in 1947, he was named a partner in 1957, then
took a two-year leave of absence to serve as assistant to Treasury Secretary
Robert B. Anderson, chief counsel and head of the legal staff. Anderson, a
Texan, is a member of the National Cathedral. He has other credentials to link
himself to the Episcocratic elite—his own finance company; Pan Am and Good-
year, which was reorganized in the twenties by Clarence Dillon; later a partner-
ship in Loeb Rhodes. Lindsay's foreign affairs outlet was the International
Development Foundation, and he was a member of the Yale Alumni Fund.
Memorial services were held at beautiful St. James on Madison Avenue, also
John Lindsay's church.

connections to work. He went to Washington—talking to no one "above the level of the career people," he said later, though his acquaintances extended higher. Coincidence or not, Burns was ordered to drop the criminal prosecution against GM and settle the case civilly. Burns sat down with Walsh to settle it on the evening of January 8, 1971. They finished about ten, and Burns brought the signed papers in to his boss, Seymour. Seymour took the papers—then fired Burns.

The firing was never explained. Seymour at first insisted that his assistant had resigned voluntarily. More than a year later, when Burns was running unsuccessfully for a congressional seat in the Hudson Valley, Seymour made a speech criticizing "certain publicity-seeking, self-styled conservation spokesmen."

Chalk up another victory for the Episcocratic law-business-government network.

The Wall Street bar, bordered on one frontier by government and on the other by business, has long been the special preserve of wellborn, well-educated, well-tailored men of Episcocratic descent whose roots in American institutions fade into the mist of three and four generations. And more. Many never doubted they would become lawyers—and damned important ones—any more than that they would marry a woman of English descent in an Episcopal church.

There is something especially congenial about the law to those descendants of Episcocratic families who might feel a touch soiled to be running a family business. At any rate, the family business had generally become a publicly held corporation by the twentieth century, making advancement harder and the company less congenial. A certain concreteness and sharpness of thought in the practice of corporate law made it perfect for men bred in the great Episcocratic tradition of pragmatism and anti-intellectualism.

George Wharton Pepper, Episcocratic U.S. senator and Philadelphia's most distinguished lawyer of the twentieth century, admitted he had to "struggle to develop a greater capacity for abstract thought." Cyrus Vance spoke of law as the profession "in which people are trained to take a great mass of facts, sift them, marshal them." One has an image of a great burrowing animal plowing unimaginatively—but profitably—ahead.

The Episcocratic business elite recognized early in the century how lucrative the corporate bar would become. Like businessmen, corporate lawyers learned quickly to scrape off the cream of prestige and money from the American industrial whirlpool. Corporate lawyers and corporate businessmen learned to change places quickly and easily at the highest levels—a movement facilitated by the Episcocratic rules by which everyone plays in both worlds. Quick perception of how discreet, well-connected lawyers can serve—and profit from—business still exists among Episcocrats. Maxwell Cox demonstrated that when he jumped the Simpson Thacher ship for a rich new world.

Cox was the brother not only of Archibald Cox, the Watergate special prosecutor and one of the most respected members of the American bar, but also of the Reverend Rowland Cox, who at the time of his death in the summer of 1977 was headmaster of the Groton School. Maxwell Cox, coming out of Harvard, soon demonstrated that he could deftly branch out to soak up the golden sunshine of a changing economy. Joining Simpson Thacher was no coup of modern thinking. Joining Howard Hughes was.

Hughes had been brought as a client into the Simpson Thacher fold by Edwin Weisl. The billionaire was on the verge of his bitter battle for control of TWA. His opponents at the airlines had retained Lehman Brothers as financial advisers. Lehman Brothers, in turn, was an old and essential client of Simpson Thacher. Chester C. Davis, the Simpson Thacher partner handling the case, was confronted with the choice of giving up Hughes or leaving the firm. Davis left—with the Hughes account. He invited Cox along for the ride. Cox, figuring that a name partner at Davis & Cox rides better than an associate at Simpson Thacher, made the switch.

It was a well-considered move. Five weeks later TWA initiated a year-long antitrust suit that earned bushels of money for Davis & Cox. When that matter was settled, along came the lawsuit over Clifford Irving's forged "biography" of Hughes. Winning cases like those, which Davis & Cox did, was an efficient way to create a third-generation Episcocratic law firm.

The history of the great corporate law firms is also the history of the response of Episcocratic manufacturing and banking enterprises to their spectacular growth. The massive concentration of wealth in the hands of the Morgans, the Mellons, the Du Ponts, the Vanderbilts, the Rockefellers—the early Episcocrats and those who founded family lines that became Episcocratic—eventually became top-heavy. They could no longer be handled by one man. The enormous economic concentrations had to be institutionalized, bureaucratized, diversified. One answer was to create banking houses that could diversify and reinvest the staggering profits that were rolling in.

Two sons of William Rockefeller, John D. Sr.'s brother and business partner, each married a daughter of James Stillman, a good friend and important connection (he was a founder of First National City Bank). The son of one of those marriages, James Stillman Rockefeller, later became chairman of the giant bank now called Citicorp. This branch of the family also became Episcopalians in religion, fully joining the ranks of Episcocrats. The present William Rockefeller and Avery Rockefeller, Jr., now belong to the Church Club.

Though many of the Rockefellers of the "main" line—John D.'s—remained Baptists, their families and business connections wove them into the network of America's intercity elite, which grows through Episcocratic institutions like the prep schools and proper marriages. With a number of families the Rockefellers have had family *and* business relationships—intermarriages and interlocking directorships. The Chicago McCormicks, one of whom married a daughter of John D., are at the core of a Rockefeller-Episcocrat group on the board of the First National Bank of Chicago that also includes retailer-publisher Marshall Field IV. The Episcocratic Aldrich family, connected since Abby's marriage to John D. Jr., linked the Rockefellers to Chemical Bank. (The current president of Chemical Bank is Episcocrat Norborne Berkeley, a Yale man and lawyer who lives in Princeton, like chief Rockefeller financial adviser

Richardson Dilworth, another Episcocrat.) Recent links to the board at Chemical also include Lammot du Pont Copeland and Robert Goelet, of august Episcocratic families in Wilmington and New York respectively.

Amory Houghton sits on the board of Citicorp, the Stillman-Rockefeller bank. So have J. Peter Grace and John Phipps, Episcocratic descendants of founders of W. R. Grace and Carnegie Steel respectively, both part of the upper-class business elite. Another Citicorp director has been George F. Baker III, whose father dominated the predecessor First National Bank of New York (he married into the upper-class Jewish Schiff family of Kuhn Loeb and, until recently, the *New York Post*). On the Chase Manhattan board (David Rockefeller, chairman) the Episcocratic tradition is represented by one of its grand products, C. Douglas Dillon.

Berkeley, Chemical Bank's president, exemplifies another device for the preservation and expansion of the family fortunes and Episcocratic tradition: the corporate law firms. The new complexity of the law, embodying issues like taxes and antitrust actions, not only helped preserve the giant corporations from potential competitors but challenged men like Berkeley, who grew familiar with the complexities of their clients' businesses—and then took them over. The bar became an agent of a fluid Episcocratic elite.

The corporate bar held a number of advantages: It was a place for the younger sons of prominent businessmen to go when they lacked either a space in or an inclination toward their fathers' firms, and it provided a natural bridge from the Episcocracy into the increasingly complex and important world of the federal government.

The corporate bar provided yet another avenue for passing "new money" through hands anointed by generations of Episcocrats. The Rockefellers were again a good example. Thomas Debevoise was their first family counsel. He married a Whitney. Their son, Eli Whitney Debevoise, another culmination of Episcocratic intermarriage, became a founding partner of Debevoise Plimpton, one of the titans of the corporate bar and an offshoot of Davis Polk, the presidential candidate's firm. Debevoise and Plimpton founded the firm because they were law school partners. George Lindsay, another of the former

New York mayor's brothers, works there today, and the clients include such high-Episcocratic institutions as McGeorge Bundy's Ford Foundation.

When Nelson Rockefeller, then governor of New York, needed someone to review the state's antidiscrimination laws, he kept his family's Episcocratic connection strong by selecting Eli Whitney Debevoise.* The Rockefellers' current family counsel, Richardson Dilworth, continues the Episcocratic tradition.

The corporate law firm, a creation of the age of Episcocratic consolidation, was a radical departure. In the old days, it was possible for a young Abe Lincoln to make his name in a country law practice in Illinois without considering a practice on Wall Street, even then perceived as the financial center of the country. For generations, countless country boys used the law to climb toward a relatively loose American aristocracy.

The Episcocratic revolution late in the nineteenth century completely changed these rules, as it changed so much else. The country lawyer all but disappeared—at least from the sight of big businessmen and national legislators. In his place appeared the well-educated, well-bred men of law who paved the way for the domination by the big Episcocratic firms.

That important development was perhaps inevitable. Law always had a sense of its own importance; as long ago as the democratic Age of Jackson, the 1830s, Alexis de Tocqueville wrote: "If I were asked where I place the American aristocracy, I should reply without hesitation . . . that it occupies the judicial bench and the bar." A historian writing later of that same time said, "There seems strong evidence that an identifiable, self-conscious, and dominant portion of the profession was found consistently in collusion with the advance guard of commercial and industrial capitalism."

It was natural that the grubby new industrial powers should seek to clothe themselves in the more seemly robes of society's law, much as they wanted to clothe their descendants in the names of the country's most prestigious families. That reach

---

* When Mayor John Lindsay needed an extragovernment official to probe possible breaches of ethics by city workers, he called first on Bruce Bromley of Cravath, Swaine & Moore, Lindsay's fellow member of the Church Club, and later, when Bromley resigned, on Plimpton.

for legitimacy also represented deliberate construction of legal ramparts against forces, economic and social, that might threaten the Episcocrats' hold on American power.

Passion for upper-class legitimacy also tended to preselect the types of men allowed to practice in the new law firms. The high executives of the new corporate behemoths, converting to Episcopalianism or marrying their daughters to it, would hardly think of dealing with a lawyer—a man giving them professional advice—who did not fairly shout the values of the British-descended aristocracy. It became a commonplace that law firms "could not afford" to hire Jewish lawyers because the clients wouldn't deal with them; just as more recently Japanese businessmen have vetoed the use of women lawyers on their accounts.

The economic, legal, and social sophistication required by the newly complex industries—besieged by income tax and antitrust legislation from the populist segments of the Congress—demanded the qualifications of proper education. This was deemed to be a college degree. Previously, lawyers had learned their trade much as carpenters—by apprenticing themselves to a practicing member. That commonsense system, which re-garded law as one more trade, changed profoundly in the late nineteenth century. The new corporate law firms began de-manding a law degree. Law schools, in turn, demanded a col-lege degree. At the turn of the century, only 4 percent of the American population had received college degrees. A simple change of rules preselected the entire reborn legal profession.

As we have already seen, admission to a prestigious college was ordinarily dependent on admission to one of the New Eng-land church schools, leaving the top of the legal profession homogeneous not only in educational attainment but in Epis-cocratic values, Episcocratic background. Overnight, law be-came an Episcocratic profession.

But as the value of a law degree became quickly apparent to many of the new immigrants, especially Jews, who entered the country during the height of the explosion of the elite, the cultural integrity of the bar had to be preserved by direct means. First came the explicit prohibition of the use of a degree from a *night* law school for admission to the bar associations, adding a family-economics nail to the coffin of immigrant hopes.

But those restrictions began leaking as immigrants' family

finances improved in the second or third generation. In response, the Pennsylvania Bar Association in the 1920s instituted what was probably the most discriminatory system of professional requirements in America. Everyone who applied to law school had to find a "preceptor" with five years' experience as a lawyer who would guarantee him a six-month clerkship upon graduation. Besides that, the applicant needed three sponsors. He also had to convince his county board of examiners before he even started law school that he would make a good lawyer. As a result, one historian of the law has written:

> At each stage in the new admissions process a prospective Jewish lawyer—the association's primary target—confronted a high wall of resistance. The Preceptorship-registration system placed a premium upon social standing, family connections, and upon those personality traits defined as desirable by examiners who were unrestrained in the power to screen candidates through their own prejudices.

In Philadelphia, which developed an Episcocratic bar even earlier and more strictly than Wall Street, no bones were made about the base of selections. Henry S. Drinker, founder of one of Philadelphia's biggest law firms, Drinker, Biddle & Reath—this prerevolutionary Quaker family had somehow become Presbyterian instead of Episcopalian, but Drinker moved in thoroughly Episcocratic circles—managed to get in a few digs at the "ambulance chasers" who were allegedly debasing the bar. They had, he said, come "up out of the gutter" and "were merely following the methods their fathers had been using in selling shoe-strings and other merchandise."

When Drinker referred more specifically to the "Russian Jew boys" he had heard complaints about, it became clear that his wounded professional pride was compounded of ethnic distaste as well as a true aristocrat's disdain for "merchandising." The preoccupation with the aristocratic rebirth of the law soon led to such measures as a ban on advertising—which did not hurt the established corporate law firms, the rulers making the rules.*

* At about this same period, other professions favored by Episcocrats, notably medicine and architecture, were fencing off their preserves through similar measures, ostensibly to preserve the "integrity of the profession," but with the

To demonstrate the closed-circuit world of the early corporate bar, two case histories from the same time and place:

John J. McCloy was a much-sobered young man when he walked out of the office of George Wharton Pepper one day in 1921. Pepper was the grandest of grand old men: His last two names belonged to the oldest families in Philadelphia; he had grown up in the privileged whirl of the Victorian Episcocracy. He was an active layman in the church; soon he would be U.S. senator from Pennsylvania without seeking the post. Before too long, people would applaud spontaneously when he entered a dining room.

Pepper had been a hero of McCloy's mother, a common enough sort of adulation in those proper times when young J. P. Morgan collected autographs of Episcopal bishops. McCloy had managed to put himself through Amherst—though fatherless since the age of six—and moved to Harvard Law School, achieving brilliant grades. All that was impressive, Pepper said when McCloy visited him in 1921, but not very germane to the question of McCloy's future employment. Somewhat more to the point was McCloy's family—he had none, except in the biological sense—and his religion—Presbyterian, unfortunately.

Pepper suggested, McCloy recalled later, "that he thought it was pretty difficult to break into the law in Philadelphia, that it was a 'family town,' a 'closed corporation.'" McCloy got no offers at all in Philadelphia. So he left his birthplace, showed his Harvard grades to the best law firms in New York, and picked among their offers.

A year earlier R. Sturgis Ingersoll set out to join the Pennsylvania bar. At Penn Law School, which was not quite Harvard, Ingersoll had not been an astounding student. He allowed in his autobiography that "the law as law never appealed to me or aroused acute curiosity or interest. . . . There were numerous

---

effect of preserving the integrity of the members' incomes and the ethnic homogeneity of their meetings. It was a classic case of "last in shut the door" and especially at the beginning of the century had the effect of creating heavy Episcocratic concentrations. Later these broke down somewhat, though architecture retains a WASPy orientation. Other professions unconcerned with ethnic composition—pharmacists and optometrists—discovered that laws banning advertising and setting up entrance "standards" kept numbers low and incomes high. Later still, this practice was expanded to the corporate level; airlines and other industries used federal "regulation" as a tool to throttle competition, preserve high prices, and choke off putative competitors.

gaps in my legal education. . . . The only course which I really enjoyed was one on criminal law, a subject of no use to me during my more than fifty years of practice."

Ingersoll did not find his relatively sparse legal knowledge to be a barrier to a successful practice. He did have to get a certificate, just like the poorest of hardworking immigrants. As Anatole France observed twenty-six years before, "The law, in its majestic equality, forbids the rich as well as the poor to sleep under the bridges, to be in the streets, and to steal bread." Ingersoll's approach to adversity was somewhat different from his poorer brethren's, though: "I knew that there were many lawyers in the Land Title Building, and on examining the directory in the lobby, I spotted the name of a lifelong friend, Percy C. Madeira."

A break. Ingersoll was certainly not hurt by being the sixth consecutive generation of Ingersolls to practice law in Philadelphia; one of them had been minister to England a century before. It was no surprise that Mr. Madeira (the Madeira School in Washington trains Episcocratic young ladies) not only signed the certificate Ingersoll needed but told him there was a new firm starting up. If Ingersoll should happen to need a job . . . ? Ingersoll did. He was approaching thirty and already had three children. It somewhat astonished even such a to-the-manner-born Philadelphian as Ingersoll, at least in retrospect, how easy it was to get started:

How different was the hiring of a lawyer in those days than it is today. He [Ellis Ames Ballard, a solid link in the Episcocratic chain, who had started the new firm a year ago with, among others, his son] did not ask me how I had done at law school or whether I had graduated, which I had not. I do not recall having disclosed to him the serious gaps in my legal education. I must assume that he took a liking to me—I certainly did to him. In any event, within forty-eight hours I received a letter from him stating a salary far beyond my expectation with an indication that within a year or so I would be a partner—a happening which occurred.

Ingersoll went on to become a name partner in the firm, a

middling lawyer, an avant-garde (for Philadelphia) collector of modern art, president of the Philadelphia Art Museum, a political figure in the Public-minded Patrician wing with men like Francis Biddle and William Bullitt, and a member of the Episcopal Church's lay board in Pennsylvania.

McCloy, on the other hand, rose to national rather than Philadelphia prominence, becoming high commissioner of Germany, head of the World Bank, and chairman of Chase Manhattan. The irony of the man whom Richard Rovere called "the Chairman of the Board of the American Establishment" starting his law career by being rejected as too unwashed for a Philadelphia firm tells much about the law during the Episcocratic age. And about Philadelphia.

The heart of the nation's economic activity, New York, was somewhat more open, but it was no Jacobin furnace. The very fact that it was more "open" in a social sense meant that the Episcocratic values developed by the combination of church schools and industrial might would be imposed the more strictly on a wider range of people. If, in fact, a Presbyterian or someone from West Virginia could replace an Ingersoll in a New York firm, the Ingersoll would be the more bound to toe the corporate line.

The effect of a touch of "outsider" mentality is evident in the career of John W. Davis. Like his cousin Cyrus Vance, Davis was an Episcopalian, but hailed from the déclassé state of West Virginia. Unlike many of his successors on Wall Street, Davis became a corporate lawyer *after* high government service, serving first as a congressman, then as Wilson's solicitor general, and finally, expectedly, as ambassador to England. Only after World War I did he return to New York to start Davis Polk, which immediately became one of the largest and most social corporate firms.

Once Davis got to the Street, he wasted no time setting standards of accomplishment that his successors could hardly hope to surpass. Davis Polk's clients included the J. P. Morgan Company, which was connected to the firm's offices by a private elevator, and Standard Oil—another example of the inevitable Episcopal connection to the country's greatest non-Episcopalian fortune. Davis was a fabulous attractor of business—a "rain-maker"—and his salary reflected it: $400,000 in those days of tap-on-the-cheek income taxes.

The financial advantages of becoming a Wall Street lawyer, especially since the great industrial fortunes would obviously be difficult to duplicate, were more and more clear to young lawyers at the height of WASP domination, the twenties. Elihu Root, Theodore Roosevelt's Episcocratic secretary of state, told Henry Stimson (later secretary of state, too) that "to have a flourishing law practice in New York was a great *point d'appui* for anything that might come up." Law was soon the destiny of the prep school grads—at least those who didn't become stockbrokers and inhabit offices next door to the law firms. In turn, the pressure of high salaries and high social prestige enforced the strictest standards of caste behavior, including anti-Semitism; when even a Presbyterian could not get a job in a big Philadelphia law firm, the prospects for Jews were virtually nonexistent.

The pull of Wall Street became so strong that Davis even refused to consider an appointment to the Supreme Court—an example of the thinking of the Refined Reactionary. "I am a hard-working lawyer with no ambition in the world except to have good clients and plenty of them," Davis wrote when he was asked if he might consider the High Court. That got Chief Justice William Howard Taft mad. Speaking as might a representative of the Public-minded Patrician, Taft complained, "If you people in New York were not so eager for money . . . you might have some representatives on our bench."

A few years later Davis succumbed to personal ambition and ran for president as a Democrat. He had not abandoned his Refined Reactionary principles; he defended them, practically campaigned on them. Instead of emphasizing his West Virginia background, Davis went out of his way to identify himself with "those who call upon him"—Morgan and Rockefeller. His candidacy quickly fell victim to what a Yale Law School teacher called "the curse of his evil associations." Davis continued to make great multiples of the president's salary and much later, arguing the losing side of the school desegregation case before the Supreme Court, was lost in the political desert facing Episcocrats who single-mindedly pursued the new corporate dollar.

The connections of Davis Polk with the financial and business worlds never suffered. Today the firm's main clients include AT&T and Morgan Guaranty—both firms that remained among the biggest in their fields since they were founded by Episcocrats, both today headed by Episcocrats (chairman Elmore Patterson and vice-chairman De Witt Peterkin of Morgan, as well as de Butts of Telephone).

Corporate law firms all around the country have been created and dominated by Episcocrats educated in the proper schools and proper manners. The firms imposed the Episcocratic values of formality, secrecy, subtlety, and disdain for abstract thought on the few associates and even fewer partners who managed to crack the barrier of direct and indirect prejudice. Those values, of course, are tailor-made for the corporate state of modern America, and apologists for the corporate law firms suggest that the "white shoe" firms grew to dominate the field because Episcocratic values suited the American economy, not because they tended ruthlessly to eliminate all potential challenge from within their own ranks—by controlling the bar associations, for example. This is largely a question of emphasis. At any rate, Episcocrats set the fundamental course for the law firms and have continued to bulk disproportionately large in the respectable bar up to the present.

The tools of Episcocratic control have changed in the past sixty years. Today there are few formal barriers against people who do not happen to belong to the Episcopal religion, by either background or conversion. Having a father named Whitney North Seymour, however, still smooths the way. The old pattern of Groton–Harvard Law, and variations on that theme, are still the best admission ticket to the profession.

The result is a still-formidable Episcopalian presence in corporate law—immensely greater than the denomination's share of the national population.

Whether that disproportion is due to subtle discrimination may be settled in court. A former associate at Cravath filed a discrimination suit in federal court in 1975, claiming he was denied partnership because he was Italian and Catholic. The disgruntled former employee alleged several instances of discrimination: once a Cravath partner told him that he "might be a partner in Sullivan and Cromwell," which he took to mean "in a Catholic firm," and he was assigned frequently to "Italian-surnamed parties" as clients.

The firm replied, in the words of partner Alan Hruska, who frequently supervised the unpromoted man, that this is a "mendacious" case prepared by a man who "really kind of bombed out," "went blooey," and caused "a real problem here." Hruska—a felicitous partner to speak for the firm, since he was of Czech ancestry—said that Cravath Swaine was "as polyglot as you can get" and had "six or seven" Catholic partners out of a total of forty-six. (He also estimated that 20 or 25 percent of the partners were Jewish; most of the remainder were WASP.) There were no Italian partners, he conceded—which was "statistically unfortunate"—but, he added, there are "no Lithuanian partners either."

Hruska was willing to concede that historically Cravath, like all the big downtown firms, set no records for evenhanded treatment of potential lawyers from outside the Episcocratic elite.

"Mr. Cravath and Mr. Swaine were probably very warped, bigoted people—so many people in that category *were* bigoted," Hruska suggested.

"But if anybody tried that now, even if he weren't stoned by the minority groups, he would not get a favorable reaction. No doubt there are still some Anglo-Saxons who emotionally have the feeling they must cling together, but they don't utter those sentiments. The thought of exercising such a grotesquely stupid standard—it's just not done. If we had any such point of view, we would very quickly lose clients and lose people from the law schools. The only standard we have is to have the best darn law firm in the country."

The founding partners were certainly mean men. All three had reputations as crusty, hard-driving curmudgeons. Almost single-handedly they created the "Cravath system," which eliminated the old apprenticeship program and decreed that a man went either "up" to a partnership or "out." The apocryphal story was told that Hoyt Moore was stopped by a partner and told that the firm was pushing its associates too hard. "That's silly," Moore replied. "No one is under pressure. There wasn't a light on when I left at two this morning."

Moore was eventually indicted for giving a $500,000 bribe to a federal judge on behalf of Bethlehem Steel, one of the firm's biggest and best blue-chip clients; he managed to avoid conviction because the statute of limitations had expired. Down to the present, Cravath lawyers have had a tendency to take controversial steps for their giant clients.

IBM is the biggest Cravath client nowadays, the biggest client in the world, with fees running to $10 million a year in an unprecedented series of antitrust actions. Episcocrat Bruce Bromley, the firm's chief litigator, has represented the computer giant. In 1973, IBM settled a massive civil antitrust suit privately with Control Data. As part of the settlement, Control Data handed over the computerized file it had built up on its opponent. The federal court ordered that the information be preserved for use in a federal antitrust suit. It was not preserved. Instead, *Fortune* magazine reported: "Papers were dropped into a mulching vat, microfilm was given an acid bath, and computer tapes were simply erased."

Chief Judge David Edelstein was furious with Cravath's team, denouncing "such unseemly behavior" and calling it "particularly distressing." Three months later Bromley was back in court, refusing to turn over 1200 documents the court had ordered produced. He asked that he personally be held in contempt, apparently to save IBM. Judge Edelstein fined the corporation anyway—$150,000 a day until it produced the documents, which it finally did.

Within the right professional and social boundaries, the normal rules of gentlemanly behavior do not always apply.

CHAPTER

20

Going About Their Business

In business, as in law, the modern corporate state changed—
though it did not eliminate—the power of Episcocratic men,
who have dominated American industry since it began.

The Searle brothers of Chicago, Daniel C. and William L., are
of good Episcocratic stock; Daniel, who lives in suburban Winnetka, is an Episcopal vestryman. The family owns one-third of
G. D. Searle & Company, one of the oldest and proudest drug
companies. Daniel is chairman; William is one vice-chairman.
Brother-in-law Wesley M. Dixon, Jr., is still another vice-chairman. An empire in the old Episcocratic tradition—but the empire crumbled underneath them.

Starting in 1976, Searle was under investigation by the federal
Food and Drug Administration, which claims the company's
records listed malignant tumors as benign and dead rats as
alive, all in an effort to rescue its new hypertension drugs from
oblivion and nonprofitability. "We have admitted to having
made some human errors," Dixon conceded disarmingly, though
the company continued the old tradition of putting most of the
blame on governmental interference.

The problem of the company, in the view of some analysts,
has been what one might term creeping aristocratization, which
strikes a family firm as its leaders turn increasingly more refined
and less hungry, encouraging shortcuts where sheer business
drive used to make the company work.

"The Searles are genuinely nice people," a Merrill Lynch analyst said. "The problem is that they're neither aggressive nor competent." *Sic transit gloria Searle.*

A sign of the times was the Searles' response. Belatedly, in the summer of 1977, they removed themselves from the daily decision-making process and called in Donald Rumsfeld, President Ford's chief of staff and secretary of defense. Rumsfeld was not a complete outsider: The Searles had helped finance his first campaign that made him a Republican congressman from the district where the plant is located. That is how intelligent old-family firms preserve their wealth, if not their personal power—by drawing in the best of the new talent.

Episcopalians have hardly disappeared from the country's executive suites. They continue to be represented greatly out of proportion to their numbers in the country; in absolute numbers they are the greatest breeding ground for American business executives, though one of the country's smallest religious denominations. When *Fortune* magazine in May 1976 disclosed that of the 500 biggest companies in the United States, more than 20 percent were run by Episcopalian chief executive officers, the magazine also pointed out that percentage was a considerable drop from 1950, when fully one-third of all CEOs were Episcopalian. But it still means that Episcocrats hold wide influence over the business world.

In commercial banking, the Episcopalian presence in the top office remained at one-third of the total—and probably more in the big, old-line New York banks. But these may well be somewhat different types of Episcopalians from those in the past; in the *Fortune* survey, the number of CEOs who said they came from "wealthy" backgrounds diminished radically: from nearly 40 percent in 1950 to only 10 percent in 1975. But perhaps it is merely the self-definition of wealth that has changed.

The combination of these trends—the persistence of Episcopalians as a group in executive suites, but injection of fresh blood from outside the old corporate elite—is exemplified in the career of Tom Killefer. Killefer is now chairman of the U.S. Trust Company—a New York investment banking firm that has the sixth-greatest total of trust assets in the country, but probably the largest collection, period, of old-line wealth, with clients the caliber of the late Joan Whitney Payson. The dominant interest in large fortunes is ensured by a simple rule: You can't invest with less than $100,000.

U.S. Trust's officers have always been cut from the established Episcocratic mold, too. Until recently, the chairman was Hoyt Ammidon, a Loomis- and Yale-educated Episcocrat who relaxed at the exclusive Links and Piping Rock clubs and was a fellow of the Metropolitan Museum and the Morgan Library, as well as a member of the Council on Foreign Relations. His executive vice-president was J. Sinclair Armstrong, a Harvard-educated banker and lawyer who had all the proper accouterments—he had been an assistant secretary of the navy and member of the Securities and Exchange Commission, and he has remained active in Episcopal Church causes in New York, including the Church Club.

Killefer is a new breed of Episcocrat, who might have to be force-grown by the Episcopal gentry to meet newer conditions in their traditional duchies of law, business, and finance. Killefer is not an old-line, prep school product; he comes from California, an area that is effectively challenging the East for domination but is sparsely populated by Episcopalians. Killefer's father was, of all déclassé occupations, a professional baseball player. Killefer came out of Los Angeles as an Episcopalian before World War II. Instead of Harvard or Yale, he was educated at Stanford ("the Harvard of the West"), then came east to Harvard Law School and moved on to Oxford University as a Rhodes Scholar.

In 1947 the bright young man joined the prestigious California law firm of Lillick, Geary Wheat, Adams & Charles. Like many other big corporate law firms around the country—King & Spaulding in Atlanta, for example, the home of Attorney General Griffin Bell—Lillick is a local focus for a city's links with the national aristocracy. During the Eisenhower administration, Killefer made the proper jump to Washington from his law firm, serving as a special assistant to the treasury secretary, as vice-chairman of the Export-Import Bank, and in other high positions in the federal government. Then the young administrator cashed in his other careers and began making real money by going to work for the Chrysler Corporation.

Killefer had become a triple threat in the modern corporate world: lawyer, government administrator, and businessman. That combination led many men to the top. Killefer went out of his way to establish a new synthesis between his California background and the older Episcocratic elite of the eastern seaboard. He married Carolyn Clothier, descendant of one of Philadelphia's most aristocratic and wealthiest (department store) families. He joined the proper clubs in New York—Links and River—while retaining membership in San Francisco's Episcocratic Pacific Union Club. He joined the National Cathedral Foundation, too.

Even when the foundering U.S. Trust Company recruited Killefer from Chrysler (where he remained a director after moving to U.S. Trust), the new banker kept a certain manner of his own, a California-style Episcocratic polish.

Killefer likes sports tremendously, a little more than many of his colleagues feel is entirely proper. Too much sports is California, not New York banker. In a world where attitudes and even trustworthiness are measured by such things, it is considered proper that Killefer wear the traditional garters to hold up his socks, but definitely shocking that he will sometimes show up at the office in a subdued Glen plaid suit. Bankers in New York wear solid or pin-striped suits, gray-black and dark blue. *Lawyers* wear Glen plaid.

The boss, Killefer made clear, wears what he wants. He seems like a revival of the strong-minded bosses earlier in the century. He is carrying on a great tradition of Episcocratic business success, while overturning stultifying Episcocratic habits—like those saying bankers have to go to prep schools and follow outmoded policies that lose money.

One important Episcocratic device for control of American business is well demonstrated by Killefer—namely, the practice of holding a network of business directorships while maintaining executive control over another company. We have seen how such links tie Rockefeller interests to a centralized Episcocratic old-family elite. The power can be even stronger when the companies are industrial concerns supposedly in competition.

The corporate power base of Thomas S. Gates, the former defense secretary, was the Morgan Guaranty Trust Company, where he was chairman. This descendant of J. P. Morgan's empire has an investment portfolio even Morgan could never have dreamed of—in the range of $30 billion. While Gates was a director of General Electric, he also remained a director of Morgan Guaranty, which held 2.7 percent of GE's stock. (Gates's other directorships included Scott Paper, Campbell Soup, INA, Bethlehem Steel—and the Foxcroft School.)

In manufacturing, Richard C. Bond, former chairman of Philadelphia's Wanamaker department store and a product of the same Episcocratic society as Gates, was at the same time a director of Kraftco, Inc., and the SCM Corporation, both giant producers of edible oils, margarine, and related food products. Bond's extension of influence was enough to prompt the Federal Trade Commission to issue a complaint against him in July 1975. The FTC also intervened in 1975 to trigger the resignation, among others, of Episcocrat Horace A. Shepard, board chairman of TRW, Inc., from his interlocking boards. The FTC felt Shepard linked Standard Oil of Ohio and the Diamond Shamrock Corporation, competing oil companies.

The economic power of the financial institutions so heavily dominated by Episcopalians was outlined by a congressional subcommittee in 1967. Under Texas populist Wright Patman, a Wall Street–phobe, the subcommittee found that the trust departments of 49 of the nation's largest commercial banks—the ones in and slightly below the *Fortune* 500—held a total of $607 billion worth of investments in American industries. Those investments were held mainly for giant institutional investors like insurance companies, mutual funds, and pension funds—companies that also tend to be dominated by Episcocratic directors, many on the banks' own boards.

Of the 49 banks, the six largest New York banks—the ones linked with the Episcocratic consolidation of Morgan, Rockefeller, Stillman, and Baker and their allies—held more than 10 percent of the total investments, or $64.4 billion. Altogether, the big banking institutions had 768 director interlocks with 286 of the 500 largest corporations, or, the subcommittee report said, "an average of almost three directors for each corporation board on which bank director representation is found." The banks also held at least 5 percent of each of 147 of the 500 largest industrial corporations, a massive proportion in the era of diversified ownership of giant corporations.

Through such arrangements, the influence of major Episcocratic businessmen and family dynasties extend throughout the economy. Non-Episcopalian establishment figures who sit on boards alongside, say, Thomas Gates, are as interested in making money for their firms and themselves as he is. But given the heavily Episcocratic development of this system of interlocking economic power and the continuing presence of large numbers of people who identify themselves as Episcopalians, it is fair to say that an Episcocratic tradition continues to pervade American economic institutions. The values nurtured in an upper-class environment of prep school, college, and club continue to run the banking-industrial structure; deals are made through friendships and mutual trust rather than through public forums. There does seem to be an old boys' network.

To come from a financial and social background that largely controls the country creates the opportunity to snub it. In this generation, as in several before, descendants of Episcocratic fixtures in the business-law-government nexus had the money and self-assurance to take flyers on a wide range of alternative activities. This generation, there is a trend among Episcocratic young men—and their rich wives—to invest in small, unprofitable magazines.

There's Hamilton Fish, who at twenty-six became publisher of the venerable journal *The Nation*. With a social and financial pedigree like Fish's, topped by a Harvard education, it is relatively easy to break into public life at the top. In 1974, barely out of college, he served as finance director for Ramsey Clark's unsuccessful run for senator from New York. Then he produced and distributed a widely acclaimed Marcel Ophuls film, *The Memory of Justice*. Then, just like that, he bought *The Nation*, with the distant goal of turning the consistently liberal and consistently money-losing magazine into a profit maker.

Hamilton Fish was following another Episcocratic tradition —owning the press. Disgruntled and anti-Semitic groups frequently accuse the Jews of holding a disproportionate control of the American media. Certainly in movies and television and some newspapers like the *New York Times*, Jews hold positions far out of proportion to their numbers. It is just as true that old-line Episcocratic families have long controlled major and minor organs of written communication. The eastern press establishment is at least as heavily Episcopalian as it is Jewish.

It is not that Episcopalians have no influence in the modern news medium, television; Walter Cronkite, probably the most authoritative television news commentator ever, is an active Episcopalian. He lent his powerful presence to the work of promoting films and causes espoused by the Episcopal Radio-TV Foundation in Atlanta. After a taping session a few years ago, Caroline Rakestraw, the foundation's executive director, exclaimed happily, "Walter, with that voice, if you'd been a priest, you could have converted the world."

Much to Mrs. Rakestraw's astonishment, Cronkite said he nearly *had* become a priest. As a cub reporter in Houston, he had covered a meeting of the Episcopal House of Bishops and been impressed enough with the consequence and interest of the matters before them to begin mulling the possibility of a new career. He gave up the idea and returned to journalism, he said, after being told that he would have to go back to school for three more years to qualify.

But newspapers have always been the forte of the upper class. Joint control of the branches of the media is one example of the similarities between Episcocrats and Jews. Episcocratic newspaper owners held sway over the *Herald Tribune.* The country's largest newspapers, including the Jewish-owned *New York Times*, have firm Episcocratic traditions, especially in higher editorial positions and foreign affairs. Some of the country's top journalists rose through the traditional Episcocratic network. The Grotonian Alsops, for example.

Ben Bradlee, executive editor of the *Washington Post*, has said that one of the key moves in his career was being taken on as a press attaché by C. Douglas Dillon, then American ambassador in Paris. That is a move open largely to people with Episcocratic connections in the State Department.

The Episcocratic influence extends to *Newsweek*, owned by the *Washington Post*. Osborn Elliott, out of St. Paul's, was editor. The managing editor, Kenneth Auchincloss, moved to *Newsweek* in 1966, after attending Groton, Harvard, and Oxford and spending several years as an assistant to Commerce Department officials.

In its Episcocratic foundation—by Vincent Astor—*Newsweek*

was like many of the great newspapers. Senator George Hearst, who started the dynasty of San Francisco newspapers that spread around the country, was a nominal Episcopalian himself, and the greatest press lord of all, his son William Randolph Hearst, attended St. Paul's—which he hated—and always considered himself Episcopalian. "Colonel" Robert McCormick, the Chicago newspaper baron, was also sent to an eastern boarding school, Groton in his case—and also hated it. Another Groton grad was Captain Joseph Medill ("Joe") Patterson, owner of the *New York Daily News*, everyone's favorite blue-collar newspaper; his empire once included the Long Island newspaper *Newsday*, the *Chicago Tribune*, and the *Washington Herald*. Whitelaw Reid, owner of the *Herald Tribune* before Jock Whitney, was allied by marriage to many of the great Episcocratic families. Whitney himself, of course, is another shining example of the Groton-educated newspaper owner.

Newsweek's competitor, *Time*, was founded by Henry Luce, a Presbyterian with strong links to the Episcocratic elite, and especially in its earlier days was staffed by Princetonian, Episcocratic types. T. S. Matthews, who eventually became *Time*'s managing editor, got his job through a friend who belonged with him to the Ivy Club, Princeton's most exclusive. The son of an Episcopal bishop who married an heiress to the Procter & Gamble fortune, Matthews was stocked up enough with the muscular Christianity of St. Paul's to despise Luce's yellow journalism—but he was also enough of a Refined Reactionary not to do anything about it.

If *Time* magazine served as a voice of the Refined Reactionary, denouncing the traitorous Roosevelt administration, there was also an opposing Public-minded Patrician strain in the world of journalism, fed by the Episcocratic men and women with a social conscience. *The New Republic* was founded in 1914 largely on money provided by Dorothy Whitney Straight, daughter of William C. Whitney, the family founder, and wife of William Straight, a liberal partner in J. P. Morgan & Company. Later the magazine was sold to Gilbert Harrison, whose wife was an heiress to the McCormick fortune in Chicago.

It is this Public-minded Patrician tradition of journalism that Hamilton Fish has been following. Despite the Rabid and Re-

Phoebe Apperson Hearst, wife of one newspaperman (George Hearst) and mother of another (William Randolph Hearst), endowed National Cathedral School for Girls.

William Randolph Hearst, St. Paul's student and purveyor of news to the masses.

Stewart (at left) and Joseph Alsop, columnists and Grotonian sages.

fined Reactionaries in his family, he considers himself a committed liberal Democrat and plans to keep *The Nation* as "pink" as ever. Fish's defeated competition for the purchase of the journal was Tom Morgan. It will never be clear if Morgan would have kept up the Episcocratic Patrician tendency, but he certainly fulfilled another tradition among Episcocratic publishers: He had a rich wife. Mary Morgan is the youngest daughter of Nelson Rockefeller and brought with her a web of Episcocratic connections. (So did Morgan, who had been Mayor Lindsay's press secretary.)

Morgan said later that his wife was more liability than help in his attempt to buy *The Nation*. "In my negotiations with *The Nation*," he complained, "it seemed that everyone thought there was unlimited money because of her family, not recognizing the difference between second- and third-generation wealth." The Morgans recovered enough to start their own magazine, *Politicks*.

Politicks went under after fourteen issues, proving that third-generation wealth is different. Enough wealth from the first and second generations of Episcocrats has gone into the press, though, to ensure that the Episcocratic voice will continue to be heard.

CHAPTER
21

Patricians as Patrons

The Met was a mess. Under its ebullient Episcocratic director Thomas Hoving, the great museum had made a couple of serious mistakes. People were beginning to wonder why they were giving it any money. The mistakes were the outgrowth of a phenomenon of the late 1960s, "radical chic."

Outside the museum field, the most notorious expression of "radical chic" was reparations—a descendant, fifty years later, of the Wobblies' march on St. John's Church in 1914. Not all the targets of the aggressive and adroit black leaders like Rap Brown—the Mau Mauers, as Tom Wolfe called them—were Episcopalians; Leonard Bernstein probably gave the largest and best-reported party ever attended by revolutionaries bearing sidearms. But by 1972, when the Episcopal diocese of New York came into the determinedly liberal hands of Bishop Paul Moore, the fashionably Public-minded branch of the Episcocratic elite was involved in strenuous attempts to redress societal imbalances earlier Episcocrats had created.

The unrest of the late sixties brought to a head the antagonism between the bedrock conservatism, even racist and anti-Semitic caste feeling, of the Rabid Reactionaries and the supremely confident, finely educated Public-minded Patricians, products of the same class but determined to show their sympathy with the oppressed.

John Vliet Lindsay, the Episcopalian Yale man and member

of wealth-encrusted St. James Madison Avenue, leading the city with the greatest Jewish, black, and Puerto Rican populations in the country, represented that upper-class reformist tradition. By the sixties, under pressure from black and student militants, the tradition had turned increasingly radical. But the Public-minded Patricians-turned-radicals retained their preference for radicals of their own class.

Lindsay ran an administration that heavily and obviously favored people from backgrounds similar to his, an administration consequently distrusted by the white ethnics who inhabited the city's outlying districts, who instinctively disliked Lindsay's patrician looks and were not fooled when he referred to Episcocratic St. Paul's School as "my high school." Neither was it too well loved by the underprivileged it vociferously supported. It was an Episcocratic government, a rich man's government, one that seemed marvelously progressive at the time and later appeared more a throwback to the massa-knows-best syndrome of the antebellum South and the Victorian North.

Sidestepping the old Tammany loyalties under which Irish bosses and Italian padrones had run the city government, Lindsay substituted an upper-class, right-schools network. When his administration removed the city's cable TV franchise from the traditional bidding procedure, distinguished personal friends of Mayor Lindsay's, such as Andrew Heiskell, chairman of Time-Life, and Bruce Bromley, Heiskell's lawyer—a leading Episcopalian and a power figure in his own right—were among the first to apply.

As Martin and Susan Tolchin related:

> Lindsay's favorite architect, Philip Johnson, has won contracts from the city for the development of Battery Park City and Welfare Island. According to Roger Starr, director of the Citizens Housing and Planning Council, "an architect has a better chance of getting a contract from the city if he calls in Johnson as a consultant." Mr. Johnson returns Lindsay's favors by hosting dinners for New York's "beautiful people" at which he enthuses about the mayor. "The people will support Lindsay in the fall because of Johnson . . . a great boulevardier," said Mr. Starr.

Robert Amory, Jr. (at left), chief finance man of the National Gallery of Art, and Trinity Church Boston (below) under construction at an Amory ancestor's direction.

William H. Vanderbilt, son of "the Commodore," caused scandal by opening his personal art collection to the press, 1884.

Paul Mellon of the National Gallery of Art.

Fairleigh S. Dickinson, Jr. (center), as chairman of the trustees at the university bearing his name, accepts the transfer of the Gallery of Modern Art (in background) from Huntington Hartford (at left), New York, 1969.

Henry Clay Frick (shown here at Palm Beach) discovered art and Episcopalianism were complementary paths to gentility. Below, interior and exterior of Frick's Fifth Avenue château, now the Frick Museum.

Boston's famed collector Mrs. Jack Gardner in one of the "risqué" poses she favored. Portrait by Anders Zorn.

The Rand Corporation, a think tank that serves as a final resting place for many of the best and brightest minds and genealogies who for one reason or another can't work in government at the moment, received an $8 million contract that a city official called "really a gift." And an employee of McKinsey & Company—the management consulting firm whose partner Peter C. M. S. Braun was on Trinity Wall Street's vestry in 1977—explained to the Tolchins how the firm came up with its $1.5 million in contracts in 1969: "We became eligible for contracts because we are the right social people, we have the right values, and we're trustworthy, just as other kinds of people, who wear different clothes and have different values, receive their contracts from the clubhouse."

Into this ferment of Episcocratic reform, Thomas Hoving fitted like an Auchincloss in Groton. Thomas's father is Walter Hoving, the colorful, curmudgeonly chairman of refined old Tiffany's on Fifth Avenue. Born in Sweden, the elder Hoving managed to become one of the more amazing Episcopalians in America. He uncharacteristically proclaims his religiosity wherever and whenever he gets a chance—including his company's newspaper ads, which frequently offer little gold pendants and pins that say "Try God." All proceeds from this "limited edition" —that is, limited to people who believe in God—go to the Walter Hoving Home in Garrison, New York, where girls afflicted with drug addiction and other serious problems "are permanently cured by accepting God into their lives." Walter Hoving now identifies himself as an evangelical Christian and claims that he used to be an "Episcopagan."

Young Thomas Hoving turned out more conventional in the Episcocratic world than his iconoclastic father—though his father's position no doubt helped him in the usual way. A graduate of the Hotchkiss School—modeled on the Episcopal prep school, though not itself affiliated with the church—and of Princeton, Hoving came into the public consciousness through his friendship with Mayor Lindsay. He had been curator of the Metropolitan Museum's Cloisters in Upper Manhattan, a creation of John D. Rockefeller, Jr.

In 1965, Hoving switched patrons by accepting Lindsay's offer of the post of parks commissioner. He wasted no time giving practical expression to Lindsay's designation of New

York as Fun City. The parks came alive with "happenings." Then the board of directors of the Metropolitan Museum, led by Douglas Dillon, selected Hoving to replace the previous director, James Rorimer. Rorimer, Rockefeller's factotum in the creation of the Cloisters, had been a stolid, solid administrator —a low-WASP administrator for the Baptist Rockefeller. Hoving was to be a big spender, a big doer, a sophisticated, splashy director. He was to be a leader and instrument of Episcocratic New York.

Hoving and the Upper East Side crowd—the new breed of radical Episcocrats—lost no time pumping up action at the Met. Their lavish expenditure of energy and money did not please everyone. Hoving laid out more than $1.4 million to buy a single Monet from the Pitcairn family of Philadelphia, the wealthy subsidizers—owners, virtually—of the tiny Swedenborgian religion. In the late sixties a small Greek horse statue in the Met took a roller-coaster ride from "best-of-its-genre" to "one of the most important classical art forgeries ever discovered" and then back again. Finally, Hoving's reputation hit bottom with the troublesome exhibition "Harlem on My Mind," an art-world answer to Leonard Bernstein's dinners. The catalog contained a schoolgirl's essay denouncing a wide range of ethnic, racial, and religious groups. Hoving's more-liberal-than-thou attitude left him for the moment alienated from the culture he was trying to lead. But he survived, and by the mid-1970s his freewheeling, mod-Episcocratic approach was generally recognized as *the* new direction in art museums.

In Washington, the Met's biggest competitor, the National Gallery of Art, was moving to displace the grand old lady of the American art world. Socially, they were hardly upstarts down there. J. Carter Brown, the director, had few peers when it came to Episcocratic background. His network of family and acquaintances was a reminder of the days before New York became too big, too diverse to operate as a purely Episcocratic city. In the field of art collecting, it was as though Washington were just coming into its own as an upper-class city.

The Episcocratic impulse to give back to the American people in art some of the vast fortunes that were taken from them benefited Washington a century after it built the palatial museums in New York, Boston, Philadelphia, and to a lesser extent all the established Episcocratic cities of the high-Victorian age. Though they served in the national government, the Public-minded Patricians gave their art to their native cities. Washington got paved boulevards in the time of Theodore Roosevelt but remained a muddy wasteland of cultural activity.

Over the past few decades, however, a select portion of the American nobility turned their attention to the National Gallery. As a result, it was challenging the Met for preeminence as the premier showcase of American culture and civilization. The National Gallery drew on the same complex of Episcocratic feelings that built all the great American museums—the family pride, the noblesse oblige, the desire to "edify."

To those traditional sources of a museum's life, the National Gallery added a powerful new force—the federal government. The government's art-finance arm is as dominated by old-line Episcocrats as is the State Department. The reasons are easy to understand: The traditional Episcocratic networks within the art-collecting world and the federal government are united by ties of family and a common quasi-religious "service" drive. The man on the leading edge of this art juggernaut in Washington is J. Carter Brown, director of the National Gallery.

Brown comes from where one would expect him to. He was born into the Episcocratic society of Rhode Island, breeding ground of such Episcocratic institutions as St. George's School and the resort of Newport, a state where a Vanderbilt can be and has been governor. Brown's mother was a Kinsolving, an old Baltimore family with a line of Episcopal clergymen.

Brown's father's family bowed to no one in its distinction. Fueled by an enormous fortune begun in the China trade and continuing in finance and real estate, they managed to act the part of dream aristocrats. They named a university after themselves, like Episcocrats Duke, Vanderbilt, Dickinson, and Mellon. The elder Brown spent his ample money on art-history expeditions, such as uncovering the mosaics in Istanbul's famous mosque Hagia Sophia. Nor did Brown's father neglect the more serious duties of an Episcocratic family; he served as Truman's assistant secretary of the navy, that post beloved of such American noblemen as the young Franklin Roosevelt.

(More recently, Virginia Episcocrat John Warner skipped the assistantship to become secretary of the navy. He had something else in common with the Brown family: At one point before Elizabeth Taylor, he married a Mellon.)

Young Carter Brown blossomed throughout a childhood that he happily concedes was privileged "in every way." He attended Groton and graduated summa cum laude at Harvard. Even before he was graduated, Brown had become well planted in the viny garden of class, family, and house-expert relationships that made and kept museum directing probably the country's most Episcocratic occupation. He went to Paris to study with Bernard Berenson, who had become one of the most famous names in the world of art by working with famous collector Mrs. Jack Gardner—and had become an Episcopalian along the way.

At Harvard, Brown was careful to specialize in the broader field of cultural affairs rather than in fine arts. Advice to that effect came from old family friend Francis Henry Taylor, who had gone from Philadelphia to Worcester and finally to the Metropolitan Museum and was one of the great Episcocratic curators of the earlier twentieth century; the academic mantle was passed from one upper-class generation to the next. (Carter Brown added a new academic wrinkle of his own, becoming one of the first potential museum directors in the country to study business administration in preparation for his administrative work. Like Polaroid or Xerox, the established line keeps ahead of potential competitors by making refinements before the competitors even develop the original product.)

Back in New York after a year studying with Berenson, Brown visited John Walker, his predecessor as director of the National Gallery. It was the only time he ever asked for a job. He got it. The career was made. Under Walker's tutelage— "It was a master-apprentice relationship," Brown has said—the young Brahmin quickly learned whatever he had failed to pick up from his wealthy family, his prep school, his college, or his years abroad. And when Walker retired in 1969, Brown was chosen his successor. Says Walker now, "I always intended that he would be heir apparent."

Envy of Brown's effortless rise has given a conspiratorial air to statements like that. No doubt Brown's contacts speeded his career. Brown's parents were friends of Walker's. The obvious conclusion is that their friendship was a key factor in gaining entrée—and perhaps favor—for the young student. Walker in turn had grown up in Pittsburgh with Paul Mellon, the National Gallery's chief benefactor, major board power, and sine qua non. There is even less doubt that the childhood friendship got Walker *his* job at the National Gallery. The mantle of power once again was passed.

Pittsburgh's fabulously wealthy and compulsively open-handed Mellon family created the gallery from scratch and continues to nurture it.* Andrew Mellon, the reclusive financier who was secretary of the treasury through the 1920s (then ambassador to England), started the gallery in 1937 with a grant of 133 Old Master paintings and sculptures—$50 million worth —plus $15 million in spending money to keep the wheels moving. Very likely Mellon's appointment as treasury secretary prompted that impressive gift, for Mellon was a man of quick decision and gratitude in his charities. He sent his son Paul to the Episcopal-modeled Choate, though the Mellon family has traditionally been Presbyterian. Just as Paul Mellon was about to be graduated, in 1926, his father paid a visit to the school. Choate's first headmaster, the Reverend George St. John, describes it :

"After an exchange of greetings, [Mellon] seemed embarrassed, shy, as a schoolboy come to ask some unusual favor. 'Would you,' he began hesitatingly, 'like a—' I had never noticed so much a hiatus in his speech. 'Would you like,' he began again, 'to have me give to the school a library?' "

Another of the elder Mellon's charities was the National Cathedral, to which he contributed the Mellon Bay and his daughter Ailsa's spectacular 1926 wedding.

Whatever his ancestral religion, Andrew Mellon loved out-churching the Episcocrats of his financial and social circles. The current arts director of the Andrew Mellon Foundation, incidentally, is David Saltonstall, from the most socially august of old Boston families.

---

* The creator of the National Collection in the Smithsonian, which preceded the National Gallery as an "official exhibition" and was later dwarfed by it, was Harriet Lane Johnston, niece of President James Buchanan and chief benefactor of St. Alban's School.

Paul Mellon, a gentle, pleasant aristocrat imbued with the give-it-away-but-get-value-for-it philosophy of the prep school masters and of his father's example, grew up to spend his way into the National Gallery in his own right. Mellon and his sister Ailsa gave $20 million to the museum in 1967 to build the just-opened East Building that is expected to make the gallery one of the great art centers of the country. That donation gave Mellon considerable leverage over the museum's policies. Now, says art critic Grace Glueck, "it is virtually the private fief of Mellon and its nine-man board, most of whom are substantial private citizens."

Mellon's colleagues on the board tend by background to hold the same art values as he and Brown. One such is S. Dillon Ripley, who sits ex officio through his post as secretary of the Smithsonian Institution, parent organization of most of Washington's museums (a post, incidentally, that rumors have put near the top of Brown's putative career ladder). Ripley is a St. Paul's old boy who later picked up degrees from both Yale and Harvard and sealed his Episcocratic credentials by marrying a Livingston. He is a strong-minded, formal, and power-interested man, very much in the solid old Episcocratic tradition.

According to a January 1978 report to the House Appropriations Committee, Ripley liked to deal privately and imperiously with the institutions under his sway. The report said he followed a deliberate policy "to avoid accountability" by mixing public and private funds. He made substantial decisions—to build a new Museum of Man, for example—completely on his own, without consulting the Smithsonian's board of regents.

Mellon says, in Episcocratic words, that the goal of all his participation in the National Gallery is "to make it live up to my father's expectations. Its mission is to have very high quality art for the public's pleasure and instruction. . . . All of the work in the gallery has been aimed toward my father's ideal." He was giving back what had been entrusted, largesse worthy of the Episcocratic titans.

Fortunately for Brown's career, he was assigned to work on the East Building right after Mellon gave the money. The similar backgrounds of the two blossomed into a close working relationship. Brown was at some pains to make it even closer.

For several years he was married to Constance Mellon, Paul's second cousin. But the Episcocratic union could not survive the weaker discipline of the modern era; divorce threatened to turn Brown's masterstroke sour. Fortunately Mellon realized the tides of the times made marital failure possible and didn't take it personally.

Brown went on to marry, in October 1976, Pamela Braga Drexel, descendant of the family of Philadelphia and New York bankers, partners of J. P. Morgan, and marriage allies of the Philadelphia Biddles—who, as a prominent art family, were Brown's match. The Brown-Drexel nuptials were performed in London's Westminster Abbey, home church of the international Anglican aristocracy.

Family connections proved extremely useful to Brown in his continuing drive to improve the National Gallery's position vis-à-vis the museum world, the Metropolitan in particular. Federal support of the gallery was bound to help negotiations to obtain foreign exhibits—one of Brown's great strengths. His upper-class background added a second level of persuasion to such effort. He was able to enlist the help of the Episcocratic State Department in persuading Egypt to lend art works for a special exhibition and similar help for another show from East Germany.

Brown's Episcocratic family connections showed their true mettle in the pursuit of the National Gallery's greatest triumph, "Archaeological Finds of the People's Republic of China" in 1974–75. Special help all through the protracted negotiations came from David K. E. Bruce, son of the Maryland senator, career diplomat out of the same Episcocratic mold as Brown. This was when Bruce headed the U.S. liaison office in Peking.* The National Gallery had a special connection to Bruce—his first wife, Ailsa Mellon. For Brown and the Far East show, it was even more helpful that Bruce happened to be Brown's mother's cousin. The National Gallery got the show.

However it was obtained, one could hardly question the value of the Chinese show, one of the greatest popular and critical successes in museum history. What of the influence of

---

* Two other heads of the China mission have also been major Episcocrats: Thomas S. Gates, Jr., and George H. W. Bush, former CIA head, who is on the board of the Episcopal Church Foundation.

this Episcocratic family-money web on the National Gallery as a whole and thereby on American taste in art? Some naturally dislike Brown and everything he stands for. Grace Glueck met one of them, a "senior member of the trade": "As for pictures, he has a combination of official and bankers' taste. I don't think he would go for anything with much *Sturm und Drang*."

To Mellon, who rose to his position as arbiter by being born a banker, such "criticism" probably sounded like praise. Mellon's assessment of Brown: "He's a very able, bright and conscientious young man, doing a good job. . . . Being on the fairly young side, he's conservative without being stuffy. His taste is good without his trying to be a great showman."

"Conservative without being stuffy"—could there be a better expression of the art ideals of the old-line Episcopalians? That characterization was no doubt Mellon's way of distinguishing between his old-line Episcocratic director and John Lindsay's flash-and-dash, radical-chic Episcocratic "degenerate," Hoving. It's the old distinction between the aristocratic and the "social," between Hoving's family fortune in jewelry (more than a little nouveau) and Brown's and Mellon's land (the noble's lifeblood) and, even—though this was a more recent development —between the no-standards social whirl of New York and the peculiarly but definitely ordered social world of Washington.

Within the museum world, Brown was the newly aggressive pusher, challenging the Metropolitan, which, despite occasionally quirky shows, remained the standard for American museums. Brown's competitiveness led Hoving to sniff, "They're touchy at the National Gallery, aren't they? They take the position they must get every exhibition first; if not, they'll take their ball away and play another game." A source of Grace Glueck's, adding up Brown's methods and tastes and supporters, damned him with this characterization: "The problem is, Carter's a symbol of the association of art with the upper classes."

Carter Brown and Thomas Hoving differed over emphasis, but art remained in the Episcocratic family. Big art in America is an Episcopal fiefdom like no other. Especially in Boston, where Isabella (Mrs. Jack) Gardner, the *enfant terrible* referred to

Episcocrats by association and taste: Judge Thomas Mellon (below, left) hammered out a fortune in Pittsburgh; his son Andrew W. Mellon (below, right), secretary of the treasury and creator of the National Gallery. Facing page: Andrew's son and heir to the National Gallery sponsorship, Paul Mellon (top), as young bridegroom and mature stable owner; Richard King Mellon (bottom), Paul's first cousin, who tends the family bank in Pittsburgh, shown on and off horseback.

by Cleveland Amory as "The Improper Bostonian Number 1," started the age of the great multimillionaire collectors, competing with J. P. Morgan. Like Morgan, Mrs. Gardner was as devoted an Episcopalian as she was an art collector. (She used to scrub the steps of Boston's extremely high Church of the Advent on her hands and knees.)

In 1903, her dream castle, which no one was allowed to see until its grand New Year's debut, opened its doors on Fenway Court, near the site of the present Boston Museum of Fine Arts. (Since no one was allowed to see the edifice until its opening, Mrs. Gardner in her customary ingenious way had the acoustics tested by blind schoolboys.)

Fourteen years before Fenway Court opened, the grand dame had been painted by John Sargent in what was then a most scandalous manner. She stands in a black dress, with short sleeves, a double strand of pearls around her hourglass waist, and a deep V neck to set off her full bust. As Aline Saarinen wrote, "The pattern made a halo behind her head, causing one gentleman visitor to remark, 'Egad, she's had herself painted as a medieval saint,' and a Unitarian minister to rejoin, 'Leave off the "medi" and you will describe it.'"

The tradition of combining art with Episcopalianism, if not with the *enfant terrible*, continues in Boston. The Boston Museum of Fine Arts, created out of Mrs. Jack's collection, continued barreling ahead with the full support of that city's small but crucial Episcocratic community. Directing the museum as it celebrated the hundredth anniversary of its founding (in the same year as the Metropolitan) was a full-blooded Episcocrat, Perry Townsend Rathbone, Harvard graduate, member of Boston's upper-class Somerset Club and also, along with Hoving and other art establishment types, of New York's Century.

Leading the fund-raising drive to expand the BMFA at its centennial was George C. Seybolt, a food products executive and perhaps the best current example of how art—and Episcopalianism—can still spring an ambitious young man into the upper reaches of even Boston's very closed society. Seybolt was not even born in Boston, nor did he go to Harvard or one of the prep schools, and he is not a gentleman of inherited wealth, a banker, or a statesman. He has achieved civic leadership by assiduously volunteering for any assignment available in the Chamber of Commerce, local government, art—and the vestry of the Episcopal Church, not to mention the diocesan committee.

In Philadelphia, the art museum board, like the directors of the orchestra and other cultural institutions, have long been even more Episcocratic than in any other cities. These prestigious boards served as homes-away-from-mansions for generations of Ingersolls, Biddles, and other Episcocratic families with artistic sympathies. Powers in Philadelphia art continue to be drawn from the Episcocratic elite.

There is the ubiquitous Dixon, widely known as the owner of the Philadelphia 76ers basketball team and the $6 million purchaser of Dr. J, but also the inheritor of the Widener (another revered art name) and Elkins fortunes, who does everything expected of an Episcocrat. When Dixon bought the famous Robert Indiana *LOVE* sculpture for $35,000 and gave it to the city, he explained his action by quoting St. John on "faith, hope and love." Dixon used to be joined at meetings of the Philadelphia Art Commission by John T. Dorrance, Jr., heir and chairman of the Campbell Soup Company and first cousin of the chairman of the big Philadelphia National Bank. Dixon and Dorrance are classic modern Episcocrats, products of alliances between third-generation industrial money and pre-revolutionary Episcocratic families.

Still another major figure in Philadelphia arts, Robert Montgomery Scott, the Groton- and Harvard-educated president of the Academy of Music and vice-president of the Museum of Art, interpreted the art-bestowing impulse for his fellow Episcocrats in a recent interview. "I went to two church schools," he explained. "I can't say I'm a reborn anything. But religious teachings imposed a very strong sense of responsibility to give with what you've got. I suppose that's one of the motivations that has led me to become as involved in civic affairs as I am, giving a fair amount back to society." Then, characteristically, he demurred, "This may sound priggish."

Chicago's art owed everything to Mrs. Potter Palmer, the colorful first lady of the "White City" at the turn of the century and Mrs. Gardner's arch rival, although the two women were as different as Boston and Chicago, Episcopalianism and midwestern Quaker-Protestantism. Mrs. Palmer and her doting husband (he bequeathed his fortune to her, telling a dubious friend that, if indeed she remarried, her next husband would need it) amassed an enormous collection of the Impressionist art that was just coming into vogue in Paris. The gossips whispered, however, that Mrs. Palmer did not really appreciate Impressionists and had once returned a Renoir because it clashed with the color scheme of her bedroom.

Mrs. Gardner's art, befitting the Episcocracy, had nothing to do with modern vogues. The differences between the two grand dames of the same era is a fable of the differences between the established Episcopalian and the parvenu. When Mrs. Palmer invited her to Chicago, in 1893, and received her in her battlemented castle, Mrs. Gardner was contemptuous of the midwestern splendor and the contemporary art. She summed up her feelings in the pantry. Mrs. Palmer's eighteen-year-old son, exhibiting the gold and silver plates and the endless towers of porcelain dishes, explained that his mother had fifty of everything.

"What does she do," Mrs. Gardner asked acidly, "when she has a really big party?"

Mrs. Gardner put her servants on rations when she wanted to buy a painting. Her refreshments at the opening of Fenway Court were of such Bostonian frugality—champagne and doughnuts—that New Yorker Edith Wharton complained of the skimpy fare in French, assuming that Mrs. Jack would not understand. She did, and merely informed Edith Wharton she would not be invited back to taste them.

It is touching that Mrs. Gardner felt so threatened by her Chicago counterpart. The name of one of these ladies has been memorialized in a specially developed white petunia; the other's name lends its majesty to Mount Gardner in Washington and the Isabella Range, extending north-northwest. As Aline Saarinen wrote: "In the end there was, of course, no question. The Palmers' ferociously turreted castle was leveled to make room for a ferociously boresome apartment house; the few dozen splendid paintings were assimilated into the vast collection of the Art Institute; and Mrs. Potter Palmer has become only a very likeable legend. But Isabella Stewart Gardner's collection, and the writings of the man who helped her form it [Bernard Berenson], set a taste in America for

Italian art that the multimillionaires of the Morgan era would follow in grand style."

In Pittsburgh, the city's museum assumed first rank among American institutions through gifts of Ailsa Mellon Bruce and Sarah Mellon Scaife, both related to Andrew Mellon and other Episcocratic family lines, the latter married into Pittsburgh's other fabulously wealthy banking family.

In Los Angeles the art movement has been the creation of such relatively new Episcocrats as the Huntington and Hearst clans. San Francisco owed much to the collections of Groton-educated Crockers.

The New Orleans Museum of Art hired a young Episcopal director who displayed possible variations on the art establishment theme. Edgar John Bullard's religion certainly worked for him, as did his five-year stint at the National Gallery with Carter Brown. But like Tom Killefer in the world of business, he had the less common birthplace of Los Angeles and studied art at UCLA—generally considered more a breeder of basketball players and surfers than Episcocratic art directors.

In all these cities by now, there has been a perception that art is such a heavily Episcocratic game that it automatically confers an Episcocratic aura on the *arriviste*. The discovery of that art aura by Henry Clay Frick and other déclassé millionaires continues to hold true. J. P. Getty was the great example in Los Angeles. He created the J. P. Getty Museum from scratch in Malibu, left the bulk of his estate to it, endured some criticism of its too-rich setting—but never saw it before he died. In Philadelphia, Walter Annenberg, son of a man who spent time in federal prison and in his own right owner of some of the less restrained newspapers in postwar America, successfully gained access to Episcocratic society by serving as chairman of the Philadelphia art museum and, more important, by financing it. The stinging criticism that forced Annenberg to withdraw the $20 million media wing he had offered to the Metropolitan Museum in 1977 must have made him—and Episcocrats—wonder whatever happened to public adulation of millionaires who create monuments to themselves.

As long as there have been museums in America, there have been Episcocrats controlling, financing, and artistically directing them—and outsiders who have used them as a vehicle to hobnob with Episcocrats and perhaps to become Episcocrats themselves. The Metropolitan and the Boston Museum of Fine Arts were created in 1870, at the beginning of the age when Episcocrats were formulating their class responses to enormous new wealth. In Europe, as Nathaniel Burt points out in *Palaces for the People,* there was no need for "museums" because they grew in the homes of the high nobility, who throughout the history of the West performed the function of patronizing artists and displaying their works. There could be no such natural palaces in America; they had to be created, just as an official religion (and "aristocratic" families) had to be willed into being.

In New York, the new museum was the work of a tight-knit group of men who wanted it as an expression of their country's glory. As William Cullen Bryant told the group that gathered in 1869 to plan the Met's creation, the richest country in the world should surely have its own great museum if even such a "third-rate" power as Spain could have one. In a concession to the stricter morality of those proto-Episcocratic first citizens, the museum must "encounter the temptations" available to New York's rapidly expanding population "by alternative entertainment of an innocent and improving character."

The idea of a museum was first voiced in 1866 by John Jay, grandson of the first chief justice and descendant of an already old line of Episcocrats. Jay's associates in the Union League Club, of which he was president, were the movers and shakers behind the museum's actual founding: Aristocratic names like Stuyvesant, Griswold, Dodge, Field, Rhinelander, and Roosevelt were among the Met's founding or early trustees. And the early years of the Metropolitan showed a distinct prejudice in favor of the "gentlemanly" at the expense of the expert—the Episcocratic trait of wanting things done tastefully, though not necessarily well.

The most famous example at the early Met was the affair of the spectacular fraud Cesnola, an Italian nobleman who unearthed early archaeological treasures from Cyprus. When he was accused of fabricating some of his "discoveries"—putting a bearded head on a breasted torso to create a peculiar Venus, for example—the board of trustees took the strange tack, not of having impartial art experts examine the collection to decide whether it was genuine, but of soliciting testimony from a group of well-known men about the "good character" of Cesnola. Swinging from elite "amateurism" to touching democracy, the museum fathers set up two of the disputed statues in the museum's Great Hall and invited the public to probe the statues—which the public did, reducing statues that might have been forgeries to useless hunks of plaster.

After a few such early missteps, the Episcocrats cleaned up their act, bending to the acquisition and classification of Art-with-a-capital-A the talents that had built them the fortunes on which their acquisitions depended. Again it was J. P. Morgan, that crusty paragon of Episcocratic values, who led the charge into Europe in quest of loot. His father, Junius, founder of the family's international banking house, had been instrumental in buying for the infant Met the Cesnola collection that caused so much trouble.

J. P., the collector of signatures of Episcopal bishops in his youth, did not become a serious adult collector of art and rarities of literature until well along in his middle age. In 1888 he bought a Thackeray manuscript from a friend of his nephew's—and was hooked. With his usual energy, Morgan began scouring Europe and Egypt for anything that looked artistic. In the process he became good at it, at least according to that chronicler of the Episcopal aristocracy Bishop Lawrence, who accompanied Morgan and his constant companion Mrs. Markoe on Morgan's last and greatest collecting expedition, the Egyptian journey of 1912. He wrote:

> It was often said of him that he could pay anything for a work of art he wanted. Here was an instance to the contrary. That boat he had wanted the year before. He had seen it and studied it; the price was exorbitant; he had returned to New York, had thought of it, and tried by correspondence for it with no result. Now he returned to the contest. . . . Mr. Morgan [attempted] to drive down the price, but with no result, and we started up the river again. The study of the Oriental and this most typical Occidental, as they met each other in the duel of a bargain for some treasure, was most interesting. At almost every place that we went objects were offered. At times treasures at a distance were offered through one of the experts of the party. If . . . an inspection was worthwhile, Mr.

Morgan halted at no difficulties to study the object for himself.

When we arrived at such a house as that at Assiut, the Oriental, to whom time is of no consideration, received his guest as if it were a day's pleasure, offered coffee, and talked of matters of health and climate. Mr. Morgan pushed through these preliminaries as quickly as was courteous and came to the point. On inspecting some of the objects, he turned his back immediately. "We do not want that." "We already have something better than that in the museum." "I bought one of those last year and it is in my collection; it is not necessary to have a second."

When, however, he saw something that he really wanted, he surprised the Oriental, unless that Oriental had had dealings with him before, by suddenly asking the price, which, of course, was double or several times its worth; and then with impatience Mr. Morgan either stood up to go, only to be called back again, or sat in silence. Gradually he drew in another treasure, and then another, and putting his hand on three, said, "How much for the lot?" This enabled the Oriental to come down with dignity and to reduce his figure. The same might happen again with an added object, with the result that either Mr. Morgan left with determination, the Oriental following him to the boat, or struck the bargain. Certain unique treasures he was bound to have if he could get them by persistence; and before we had left Egypt, he had, through the agency of an Assiut banker and the members of our party, bought the boat that he first sought, another boat, a very rich mummy, and other valuable objects which separately would have been gained at much greater cost.

As in everything else, Morgan made a point of doing his collecting more seriously and carefully than most other American collectors. Many new millionaires and their agents were unquestionably fleeced by Europeans and "Orientals" who quickly perceived that their art "treasures" were just that and that their value was whatever someone would pay. Bishop Lawrence points out that Morgan, unlike the early Met board, consulted "experts" before acting and also managed to sharpen his own judgment to competence.

Even Morgan's incredible wealth could not bring art objects back home through the prohibitive tariffs that manufacturers of his class had passed to protect their monopolies. Not, at least, until Senator Aldrich, father of Abby Aldrich Rockefeller, pushed through the tariff bill in 1909 that permitted works of art more than 100 years old to come into the country duty-free. That decision was a sacrifice of public money for public palaces created by the Episcocrats, a forerunner of today's tax laws that allow Episcocratic-endowed and -run foundations to exert their influence without paying taxes. The Aldrich tariff was certainly influenced by Morgan.

J. P. had, by the time of his death in 1913, as much of a hold on the American art establishment as on Wall Street, since he was chairman of the Metropolitan as well as its chief donor. He bought art experts and paintings in his inimitable but typically Occidental manner. Such was the case with Sir Caspar Purdon Clark, of the Victoria and Albert Museum in London, the great exemplum of the Victorian aristocracy's museum movement. The secretary of the V and A was supposed to have gone on a trip, leaving behind a bid on some porcelain and tapestries. When he got back, he asked about the porcelain. Morgan had bought it. The tapestries? Morgan bought them, too. "Good God! I must speak to Sir Purdon," the secretary supposedly exclaimed. "Sorry, sir, but Mr. Morgan bought him, too." Under Morgan's command, the Met grew great at the expense also of the Boston Museum of Fine Arts, plucking off top figures one by one.

Morgan was not foresighted enough to die before death duties had become a definite, though by no means heavy, burden for millionaires like himself. Since much of his $68 million estate was tied up in the art objects, and since they that live by the sword will die by the sword, a good portion of the Morgan collection had to be sold, at what in retrospect seem steal prices. Such Episcocrats as the Havemeyers and Peter Widener took valuable pieces and later contributed them to the National Gallery—helping lay groundwork for the conflict between the Met and Carter Brown.

First on line at Morgan's deathbed was his former protégé Henry Clay Frick, the Coke King, who ended up with the Fragonard panels and the best of Morgan's collection of Renaissance bronze. Frick's interest in art collecting, art exhibiting, and architectural display came as late in his life (and was as out of character) as his conversion to Episcopalianism. Like many lesser American barons, Frick's art collecting—as well as his Episcopalianism—had two motives: a fascination with the ordered legitimacy of the medieval European civilization and the patrician generosity that massages the ego. Frick, whose middle name described the composition of his soul, felt compelled to outdo Morgan in art collecting as he did in everything. And so he built what became the fabulous Frick Museum on Fifth Avenue. Though it did not by any means reflect the "real" Frick, the château is nevertheless a grand expression of Episcocratic aspirations.

Nathaniel Burt noted, "Artificial as the Frick hotel may be, reflecting in no real way the personality of its builder, the rarefied product not of the native soil of Mennonite Pennsylvania but of the world's most expert art dealers, it is nonetheless a very perfect blossom of taste and expertise, a true expression of New York's ability to buy the best of Europe."

In a negative way, the continuing association of Episcocratic values and institutions with the world of art collecting changed the course of art history. Peter A. B. Widener was a butcher's son. After he made his millions in streetcars and his descendants gave a library to Harvard and something else to just about everyone, the Wideners were still not accepted by the Episcocratic establishment in Philadelphia. Later than anywhere else, it was not enough in Philadelphia even to be rich and refined; one at least had to marry into an old family.

Joseph Widener, Peter's son, was not accepted socially— though he was accepted civically; he was selected for every board of directors in the hope he would eventually do something for the selecting institution. Finally, though, Philadelphia reaped the wages of its social sins—and lost the incredible Widener collection of Old Masters. Joseph Widener gave them to the National Gallery, which was founding a newer Episcocratic tradition out of more broad-minded and public-spirited people than the Philadelphia establishment.*

---

* It is not only Philadelphia where big art can lead to harsh actions among Episcocrats. Not long ago New York was presented with the spectacle of the courtly Douglas Dillon, chairman of the Metropolitan, going to court to argue that the estate of Joan Whitney Payson still owed $1.5 million on a pledge. As a sign of the times, the estate's lawyer implied that the pledge by this lady who owned six homes was a burden on her children.

By now, of course, Philadelphia has accepted the Widener descendants (the most prominent is Dixon) because they married into the proper families. But it was too late to get an art collection. On the other hand, Dixon has given Philadelphia Dr. J and Widener College, formerly a military college going out of business; between them, these two institutions no doubt please and benefit a considerably more democratic selection of people than does the Widener collection in the National Gallery.

Livingston L. Biddle, Jr., a Philadelphia Biddle, is proud of the fact that Americans no longer have to go to Europe to be "cultured."

That view is important because in 1977 Biddle became chairman of the National Endowment for the Arts, the government's shot-in-the-arm to artists. He is also a great-grandson of Nicholas Biddle, the banker who nearly bought the United States, and thus as true an aristocrat as any of the European counts who run *their* countries' art establishments. Between the two qualifications, Biddle is a flowering of the new Episcocratic synthesis between the amateur gentleman-artist and the government official. His presence in the job, the most influential of its kind in the country, was a visible symbol of the continuing domination of the arts by Episcopalians.

Biddle's roots in the government establishment run deep, to more recent generations than Nicholas's. His cousins include Roosevelt's attorney general Francis Biddle, noted sculptor George Biddle, former ambassador to Spain and Poland A. J. Drexel Biddle, and finally, more recently, Angier Biddle Duke, product of the Biddles' union with one of the country's richest families, the youngest ambassador in United States history (to San Salvador) and later the State Department's chief of protocol. Nor has he neglected the new and important intersection, a very Episcocratic corner of the world, between government and the arts. Biddle comes into the job naturally enough; in 1965 he wrote the legislation creating the endowment. He has been its deputy chairman and congressional liaison officer. Until he was appointed chairman, Biddle was staff director of the Senate's Subcommittee on Education, the Arts, and Humanities. The head of that subcommittee was

Claiborne Pell, of the wealthy and Episcocratic Rhode Island family—and Biddle's college roommate.

Biddle's own background and achievements combined to make clear why such an Episcocratic background almost eliminated other applicants from the arts-management field. The living room of his Georgetown town house is thick with Oriental antiques brought back by his father from an around-the-world collecting trip. He has been deeply involved in an effort to finance the Pennsylvania Ballet. He has even written four novels, the first of which bore the appropriate title *Main Line*. His family surrounds him with art—wife Catharina Baart Biddle is a painter, son Livvy Biddle IV is in architecture, and daughter Cordelia Biddle Dietrich is a drama student. (Cordelia also carried on the long Episcocratic tradition of marrying into newer and somewhat less respectable families with newer [and more] money.)

Biddle will be the key figure in the endowment's relatively easy, though admittedly sensitive, job of giving away $115 million annually. He will inevitably be criticized for being either too "elitist" or too "populist," for "politicizing" the arts one way or another. As backgrounds in the arts and Episcopalianism teach one, Biddle airily dismisses suggestions of conflict, calling the potential problems a matter of "semantics" and expressing a wish to create "a new spirit of unity" in the art world.

That is not liable to happen. Large Episcocratic institutions like the Metropolitan Museum and the Metropolitan Opera—whose guild is chaired by Michael V. Forrestal, the Episcocratic son of the first secretary of defense—are fearful they will lose funding to smaller, "alternative" manifestations of art.

Certainly the Episcocratic institutions could hardly muster people with a better understanding of their own values to plead their case to than Biddle and Senator Pell. If minor shifts in arts funding come in the next few years, it will be true in this field, as in so many others, that Episcocrats are on both sides of the negotiating table. Whichever way the discussions go, Episcocrats will control much future arts funding.

CHAPTER
22

The Unfinished Cathedral

It started, in a way, on the gloomy afternoon of March 5, 1969, when Fairleigh S. Dickinson III was found dead in the dormitory room of a fellow freshman at Columbia University. Dickinson had taken opium and LSD, popular pastime of the period.

What made the death important to people outside the family was the family. Young Dickinson did seem to have everything to live for. His father, Fairleigh S. Dickinson, Jr., was one of the richest, most powerful, and best-known men in New Jersey, even in the country. There was the university of the same name, begun under the original Fairleigh Dickinson in 1942 and since grown into the eighth largest private college in the country. Dickinson was also a state senator. He was chairman and president of Becton, Dickinson & Company, a giant manufacturer of medical supplies, and of the National Community Bank of Rutherford. The Dickinson family owned more than 800,000 shares of Becton, Dickinson outright, another 127,000 in trust. It all produced some $500,000 a year in income, to which was added Dickinson's $150,000-a-year salary and more income from the bank holdings.

Dickinson is also one of the leading modern Episcopal laymen, a religious rich man in the tradition of a J. P. Morgan. His response to the death of his son was an immediate turn to the church. But that signal of his own confidence in the church

The National Cathedral towers over the nation's capital.

was matched by a series of events that indicated how the great financial power has declined since the days of Morgan—though they also point to the persistent visibility and influence of the Episcocrats of today.

Fairleigh Dickinson, Jr., a shy, courteous gentleman who sometimes came to work in baggy flannels and a yachting blazer, was as shocked and puzzled as the outside world at his son's incredible death. Shortly afterward everything started to sour for him. He declined to run for reelection when his term in the state Senate expired in 1971. In 1972 he was removed as president of Becton, Dickinson, though he retained his chairmanship; it was the first step in a chain leading to his bitter and losing fight to keep his grip on the firm. Increasingly, his attention and that of his mother turned toward the numerous charitable activities that the family had long been known for. They began giving out money in a grand manner.

Shortly after Fairleigh III died, Mrs. Dickinson, Sr., gave millions to found the New York Gallery of Modern Art and promised more if it needed it. She and Fairleigh Jr. persuaded Huntington Hartford to give Fairleigh Dickinson University a gallery of modern art and promised to subsidize *that*. The public library in Rutherford, the company's home, and the civic institutions around their hometown of Ridgewood were recipients of redoubled largess. Dickinson became president of the corporation of the Kent School in Connecticut, which, like most school boards, favors actual and potential big contributors to fill its seats.

One of the people who was a special help to the bereaved father in the rocky period after the death of his son and namesake was Francis B. Sayre, Jr., dean of the Washington Cathedral. Sayre is an extraordinary man, beloved of all except those, like Lady Bird Johnson, for example, whom he alienates with his moral stances.* On a personal level he is a phenomenon— gentle, clever, loose-limbed, warm, boyish (though over sixty), down-to-earth (though a White House–born grandson of President Wilson), and deep of feeling. Dickinson appreciated all that when the men got together. Gradually, the idea became more fully formed: He would do for Frank Sayre something of what the dean had done for him. Sayre had helped him back to his feet after the rough period following the death of his son. Now he would help Sayre achieve the dream of a lifetime: to finish the cathedral.

Towering above Washington, the highest point in the city, the most visible landmark for landing planes, more graceful and subtly beautiful than the elephantine official architecture downtown, the great cathedral is a massive and appropriate symbol of Episcopalians and their church in America today. They have always thought of it as America's Westminster—a great expression of national unity, a burial place for great national heroes, a combination of the best that American money and technology can make of the great arts of the ages.

From the time the great stone feet were buried on Mount St. Alban in 1907, at the height of the great age of Episcocratic supremacy, the cathedral has risen steadily higher over a cen-

---

* He was opposed to the war in Southeast Asia and so opposed to her president husband.

tury of Episcocratic rule in the American capital. In enclosed square footage it is already the sixth largest cathedral in the world—only the Cathedral of St. John the Divine, the seat of the New York Episcopal bishop, is larger in the Western Hemisphere. The Gloria in Excelsis tower soars 301 feet above the base of the cathedral itself; St. Alban's and the Cathedral schools nearby, and the rest of Washington, falling off into the distance. The high and glorious church even now suggests the majesty of God and of His chosen servants, the Episcopalians on earth. When it is finished, it will be a miracle of taste, dedication, and money.

When it is finished. That subordinate and annoying clause troubled Sayre since he became dean of the cathedral in 1952.

A cathedral is, by definition, one of the most monumental undertakings on God's earth. The founders of the National Cathedral imitated the great medieval cathedrals by planning construction for a long and indefinite period—the work of generations of Christians. That was really not their choice; money, skilled craftsmanship, and cathedral technology were and remained scarce enough to stretch the huge work over decades. Directing such a task demands enormous reserves of patience, ambition, and administrative skill from a dean—a demand that wore out several of them.

Early in his tenure, Sayre made it clear he would use his position for all it was worth, in two directions: to base political and social action in the cathedral and to finish the stone building itself. Sayre, grandson of the visionary President Wilson, son of the personal agent of the king of Siam, had a sweep of vision and a grasp of potential that made completion a good bet. The completion of the great central tower in 1964 was the great event of his tenure. Sayre also installed half the stained glass in the cathedral—including the breathtaking west rose window, forty-five feet high, with figures as big as a man —and finished 30 percent of the entire cathedral. Only about 6 percent now remains unfinished, chiefly the west towers.

Very early in his career, too, Sayre made the decision to present his eventual successor with a fait accompli. Someday a "hardheaded" dean would decide to do without, say, the central tower. Sayre decided to take all choice out of his hands. No one would tear down a cathedral already built. Sayre was well aware of the decision made at New York's "St. John's the

Unfinished" near Columbia University—that in an age of political and social strife, cathedrals should remain a relic of the Middle Ages, not something to spend good current dollars on. Sayre wanted it all: social works, social preaching, and a great stone monument to his church, his people, and, well, himself.

For what will almost certainly be the last pure Gothic structure ever built, Sayre says, "We have sought after the utmost excellence—in stained glass, sculpture, carving, and all the arts that make a cathedral. This effort is rare; no magnificence has been spared. When the stained-glass windows weren't right in the west rose window, we took them out and threw them away —spent another forty or fifty thousand dollars to get it right."

In 1969, Sayre landed the man who, as treasurer, could do the job for him: Amory—lawyer, accountant, intelligence chief, knower of all things and all men. Amory's great contribution was to stabilize the cathedral's funding sources so building could proceed steadily. Previously work had been done as money arrived in contributions—a bay as Andrew Mellon and his group paid up, a memorial to a Pennsylvania bishop as a group headed by Senator George Wharton Pepper came through, a Folger Bay for the Shakespeare Library people, contributions in the name of Du Ponts and other industrialists and politicians. That had been a painful, halting process, annoying to the dean, mean to the rare artisans who had to be either kept on during slack months with no work or told to go home.

Amory fixed all that. A good friend in New York introduced him to the Marine Midland Bank, for a long time bankrollers of the Roman Catholic archdiocese of New York. Episcopalians should have the same access to money at half a point above the prime rate, Amory told them with typical aplomb: "It's the same creed, just a small difference over who's the head man."

The bank extended the money. Amory began engineering the greatest fund-raising drive the cathedral had ever seen, the one that would put it over the top.

Through the early 1970s the drive continued to accelerate. Amory was aware of Dean Sayre's desire to finish as much as possible before he had to retire, and he knew the dean wanted to finish the west wall windows and hopefully the entire nave (body of the church) before Queen Elizabeth arrived for the Bicentennial activities on July 4, 1976. In the summer of 1975,

Amory's bank loans and carefully balanced budgeting coalesced as Fairleigh Dickinson, Jr., walked onto the scene with a long, long shadow and proclaimed, "This cathedral will be built."

Specifically, Dickinson intended to give fully $5 million. Even for an institution with the cathedral's enormous and insatiable appetite for money, that was an impressive sum—and a decisive one. The entire debt for the incredibly intricate and expensive work so far was in the range of $7 million. Amory had been budgeting several million dollars a year for construction, in addition to $1.5 million to operate Sayre's wide-ranging program of services, musical and artistic events, community-involvement projects, and general upkeep of the building and grounds. With careful budgeting and continual hard fund raising on the part of Amory and Sayre—charming, hardheaded men in the great tradition of Episcocratic money gatherers—completion of the nave was set before the Bicentennial, and the Sts. Peter and Paul towers on the west end, the final pieces, would be in place by 1980. Now, with Dickinson's unprecedented and apparently open-ended gift in hand, Amory threw on full power and began reaching for completion as soon as stone could be piled on stone. Dickinson's entire gift was budgeted for 1976.

The reach far exceeded the grasp, perhaps more sadly than before. Dickinson's efforts came to naught. Soon he had to explain that the money was not immediately available. The man worth an estimated $75 million could not readily put his hands on $5 million because of an unforeseen worsening of his relations at Becton, Dickinson. Unknown to outsiders, Dickinson had sunk increasingly deep into a feud over expansion policies and executive performance at the company his father had founded at the turn of the century. The medical-supplies king and financial angel of the cathedral suddenly found himself forced to marshal his 810,000 shares of the company's stock for what looked more and more like a battle for control of the company. Soon, Dickinson kept expecting, we'll have this settled and you can have the money.

Unhappily, came April 20, 1977, and Dickinson's rebellious board of directors removed him as chairman, kicking him upstairs to "honorary chairman" and adding insult to injury by replacing him with Henry P. Becton, son of the *other* founder.

On November 1, the board unceremoniously booted Dickinson out of his office for good, taking away his $165,000 salary. Dickinson faces a foreseeable future in which he may be forced to hold on to his cash and defer the gift which he still expects to bestow on the Cathedral.

Dickinson was not the only disappointment. For one reason or another, the huge bequests of past years no longer came through. "The years you could use a death, you don't get one," Robert Robinson, an old-time New Yorker with interests in insurance, publishing, and Episcopal fund raising who was called in to take command of the sinking ship, says with a sigh.

All of which had a sad, near-disastrous effect on the glorious National Cathedral. Since construction had gone ahead with a damn-the-torpedoes euphoria, the outstanding debt leaped heartbreakingly in the single year 1976 from $7 million to $11 million. The lights inside the cathedral were shut off, aside from services. One of the four clerics was dismissed. The non-clerical staff was slashed drastically. The building program was severely curtailed. As the extent of the shortfall, the massiveness of the $900,000-a-year debt payments, became soberingly clear during 1976, the cathedral chapter (its governing body) and the National Cathedral Association, the umbrella fund-raising organization, were shaken by bitter internal fights. William Creighton, the soon-to-retire Episcopal bishop of Washington, demanded Amory's resignation outright. He was joined in the showdown by Charles McC. Mathias, latest in a long line of patrician Episcopalian senators from Maryland. Amory had no intention of leaving under fire—his term had only another year to run anyway—and managed to gain enough time to persuade Marine Midland Bank to extend the loans indefinitely. Dickinson and others would come through eventually, Amory and Sayre were convinced. Since the bank would have little to gain by forcing the cathedral into bankruptcy—there isn't much market for secondhand blocks of marble and limestone —it agreed to go along.

So some construction continues. Eli Lilly, of the huge drug company, died conveniently in January 1977, the depth of the crisis, and left a blessed $2-million bequest that was rushed into the fiscal gap and closed it sufficiently to allow token work to proceed. But Amory has gone. So has Sayre. He announced his retirement in June 1977, shortly after the extent of the cathedral's troubles—and the far-off time of its completion—became public.

Along the way, the cathedral was subject to bizarre and distinctly non-Episcopal occurrences, which added to the ignominy of the non-Episcopal inability to procure money. One of the tense chapter meetings at the height of the crisis was invaded by Lester Kinsolving, a priest, right-wing commentator for a Washington radio station, and descendant of a noble long line of Episcopal clergymen from Baltimore. The chapter was wary, for Kinsolving already had a certain reputation, and soon thereafter he was banned from State Department press briefings.*

Kinsolving not only wanted to sit in on what the chapter thought should be a private meeting, but wanted to put it all on his radio shows and seemed ready to filibuster for days as long as he was there. When some members began muttering about banishing him, he protested that his First Amendment rights of free speech were being violated. Amory, much to Kinsolving's surprise, agreed with him and told the dissident he could stay on the cathedral grounds. Then, as the chapter retired, the former military engineer pointed to a row of trees and gave strict orders to arrest Kinsolving for trespassing if he went beyond them. There were only internal disruptions for the rest of the meeting.

That public display, caused by one of their own Episcopalians, was not nearly so troubling to some of the old-line cathedral members as the obvious inability to produce the money for which they have long been so famous. There have always been a few priests along the lines of young Kinsolving, gadflies to the serious-minded in the church hierarchy. But the discovery that Fairleigh Dickinson was no ready-money tiger rocked the cathedral chapter to the roots of its self-assurance.

Dickinson appeared to be in a grand tradition—the businessman who is also a Public-minded Patrician, vitally concerned with the community around him, including the church, and ready to back up his convictions with baskets of money. Differ-

---

* Kinsolving was readmitted to the press briefings but continued to badger State Department spokesman Hodding Carter, another Episcopalian, so insistently that on May 3, 1978, Carter reached under his lectern for a rubber chicken he had secreted there and hurled the bird at the radioman, declaring, "You have plucked me, and you have plucked me enough."

ent as they were, J. Pierpont Morgan, the two Roosevelt presidents, the Astors and Vanderbilts, had important qualities in common. Each was pushed by an internal sense of self-worth and by the pressures of their Episcocratic societies to take the burdens of the world on their shoulders and help relieve them. This tradition of the broad-shouldered Titan, the Strong Man, the Captain of Industry, the American Aristocrat, sustained not only the church itself but all Episcocratic society—its schools, its cultural institutions, the style of its life.

Dickinson had the money; he had the breeding; he had the family tradition of service—the father with the university named after himself, the mother contributing not only art galleries but some $4 million to the National Cathedral. He had the strong commitment to the church, the personal friendship with leading churchmen like Sayre, the leadership of a great prep school's board of directors at Kent. Still, in the end Dickinson had been powerless to deliver. His unintentional delay was an unintentional reflection of the present state of the Episcopal Church in America.

"The important people who are Episcopalians simply feel that the church has a minor claim on their energy and time," observed David Acheson, an important person himself and one who must be concerned with such matters, since he is the new president of the National Cathedral Association. "They have a loose attachment; it doesn't seem to be part of their lives. As a result, the active people we do have tend to be retired people, nonworking people for one reason or another, or 'society' people."

There are, it is true, substantial, committed Episcopalians to whom the church will continue to turn for advice and, it hopes, large financial assistance. There are Senator Mathias and former senator Stuart Symington, the rich, aristocratic, and social former presidential aspirant from Missouri, who has also been head of the NCA. There is a bright new prospect in Washington now in the person of Joseph Allbritton, who loves to attend meetings of the cathedral chapter. Allbritton used to own the *Washington Star* until he sold the newspaper to *Time* magazine early in 1978. What makes him even more interesting *after* that sale is that he now has $20 million that he has to put *somewhere*.

In New York, Tom Killefer, the California-born chairman of

the Episcocratic old investment banking firm U.S. Trust, has also been active in the church, including the cathedral chapter (though he has been a financial disappointment there). But New York holds several other interested Episcocrats who might help keep the cathedral rolling, like Charles Scribner, Jr., of the publishing company, and the two Rockefellers from the Connecticut (that is to say Episcopalian) branch of the family. In Princeton, New Jersey, George Gallup, Jr., who almost became an Episcopal priest as a young man, helps through his polling organization to analyze the church's troubles and recommend improvements. Gallup's close friend and fellow pillar of Trinity Church Princeton is Lee Hastings Bristol, Jr., heir to the Bristol-Myers fortune, who for years has dedicated his business life to working for Episcopal organizations—for free. (He and Gallup take breaks from their church work to sing together in a Gilbert and Sullivan group; Bristol is a published composer.)

But the old solid family-and-peer-group social structure that used to dictate at least a token effort of support for the church is breaking down. Modern life is disrupting the old fabric. In March 1978 the cathedral chapter read with sinking hearts front-page stories in the *Washington Post* about the travails of G. William Middendorf. The Securities and Exchange Commission accused Middendorf in a civil complaint of violating the securities laws during a subterranean struggle for control of Financial General Bankshares, Inc., a bank holding company in Washington of which Middendorf was president.

Middendorf had been an active Episcocrat, former secretary of the navy, a prime target for fund raisers at the National Cathedral. Then, suddenly, he was involved in a financial quagmire frighteningly similar to Dickinson's. Even more depressing were the people he had got into it with, according to the SEC: Bert Lance, Jimmy Carter's disgraced budget director, and several Arab potentates. Gone were the days when gentlemen made business deals in clubs and yachts with other gentlemen, not with non-northerners, non-Ivy men, non-Americans, and non-Christians.

If lay Episcocrats failed the church, much of the church's high clergy also failed to attain the modern equivalent of the business skills of a Bishop Lawrence. When Paul Moore came to Washington as suffragan bishop in the early 1960s, he carried with him a twin reputation that represented divergent and competitive trends in the church. He was a well-educated, broad-minded liberal, like a long line of churchmen before him, and a personally wealthy young man from a distinguished family, like a substantial percentage of the church as a whole. Moore and his wife moved easily into the upper ranks of Washington society, inviting and being invited, reestablishing old contacts and friendships, being led to new ones.

One of the old acquaintances was a roommate at St. Paul's who had gone on to become an assistant secretary of defense. Assistant secretary, especially in the departments of State, Defense, and the Treasury, is a prestigious, influential post frequently filled through the family-and-friends network with its outposts in the prep schools, the Ivy colleges, and the New York law firms. Dr. John Harper, who from his office in St. John's Church, across the square from the White House, felt very acutely the talent and influence that come with assistant secretaries, tried to persuade Bishop Moore to put a little political pressure on the assistant secretary to deploy his administrative and fund-raising talents for the cathedral or the diocese of Washington or both. Moore, though he remained personally close with the man, declined to inject church business into the relationship. The man continued to have no substantial role in the church.

Some fifteen years later, on the night of January 23, 1978, Paul Moore, now bishop of New York, walked into the Plaza Hotel to try to repair some of the fences he had managed to break during his highly publicized career as a bishop, tearing down old church traditions, culminating in that awesome and troubling occasion early in 1977 when he ordained Ellen Marie Barrett, a self-professed lesbian, into the Episcopal priesthood. That action led several churches in his diocese to withhold their contribution to the diocesan headquarters and helped give added momentum to a secession movement that had already affected some fifty parishes around the country.

On this night, speaking in a giant banquet hall at the elegant old Plaza after an exercise in the quintessential Episcopal social occasion—cocktails—Moore was his charming, story telling, old-family best. Everybody laughed as Moore recalled the traditional image of Episcopalians as "the Tory party at prayer." It was even jollier when he recalled the reply of Bishop William T. Manning, a predecessor who ruled the New York diocese during the less chaotic years from 1921 through 1946, to a young man who asked whether there is salvation outside the Episcopal Church.

"Perhaps so," the bishop replied after a long, puzzled pause, "but no gentleman would avail himself of it."

One of the rich ironies of this situation—and there are always ironies with Episcopalians—was that Paul Moore was addressing the Church Club of New York, considered one of the more backward organizations in the church in terms of social consciousness, with a thinly disguised longing for precisely the days when the church not only was composed of gentlemen but supported their right to continue to be gentlemen and to remain at the top of society. The tuxedoed gentlemen and their horsy, sophisticated-looking wives looked like nothing so much as a dinner meeting of the House of Lords. Though they were not at prayer—they were at Petite Marmite Henri IV and petits fours—they looked and acted like English Tories.

(In its history in the United States the social effect of Anglophilia has made a notable impression on the church. Episcopalians have always loved things English—the language, the form of service, the manner of speaking, the fox hunting and polo and horse racing, the gin, the outdoors, the country houses, the big-boned men and handsome women, the sophisticated business leaders.)

The banquet room at the Plaza was filled with big-boned, well-educated, sophisticated business leaders. Gathered in this one room for the Church Club's annual dinner was good sprinkling of America's banking, industrial, and legal elite—such as Armstrong, the executive vice-president at Killefer's U.S. Trust Company; Eugene Banks, head of the investment division at another important Episcocratic investment banking house, Brown Brothers Harriman; and the secretary-counsel of both the Long Island Railroad and the huge American Can Company.

They listened politely, sipped some wine, and some fell asleep; 400 well-dressed, self-assured, wealthy people breathed heavily after dinner as they listened to Bishop Paul Moore, the social and financial equal of them all, speak in toned-down terms about the church's role in a too rapidly changing society.

Episcopalians may no longer support monuments to themselves; they may no longer even be at prayer; they do remain the Tory party.

CHAPTER
23

"*The Episcopal Church Welcomes You*"

William Appleton Coolidge has the look of a superannuated Yankee sea captain enjoying the flowers of his (and his ancestors') labors. His house in Boston's rolling North Shore section glows and smells with dozens of large full-formed plants blossoming with Tahitian intensity. Coolidge claims not to know the name of a single one for fear that they will take hold of him. He does, however, know his paintings; he points out why the Van Gogh works well in the blond wood above the dining room's mantelpiece, details of the Utrillos and Sisleys, and hardly bothers to note the Rembrandt in a corner of a hallway, which is, after all, just a Dutch burgher portrait like many others.

Outside, the first warm sun of spring bathes the graceful steps of Coolidge's land, which turns wild fifty yards from the house and runs unshackled down to the Ipswich River. It is in flood tide, he explains. Across the glinting full river, four riders are cantering up the slope of Coolidge's land on the other side of the river. Coolidge is an old man with a mane of white hair, whose typical attitude is staring through the French doors over the land he has known and held and cultivated for three decades.

Coolidge lived a life rooted in the turn-of-the-century glory of Episcocratic culture; he has been a Harvard and Oxford student, a stockbroker, a lawyer, a Navy Department official during World War II, and, since 1948, the leading citizen and landowner of Topsfield, some twenty miles north of Boston, as well as the largest contributor to the diocese of Massachusetts, retired president of the boards of both St. Mark's School and the Episcopal Divinity School, and, without question, one of the most popular members of corporate boards in the United States.

Coolidge is a "churchman" in the old sense, a concerned, active, refined, and very rich reminder of the glory that was the Episcopal Church. Growing up on Brimmer Street at the intersection of Boston's two great Episcocratic neighborhoods, Back Bay and Beacon Hill, the young Coolidge went with his parents, converts from their parents' Unitarianism during the mass apostasy of Victorian days, to Boston's gilded, cavernous Trinity Church on Copley Square. For fifty-six years Coolidge sat in the same pew every Sunday, surrounded by the cream of Boston society, nearly all of whom were related to him one way or another.

Casually he refers to "Cousin William Lawrence," the great aristocratic bishop who, along with Phillips Brooks, helped persuade Boston to join the Anglican Communion. Rooted in that refined past, Coolidge is carrying a lonely beacon into an age that seems sometimes not to care for his treasures of style and memory. Fewer and fewer are the people whose lives are built on the pillars of service to man, gentlemanly refinements, and staunch adherence to a hereditary creed; fewer still those who will say with Coolidge at his age, "I've given up everything except church and Coca-Cola."

So little has the weathered Brahmin given up the church that he built his own church on his own land in Topsfield and, with a nod toward his past, called it Trinity, too. It is a small but thriving parish, a reminder of the power that once enabled the church to capture the allegiance of the country gentlemen of Coolidge's breed. In his spare time from heading the boards of St. Mark's School and other church institutions, Coolidge also led a drive to raise some $3 million to make the church grow in similar ways. It did not have his golden touch.

"Those silly bishops," he says. "They just squandered all the money. They hired three archdeacons to find places to build new churches. The result was absolute bedlam. Now you have about twenty-five incompetent, bankrupt parishes; some of them are now closed, and some ought to be." In these days of religion's drought, the Coolidges who can build their own churches are not enough to keep the institutions growing.

In every major city there is at least one parish—in eastern cities a number of parishes—with large endowments, cultured priests, powerful parishioners, and awesome social clout. In downtown Boston, Trinity on Copley Square still has nearly 1500 members and the solid allegiance of a network of aristocrats, even though the building is sinking a few inches a year because the gleaming Hancock Tower on its flank drastically lowered the water level. The Church of the Advent on Beacon Hill is another Gothic-revival symbol of Boston's upper-class conversion; it remains the most orthodox of Anglo-Catholic churches, perhaps the only regular parish in the country where an Episcopalian can go into a confessional like a Roman Catholic and confess his sins to a priest. (Mainstream Episcopalianism provides for group absolution.) The rich, refined suburban parishes around Boston include St. Andrew's Wellesley and St. John's Beverly Farms (on the North Shore).

Most cities, especially Boston's old eastern sisters, poured their Episcocratic strength primarily into parishes in the most expensive and oldest surburbs because the Episcocratic revival of Victorian times was followed over the next few decades by the mass relocation in the suburbs of the newly converted business classes. In Philadelphia, with more Episcopalians per capita than any other city, the huge and vigorous parishes therefore came to rest in the legendary communities: Redeemer Bryn Mawr; St. Paul's and St. Martin's-in-the-Field, both Chestnut Hill; and St. Thomas Whitemarsh, where Fitz Dixon worships.

Philadelphia witnessed another sharp turn beginning in the fifties, with an extensive and successful urban renewal project that included, among other areas, what had once been called Society Hill. The site of the signing of the Declaration of Independence and its immediate environs, after centuries of neglect, once again became one of Philadelphia's "best" places to live. It is again called Society Hill. St. Peter's Church, one of the most exclusive during revolutionary times but slowly abandoned as society moved countryward, suddenly found its school becoming, again, Episcocratic. Not only that—the school is now a favorite educational institution for many of the upper-middle-class Jewish professionals who live side by side with Episcocratic professionals in the exclusive area. The same youths who attend the Society Hill Synagogue on weekends can be seen going to compulsory chapel in their St. Peter's School uniforms during the week. It is a clear example of the influence Episcocrats have upon the upwardly mobile. One suspects it is not unique to Philadelphia.

Wilmington enjoyed the Du Pont church—Christ Church Christiana Hundred, in the suburban area locals call Château Country. Another Christ Church, in Shaker Heights, became the most upper-class church in Cleveland, and still another church of the same name serves the many Episcocrats of Winnetka and surrounding suburbs of Chicago. Christ Church Cranbrook in Bloomfield Hills, Michigan, ministers to the old social aristocracy of Detroit together with the cream of the automobile aristocracy. All Saints Pasadena is one of the largest congregations in the country, serving the elite of Los Angeles, which has a surprisingly substantial Episcopal minority. In central California, both St. Andrew's Saratoga and St. Matthew's San Mateo are large and socially prominent parishes.

The South is not only the fastest-growing area of the church—the only growing area, actually—but is home of the country's two largest parishes. Both the Cathedral of St. Philip on Peachtree Road in Atlanta's exclusive Northwest section and St. Michael and All Angels Dallas are beneficiaries of the new prosperity and social consciousness of their urban centers, combined with the southerner's fascination with joining organized churches. The Park Cities section of Dallas held not only St. Michael's, the largest Episcopal parish in the country, but the largest Presbyterian, Methodist, Baptist, and Church of Christ congregations as well.

St. Michael's rector, Robert Estill, refers to his church as "St. Mink's and All Cadillacs"; it stands at the pinnacle of the increasingly complex social heap that is Dallas. The Presbyterian Church in Park Cities is more important for business prestige, according to Estill, while the Baptists claim most of the important politicians. When Episcopalian President Jerry Ford visited Dallas during his 1976 campaign, he pointedly stayed away from St. Michael's and spent time with the Baptists instead.

St. John's Lafayette Square is the best-known and historically most prestigious church in Washington, as Trinity Copley Square is in Boston, but St. John's has competition from the suburban parishes in Maryland, Virginia, and Georgetown. St. Dunstan's McLean and the two giants of Chevy Chase, All Saints and St. John's, are the big ones outside the district. Georgetown contains two relatively small but prestigious churches only two blocks apart on "O" Street. Christ Church is the Victorian, bourgeois-brick home of generals and other old-line Episcocrats.

St. John's Georgetown, though, occupies a graceful colonial structure built by an original vestry that included Thomas Jefferson and Francis Scott Key, and is an intriguing, modern-Episcocrat mixture. Parishioner Carol Clendenning Laise, as director general of the foreign service, was responsible for the assignment of every member of the foreign service. In 1967, Carol Laise married distinguished businessman-diplomat Ellsworth Bunker just before she became ambassador to Nepal and he ambassador to Vietnam; she is also the sister of Frederic Stevens Laise, senior vice-president of the Episcocrat-dominated American Red Cross, where Bunker was president from 1953 to 1956.

Yet Ms. Laise's rector at St. John's was a young man named Peter Winterble, whose clothes have Italian and French cognomens, who drives a Porsche, is divorced from a Jewish woman, used to be a newspaper reporter, and makes no secret of his affection for Clyde's, one of Georgetown's watering holes for the foreign service and government lawyer crowd. Winterble is a symbol, in short, of the possibility that Episcopalianism's

future is not Coolidge's churchman model but as a religion
to provide initials for expensive T-shirts.

"I don't know what is happening," said John Davis Lodge,
former governor of Connecticut, a former ambassador, descendant and brother of two Senator Henry Cabot Lodges. "Last Sunday, the service was stopped while these two young people stood
up—he had no tie on and she had stringy yellow hair—and they
asked for money for some sort of center for young people. This
is not what the church should be doing."

Ambassador Lodge attends, with some reluctance, the Church
of Christ and the Holy Trinity in Westport, Connecticut—one
of the rich and exclusive parishes that New York suburbs grow
like giant oaks. The complaints of Lodge and a few more conservative Episcocrats aside, the important parishes do not seem
in danger of losing social cachet or Business Aristocracy adherents. Greenwich, the other big name in Connecticut suburbs,
features its own Christ Church, one of whose parishioners is
Avery Rockefeller, Jr. (William Rockefeller, another member
of the Connecticut Rockefellers that, unlike the Westchester
branch, turned Episcopalian in Victorian times, belongs to
Christ Church Rye.) St. James the Less, Scarsdale, is the dominant church of the wealthy rolling Westchester countryside.
In New Jersey there is St. John's-on-the-Mountain for the
country crowd of Bernardsville; a bigger and more important
church is Trinity Princeton, whose current rector, the Reverend
John Crocker, is the son of former Groton headmaster "Black
Jack" Crocker and was the captain of the Harvard hockey team
in 1950.

The biggest congregations with the biggest churches and the
biggest names and the biggest treasuries are all on Manhattan's
Upper East Side—churches that hardly lost an ounce of wealth
or social prestige from the days when the Vanderbilts used to
be able to see J. P. Morgan's car arriving behind theirs for
services at St. Thomas's Fifth Avenue (at Fifty-third Street).
St. Thomas's still is home to Episcocratic names like Gardiner
and Root and Gallatin. On Park Avenue and a few blocks uptown stands the rambling mass of St. Bartholomew's, where
the publisher Charles Scribner, Jr., worships. Perhaps an even

more splendiferous parish register belongs to St. James Madison Avenue, again slightly farther uptown at Seventy-first Street. Here, aside from the expected old-family Business-Aristocracy names like Havemeyer and Hay, the parishioners include Bruce Bromley, the Cravath Swaine partner who is leading the defense for IBM in the biggest lawsuit in history, and former Episcocrat-chic Mayor John Lindsay. All three churches, at about 3000 members each, rank among the largest in the country, and the combined wealth of their parishioners is unquestionably larger than any other churches' in the country. St. Thomas's and St. Bartholomew's, with St. John's Lafayette Square and Trinity Boston, are generally considered the Episcopal Church's four "cardinal churches." It is no social mistake to belong to them.

Not quite as grand as the big three, but in some ways more interesting, is their uptown neighbor at Fifth Avenue and Ninetieth Street.

The Church of the Heavenly Rest was built in 1929, just before the stock market crashed and Roosevelt became president. Inside the church, it is as if 1977 were still 1929. Two women sit in a high-ceilinged room near the entrance working on a dossal, a magnificent sewn cloth about as large as a clipper's sail whose purpose is to decorate the area behind the altar. They have been working on it for two years.

The Reverend Alanson B. Houghton, the current rector of this magnificent Episcopal parish, wears the clothes of his predecessors—a continuity of taste that has kept Brooks Brothers in business since before the Civil War. Houghton's cigars don't come from Cuba, as his predecessors' did, but they smell masculine and refined, hang in the air like delicate thoughts, and add an extra length to the long, tall, slim rector. For a millionaire capitalist, Alan Houghton is an exceptionally warm and good-humored man. He cheerfully reminds visitors of Heavenly Rest's nickname—Celestial Snooze.

People like Houghton make today's Episcopal Church the House of Lords among American religious groups. *Aristocratic* is too weak a word for him. From the well-mellowed tips of his penny loafers to the perfectly combed hair, strands of old silver, Houghton is a breathtaking reminder of the civilization that the Episcopal Church helped achieve. His career is a classic example of the timeless continuity in the fabric of the church of wealth, culture, and aristocratic lineage. He is Coolidge's New York counterpart.

Alanson Houghton is the son of Amory Houghton, former ambassador to France—a diplomatic post second only to the Court of St. James's as the ultimate jewel in a business-diplomatic career. Amory Houghton fully participated in the business side of that career: Until his son and namesake took over in 1964, he was chairman of Corning Glass, a business that made every member of the Houghton family many times a millionaire. The former ambassador holds a handful of typically Episcocratic directorships, including Morgan Guaranty, New York Life, the Morgan Library, the Metropolitan Museum, and the Council on Foreign Relations.

The elder Houghton has also been for many years one of the great lay leaders of the Episcopal Church; so is Mrs. Amory Houghton, an honorary director of the Episcopal Church Foundation. "They are not only regular attenders at church," notes their son. "They have great faith." Nor has Amory Houghton, Jr., Amo as he is called, neglected the links that made the Houghtons one of the most important Episcocratic families in the country. A Harvard classmate ('50) of Stephen Howe, the chancellor (lawyer) of the diocese of Massachusetts, Amo also has on his board at Corning Glass John B. Coburn, the bishop of Massachusetts. Amo was the featured speaker when Coburn was consecrated bishop after being called from his former post as rector of St. James Madison Avenue.

As a young man, Alanson Houghton did not have great faith. He did not even have great respect. He was, he says without being specific, "thrown out" of St. Paul's School, alma mater of his father and brothers. It was part of the youthful high jinks always part of the upper class's growing-up pangs. Young Alanson soon settled down to a respectable college career, a Harvard Business degree, and then the expected executive position at Corning Glass.

"I enjoyed business," he recalls—but. At the age of thirty-four, Houghton says, "I just began to feel there was something I had to do." It had always been somewhere in the back of his mind, surfacing at intervals of years, that he might someday want to enter the ministry. He went to see Horace Donegan, bishop of New York from 1950 to 1972. (When you are a Houghton, you go to the bishop, not the parish priest, for advice.)

"If you love your Lord and love people, the ministry is an option," the bishop told him.

Houghton opted for it, was ordained two years later, and since then has "had no regrets." "Sure, some people just said, 'You're nuts,'" he remembers. "But others gave three cheers. There are a lot of people out there who have toyed with the idea and not done it."

A surprisingly large number of Episcopal priests, like Houghton, came into the clergy from other occupations—frequently, business, teaching, and, for some reason, journalism. It was, many found, a liberating alternative to the deadening lockstep of a business career. What made it a real option for discontented Episcopalians was the lack of a celibacy requirement. Catholics would have to shuffle off a family to sign up for their clergy; there aren't many willing to do that, much less promise the questionable virtue of lifelong celibacy.

For the most part, Episcopalians expect their priests to be employees like anyone else. They even pay fairly well, from approximately $15,000 for a parish priest to about $30,000 to $35,000 for a dean or bishop. Clergymen also get such fringe benefits as housing, often lovely, in the rectory. The idea lately has seemed so attractive to many searching Episcopalians that the church has encountered a severe glut of clergymen—and now, making the crunch greater, clergywomen. Half or more of all current graduates of the seminaries find no parish. And most dioceses will no longer ordain a priest unless he has some job waiting.

Houghton's background and education helped him avoid unemployment. His first job was at Christ Church in Shaker Heights, a church that holds the same position in Cleveland as St. James the Less Scarsdale does in New York—a large, prestigious suburban congregation. Houghton found his parishioners in Shaker Heights very much like the congregation he inherited when he accepted Heavenly Rest's call in 1975—partners in the national upper-class mores of Episcopalians, distilled through the years and changing slightly with the times.

Heavenly Rest has something over 1000 communicants, a

medium-large congregation for a New York Episcopal church. It is behind the giants like St. Bartholomew's Park Avenue, St. Thomas's Fifth Avenue, and St. James Madison Avenue. Since its founding, Houghton claims, the parish has "struggled over its identity—we're a family parish in the middle of New York." The church stands grand and imposing in post-Gothic glory across from a verdant Central Park, very much a reminder of the concentrated wealth that traditionally reposed in the Episcopal Church. It is a beautiful, tasteful, and grand church—adjectives that also fit its residential surroundings, the block on block of massive town houses and towering, elegant apartment houses of the Upper East Side. On Ninetieth Street, Heavenly Rest stands as a border outpost for white, upper-class East Side Manhattan; six blocks to the north begins the grim stretch of Harlem.

Heavenly Rest's congregation reflects its guarding-the-marches geographical position; very few blacks cross Ninety-sixth Street to attend services there, while it draws a considerable number of white communicants from farther down on the East Side, across the park on the West Side, and even Queens. "There are not as many [blacks] as I thought there'd be," Houghton concedes, adding, "If I were black or Puerto Rican, I don't know that I'd come here."

Even without seeing any parishioners (except the two ladies determinedly sewing the dossal in the front of the church), one can understand what Houghton means. He is not dressed in a style that many blacks would feel at home with: polka-dot tie, straight-leg cuffed wool slacks, button-down shirt, and button-down hair.

Houghton's religion is as cut-and-dried, as rationalistic, as he is. He believes in his Creator and in praying by the prayer book—the modern translation of the Book of Common Prayer that has caused some discussion in the church as a whole. The parish engages in the fourteenth-century-Flemish-convent ceremonial represented by the dossal-weaving women. But Houghton says he hates "to see people make it a sort of mystical trip." Heavenly Rest practices mainstream contemporary Episcopalianism: a determination to maintain that there is a living, caring God, combined with a bland conviction that He is not, somehow, a thing one mentions in company.

It fits in very well with good society, this religion. Houghton maintains it should be part of daily living, relaxed, informal. Blacks and other relatively deprived people, on the other hand, do not want a religion that is part of daily life. They want a religion that assures them there is something different from, better than, daily life and provides a bit of it every Sunday morning. For Houghton's congregation Sunday morning is a social gathering, an intensification of their normally pleasant lives; for people who would never think of joining the Episcopal Church—blacks, Eastern Europeans—church provides a needed escape.

Houghton describes his congregation as "basically middle-class," but middle-class for Upper East Side Manhattan is well above the national average in education, income, and éclat. "It's not any one economic group, social group," the rector says. "Some of them are very hard-up—though I guess there aren't any actually unemployed. I suppose some are very rich. I don't want to know. Everybody's treated exactly the same."

One can get an idea of the parish's composition from the people Houghton calls his "free priests"—men with some the-ological training who stand in for him as a preacher at least two Sundays a month. They include the head of the appraisal department at the giant auction house Sotheby Parke-Bernet, a well-known stockbroker, the head of a textile company, a retired glass manufacturer, and several notable lawyers and bankers. This is the familiar catalog of Episcocratic occupations, and it is their values—the values of the Business Aristocracy—that are encouraged and reflected by the church.

Who better to lead such a parish than one of America's great family businessmen? Too much can be made of that back-ground, Houghton insists. "Very few people come up to me and say, 'How can I get a job with Corning?' The Corning thing is something they and I are very unconscious of." Houghton did note that he is able to counsel his parishioners on problems not only of God but of Mammon. "When we talk about business and financial problems," he says, smiling, "people know that I know what I'm talking about. I can be helpful in that area if it comes up." Better to join the Church of the Heavenly Rest than to hire a business consultant.

Like most other congregations of most other American de-nominations, Heavenly Rest is crowded—increasingly—with young families who join the church largely for their children's upbringing. Many of Heavenly Rest's parishioners, Houghton says, are families on their way up, economically and socially. Many will eventually move to the suburbs, perhaps to one of the great suburban parishes, after the children have been christened and reared through the formative years. By the time they reach teen-age years, Houghton notes, it becomes something of an event to see the young Episcopalians in church. That teen-age lack of interest in religion goes for Houghton's own sons—went for himself, for that matter.

Teen-agers do not go to church. Partly that is because they are away at prep school and then college, but the prep schools know they are not exactly afire with religious fervor either. Teen-aged Episcopalians are in a well-known religious slump that generally levels out with marriage (almost invariably in an Episcopal church) and the birth of children, who in turn are reared in the church.

It is still generally considered a good idea for Episcopal children to have some training in the church. What that training is varies from church to church. In the Church of the Heavenly Rest, religion in the old form is not neglected—prayer books and real services still exist—but there is also a firm emphasis on what used to be called good works. These days good works have a stronger flavor of civic duty, of public service. It is a church for Civic-minded Patricians. One of Houghton's recent projects was a volunteer program in which the 170 or so participants agreed to give one day a month to financially lame New York City—cleaning up Central Park or working free at city institutions. A child growing up in this particular Episcopal church absorbs the idea that his religion is something to be used in everyday life, something that brings him even closer to the city and society. That it is his duty, somehow, to help.

At the Church of the Heavenly Rest, the tone of the place can hardly be lost on young Episcopalians. Church is a place full of friendly, worldly, well-dressed people gathered in an elegant building in the midst of an interesting neighborhood, from which they go out to fulfill themselves and their world. It is a place full of people who can tell you just about anything you want to know and make it easier for you to do what you want. It is a place of elegance and beauty and self-possession; when the time comes to return to it later, the return can be made with confidence and ease. Even if you never return, you are left with the abiding conviction that Episcopalians are people who well know what they're doing. You know whom to turn to.

On Lattingtown Road, there are none of the familiar signs with St. George's cross and the legend "The Episcopal Church Welcomes You." There are only small roads branching off between tall trees, marked "Private." There is the entrance to the Creek Club, the sporting club for Astors and better, and nearby the entrance of the Piping Rock Club, where the driveway is so long cars have been known to run out of gas between the road and the clubhouse. Much of the rest of the land in Locust Valley, a craggy corner of the North Shore of Long Island that is not on the road to anywhere, is in the old-family hands of the most important people of New York.

Eight hundred souls belong to St. John's of Lattingtown Church, which became the most exclusive church in the country at about the time that J. P. Morgan the younger—"Jack"—transferred his allegiance there.

Inside, the church holds only perhaps 200 people, with the proudly humble air of a nobleman's private chapel. It is clean, pretty, genteel. At weddings, which take place every Saturday afternoon at three o'clock and appear just as regularly on the society page of the *New York Times* the next day, the ushers dress in high stiff collars. The guests park their cars in the church lot across Lattingtown Road and next to the road that says "Private No Trespassing"—small cars, fashionably old, young-prep-school-grad cars. The tall young women wrap themselves in crocheted shawls for the ceremony.

The church's inner warmth and privacy are belied by its imposing, rambling stone exterior. It has the same feeling as the massive crags like the one that props a huge Locust Valley mansion protectively above St. John's. A silver limousine crawls down the steep hillside to let the bridal party out at the church door. As the guests walk across Lattingtown Road, their view of the church, like that of casual drivers headed toward Lattingtown, is dominated by a huge traffic sign that seems to apply more to the church than to its little road:

"Do Not Enter."
"The Episcopal Church Welcomes You."
It is a church of contradictions.

The Thread

Perhaps the most attractive quality in Episcopalians as a religious denomination and Episcocrats as a social elite is their unobtrusive, good-humored way of maintaining their morale—and their power. They love to poke gentle fun at themselves. Telling jokes about how exclusive Episcopalianism used to be is *de rigueur* at church functions. Nicknaming churches is almost a mania—"Celestial Snooze" for Heavenly Rest, "St. Mink and All Cadillacs" for the rich Dallas parish St. Michael's and All Angels. Episcopalians talking about themselves love to remind visitors they have been nicknamed "the frozen few" or that Episcopalianism "has a lot of piss in it."

A man who quit the church once said, piqued, that Episcopalianism "has more charming Christians" than any other denomination. He meant it as a criticism of their lighthearted approach to religion, and certainly there is ample evidence that many Episcopalians do not feel very close to God. They do feel very close to man. They tend to be extremely friendly, insistently talkative, but not in a nagging way—good conversation is a skill that Episcocratic parents tend to drill into their children.

"We weren't allowed *not* to talk," recalls an Episcocratic Philadelphia woman who learned her lesson. In conversation, in behavior, Episcocrats practice understated charm.

Even their clothing bespeaks low-key appeal—the women

wear simple tweeds and cashmeres for the winter, Lily Pulitzers for the summer. These are not styles that change with the breezes of Seventh Avenue or Paris. The men, who look forever as though their hair had just been combed and rigorously brushed, wear unchanging Brooks Brothers lapels and button-down shirts from one year to the next. They wear their clothes as though they had been born into them.

These are rugged people; they love to ride, to hunt, sail, sweat at tennis. These are also people of elegance; they are attached to their Chippendale furniture, no matter how scuffed. Through all the wear of life, they quietly exude the comfortableness of people who love exactly what they are doing and who they are. This is their charm and the Episcocratic style.

The obverse side of charm and style, some have suggested, is that Episcocrats as a rule are not deep thinkers and tend to shrug off serious human feelings. There may be some truth to that charge, at least compared with ethnic and social groups that place a greater premium on emotionalism. But Episcocrats would not consider lack of emotion a "charge." It is good form. One does not make people uncomfortable by crying in front of them, nor does one try to think up thoughts that will merely confuse others.

What Episcocrats spend their time doing when they're not making other people comfortable is succeeding. Their great achievement is not merely to succeed, to rise to heights of prestige and influence, but to do that with style, too, without the appearance of nasty, driving—and, above all, obtrusive—ambition. It is as though success were as much a part of their natural habitat as rolling hills and Ivy campuses—a quality, like those of nature, to make one relaxed, not nervous.

It is in their sense of their own caste that Episcocrats differ most from their surprisingly similar cousins the Jews. As we have seen, the two groups are amazingly alike in their total numbers in this country and in the outstanding degree of success both have achieved. There is even a fundamental affinity between Judaism and Episcopalianism as modern religions; based on elaborate religious and ethical strictures, both codes have by now lost much of their suggestion of the divine and are treated by both denominations as friendly bits of human thought that fit into one's life quietly and intermittently.

But where the determination of the Jewish parent for his

child to succeed is—at least in the stereotype—an irresistible
and inescapable force, the Episcocratic success ethic works
much more quietly, more subtly.

Episcocrats, after all, have arrived. Jews are still arriving.
Young Episcocrats grow out of the shelter of centuries of acceptance and rule. Young Jews emerge from the shadow of
persecution, the ghettos and the Holocaust still within memory
of many parents or grandparents. It is a wonder that Episcocratic rule works at all, for Episcocratic parents take pains not
to make children more uncomfortable over not succeeeding than
they would make a neighbor. That relaxed stance leads to the
parent's acceptance of the child's rebellion.

In the early 1900s, that meant the son would date an Irish
Catholic girl before finally marrying a roommate's sister. In the
1930s, it meant oceanic drinking and many demolished cars at
college. In the 1960s, it meant drugs—and sometimes tragedy.
But after all those formula rebellions, the great mass of each
Episcocratic generation ends up studying law or business and
taking over positions much like its fathers'. The common thread,
the redeeming factor, is the well-disguised but irresistible assurance in self and background that is the most common part
of an Episcocratic upbringing.

That pride of class has been one of the major and probably
one of the best factors in American life for a century. It was,
perhaps, responsible for discriminatory distribution of vast
wealth, for disdain for anything alien. It was also the cause of
great opportunity in the United States, the foundation of public
service, of a massive tradition of private support of irreplace-
able public institutions, the root of much that was best in political thought and practice. At least with those it accepted,
that Episcocratic pride produced an urbane, pleasant, humorous social life and an ameliorative, civil-libertarian political
life.

To a large degree it produced, like it or not, America.

Bibliography

Church History

Agee, James. *Letters to Father Flye*. Boston: Houghton Mifflin, 1971.

Ahlstrom, Sydney. *A Religious History of the American People*. New Haven: Yale University Press, 1972.

Dawley, Power Mills. *The Episcopal Church and Its Work*. New York: The Seabury Press, 1961.

Glock, Charles Y., and Rodney Stark. *American Piety: The Nature of Religious Commitment*. Berkeley: University of California Press, 1970.

Glock, Charles Y., Benjamin B. Ringer, and Earl Babbie. *To Confront and to Challenge: A Dilemma of the Contemporary Church*. Berkeley: University of California Press, 1967.

Gray, William and Betty. *The Episcopal Church Welcomes You*. New York: The Seabury Press, 1974.

Hamilton, Kenneth. *God Is Dead: The Anatomy of a Slogan*. Grand Rapids: Eerdmans Publishing Co., 1966.

May, Henry F. *Protestant Churches and Industrial America*. New York: Harper & Brothers, 1949.

Van Buren, Paul M. *Theological Explorations*. New York: Macmillan, 1968.

Prep Schools

Auchincloss, Louis. *The Rector of Justin*. Boston: Houghton Mifflin, 1964.

Hall, Edward Tuck. *Saint Mark's School: A Centennial History*. Southborough, Mass.: Saint Mark's Alumni Association, 1967.

St. John, George. *Forty Years at School.* New York: Henry Holt, 1959.
————. *Views from the Circle: Seventy-Five Years of Groton School.* Groton: The Trustees of Groton School, 1960.

RESORTS

Amory, Cleveland. *The Last Resorts.* New York: Harper & Brothers, 1948.
Birmingham, Stephen. *The Right Places (for the Right People).* Boston: Little, Brown, 1967.
Domhoff, G. William. *The Bohemian Grove and Other Retreats: A Study in Ruling-Class Cohesiveness.* New York: Harper & Row, 1975.
Rasponi, Lanfranco. *The Golden Oases.* New York: G. P. Putnam's Sons, 1968.

LAW

Auerbach, Jerold S. *Unequal Justice.* New York: Oxford University Press, 1976.
Goulden, Joseph C. *The Benchwarmers.* New York: Weybright and Talley, 1974.
————. *The Superlawyers.* New York: David McKay Co., 1971.
Hoffman, Paul. *Lions in the Street.* New York: E. P. Dutton, 1973.
Smigel, Erwin O. *The Wall Street Lawyer.* Bloomington: Indiana University Press, 1964.

JOURNALISM

Bradlee, Benjamin C. *Conversations with Kennedy.* New York: W. W. Norton & Co., 1975.
Roberts, Chalmers M. *The Washington Post: The First 100 Years.* Boston: Houghton Mifflin, 1977.

ART

Burt, Nathaniel. *Palaces for the People.* Boston: Little, Brown, 1977.
Glueck, Grace, "Moving in on the Met," *The New York Times Magazine,* February 27, 1977, pp. 20–24.
Saarinen, Aline. *The Proud Possessors.* New York: Random House, 1958.

FINANCE

Brooks, John. *The Go-Go Years.* New York: Weybright and Talley, 1973.

Galbraith, John Kenneth. *Money: Whence It Came, Where It Went.* Boston: Houghton Mifflin, 1975.

Gunther, Max. *The Very, Very Rich: And How They Got That Way.* Chicago: Playboy Press, 1972.

Lamott, Kenneth. *The Moneymakers* or *The Great Big New Rich in America.* Boston: Little, Brown, 1969.

Lundberg, Ferdinand. *The Rich and the Super-Rich: A Study in the Power of Money Today.* New York: Lyle Stuart, 1968.

Mintz, Morton, and Jerry S. Cohen. *Power, Inc.* New York: The Viking Press, 1976.

Myers, Gustavus. *The Ending of Hereditary American Fortunes.* New York: Augustus M. Kelley, 1939.

SOCIOLOGY

Amory, Cleveland. *The Proper Bostonians.* New York: E. P. Dutton, 1947.

———. *Who Killed Society?* New York: Harper & Brothers, 1960.

Baltzell, E. Digby. *The Protestant Establishment: Aristocracy and Caste in America.* New York: Random House, 1964.

———. *Philadelphia Gentlemen: The Making of a National Upper Class.* Chicago: The Free Press, 1958.

Birmingham, Stephen. *Our Crowd.* New York: Harper & Row, 1967.

———. *The Right People.* Boston: Little, Brown, 1958.

Burt, Nathaniel. *The Perennial Philadelphians: The Anatomy of an American Aristocracy.* Boston: Little, Brown, 1963.

Davis, Allen F., and Mark H. Haller, eds. *The Peoples of Philadelphia: A History of Ethnic Groups and Lower-Class Life 1790–1940.* Philadelphia: Temple University Press, 1973.

Demerath, N. J., III. *Social Class in American Protestantism.* Chicago: Rand McNally & Co., 1965.

Domhoff, G. William. *The Higher Circles: The Governing Class in America.* New York: Random House, 1970.

Jaher, Frederic Cople, ed. *The Rich, The Wellborn, and the Powerful. Elites and Upper Classes in History.* Secaucus: The Citadel Press, 1975.

Jones, Howard Mumford, and Bessie Zaber Jones, eds. *The Many Voices of Boston: A Historical Anthology, 1630–1975.* Boston: Little, Brown, 1975.

King, Florence. *Wasp, Where Is Thy Sting?* New York: Stein and Day, 1977.

Laumann, Edward O., ed. *Social Stratification: Research and Theory for the 1970's.* New York: Bobbs-Merrill, 1970.

Packard, Vance. *The Status Seekers.* New York: David McKay, 1959.

Petshek, Kirk R. *The Challenge of Urban Reform: Politics and Progress in Philadelphia*. Philadelphia: Temple University Press, 1973.

Rasponi, Lanfranco. *The International Nomads*. New York: G. P. Putnam's Sons, 1966.

Simon, Kate. *Fifth Avenue: A Very Social History*. New York: Harcourt Brace Jovanovich, 1978.

Thometz, Carol Estes. *The Decision Makers: The Power Structure of Dallas*. Dallas: Southern Methodist University Press, 1963.

Wecter, Dixon. *The Saga of American Society*. New York: Charles Scribner's Sons, 1937.

Zerbe, Jerome. *The Art of Social Climbing*. Garden City: Doubleday, 1965.

Sociology-Politics

Dowdey, Clifford. *The Virginia Dynasties*. Boston: Little, Brown, 1969.

Halberstam, David. *The Best and the Brightest*. New York: Random House, 1969.

Tolchin, Martin and Susan. *To the Victor . . . Political Patronage from the Club House to the White House*. New York: Random House, 1972.

Weil, Martin. *A Pretty Good Club: The Founding Fathers of the U.S. Foreign Service*. New York: W. W. Norton, 1978.

Biography and Autobiography

Acheson

Acheson, Dean. *Morning and Noon*. Boston: Houghton Mifflin, 1962.

Biddle

Biddle, Cordelia Drexel. *My Philadelphia Father*. Garden City: Doubleday, 1955.

Biddle, Francis. *A Casual Past*. Garden City: Doubleday, 1961.

Biddle, George. *An American Artist's Story*. Boston: Little, Brown, 1939.

Govan, Thomas Payne. *Nicholas Biddle—Nationalist and Public Banker 1786–1844*. Chicago: The University of Chicago Press, 1959.

Kahn, E. J., Jr. "Plenipotentiary." *New Yorker* magazine. May 3 and 10, 1952. (Two-part series on W. Averell Harriman.)

Wainwright, Nicholas B. *Commodore James Biddle and His Sketch-Book*. Philadelphia: The Historical Society of Pennsylvania, 1966.

Bullitt

Bullitt, Orville H., ed. *For the President: Personal and Secret.* Boston: Houghton Mifflin, 1972.

Lawrence

Lawrence, William. *Memories of a Happy Life.* Cambridge: Houghton Mifflin, 1926.

Hearst

Swanberg, W. A. *Citizen Hearst.* New York: Charles Scribner's Sons, 1961.

Ingersoll

Ingersoll, R. Sturgis. *Recollections at Eighty.* Philadelphia: National Publishing Co., 1971.

Lodge

Garraty, John A. *Henry Cabot Lodge.* New York: Alfred A. Knopf, 1953.

Mellon

Koskoff, David E. *The Mellons: The Chronicle of America's Richest Family.* New York: Thomas Y. Crowell, 1978.

Morgan

Wheeler, George. *Pierpont Morgan & Friends: The Anatomy of a Myth.* Englewood Cliffs: Prentice-Hall, 1973.

Post

Wright, William. *Heiress: The Rich Life of Marjorie Merriweather Post.* Washington, D.C.: New Republic Books, 1978.

Rockefeller

Lundberg, Ferdinand. *The Rockefeller Syndrome.* New York: Kensington Publishing Corp., 1976.

Roosevelt

Brough, James. *Princess Alice: A Biography of Alice Roosevelt Longworth.* Boston: Little, Brown, 1975.

Lash, Joseph P. *Eleanor and Franklin.* New York: W. W. Norton, 1971.

Roosevelt, Eleanor. *The Autobiography of Eleanor Roosevelt.* New York: Harper & Brothers, 1937.

Roosevelt, Elliott, and James Brough. *The Roosevelts of Hyde Park: An Untold Story.* New York: G. P. Putnam's Sons, 1973.

Schlesinger, Arthur M., Jr., *The Coming of the New Deal.* Cambridge, Mass.: Houghton Mifflin, 1959.

Vanderbilt

Vanderbilt, Cornelius, Jr. *Man of the World: My Life on Five Continents.* New York: Crown Publishing Co., 1959.
————. *Queen of the Golden Age: The Fabulous Story of Grace Wilson Vanderbilt.* New York: McGraw-Hill Book Co., 1956.

PARISHES

Harper, John C. *Sunday. A Minister's Story.* Boston: Little, Brown, 1974.
Morehouse, Clifford P. *Trinity: Mother of Churches.* New York: The Seabury Press, 1973.

Acknowledgments

We have tried in this book to portray a living institution, an organism with roots running deep in American history and with branches spreading over the country. To bring it to life rather than dissect it, we have avoided resorting only to single-minded academic disciplines or journalistic techniques. Instead, we have taken up any available brushes that could help depict the strength, the wide influence, the variety, and the fascination of a unique group of people bound by a religious heritage.

We found many of our materials in a spectrum of fascinating people; the book would not have been possible without their cooperation. They contributed, of course, only to the book's substance, not to any errors in interpretation.

First, there were friends who provided direction in the beginning, and throughout: Ruth Malone, an inexhaustible fund of information and ideas; Kathryn Malone, who not only supplied facts but carefully read the manuscript; Jean Stroud, Ellen Gross Miles, Sally Lyon Ford, Martha Koock, Harris Wofford, and Arthur Newbold IV, all keen observers of our subject.

Officials of Episcopal institutions were indispensable—and invaluable. Henry McCorkle, editor of *The Episcopalian*, provided a superb foundation. Caroline Rakestraw, executive director of the Episcopal Radio–TV Foundation, described her organization's work and workers. Nancy Montgomery and

Margot Semler of the National Cathedral tirelessly answered extensive queries. The staff of the Episcopal Church Foundation, Anne Simpson of the Church Club of New York, and officials of numerous church schools shortened many a long research path. And special gratitude to George Gallup, Jr., who put his polling organization and his own formidable experience in the church at our disposal.

We interviewed dozens of clerical and lay Episcopalians (and some non-Episcopalians) and were impressed by, and grateful for, their consistent candor and clarity. These deserve mention in Washington: former dean Francis B. Sayre, Jr., of the National Cathedral; David Acheson, president of the National Cathedral Association; Robert Amory, Jr., Senator Charles McC. Mathias, the Rev. Dr. John Harper of St. John's Lafayette Square, the Rev. Richard Downes of St. Alban's School, the Rev. William Wendt of St. Stephen's and the Incarnation, the Rev. Peter Winterble of St. John's Georgetown, and the gracious and interesting June Bingham.

New Yorkers generous with their time were the Rev. Alanson B. Houghton of the Church of the Heavenly Rest; the Rev. William Gray of Trinity Parish (who also wrote a helpful book on the church); Gray's former colleague at Trinity, the Rev. Peter Camp, who became acting headmaster of the Groton School; Sheila Wahlers of the Knickerbocker Greys; and Robert Robinson.

In Philadelphia, still the most Episcopal of cities, Lyman Ogilby, bishop of the diocese of Pennsylvania, contributed personal and ecclesiastical insights. So did the Rev. David Rivers of Gloria Dei church—as well as his wife, Elizabeth—and the Rev. John Schultz of Trinity Church Ambler.

We were privileged to talk to a number of Bostonians, including the consummate host William Appleton Coolidge, the diocesan chancellor Stephen Howe, George Kidder, and Henry Cabot Lodge.

Lodge's brother and fellow former ambassador, John Davis Lodge, spoke to us of the church today. The Rev. Robert Estill of St. Michael's and All Angels, Dallas, provided detailed information about that city's religious life. And we spoke all too briefly by telephone with the Rev. Malcolm Cox, headmaster of Groton, shortly before his death in the summer of 1977.

This book was helped into existence by Merrianne Reagin, who performed a variety of editing and publishing services; Ann Novotny, who dug up the frequently buried but always lively pictures; Kathy Boyoko, who provided logistical support; and the editors of the *Philadelphia Daily News*, who supplied critical free time when called upon.

And it is fair to say the book would not have been done at all without Peter Wyden, who had the original idea and arranged for further ideas to emerge out of the manuscript by close and painstaking editing.

To all these people, our deep thanks for contributing their very different colors to our picture. We hope it is as interesting and accurate as most of them were.

Our final thanks are expressed in the dedication for the patience and good humor of a five-year-old, who suffered our calling and clicking for some mysterious project in which he was not a communicant.

Index